ECONOMICS, POLITICS AND SOCIAL ISSUES IN LATIN AMERICA

Economics, Politics and Social Issues in Latin America

Mary P. Lassiter
Editor

Nova Science Publishers, Inc.
New York

For permission to use material from this book please contact us:
Telephone 631-231-7269; Fax 631-231-8175
Web Site: http://www.novapublishers.com

Library of Congress Cataloging-in-Publication Data
Available upon request.

ISBN 13 978-1-60021-182-9
ISBN 10 1-60021-182-8

Published by Nova Science Publishers, Inc. ✢New York

CONTENTS

PREFACE

Latin America is a diverse group countries with extremely diverse economies and political dynamics. Some are heavy in poverty and others are booming with petrodollars. They speak Spanish, Portuguese, and French. This new book brings together analyses detailing crucial issues at the beginning of the 21st century.

Chapter one states that in the aftermath of the September 2001 terrorist attacks on New York and Washington D.C., U.S. attention to terrorism in Latin America intensified, with an increase in bilateral and regional cooperation. Latin American nations strongly condemned the attacks, and took action through the Organization of American States (OAS) to strengthen hemispheric cooperation. In June 2002, OAS members signed an Inter-American Convention Against Terrorism. President Bush submitted the convention to the Senate in November 2002; on October 7, 2005, the Senate agreed to the resolution of advice and consent on the convention. In its annual report on global terrorism, the State Department highlights threats in Colombia, Peru, and the tri-border area of Argentina, Brazil, and Paraguay. The State Department also has designated four terrorist groups (three in Colombia and one in Peru) as Foreign Terrorist Organizations, and Cuba has been listed as a state sponsor of terrorism since 1982. In the second session of the 1 09th Congress, issues of concern will likely include continued Latin American cooperation on terrorism and oversight related to the release of the State Department's annual report on global terrorism expected in April 2006.

What are the dynamics of the political crisis of the post-64 Brazilian dictatorship? What place do intra-military processes have in the configuration of these broader dynamics? What types of divisions took shape within the military field during the dictatorship? These are the questions that guided my research on the political processes of the Brazilian dictatorship in the period of its consolidation (1964-69) in chapter two. The approach that I propose here focuses specifically on the political dynamics of the regime. The relationship between these two terms – political dynamics and regime form – both defines the field where my general concerns lay and calls for a review of the most relevant literature about the Southern Cone military regimes of the 1960s and 1970s. In this regard I will suggest that the dominant theses on those military governments lead to a series of difficulties in our understanding of the political process of the dictatorships, insofar as they underestimate the role that military processes played within them.

Chapter three shows how Brazil, as the largest and one of the most influential countries in Latin America, has emerged as a leading voice for developing countries in setting regional and multilateral trade agendas. The United States and Brazil have cultivated a constructive relationship in pursuit of their respective efforts to promote trade liberalization, including attempting to broker a compromise with the European Union in the World Trade Organization (WTO) Doha Round and forming bilateral working groups on trade (and other) issues. Still, they approach trade policy quite differently, are at odds over how to proceed regionally with the Free Trade Area of the Americas (FTAA), and share concerns over specific trade policies and practices.

Brazil's trade strategy can be explained only in part by economic incentives. Its "trade preferences" also reflect deeply embedded macroeconomic, industrial, and foreign policies. Whereas U.S. trade strategy emphasizes the negotiation of comprehensive trade agreements on multiple fronts, Brazil is focused primarily on market access issues as they pertain to its economic dominance in South America. Brazil exercises this priority in all trade arenas, such as pursuing changes to agricultural policies in the WTO, expanding the Southern Common Market (Mercosul) in South America, and resisting the FTAA for lack of a balance conducive to Brazilian interests.

Brazil has a modern, diversified economy in which services account for 53% of GDP, followed by industry and manufacturing at 37%, and agriculture at 9%. Agribusiness (commodity and processed goods) account for some 30% of GDP, explaining Brazil's emphasis on agricultural policies in trade negotiations. Brazil is the world's largest producer of sugar cane, oranges, and coffee, and the second largest of soybean, beef, poultry, and corn. It is also a major producer of steel, aircraft, automobiles, and auto parts, yet surprisingly, a relatively small trader by world standards. The United States is Brazil's largest single-country trading partner.

Brazil is critical of U.S. trade policies such as the Byrd Amendment (repealed, but program in effect until October 1, 2007), which directs duties from trade remedy cases to affected industries, the administration of trade remedy rules, and what it considers to be discriminatory treatment in the U.S. expansion of free trade agreements in Latin America. It also objects to product-specific barriers such as tariff rate quotas on sugar, orange juice, ethanol, and tobacco; subsidies for cotton, ethanol, and soybeans; and prolonged antidumping orders on steel and orange juice. U.S. concerns focus on Brazil's comparatively high tariff structure, especially on industrial goods, Mercosul's common external tariff program, and Brazil's refusal to address issues of critical importance to the United States such as services trade, intellectual property rights, government procurement, and investment.

Despite these differences, both countries recognize the potential for important gains to be had from mutually acceptable trade liberalization at all levels. As a developing country with an opportunity for considerable growth in both exports and imports, however, Brazil may have the most to gain from addressing both foreign barriers to its trade, and unilaterally opening its economy further.

Chapter four focuses on one of these standards by shedding light on the economic facets of the freedom of association. While the human rights argument in support of freedom of association and the right to collective bargaining is compelling, the question from an economic point of view is to what extent these standards contribute to economic development and performance. Answering this question would, in principle, require a comparison between countries with and without unions. This is, however, impossible as in virtually all countries – even those which suppress labor – unions and employers' organizations play a (sometimes important) role in industrial relations.

In this chapter, two related questions are considered that *indirectly* can help to disentangle the economic effects associated with freedom of association and the right to collective bargaining. These questions are: (a) what are the microeconomic effects of unions and employers' organizations (unionism); and (b) how do different institutional approaches to collective bargaining affect macroeconomic performance?

The majority of the evidence that addresses various aspects of these questions comes from OECD countries, though available evidence from developing countries will also be presented. This evidence will inform us about the economic consequences of different types of unionism as well as the interaction between unionism and the economic, political and institutional environment in which collective bargaining takes place. The aim of this review is to summarize the empirical evidence and draw some lessons of experience.

The chapter is organized in the following sections: (a) presenting some data on unionism; (b) providing a brief theoretical overview of unionism and collective bargaining; (c) reviewing evidence derived from microeconometric analysis of the economic impact of unions; (d) reviewing evidence derived from econometric studies focusing on the relationship between different systems of collective bargaining and macroeconomic performance; and (e) conclusion and lessons. The evidence presented in this paper draws heavily on a recent comprehensive study of the issues *Core Labor Standards and the Freedom of Association: Economic Aspects* by Aidt and Tzannatos (2001).

Surprisingly absent from the literature on spatial market integration are studies that seek to identify factors that increase the degree of market integration. In Chapter five, a conceptual framework for analyzing these determinants is provided. It is argued that the degree of integration is principally a function of the transactions costs related to the spatial flow of goods and information. For the Brazilian rice market, it is found that the degree of market integration is positively associated with spatial differences in physical capital, human capital, and the level of development. These are among the most important factors identified as contributing to lower transactions costs. The empirical analysis is the first to provide a link between spatial integration of agricultural markets, human capital, and the level of development.

Although labor unions are considered one of the most important institutions of modern capitalism (Freeman, 2000), the literature in chapter six shows that their mode of operation and impact on the economy vary from country to country. Although there is a wide variety of systems, institutions, and union action strategies in the different countries, an important stylized fact in the literature is that labor unions reduce wage dispersion through collective bargaining processes. This has led Metcalf et al. (2000) to refer to them as a "sword of justice." According to Freeman (2000), this phenomenon is actually more widespread than the more thoroughly researched effect of unions on wages, namely their ability to raise the relative wages of their members. The literature shows that: (i) the distribution of wages among unionized workers and/or those covered by collective bargaining is more concentrated than the wage distribution for other workers, even when demographic and productive characteristics are controlled for in the corresponding regressions; and (ii) collective bargaining diminishes the importance of merit in wage formation, thereby narrowing the wage spread between jobs (Freeman, 1980, 1992; Hirsch 1982; Card, 1992; DiNardo et al., 1995; Gosling and Machin, 1995; Blau and Kahn, 1996; DiNardo et al. 1997; Metcalf et al., 2000, among others).

This chapter seeks to answer the following questions: (i) How do employment and union laws affect collective bargaining processes? (ii) Do unions affect wage formation and income distribution? (iii) Do unions increase the rigidity of the labor market? It is concluded by some suggestions for enhancing collective bargaining and unions in Brazil.

The chapter is organized as follows: Section 2 describes labor laws and union legislation in Brazil. Section 3 describes the characteristics of unionized and non-union workers, union density, and the determinants of unionization. Section 4 investigates the effects of unions on wages and income distribution. Section 5 discusses the results obtained and seeks to demonstrate the effects of employment and union laws on collective bargaining processes and union behavior. Section 6 offers some recommendations for improving labor relations in Brazil.

Chapter seven shows that over the last two decades, most Latin American countries went through the experience of fiscal adjustment, stabilization and trade liberalization along the lines of the so-called Washington Consensus. Recently, growing attention has been devoted to assessing the role of the labor markets in the transmission process of such economic policies to the population's standards of living, in particular the poor (e.g., Horton and Mazumdar, 1994). One of the main conclusions of studies of this sort is that market imperfections prevent an efficient allocation of resources, and hence are likely to mitigate the success of such policies and a fair distribution of their potential benefits.

The chapter also uses this approach to briefly contrast labor market functioning in three Latin American countries — Mexico, Colombia and Brazil — in order to draw policy lessons in specific settings. The result of the exercise is that Mexico appears to have had the most "flexible" or integrated labor markets until the mid-1990s, Colombia exhibits traits that can be better classified as segmented or dualistic, and Brazil appears to oscillate between these two forms during the 1990s. The case of Brazil is examined further in some detail and policy implications are drawn.

The remainder of the chapter is organized as follows. Section 2 provides the conceptual and empirical background of the study, and also presents additional evidence for other Latin American countries. Section 3 presents detailed empirical findings for the Brazilian economy and relates the Brazilian experience to conceptual insights. General and Brazil-specific policy implications are developed in section 4. Finally, section 5 summarizes the main results of the study and concludes.

Chapter eight reviews the literature on the poverty effects of minimum wages to determine whether or not the minimum wage is an effective and efficient poverty alleviation tool. Lessons are drawn from developed and industrialized countries to build a picture of the impacts of minimum wages on employment, the wage distribution, household income level and inequality, and fiscal balances. To capture the developing country model, particular focus is given to the structure of the labor market in terms of its implications for coverage of minimum wage laws and risk pooling at the household level.

The chapter is structured in 8 sections. After this Introduction, Section II discusses the conceptual framework used in the analysis of the poverty impact of minimum wages. Section III analyses different measures as regards the definition of the correct minimum wage level. The impacts of the minimum wage on the wage distribution, employment, poverty and fiscal balance are assessed in the remaining sections. Finally, Section VIII presents some conclusions.

In Chapter nine, Rural development begins in Argentina together with the restoration of democracy in the 1980s, but the first actions only started to be developed in the 1990s. Since then, different programs have followed and overlapped. These programs are precisely the purpose of this study.

This paper discusses the resultant rural strategies of the main rural development programs of Argentina in the context of the neoliberal macroeconomic adjustment. It identifies its institutions and analyses whether the actions that are being carried out are suitable or not, and if the assistance to help the rural poor (promoted by international financing organisms) is feasible in face of the negative impact of the neoliberal policy over the small and medium farmers. Besides, this paper looks into and develops questions about the suitability of local and provincial institutional structures for satisfying the institutional demands of rural development programs.

The starting point is the macroeconomic transformation of the 1990s, which affected the agricultural activity and brought about permanent processes of re-structuring and de-structuring of the public and private institutions linked with rural development management.

The purpose of chapter ten is to review the international experience with active labor market policies and to discuss their applicability in developing countries. The empirical literature on evaluations of ALMPs is vast and often provides contradictory conclusions depending on country, time period and specific program characteristics under consideration. The aim of this review is to provide a summary of these evaluations and attempt to draw some lessons.

This chapter is structured as follows. In the next section is a brief overview of active labor market programs and the level of expenditures on these programs. Section 3 briefly discusses the techniques used when evaluating ALMPs. The evaluation evidence on the impacts of ALMPs is reviewed in section 4 and the key variables associated with successful outcomes are identified. Finally, in section 6, the applicability of ALMPs to these countries is discussed and the key considerations involved in balancing active and passive policies are assessed.

Chapter eleven shows how in the political sociology, the conservative thought always indicated a direct correlation between social mobilization and the appearance of systemic political troubles, with disorganizing and separative characteristics.

Samuel Huntington, who had a strong influence in the Brazilian debate since the sixties, proposed a model – in line with several other researchers – according to which the processes of socioeconomic modernization would generate a fast dissemination of certain aspirations (consumption, well-being etc) in the lower layers of society. This would cause an overload of unprocessed and not attended demands on the political system in developing countries. Consequently, would cause an anomic political mobilization. "The relationship between social mobilization and political instability seems to be reasonably direct. The urbanization and the increase in the indexes of literacy, education and exposition to the mass media provoke an increase of aspirations and expectations which, if not satisfied, galvanize the individuals and the groups to the politics. In the absence of strong and adaptable institutions, such increases of participation produce instability and violence. (...) The faster the instruction of the population occurs, more frequent is the government brought down" (Huntington, 1975, p. 60).

The social bases of the Brazilian political conflict were separated, at that time, between an organized section, which had its autonomous participation expanded – from localized claims to the participation in the public space at national level –, and a disorganized section, that was maintained as object of the populist manipulation or "new" types of use. During the transition to the democracy, those new outlines of the political practices of the society interacted strongly with the process of reorganization of the institutional order. Once again, there was a counterpoint between the demands expressed by the political mobilizations of the organized society and the "objective needs" defended as a governance issue, by the technocracy. The point, according this technocracy was to combat the economical crisis associated with the growing inflation and the external debt.

The objective of this article is – based on the context described above – to identify analytical elements to understand the social mobilizations in a different perspective, rather than the view of sociological conservatism. A perspective which sees mobilizations and demobilizations of the organized society as the compensation of the enlargement and narrowing processes of the political system or, in other terms, as movements of "socialization" or "privatization" of the sociopolitical conflict. Also, based upon the Brazilian process of democratic "transition" and "consolidation", some elements related to the tension between the processes of social mobilization and the construction of the new political institutions of the democracy are identified.

Chapter twelve presents a synthesis of doctoral research on this singular political phenomenon. It poses the question of how the leaders of the authoritarian regime were able to obtain results similar to those that they had in mind when they began the liberalization process in the early seventies, in spite of the large growth and diversification of the opposition during the period, the resistance of "hard-liners" to the political opening, and the difficult economic constraints they had to face.

To answer this question also means making a contribution to theoretical knowledge and scientific debate on political regime transition processes.. Academic production on processes of transition in political regimes come up against a series of obstacles, originating from insufficient empirical research and methodological difficulties linked to the absence of a general theory of political change (Nohlen and Thibaut, 1994). In this regard, the "third wave" of democratization (Huntington, 1991) produced a particular slant in the theories of political transition, as well as a series of generalizations on the topic, that need to be tested and honed by case studies, as is done in this article through the study of the Brazilian experience.

The main hypothesis of this paper is that the major constraints in consolidating the democratic regime in Brazil are due to the successful strategy of regime liberalization that was implemented under the Geisel and Figueiredo administrations, maintaining a high degree of voluntarism and control over political processes. Such is the case, in spite of the difficulties that General Figueiredo encountered in guiding the political process and its succession in the final years of his government, resulting from the pressures and growing mobilization of the opposition and the broad social sectors that were demanding the effective and immediate democratization of the country. As a complementary hypothesis, the long duration and extremely gradual evolution of the phase of political liberalization as well as the use of electoral competition as a privileged political transition are examined. The notion that these factors created in the Brazilian political arena the impression of a "normalization" of the process as it was being conducted under the control of and according to the rules unilaterally imposed by those in power is considered. These rules were in effect "naturalized" in the evaluations, calculations and elaboration of strategies by the main political actors of the period. This “time factor” has shown to be fundamental in the progressive widening of the moderate sector of opposition as well as the reformist wing of the regime. In this regard, the loss of control over the transition process, at the end of the Figueiredo presidency, meant that the logic of the process became more autonomous. It derived from the voluntarism of the regime’s leaders and was modeled on the most traditional characteristics of Brazilian political life: an “authoritarian praxis associated with a liberal logic” (Trindade, 1985), the political centrality of the military and the tradition of conciliation “at the high levels” of the political elite.

In: Economics, Politics and Social Issues in Latin America
Editor: Mary P. Lassiter, pp. 1-7 ISBN 1-60021-182-8

Chapter 1

LATIN AMERICA: TERRORISM ISSUES*

Mark P. Sullivan

ABSTRACT

In the aftermath of the September 2001 terrorist attacks on New York and Washington D.C., U.S. attention to terrorism in Latin America intensified, with an increase in bilateral and regional cooperation. Latin American nations strongly condemned the attacks, and took action through the Organization of American States (OAS) to strengthen hemispheric cooperation. In June 2002, OAS members signed an Inter-American Convention Against Terrorism. President Bush submitted the convention to the Senate in November 2002; on October 7, 2005, the Senate agreed to the resolution of advice and consent on the convention. In its annual report on global terrorism, the State Department highlights threats in Colombia, Peru, and the tri-border area of Argentina, Brazil, and Paraguay. The State Department also has designated four terrorist groups (three in Colombia and one in Peru) as Foreign Terrorist Organizations, and Cuba has been listed as a state sponsor of terrorism since 1982. In the second session of the 1 09th Congress, issues of concern will likely include continued Latin American cooperation on terrorism and oversight related to the release of the State Department's annual report on global terrorism expected in April 2006.

TERRORISM IN LATIN AMERICA: U.S. CONCERNS

Over the years, the United States has been concerned about threats to Latin American and Caribbean nations from various terrorist or insurgent groups that have attempted to influence or overthrow elected governments. While Latin America has not been the focal point in the war on terrorism, countries in the region have struggled with domestic terrorism for decades and international terrorist groups have at times used the region as a battleground to advance their causes. The State Department's annual report on international terrorism, recently re-titled *Country Reports on Terrorism,* highlights U.S. concerns about terrorist threats

* Excerpted from CRS Report RS21049 dated January 18, 2006.

around the world, including in Latin America. The 2004 report, issued in April 2005, notes that the international terrorist threat in the Western Hemisphere remained low in 2004, compared to other regions of the world, but also maintained that "terrorists may seek safe-haven, financing, recruiting, illegal travel documentation, or access to the United States from the area and pose serious threats." The report describes terrorist activities in the region in 2004, most notably in Colombia, Peru, and the tri-border area (TBA) of Argentina, Brazil, and Paraguay. The report also examines activity by Cuba, which has been designated by the State Department as a state-sponsor of terrorism since 1982.

In the aftermath of 9/11, U.S. attention focused on potential links in the region to the Al Qaeda terrorist network, but the State Department's 2002 report on terrorism maintained that "there was no confirmed credible information" of an Al Qaeda presence in Latin America. The 2003 State Department report on terrorism maintained that reports of an Al Qaeda presence in the TBA remained "uncorroborated by intelligence and law-enforcement officials," while the 2004 report asserted that there was no credible evidence of operational Islamic cells in the TBA countries. There were increased concerns in 2004 by some Central American officials about potential Al Qaeda threats in the region, although U.S. officials maintained that there was no evidence supporting such concerns.[1] The State Department's 2004 report maintains that there were "widespread, unfounded media reports alleging formal links between transnational criminal gangs and Islamic extremists" in Central America.

Colombia

Colombia remains of paramount concern to the United States because of the threat to democracy posed by three groups that have been designated by the Secretary of State as Foreign Terrorist Organizations (FTOs): two leftist guerrilla groups, the Revolutionary Armed Forces of Colombia (FARC) and the National Liberation Army (ELN), and a rightist paramilitary group, the United Self-Defense Forces of Colombia (AUC). According to the 2004 terrorism report, the three groups continued to conduct car bombings, political murders, and indiscriminate use of land mines, and also targeted critical infrastructure, public recreational areas, and modes of transportation. Colombia has the highest kidnapping rate in the world, with over 1,500 in 2004. Nevertheless, the Colombian government has made significant progress in regaining control of national territory, promoting desertion and reintegration of former illegal armed militants, and demobilizing the AUC. In 2004, acts of terrorism dropped by 42.5%, murders by 13.2%, massacres by 42.4%, and kidnappings by 42.4%. The FARC and AUC have been heavily involved in drug trafficking, which has been the key to their growth over past decade. In February 2003, a U.S. civilian contractor and a Colombian national were murdered by the FARC after their plane crashed. The FARC continues to hold hostage three U.S. contractors from that plane crash. All three Colombian FTOs reportedly exploit the Venezuelan side of the border with Colombia as a safe area to transship arms and drugs, rest, secure logistical supplies, and commit kidnappings. The State Department report indicates that "it is unclear to what extent and at what level the Venezuelan

---

[1] "U.S. Officials Dispute Al Qaeda Role in Hemisphere," *Homeland Security Monitor* (Intellibridge), September 30, 2004; Jerry Seper, "Al Qaeda Seeks Tie to Local Gangs." *Washington Times,* September 28, 2004.

government approves of or condones material support to Colombian terrorists." (For more on Colombia, see CRS Report RL32250, *Colombia: Issues for Congress.)*

Peru

Peru is another country of concern. The brutal Shining Path (Sendero Luminoso or SL) insurgency, which the Department of State has designated an FTO, was significantly weakened in the 1 990s with the capture of its leader Abimael Guzman. In 2001-2003, terrorist acts committed by the group increased from previous years, but in 2004 annual terrorist incidents dropped to 40 from 100 in 2003. According to the State Department terrorism report, SL has a few hundred armed members concentrated in the coca-growing valleys where they are reportedly increasing their involvement in the drug trade; the group also reportedly is trying to rebuild support in the universities where it had considerable influence in the 1 980s.

Tri-Border Area

In recent years, U.S. concerns have increased over activities of the radical Lebanon-based Islamic group Hizballah (Party of God) and the Sunni Muslim Palestinian group Hamas (Islamic Resistance Movement) in the tri-border area of Argentina, Brazil, and Paraguay, which has a large Muslim population. According to the 2003 terrorism report, the TBA "has long been characterized as a regional hub for Hizballah and Hamas fundraising activities, but it is also used for arms and drug trafficking, contraband smuggling, document and currency fraud, money laundering, and the manufacture and movement of pirated goods." The 2004 report asserts that was no credible evidence that operational Islamic terrorist cells exist in the TBA countries.

Allegations have linked Hizballah to two bombings in Argentina: the 1992 bombing of the Israeli Embassy in Buenos Aires that killed 30 people and the 1994 bombing of the Argentine-Israeli Mutual Association (AMIA) in Buenos Aires that killed 86 people. As noted in the 2004 terrorism report, all 22 Argentine defendants charged in the 1994 bombing were acquitted by a three-judge panel that faulted the investigation of the original judge and prosecutors. The acquittal prompted protests by Argentina's large Jewish community. (For additional information on Argentina, see CRS Report RS2 1113, *Argentina: Political Conditions and U.S. Relations.)*

Cuba

The Department of State includes Cuba among its list of six states sponsoring terrorism (the other five states are Iran, Libya, North Korea, Sudan, and Syria). Cuba was added to the list in 1982. The Communist government led by Fidel Castro had a history of supporting revolutionary movements and governments in Latin America and Africa, but in 1992, Castro said that his country's support for insurgents abroad was a thing of the past. Most analysts accept that Cuba's policy generally did change, largely because the breakup of the Soviet Union resulted in the loss of billions in subsidies.

The State Department's 2004 terrorism report maintains that Cuba continues to actively oppose the global war on terrorism. The report asserts that Cuba's "actions and public statements run contrary to the spirit of the UN conventions on terrorism that it has signed." (Cuba has ratified all 12 international conventions on terrorism.) The report also maintained that Cuba continued to provide limited support to FTOs as well as safe haven for terrorists. It asserted that Cuba provides safe haven to various Basque ETA members from Spain despite a November 2003 request from the Spanish government to deny them sanctuary. The report also maintained that Cuba provided safe haven and some degree of support to members of two Colombian insurgent groups, the FARC and ELN. (The State Department's 2002 and 2003 terrorism reports acknowledged, however, that Colombia acquiesced to this arrangement and that Colombia publicly said that it wanted Cuba's continued mediation with the ELN in Cuba.) The 2004 report also noted that more than 70 fugitives from U.S. justice had taken refuge in Cuba. Many of these are accused of committing violent actions in the United States, including Joanne Chesimard, who is wanted for the murder of a New Jersey State Trooper in 1973.

In general, those who support keeping Cuba on the terrorism list argue that there is ample evidence that Cuba supports terrorism. They point to the government's history of supporting terrorist acts and armed insurgencies in Latin America and Africa. They point to the government's continued hosting of members of foreign terrorist organizations and U.S. fugitives from justice. Critics of retaining Cuba on the terrorism list maintain that it is a holdover of the Cold War. They argue that domestic political considerations keep Cuba on the terrorism list and maintain that Cuba's presence on the list diverts U.S. attention from struggles against serious terrorist threats. (For further information, see CRS Report RL3 225 1, *Cuba and the State Sponsors of Terrorism List,* and CRS Report RL32730, *Cuba: Issues for the 109th Congress.)*

U.S. Policy

As in other parts of the world, the United States has assisted Latin American and Caribbean nations over the years in their struggle against terrorist or insurgent groups indigenous to the region. For example, in the 1 980s, the United States supported the government of El Salvador with significant economic and military assistance in its struggle against a leftist guerrilla insurgency. In recent years, the United States has employed various policy tools to combat terrorism in the Latin America and Caribbean region, including sanctions, anti-terrorism assistance and training, law enforcement cooperation, and multilateral cooperation through the OAS. Moreover, given the nexus between terrorism and drug trafficking, one can argue that assistance aimed at combating drug trafficking organizations in the region has also been a means of combating terrorism by cutting off a source of revenue for terrorist organizations. The same argument can be made regarding efforts to combat money laundering in the region.

Although terrorism was not the main focus of U.S. policy toward the region in recent years, attention increased in the aftermath of the 9/11 terrorist attacks on New York and Washington. Anti-terrorism assistance has increased along with bilateral and regional cooperation against terrorism. In 2002, Congress approved the Bush Administration's request to expand the scope of U.S. assistance to Colombia beyond a counternarcotics focus to also include counter-terrorism assistance to the government in its military efforts against drug-financed leftist guerrillas and rightist paramilitaries.

As noted above, the United States has imposed sanctions on three groups in Colombia (ELN, FARC, and AUC) and one group in Peru (SL) designated by the Department of State as Foreign Terrorist Organization (FTOs). Official designation of such groups as FTOs triggers a number of sanctions, including visa restrictions and the blocking of any funds of these groups in U.S. financial institutions. The designation also has the effect of increasing public awareness about these terrorist organizations and the concerns that the United States has about them.

Through the Department of State (Diplomatic Security Office, Office of Antiterrorism Assistance), the United States provides Anti-Terrorism Assistance (ATA) training and equipment to Latin American countries to help improve their capabilities in such areas as airport security management, hostage negotiations, bomb detection and deactivation, and countering terrorism financing. Such training was expanded to Argentina in the aftermath of the two bombings in 1992 and 1994. Assistance was also stepped up in 1997 to Argentina, Brazil, and Paraguay in light of increased U.S. concern over illicit activities in the tri-border area of those countries.

ATA funding is generally provided through the annual foreign operations appropriations measure. For FY2001, \$4.7 million in ATA training was provided to Western Hemisphere countries. In FY2002, a total of \$27.5 million was provided for the region, with \$25 million for an anti-kidnapping program in Colombia (appropriated through an FY2002 supplemental appropriations measure, P.L. 107-206) and \$2.5 million for the regular Western Hemisphere program. For FY2003, the Administration's \$3.6 million in ATA assistance was provided for the region, with \$3.3 million of that for Colombia. For FY2004, \$5.3 million in ATA assistance was provided for the region. For FY2005, an estimated \$1 1.1 million in ATA is being provided for the region, with \$3.9 million for Colombia and \$0.5 million for the tri-border area of Argentina, Brazil, and Paraguay. The FY2006 ATA request for Latin America is \$9.7 million, again with \$3.9 for Colombia and \$0.5 million the tri-border area.

The United States also works closely with the governments of the tri-border region — Argentina, Brazil, and Paraguay — through the "3 + 1 regional cooperation mechanism," which serves as a forum for counterterrorism cooperation and prevention among all four countries.

Money laundering in the region has been a major U.S. concern for some 20 years, largely because of its association with drug traffickers, but terrorist organizations may also be involved in money laundering as a means of hiding their financial assets. The United States works through the Financial Action Task Force (FATF), a multilateral anti-money laundering body, to help develop and promote policies to combat money laundering worldwide. According to the Department of State's March 2005 *International Narcotics Control Strategy Report,* 14 nations in the region are jurisdictions of primary concern to the United States because of their vulnerability to money laundering. These are Antigua and Barbuda, Bahamas, Belize, Brazil, Cayman Islands, Colombia, Costa Rica, Dominican Republic, Haiti, Mexico, Panama, Paraguay, Uruguay, and Venezuela.

Increased Regional Cooperation Since 9/11

Latin American nations strongly condemned the September 2001 terrorist attacks on New York and Washington and took action through the OAS and the Rio Treaty to strengthen hemispheric cooperation against terrorism. The OAS, which happened to be meeting in Peru at the time, swiftly condemned the attacks, reiterated the need to strengthen hemispheric cooperation to combat terrorism, and expressed full solidarity with the United States. At a special session on September 19, 2001, OAS members invoked the 1947 Inter-American Treaty of Reciprocal Assistance, also known as the Rio Treaty, which obligates signatories to the treaty to come to one another's defense in case of outside attack. Another resolution approved on September 21, 2001, called on Rio Treaty signatories to "use all legally available measures to pursue, capture, extradite, and punish those individuals" involved in the attacks and to "render additional assistance and support to the United States, as appropriate, to address the September 11 attacks, and also to prevent future terrorist acts."

In another resolution, the OAS called on the Inter-American Committee on Terrorism (CICTE) to identify urgent actions aimed at strengthening inter-American cooperation in order to combat and eliminate terrorism in the hemisphere. The CICTE was reinvigorated in the aftermath of 9/11, and has cooperated on border security mechanisms, controls to prevent funding of terrorist organizations, and law enforcement and counterterrorism intelligence and information. At a January 2003 CICTE meeting in El Salvador, OAS members issued the Declaration of San Salvador, which condemned terrorism and pledged to strengthen hemispheric cooperation through a variety of border, customs, and financial control measures. At the conference, the United States pledged $1 million to the OAS to help the growth of CICTE "as a technical body devoted to increasing counterterrorism expertise in the Americas."[2] At the February 2005 CICTE session held in Trinidad and Tobago, OAS members reaffirmed their commitment to deepen cooperation in the fight against terrorism.

In June 2002, OAS members signed a newly completed Inter-American Convention Against Terrorism. Signing the treaty for the United States, Secretary of State Powell said that the OAS had "produced the first new international treaty since September 11 targeted at improving our ability to combat terrorism."[3] The Convention, among other measures, would improve regional cooperation against terrorism, commit parties to sign and ratify U.N. anti-terrorism instruments and take actions against the financing of terrorism, and deny safe haven to suspected terrorists.

On October 27-28, 2003, the OAS held a Special Conference on Security in Mexico City that focused on identifying new threats, concerns, and challenges facing the hemisphere and agreed on a cooperative approach toward addressing them. Among the threats identified in the adopted Declaration on Security in the Americas were "terrorism, transnational organized crime, the global drug problem, corruption, asset laundering, illicit trafficking in weapons and the connections among these activities."[4]

---

[2] U.S. Department of State, International Information Programs, "U.S. Donates $1 Million to Combat Terrorism in Western Hemisphere," *Washington File,* January 22, 2003.

[3] U.S. Department of State, International Information Programs, "Transcript: Powell Stresses Security at OAS General Assembly," *Washington File,* June 3, 2002.

[4] Organization of American States. Declaration on Security in the Americas. October 28, 2003.

Congressional Action

President Bush submitted the Inter-American Convention Against Terrorism to the Senate on November 12, 2002, for its advice and consent, and the treaty was referred to the Senate Foreign Relations Committee (Treaty Doc. 107-18). The committee held a public hearing on the treaty on June 17, 2004. In the 109th Congress, the committee formally reported the treaty on July 28, 2005 (Senate Exec. Rept. 109-3), and on October 7, 2005, the Senate agreed to the resolution of advice and consent.

The 1 08th Congress called for two reports from the Administration regarding terrorist activities in Latin America. The FY2005 Ronald W. Reagan National Defense Authorization Act (P.L. 108-375) required a report on the activities of Al Qaeda and associated groups in Latin America and the Caribbean (Section 1047) and a report regarding any relationships between foreign governments or organizations and terrorist groups in Colombia (Section 1021). The 1 08th Congress also expressed concern regarding the investigation into the July 1994 AMIA bombing in Buenos Aires. Both houses approved similar resolutions — H.Con.Res. 469 (Ros-Lehtinen) and S.Con.Res. 126 (Coleman) — that, among other provisions, urged Argentina to provide resources to investigate all areas of the AMIA case, encouraged U.S. law enforcement support, and encouraged the establishment of an OAS task force to assist in the investigation.

In: Economics, Politics and Social Issues in Latin America ISBN 1-60021-182-8
Editor: Mary P. Lassiter, pp. 9-28

Chapter 2

State and Regime in Post-64 Brazil: Bureaucratic Authoritarianism or Military Dictatorship?[1]

João Roberto Martins Filho
Department of Political Science at Universidade Federal de São Carlos, Brazil

Introduction

What are the dynamics of the political crisis of the post-64 Brazilian dictatorship? What place do intra-military processes have in the configuration of these broader dynamics? What types of divisions took shape within the military field during the dictatorship? These are the questions that guided my research on the political processes of the Brazilian dictatorship in the period of its consolidation (1964-69). The approach that I propose here focuses specifically on the political dynamics of the regime. The relationship between these two terms – political dynamics and regime form – both defines the field where my general concerns lay and calls for a review of the most relevant literature about the Southern Cone military regimes of the 1960s and 1970s. In this regard I will suggest that the dominant theses on those military governments lead to a series of difficulties in our understanding of the political process of the dictatorships, insofar as they underestimate the role that military processes played within them.

---

[1] This chapter is an abridged version of the first chapter of my book *O Palácio e a Caserna: a Dinâmica Militar das Crises Políticas da Ditadura, 1964-1969*, published in Brazil in 1995. My research was supported by the Fulbright Foundation, as well as the Brazilian CNPq and CAPES. As a Fulbright scholar I benefited from a stay at the University of California, Riverside, in 1991, where I was hosted by my then advisor and now close friend Ronald Chilcote. A different version was published in *Revista de Sociologia e Política*, v. 2 , p. 7-23, june 1994. Translated by Meryl Adelman.

Perspectives from Political Science

I suggest to start from one of the fundamental models of Comparative Politics, and more specifically, from the well-known dichotomy that it establishes between "civic" and "praetorian" societies. According to the master of such explanations, in contrast to civic systems, with their high correlation between institutionalization and participation, praetorian systems correspond to societies "with low levels of institutionalization and high levels of participation ... where social forces, using their own methods act directly in the political sphere". (Huntington, 1968, p. 80) In the context of the polemic that began, in the mid-1960s, on the relationship between processes of economic and political modernization in developing societies, these authors went on to argue that within them, processes of economic change would not necessarily lead to the perfecting of political institutions. Concerned with the pressing problem of stability and order in societies "undergoing rapid and disruptive social and economic change" (Huntington, 1968, vii), they argued that within them, "the rates of social mobilization and the expansion of political participation are high; the rates of political organization and institutionalization are low. The result is political instability and disorder". (Huntington, 1968, p. 5) Brazil in the sixties then becomes one of the most notable examples of their notion of praetorian mass societies or political societies reminiscent of the perverse constitutions and degenerated states mentioned by the classics of political theory. These theses influenced an entire generation of experts on Latin America that produced particular resonance within the US inspired current of Brazilian Political Science.

My interest here lies in identifying how these writings dealt with the issue of political crisis in praetorian societies. Legitimate heir to the long-standing concern of elitist theorists regarding popular political participation, this current states that mass societies, given their inability to reconcile high levels of mobilization with strong institutions were characterized by endemic political crisis. "In a praetorian system social forces confront each other nakedly. ... Each group employs means which reflect its peculiar nature and capabilities. ... The absence of effective political institutions in a praetorian society means that power is fragmented: it comes in many forms and in small quantities" (Huntington, 1968, p.196-197). The fragility and transitory nature of all forms of authority are their trademark and military "are seen as only one specific manifestation of a broader phenomenon in underdeveloped societies: the general politicization of social forces and institutions". (Huntington, 1968, p. 81 e 194)

As some analysts have realized, this approach was deeply rooted in the methodological emphasis that this school explicitly placed on the degree, rather than the on forms or on the nature of power. Within the field of Comparative Politics, as one critic of such positions has already argued, this leads to the conclusion that "the accumulation of power is the alpha and omega of 'political development'", and to a strong tendency to legitimate all forms of power upon emphasizing "any consolidation of political power which is capable of exercising effective control" (O'Donnell, 1977, p. 52). This is said explicitly in the opening paragraph of Huntington's *Political Order in Changing Societies*:

> "The most important political distinction among countries concerns not their form of government but their degree of government. The differences between democracy and dictatorship are less than the differences between those countries whose politics embodies

consensus, community, legitimacy, organization, effectiveness, stability, and those countries whose politics is deficient in these qualities". (Huntington, 1968, p. 1)

What we see clearly manifested there is a tendency to analyze political processes at a very high level of generality which does not seem to leave any room for the topic of the relationship between political crises and different types of power. In this regard, and moving on to another current of analysis that has heavily influenced the study of the dictatorships under consideration here, the theory of authoritarianism can be seen as an attempt to overcome such limitations. One of its most important characteristics is its effort to perfect the traditional dualism of Political Science, centered on an opposition between democratic and totalitarian systems. For the authors belonging to this school, the situation of a whole group of contemporary societies calls for the definition of an intermediate type of regime, with a life and features of it own, that can neither be considered democratic nor totalitarian (Linz, 1970). However, in terms of what interests us here, a more attentive examination reveals the limitations of such an effort to analyze forms of domination, as part of the task of understanding political crises. Its central tenet seems precisely to be the refusal of any form of structural determinism; its cornerstone, the methodological precedence of elite political action for the comprehension of processes of crisis. This is the case for Juan Linz' model for deciphering the crises of democratic regimes and the consideration of their alleged inevitability.

Regarding the problems of political crises in dictatorial regimes, we should still recognize that within the limits of the Political Science mainstream, certain authors explore possibilities that distinguish them from the authors discussed above. In this regard, it has remained up to a variety of corporatist approaches, concerned with the critique of the culturalist tradition of this school, to bring to the debate on the authoritarian regimes a particular topic that was uncommon in the American literature: the relevance of historical and structural factors for the differentiation of forms of political domination. These theoreticians set out to build an elaborate typology of modern arrangements for "interest representation" that would be able to go beyond the classic pluralist paradigm. In this effort, representatives of this current of thought show a rare sensitivity for issues of political and social structure.

Alongside other types of modern arrangements, such as pluralism, monism, and trade unionism, corporatism is seen as one of the possible institutional forms for the linking of the socially organized interests of civil society to the decision-making structures of the State. Sharing a basic structural similarity, the set of contemporary arrangements for the corporatist system of interest representation were seen to hold within different subtypes that were a product of highly varied "social, political and economic processes". It is precisely in this effort to define the contrasts between "societal" and "statist" sub-types that authors such as Philippe Schmitter (1974, p.105) introduce the subject of historical and structural factors. In his view, it is a matter of considering the constraints, opportunities and contradictions that the operation of the economic system creates for political actors, which means that the basic institutions of capitalism and the class structure of power and property that it generates must be examined. (Schmitter, 1974, p. 107)

The diverse origins of corporatist modes are seen as related to certain basic needs of capitalist reproduction in different phases of its international context. The societal subtype is seen as a component of post-liberal advanced capitalism and it statist variant as an element, if not a structural need of the late capitalist, anti-liberal, authoritarian and Neo-mercantilist State. (Schmitter, 1974, p.105)

This dislocation of the field of analysis from action to structure was all the clearer in the works of the Argentine political scientist Guillermo O'Donnell. In proposing a revision of corporatist perspectives, he draws attention to the "exclusion of the historical-structural factors" as their main limitation, as well as their inability to understand corporatism as "a set of structures which link society with the state". (O'Donnell, 1977, p. 49, 47). The path that O'Donnell took can be seen as an exemplary case of the tendency to reconcile concepts of mainstream Political Science with Marxist theories of the State.[2] Although this feature was hardly noted, his work can be divided in two periods: an initial analysis focused on a "genetic explanation of certain fundamental characteristics of contemporary South American political systems" and later attempts to define bureaucratic authoritarianism – a notion to which I will return further on – as "a type of capitalist state (that) should ... be understood in light of the distinctive features of capitalist states in general". (O'Donnell, 1973, p. 53 and 1988, p. 2). In this vein, the author goes on to develop a historical-structural approach that involves investigating "the temporal relations between a system of forces and social relationships – capitalism – and its mutually consonant patterns of political domination". (O'Donnell, 1980).

Having carried out this evaluation of the hegemonic views within the debate on military dictatorships, we can then move on to the issue of the obstacles that its categories create for understanding the issue that interests us here. Once again, I suggest starting from Huntington. His theses on the endemic political crises and endemic militarism of societies that are undergoing modernization processes seem to neglect the particular power structures that were implemented as of the 60s in a variety of Latin American countries. In this sense, it is worth noting that the authors who belong to this current are so preoccupied with the question of the viability of the role of the military as institution builder that they seem to have forgotten the real changes in the State apparatus that were made in the aftermath of the military coups, as was the case for post-64 Brazil. It is no coincidence that many of the analyses made by so-called Brazilianists took on a normative tone, positively evaluating gains in terms of economic development, order and stability, while at the same time expressing reservations for what they saw as the negative side of the phenomenon: its inability to create true political institutions, in the shape of the political party system of civic societies.[3] In other words, in focusing their attention on political institutions that did not emerge, these scholars turn their eyes away from the whole dictatorial structure that was thus built "behind their backs." Whether stable or not, regimes like the Brazilian one created effective power structures. In my opinion, it is to the study of the latter that we must turn.

Furthermore, elitist approaches' neglect for the forms of power became a specific obstacle to the analyses of crisis dynamics. It is no coincidence that representatives of this perspective that turned to the specific case of post-1964 Brazil were unable to make progress in their understanding of the concrete content of the conflicts that structured the political crises of the military regime. Within the context of neglect for structural determinations, their emphasis on projects, discourse and ideologies ran up against the need for constant reconstruction of predictions on the direction of leaderships' actions; they were frequently

---

[2] This move toward Marxist theory was denied by commentators of O'Donnell's work. In David Collier's words (1982, p. 31), there was not more than a simple "change in terminology: the substitution of the concept of political system for that of the State.

[3] This is the case of Schneider (1971), Roett (1973), Perlmutter (1969), Feit (1973) and Rowe (1966).

lost in the precarious visibility of analyses that had been carried out in the "heat of the moment". (Mendes, 1966 and 1967). Following another route, attempts to define the post-1964 regime through research on selection criteria, attitudes and values of the power elite contributed little regarding the specific dynamic of the political conflicts, which marked the crisis of the period. (Druckman and Vario, 1983). Lastly, in their analysis of the Brazilian case, the corporatist perspectives discussed above seem, although remaining within the interest representation paradigm, to go beyond some of the most visible limitations of the debate on "incomplete institutionalization", making it possible to consider actual modifications of power structures post-1964. For example, in posing the question, "What did the military do to alter the type of authoritarian domination developed under Getúlio Vargas?", authors such as Philippe Schmitter make progress in the study of power arrangements.

From this vantage point, institutionalization comes to be seen in terms of effective processes rather than absent processes. Nonetheless, Schmitter's propositions on the corporatism of the Brazilian state, although not blocking analysis of the structural modifications that mark the processes of political crisis, do present some limitations to deepening our understanding of these processes. The idea that corporatism is compatible with several types of regime does not lead to greater exploration of the specific nature of the power arrangements that were gradually implanted after 1964. Symptomatically, in analyzing the processes of power centralization and control over the political system periphery – with emphasis on the National Information Service (Serviço Nacional de Informações, SNI) this author also seems to be unable to resist the "sirens' call" of institutionalization.

Political Crisis and State Forms

We may perhaps define the argument presented here in a single statement: the study of processes of political crisis requires analysis of the structural forms of political power. In the field of Marxist theory of the State, this means returning to the classic concern with the variation of bourgeois power: the different "forms of government", as brought out in Marx, Trotsky and Gramsci's writings on Bonapartism, fascism and Caesarism. On other occasions, it should be added, this topic reappears in the Marxist analysis of "typical" and "atypical", "complete" and "incomplete" forms of bourgeois power. (Guimarães, 1988). Later, Nicos Poulantzas' work took up the Marxist theory of the State and politics again, seeking to systematize and develop it through his new propositions on regime and State types. Through a particular reading of Poulantzas' work (1977, 1978, 1978a), I attempt to present a proposal for the analysis of the critical processes of military dictatorships.

Through his pioneering attempt that develops the idea of the political as a regional level of the capitalist mode of production and an analysis of the bourgeois State as a specific form of juridical and political apparatus, Poulantzas' work produces several decisive ruptures. This however is not the appropriate place to discuss the development of his work; rather, I shall limit myself to his reflections on "exceptional" forms of State and regime. In looking at those latter, he sought to demonstrate that the variation in those forms of the State are the result of specific political crises. Bonapartism, fascism and military dictatorship can be considered to be *critical forms of the State.*

In this sense, the focus of my work here is not the study of the political crises that are at the root of transition from one form of State to another. Rather, the processes of crisis occurring after the implantation of the military dictatorships turn our attention to the concept of "forms of exceptional regimes" which means *critical forms of regimes*. Thus, the brief examination of the issue of forms of State that I will engage in here has the aim of introducing the question of the relationship between regime forms and political crisis.

From the start, one essential aspect of this issue must be kept in mind: exceptional forms of the State regard a situation of rupture in the State apparatus – a crucial reorganization of State apparatuses. In this sense, students of the post-1964 Brazilian political process will certainly recognize the pertinence of Poulantzas' characterization of the basic features that underlie the changes taking place in those arrangements. For our purposes here, it should be enough to enunciate the following: a tendency to control the entirety of State and non-State apparatuses, by one apparatus alone; the workings of the sub-ideology of this dominant apparatus in legitimating repression and obtaining the submission of other apparatuses; the "dislocation of dominance" from within the State as a whole to the site of a specific apparatus within which a previously secondary aspect – the ideological – becomes primordial; significant changes in the juridical system (public law no longer exercising a role in regulating and establishing limits); modification of the principle of suffrage, with the crisis of political party representation and the curtailment of voting rights; higher rates of bureaucratization; parallel chains of power, meaning the end of discrete spheres of competence, with the dislocation of contradictions to the interior of State apparatuses themselves. (Poulantzas, 1978a, p. 335-353)

Poulantzas' scholars will certainly note that here the concept of the ideological apparatuses of the State is missing. Actually I do not consider all the political parties, the educational system and the Church as *State* apparatuses. So, I have concentrated on Poulantzas' analysis of the apparatuses and branches of the State per se[4]. My focuses of attention are the exceptional forms of regime. Thus, although in *Fascism and Dictatorship* the criteria for distinguishing between fascist, Bonapartist and military dictatorship regimes lies mainly in the relationship between repressive and ideological apparatuses – "the dominance of one or the other specifying the forms that regimes or States of exception take on" – I will restrict myself to the notion that the dominance of a fascist party, civil administration or the Army, *as branches of the State*, and that the relationship between these branches and non-State apparatuses is what distinguishes these forms.

A more in-depth analysis of the problem of the specificity of regime forms requires a return to some of the observations that Poulantzas put forth in his book, *Political Power and Social Classes,* in which he seems to be suggesting a different approach. State forms, he argues, can only be studied in conjunction with *regime forms*, which are related to the political scenario and to periodization. From my perspective, it is here where a more interesting possibility for the study of regime forms can be found. I suggest that it is possible to make progress in the understanding of the military dictatorial regime through the analysis

[4] In my opinion, Poulantzas' book, *Political Power and Social Classes* does away with the distinction between the 'repressive' and 'ideological' State apparatuses. This distinction, which appears in the famous Poulantzas-Miliband debate and in *Fascism and Dictatorship,* sets forth two problems which I will only mention here: if in *Political Power and Social Classes* the definition of the capitalist State is based on its specific dual function in isolating and representing unity, then why are the school system, leftist parties and the State considered "State apparatuses"? Do they really carry out this dual function, and if so, how?

of the dynamics of its political crises. This perspective should become clearer through the following evaluation of analyses that have been made on the nature of the regimes that emerged from Latin American military coups of the sixties and seventies.

To do this, I will return to the debate on the autocratic form of the State and on the regimes that were the result of military coups in Latin America in the sixties and seventies. To remain within Brazil, the definition of the military dictatorship as fascist was, for a time, well accepted (Jaguaribe, 1968). In order to refute this perspective, it should be enough to take a look at the distinctive characteristics of fascism according to Poulantzas, or to turn to the Latin American literature that criticized that type of interpretation.[5]

But the problem seems to be more complex in the case of Bonapartism. Even if we were able to return to the specific nature of the political crisis that leads to this type of State, Marxist analyses seeking to understand the post-64 regime in terms of this framework bring out a crucial point in our approach to the political dynamics of dictatorship (Antunes, 1988, p. 112-26) I refer to the issue of the bureaucratization of the State and the autonomy that bureaucracy obtains, as fundamental characteristics of regimes like the one established in post-1964 Brazil. In effect, even the quickest examination of the literature on "military authoritarianism" reveals that one of the dominant perspectives is the one that gives salience to bureaucratic elements in defining the characteristics of this type of regime.

CRITIQUE OF BUREAUCRATIC AUTHORITARIANISM

Actually, at least within academic discussion, the work of Guillermo O'Donnell has long been regarded as a point of reference for studies on the new type of military regimes that emerged in Latin America. In his earlier writing – works published originally in 1972 – he attempted to construct an explanation of this type of "political system" in terms of David Apter's analyses of modernization processes and Samuel Huntington's thesis on the "political gap" of praetorian societies (O'Donnell, 1973 and 1986a). Later, as we already have seen, this author modified his perspective, first in the sense of incorporating a Marxist variety of corporatism (O'Donnell, 1974) and then, a historical and structural view of the capitalist State. At this point I would like to examine his work in terms of another key issue: why should the Brazilian and Argentine regimes be characterized as bureaucratic rather than military? Why the emphasis on processes of bureaucratization rather than militarization?

In this regard, even the slightest look at the writings of this Argentine political scientist is enough to reveal that the shifts in his general perspective coexist alongside strong elements of continuity. The basis for that analytical continuity can be found, in my opinion, in the notion of *bureaucratization.* It is no coincidence that the cornerstone of his first important study, in which he proposes a genetic explanation of the political systems of countries such as Argentina and Brazil, was the hypothesis of the "penetration of technocratic roles" in societies with high levels of modernization. It is within this context that he offers the concept of bureaucratic authoritarianism, through the twin borrowing of notions from Juan Linz (autocratic regime) and David Apter (bureaucratic system). In his own words,

[5] To mention just a few examples, we have Quartim's work (1971) on the role of the army in political dictatorships as the political party of the bourgeoisie and the analyses of the lack, in such regimes, of a party capable of mobilizing the masses, in Borón (1977) and Cardoso (1982).

> this awkward term [is used] because it facilitates the use of the term "authoritarian" as a genus that includes other types of non-democratic South American political systems associated with lower levels of modernization. The term "bureaucratic" suggests the crucial features that are specific to authoritarian systems of high modernization: the growth of organizational power of many social sectors, the government attempts to control by "encapsulation", the career patterns and the power bases of most incumbents of technocratic roles, and the pivotal role played by large (public and private) bureaucracies. (O'Donnell, 1973, p.95).[6]

In my opinion, the later shifts in O'Donnell's work do not change this analytical hardcore of his work.

Summarizing then in this way the most consistent attempt that was made to provide a definition of the regimes that are at issue here as "bureaucratic", the following question remains: does such a definition adequately cope with the nature and dynamic of the dictatorships like the Brazilian and the Argentine in the 60s? The answer, which I will attempt to develop below, can initially be responded to as follows: the "bureaucratic" approach leaves out a key element of this type of political arrangement: its military-dictatorial nature. That is, the military nature of such dictatorships can be lost if they are defined primarily in terms of their aspects of bureaucratic rationalization. In this way, comprehension not only of their nature but their political dynamics is blocked.

In order to develop this critique, we need to return to Poulantzas' analyses. It is there that the distinction between "bureaucracy" and "bureaucratism" emerges clearly. The first term refers to a social category that has the responsibility for managing the State; the second, to a "specific system of organization and internal functioning of the State apparatus". (Poulantzas, 1977, p. 328) Along these lines, when O'Donnell refers to the bureaucratization that characterizes the deepening of modernization processes in countries such as Brazil and Argentina, he is able to account for a real process, visibly intensified in the mentioned countries after the military coups: we are dealing here with "bureaucratism" as a constitutive feature of capitalism (Weber) or of the capitalist State apparatus (Marx). In Poulantzian terms, bureaucratism makes up part of the juridical and political structure of the bourgeois State (Saes, 1982). Thus, to see the political arrangements under consideration here as "bureaucratic" does not contribute to our understanding of the specific form of State that characterizes the Argentine and Brazilian situations. The specificity of the State form that is consolidated in these two cases does not lie in the advance of bureaucratization, which is a general characteristic of capitalist societies, but in the further militarization of the State, and in the special place that the Armed Forces come to occupy within the new power structures.

Nonetheless, this matter alone does not in itself exhaust the authoritarian-bureaucratic hypothesis. The latter is also founded on the idea that the regimes under consideration here are defined by the central role of bureaucracy, as a social category. It is on this point that the bureaucratic thesis has several variations (which in turn, serves to show how well received it has been in studies on these dictatorships.) For some of these authors, among which O'Donnell himself stands out, the undeniable preponderance of the military in the new technocratic arrangement does not stop us from defining these forms of power as

[6] With this I explain my option for not using the term "bureaucratic-authoritarian State" that was predominant in the Spanish and Portuguese language versions of O'Donnell's work. In effect, in the author's own words, this concept sought to define a "bureaucratic" variety of the "authoritarian" type of political system.

bureaucratic, to the extent that they take the Armed Forces primarily as a bureaucratic organization; for others, heirs of the theory of the elites, regimes such as the Argentine and the Brazilian can be defined through their alliance between civil (technocratic) and military bureaucracies. (Mendes, 1967) A Marxist variation based on the concept of Bonapartism sees the governmental counter-revolutionary elite that came to power with the coups that took place in the 1960s as military and techno-bureaucratic currents. (Martins, 1977). All of these variations have a point in common: insofar as political representation is concerned, the bureaucratic nature of these regimes subordinates their military aspects.

In order to perform a more in-depth critique of such a view, I would like to take a closer look at the work of an author whom, although still working within the bureaucratic hypothesis, also considers elements that in my opinion permit an alternative approach to the study of the regimes examined here. I refer to Fernando Henrique Cardoso and his work on the "Brazilian political model" (1979). In that piece, he offers an analysis of the post-1964 regime that emphasizes its "hybrid aspects" or its "contradictory duality", referring to the special autonomy that economic policy maintains in relation to specifically political aspects. According to Cardoso, in Latin America, regardless of the type of State that prevails, countries with similar levels of industrialization present evident similarities in the content of their economic policies. Thus, in "bureaucratic-authoritarian" regimes, economic dynamics would maintain significant autonomy in relation to specifically political aspects. "In this regard, the militarization of power played a lesser role than we would have expected", Cardoso concludes, while at the same time affirming: the military "is in command. They control the State. But this command and control do not determine the central policies of government." (1984, p.48)[7] This seems to be the basis of Cardoso's approach to bureaucratization, which follows closely along the lines established by O'Donnell's analyses. And this is also the framework within which he introduces his famous concept of "bureaucratic rings" which cut horizontally across the two bureaucratic structures that are present on the Brazilian political scenario: the large private firm and the public bureaucracy (1975a).

Up to this point, Cardoso's argument fits within the boundaries of the bureaucratic paradigm for the analysis of political regimes. Nonetheless, in his own analyses, elements can be found that point toward the centrality of the military aspect of political arrangements. Thus, in criticizing the elitist bias of authors such as Cândido Mendes, who have taken the projects and ideology of political actors themselves all too seriously, Cardoso suggests to "rescue the nerve of politics, in other words, conflict", which means to pay attention to "opposition between groups within the system of power and between them and those who are outside of it." The analyst's task thus becomes the "identification of existing political forces, demarcating the area in which they operate and evaluating the results of their action". Furthermore, it becomes necessary to recognize the "zigzags" of politics that "create a margin for the formation of power structures that, although neither foreseen nor intended by political actors, must bear some relation to existing political forces."(1979, p. 72-74)

Such observations seem fundamental for the analysis of the military regimes and their political dynamics. Let us begin with the issue of power structures. In my view, Cardoso

[7] In this same sense, Cardoso proposes that these arrangements be understood in terms of a contradictory duality, "the creation of two guidelines for decision-making, one that is political/administrative/repressive and the other that it political/economic", with the military president as arbiter. (1975, p. 209)

himself does not give adequate consideration to the central characteristics of the transformation of political arrangements in post-1964 Brazil. In the period that follows the military coup, the new form of political representation that is a result of the ensuing crisis of bourgeois hegemony seems to point less to a process of bureaucratization than one of militarization of the State apparatus. In other words, the role that the Armed Forces come to play as the "political party of the bourgeoisie" upon the withdrawal of properly political representatives has as its institutional expression the emergence and consolidation of seats of military power – the presidency and its organs of military advisory, the three military ministries, as well as the Army commanders, the chiefs of staffs, and, after 1967 the High Command of the Armed Forces – that, in their political dimensions, are marked by a sharp "structural inequality" in relation to other branches and apparatuses of the State. In this regard, the preponderance of the military bureaucracy within the whole of the bureaucratic structure leads the analyst to emphasize, above all, the specific characteristics of this sector, insofar as it is the dominant branch of the repressive apparatus amongst all the branches that make up this form of dictatorial State. Thus, the concept that is most pertinent for our understanding of these regimes is that of military dictatorship, rather than bureaucratic autocracy.

Furthermore, Cardoso seems to pointing in this very direction himself, in his attempt to answer the question "What regime is this?", posed in relation to the election of General Medici (1969). On that occasion, he states that the "fundamental decision ... had the following characteristics: a) it was taken by the upper strata of the military bureaucracy (four star generals); it followed bureaucratic criteria of hierarchy and corporate representation; c) it put a damper on the greatest risk that the Army as dominant bureaucratic force had to face: a disunion produced by the proliferation of tendencies and factions; d) it thus led to conciliation among groups within the Army (1979, p. 78).

On this issue, a critique of dominant hypotheses will demand that we consider the consequences they imply for the analysis of the dynamics of political crises in dictatorial regimes. For such purposes, I propose focusing attention on the way in which this issue appears in analyses of the post-1964 Brazilian military dictatorship.

Bureaucratic Elitism and Political Dynamics

From my point of view, examining the dynamics of political crises is a privileged resource for the study of certain characteristics of the Brazilian military dictatorship. My central hypothesis is that an underestimation of its fundamentally military nature will lead to particular difficulties in understanding the political processes of the dictatorial regime. This is the context in which I will return to the critique of the elitist bureaucratic paradigm.

In his first book, O'Donnell has tried to take up the issue of the evolution of bureaucratic authoritarian regimes focusing his attention on the political interplay of domestic social actors, that is, on the values and the actions of the "technocratic elite". (1973, p. 106-109)[8]

[8] Within the framework of "game theory", the author proposes understanding political action as "action in a situation (policy issues, type of political system and rules of competition, and set of players) that must be taken into account at least by 'players' trying to achieve goals." (O'Donnell, 1973, p. 106) In a later text, he would see this approach as indispensable for "an adequate analysis of the dynamic, evolution and impact" of such arrangements. (O'Donnell, 1982, p. 41)

His analysis of the viability of the coalition that led the coup is thus based on the criteria according to which those who were "in pivotal technocratic roles" evaluated governmental performance. In his hypothesis, the government's "success" or "failure" in suppressing resistance from the social sectors t hurt by the authoritarian economic policy creates two possible routes of political evolution. In the "successful cases", support for the technocratic elite would be reinforced, at the cost of isolation from the affected social strata; government policies are employed in the sense that was previously noted and chances of dissidence are minimal. The process only looses intensity when technocratic criteria themselves are no longer able to sustain growth. At that point, however, the system has already been implanted and a new type of "political game" has been initiated.

On the other hand, in the case of "unsuccessful systems" (incapable of applying coercion efficiently) a wide range of consequences emerges. The search for technocratic goals generates effective social resistance but the government has no choice but to reinforce technocratic policies. New measures of this sort increase resistance and repression, which in turn make inevitable the reappearance of mass praetorianism and of political instability within the authoritarian context. This process also tends to split the dominant coalition in two: one sub-coalition that seeks to maintain continuity and a second one open to external alliances. If the former prevails and the process is thus continued along earlier lines, this will occur only until a new impasse is reached. On the other hand, the possibility of return to a democratic system means the return to the well-known conditions of mass praetorianism.

This framework of analysis refers explicitly to the case of the "successful" Brazilian dictatorship and the "failure" of the 1966 Argentine military regime. Nonetheless, this is not the place to go into greater detail on this hypothesis of comparative politics. The point to be made is that in this light, the Brazilian and Argentine military dictatorships appear to be voided of any specifically military dynamic. Such effects of the elitist bureaucratic approach appear clearly in other analyses. One example should be enough: Cândido Mendes' work on the dynamics of the post-64 Brazilian political system, whose cornerstone is the technocracy as a sort of classic sub-species of the power elite. The characteristics that define these groups are then relative social neutrality, ideological homogeneity, rationalist ideologies and ideologies of salvation. (Mendes, 1966). It is not quite surprising that authors that conceive of the new type of military regime as "authoritarian and bureaucratic" or that define them as "systems of the power elite" do not emphasize military processes in the general dynamics of these regimes. Less evident is why the elitist-bureaucratic paradigm is so strong in some of the main studies of the political role of the Armed Forces in Brazil and Argentina during the sixties. In this regard the most significant case is that of Alfred Stepan, whose views on the changing role of the military in countries with high levels of modernization, have been heavily incorporated by Guillermo O'Donnell (1986a).

Since its first edition in 1971, *The Military in Politics: Changing Patterns in Brazil,* the book that brought Stepan his fame, was welcomed as an undeniable step beyond the reigning theses on the military in modernizing countries. In opposition to ideas that until then had been widely accepted regarding the unity and self-isolation of the military corporation, Stepan suggested focusing research not on the institutional characteristics of the Armed Forces but on the interaction between the "military subsystem" and the wider political system. This was the framework within which he carried out his discussion on the changing political role of the military in Brazil. It thus seems natural that both critics and fans of Stepan's ideas have focused on his thesis on the "moderating pattern" of civil-military relations. Nonetheless, in emphasizing this aspect they have left the issue that interests us more specifically here on a lesser level: the consequences of Stepan's methodological approach for the analysis of the post 1964 Brazilian military regime.

In order to make progress in this direction, let us start from a first notion that can seem provocative: the hypothesis that the moderating pattern is not the most original aspect of Stepan's work.[9] Actually, the object of this research seems to lead us less to the moderating model than to the processes that were at the origin of its break-up and the implantation of a new "pattern" or "model" of civil-military relations. More precisely, it locates here – in the hypothesis of the emergence of a military ideology marked by a "new professionalism" – not only Stepan's most original contribution but also the key to understanding the limitations of his approach to post-1964 military processes in Brazil. In order to move ahead in this regard, I propose a reading of that author's propositions that focuses attention not only on his explicit theses but also in what the latter actually keep hidden.

In *The Military in Politics,* Stepan argues that the key element to understanding the role of the military lies in the examination of their interaction with the civil elite or, to use his own terminology, the relationship between the military subsystem and the global political system (54-55). The Armed Forces in his approach thus constitute "more of a dependent than an independent variable"(p.80). In building his moderating model, Stepan sought to attribute to the civilian elite a major role in the configuration of military behavior, through his hypothesis of the role of civil legitimacy in the success of Armed Forces intervention (66). Within this general context, the idea that the institutional characteristics of the military, although not "politically irrelevant", are subordinate to the interaction of the civil sphere in defining the behavior of the Armed Forces, seems coherent with his analytical framework (54-55). This is so to the point that, upon a first reading, Stepan's approach cannot be seen as "organizational". It is no coincidence that, upon examining the literature on the Brazilian military as it can be classified into "instrumental" and "organizational" approaches, some analysts have associated his moderating model with the first category, insofar as he suggests "that the arbitration of conflicts between classes and groups is carried out in consonance with the prevalent currents in public opinion." (Coelho, 1976, p. 19)

My approach here contests such a vision. In my hypothesis, although Stepan has sought to distinguish his studies through the emphasis given to the civil-military interaction, we can detect -in the very way in which he conceives of the two subsequent patterns of civil-military relationship – the need for a particular concept of military institution. In order to explain this point, it is necessary to go back to the issue of the "changing patterns" in military behavior. As is known, Stepan's point of departure was Samuel Huntington's thesis on the "professional" model of civil-military relations (Stepan,1973a) Stepan has presented his reasoning as an effort to break with that model on basically two accounts. To begin with, his critique of the Huntington model of civilian control over the military through professionalization is an important part of the building of the moderating model and is the basis of the idea that in praetorian societies the military is politicized and that civilians

[9] The author himself in the preface to his work recognizes his indebtedness to two Brazilian analysts: Fernando Pedreira and Cândido Mendes. In fact, as early as the mid sixties the two of them were widely advocating the notion of the moderating pattern. Perhaps it is enough to remember the text of the latter of these two authors published in 1966 in the Brazilian journal *Dados,* in which the Costa e Silva candidacy was considered to be major evidence of a "change in the role of the Armed Forces, from a moderating and arbitrating function to the open assuming of responsibilities in national political decision-making." (1966, p. 16)

concede a "partial legitimacy" to military participation in politics (1974, p. 49) At a following moment, the Huntington model becomes a reference for his construction of the concept of a "new professionalism" of the military. Thus, a change in military ideology is identified as being at the roots of the erosion of the moderating pattern and the emergence of a "new attitude" toward politics on the part of the military. (1973, p. 50)

The emphasis that Stepan places on this divergence can distract us from the convergence of the various models that we have analyzed. In effect, belying the definition of moderating, professional and leadership (or "new professionalism") patterns is a conception of the Armed Forces as a bureaucratic elite, in the terms of a systemic analysis of the military apparatus. Huntington's model seems to dispense with further explanations in this regard.[10] Regarding the moderating model, several analysts have identified the secondary role that it assigns to the military vis-à-vis the civilian elite (to whom the taking of initiatives is always attributed) as one of its most fragile points.

In my opinion, however, what these critics have not perceived is that it is the very "bureaucratic" conception of the military institution that lies at the heart of the "passive" role attributed to the Armed Forces. This point becomes more clearly evident on the issue of changing patterns of military behavior. There, Stepan's analysis of the change in military ideology and the emergence of a new military professionalism seems to be founded on a overestimation of the effects of the 1961-64 Brazilian crisis on military behavior. That critical juncture is seen as having had a double impact: on the one hand, it dissolved the "liberal" scenario in which the elite situated the moderating role of the Armed Forces; on the other hand, it sharpened the military's sense of institutional insecurity resulting from the presence of threats to military unity. These processes led to a change in the military's attitude regarding politics. And, as an analytical framework, it lends support to the central argument behind my critique of Stepan. It brings to the forefront an evident underestimation of the previously established ideological orientation of the Brazilian Armed Forces.[11] In such a view, the situation is portrayed as if it were only at this point that the Brazilian military as a corporatist entity "discovers" political ideologies. Thus, notwithstanding his reservations regarding Huntington's professional model, Stepan's conception of the military attitudes that characterize the moderating pattern seemed to be founded on a view of these sectors as a "professional" or "bureaucratic" elite.

This attribute stands out clearly in the second effect of the 1961-64 crisis on military attitudes: institutional reaction to political and social uncertainty. Referring to the military perception of the uncertainty reigning prior to the coup, in a text in which he reproduces Stepan's arguments, O'Donnell asserts: "organizations try to reduce uncertainty perceived as affecting the internal state and/or viability of the organization. ... the organization's directors operate through concepts and strategies which reflect their bias in perception and evaluation, as well as the patterns of decision-making which result from organizational specialization in certain types of activity". (O'Donnell,1986, p. 118)

Through these observations I have advanced the central elements of my critique. In both Stepan and O'Donnell, there is a prevailing definition of the military as basically an elitist and

---

[10] I refer here to the characteristics of role exclusivity, military specialization, ideological neutrality and homogeneization through professionalization that are present in the "professionalization pattern".

[11] For more on this question, see João Quartim (1985, p. 177) on the substition of "politics within the Army" for a "politics of the Army", as well as a discussion of the importance of the anti-Vargas sentiments that since 1945 were a component of the ideology of the Brazilian military.

bureaucratic group, with modifications in military ideology as a result of the ascendance of the National Security Doctrine. Emphasis placed on elements of variation undermines the importance of that which is held constant. This point established, we can go on to take a look at the effects that this paradigm has on the analysis of the military dynamics that follow the coup.

Other scholars have also perceived the tendency pertaining to the explicitly organizational paradigm to overestimate the homogeneity of the military and to put the divisions within the military camp in the background, whether before or after their coming to power. From my point of view, emphasis on military homogeneity is one of the most visible results of the bureaucratic and elitist paradigm.

Further demonstration of my argument would require a deeper examination of such results both for the "moderating" as well as the post-coup periods. In the first example, it takes me back to the notion of the military as a "professional group" and to the centrality of such a notion for Stepan's idea of the unilateral civilian co-optation of the military. For my purposes here, it seems more relevant to focus attention on the effects that the elitist and bureaucratic paradigm have over the analysis of the post-coup military dynamics. The aspect to be emphasized is the need that such a model creates to identify a *paradigmatic elite* corresponding to the ideal type that underlies it and that materializes its premises of the homogeneity, rationality and foreseeable behavior associated with the military and bureaucratic elite. This in my opinion is the bases of the analyses that take the ESG, the group represented by the *Escola Superior de Guerra*, as the main actor behind the coup movement, followed by the choice of the *Castelista* current as the paradigmatic elite and central agent of post-64 processes.

The fundamental point here is that the search for a paradigmatic elite leads these authors to overestimate a series of aspects including military project, discourse and ideology, in detriment to another series of processes linked to the practices, conflicts and actual balance of forces within the Armed Forces. In my opinion, therein lies the basis of the over-estimation of the role of chosen sectors of the military as paradigmatic: in the Brazilian case, the group belonging to the *Escola Superior de Guerra*.[12] Such studies tend to lose sight of the complex configuration of the whole of the Armed Forces during the military period and the specificity of the practices of the various political currents of the military. At the same time, it is precisely the need to recover aspects ignored by dominant paradigms that justify the search for an analytical alternative for understanding the political and military dynamics of the post-64 Brazilian regime.

An Alternative Hypothesis

In the simplest terms, the perspective that I advocate here emphasizes the military aspect of military bureaucracies. In opposition to the thesis of a bureaucratic elite – which gives salience to bureaucratic homogeneity – I try to reveal the nature of the specifically military heterogeneity, internal division and fluidity that characterize military political practice.

[12] In this regard, see O'Donnell's view of the Ongania administration as a "demilitarized military government" and his emphasis on the role of the "paternalist" current as the Argentine paradigm of military professionalization.

In general terms, this viewpoint is not new in the field of analyses on the role on the Armed Forces in countries such as Brazil. For example, this seems to be the sense that is given to the concerns of authors who proposed the hypothesis of military parties in order to take up the specificities of the political behavior of the military institution. As the French sociologist Alain Rouquié notes: "The Armed Forces may be seen as political forces that carry out, through different means, the same basic functions as political parties and that include – just as parties do, but with a different logic – processes of deliberation, of decision-making and even of social articulation and unity." (Rouquié, 1991, p. 12)

In proposing this type of idea such analysts seek to question "the common sense notion (encouraged by the military itself) of the Armed Forces as a unified, if not monolithic action. This notion was inspired by a simplistic sketching of the organizational traits that characterize military institutions (discipline, hierarchy, verticality)". (Rouquié, 1991, p. 13)

The hypothesis of military heterogeneity only makes sense when complemented by an analysis of the particularity of the specifically military features that serve to define the military's political action. According to Rouquié himself, the Armed Forces, a "hierarchical and bureaucratic institution", do not react as a political party, and its intervention in political life is neither the "impersonal, mechanical and unanimous action of a monolithic structural organization nor the docile instrument of formal hierarchical leaders." Military and political cleavages "obey properly institutional mechanisms: thus their fluid boundaries and tendencies." (Rouquié, 1978, p. 661)

The processes that Rouquié analyzed for the Argentine case seem relevant for those who study the Brazilian military. The analysis of the first Brazilian military governments should reveal the relevance of characteristics such as the following: principles of co-optation and verticality that preside in military promotion and nomination and the relation they maintain to the creation of networks of loyalty and the formation of a veritable "clientele" within army ranks; the political reformulation of military hypothesis elaborated at the highest levels as a basis for the contradictory and essentially negative character of military opinion; the military vision of the strategic enemy as the basis of the fluidity of military divisions; the influence of the martial conception of the social universe on military ideology and concerns with unity and unanimity (Rouquié, 1978, p. 662-670). Following in a similar vein, several empirical studies demonstrate it is impossible to understand military practice simply in terms of bureaucratic characteristics (Peixoto, 1991; Varas, 1992).

Nonetheless, the acceptance of these theses on the specific nature of military political practices, according to the hypothesis of my work, depends on the re-examination of the problematic of the relationship between processes of political crisis and structural forms of State power. In other terms, it is not enough to assert the specificity and autonomy of the military: it has to be understood that the action of military parties takes on different meanings in different forms of State and regime. In order to make this fundamental point clearer, we need to return to the question of the forms of State of crisis or of "exception", as it appears in Poulantzas' work (1978a). There we can find some basic distinctions that, although maintaining a high level of abstraction, point to the fundamental processes for an analysis of the political crises of dictatorships. We should begin with an examination of Poulantzas' distinction between the fascist and Bonapartist or military dictatorship forms of States of exception. For Poulantzas, the dominance of the fascist party, as an ideological State apparatus, allows the fascist State a specific stabilizing element; the military and Bonapartist dictatorships in which dominance is dislocated to a branch of the repressive apparatus (specifically, to civil administration and the Armed Forces) do not possess this specific stabilizing element.

Next, we go on to consider the opposition that Poulantzas establishes between the entirety of forms of the State "of exception" and the democratic form of capitalist State. According to that hypothesis, what distinguishes parliamentary democracies is their ability to allow "organic representation" or the "organic circulation of hegemony". In other words, to use "a skeletal organization that allows for the functioning and organic circulation of hegemony through fractions of the bloc that is in power, through their political representatives, and even a certain regulated ventilation of power within the ruling classes and dominant fractions". In crisis forms, "such a situation is completely impossible". (1978, p. 72)

These two structural distinctions make it possible to put forth the central hypothesis that I have but outlined in the first part of this article: the political crises of military dictatorships maintain a characteristic specificity. Returning to Poulantzas: "the political crises that mark States of exception are feared much more by the latter than they are within parliamentary democracy, which usually possess the institutional means to manage such crisis".(1978, p. 72) But the political instability that characterizes dictatorial forms acquires special significance in the case of military regimes. In this case, the inability to articulate their hegemony, which is common to crisis forms, joins the absence of a fascist party as a stabilizing element and is accentuated by the role of the Armed Forces, as the "dominant apparatus" in these arrangements. (1978, p. 82) This new role played by the Army distinguished dictatorships of this type from fascist ones. As Poulantzas says:

> "the internal contradictions of these regimes were manifested par excellence within the military apparatus (which, precisely and further, possesses the power of armaments) and not within the party and the bureaucracy, which are the dominant apparatuses of fascist regimes. These makes the internal contradictions of the former type of regime much more fearsome in their case than in the latter type." (1978, p. 82)

On this point, however, an important distinction should be made that points precisely to the peculiarity of dictatorships of the Brazilian type. In his analysis of European cases, Poulantzas asserts that the crisis of hegemony that led to the emergence of military dictatorships corresponded to important dislocations in the relationship of social forces, a process that was carried out, within the State, through a profound change in its apparatuses: Thus, he argues, "it is essentially toward the Army, or more precisely those who are at its head, toward whom the role of the political parties of the bourgeoisie is re-located, making this former group the political party of the entire bourgeoisie under the guidance of its hegemonic fragment." (1978, p. 82)

In an analysis of the new types of dictatorship in Latin America, such observations must be considered with some fundamental reservations. In these countries, it is not that the military should not be considered as making up the political party of the bourgeoisie, if we consider their role in the maintenance of the bourgeois order and the phenomenon that some Marxist theoreticians have referred to as "substitutionism". Nonetheless, study of the Brazilian case leads to some frontal questions regarding the feasibility of interpreting this intra-military division as intra-bourgeois divisions. In other words, I don't think it is viable to analyze post-1964 Brazilian military parties as an expression in the military realm of wider social divisions, as Poulantzas does for the Greek, Spanish and Portuguese cases or

O'Donnell for the Argentine case. In this case, it is impossible to interpret these military currents as political parties of the bourgeoisie.

Further explanation of this issue allows us to move forward on the central hypothesis of this article. In effect, one of the characteristics that stands out in our examination of the political conflicts surrounding the consolidation phase of the Brazilian military regime is precisely the critical unity of the Armed Forces once it was purged of popular and nationalist elements. This unity was built through a unanimous opposition, amongst officials and hierarchy, to returning power to civilian hands. This characteristic brings out a feature that is peculiar to societies of the Brazilian type. Within the latter, given the nature of the process through which popular masses have been brought into political life – referred to generically as "populism" – the emergence of a military ideology based on a strong rejection of civil politics was possible. The latter were seen as the equivalent of a "populist demagogy" that was associated with social instability and risks of a breakdown of order.

This equation of "politics" and "populism" came to express itself, after the Brazilian military took power, in a particular military impenetrability regarding divisions emanating from the "civil world'. In other words, the preventive strategy of refusal of any possibility of a populist "return to the past" created a scenario of military unity which was to define, in the broadest sense, the political dynamics of the post-1964 regime. On a first level, the unitary process led to increasing militarization each time a threat to the military regime was perceived; the same can be said regarding the processes of division within the Armed Forces themselves, that is, with each successive political and military crisis. The crucial unity thus created in opposition to the "political world" thus coexists with constant military strife. It is in effect, a situation of unity within division. In more specific terms, this refers to two relatively separate processes: disunity expresses itself differently within the hierarchy (discord regarding presidential succession) and within officialdom (divisions in the barracks, related to expectations of direct influence on the government).

Thus qualifying Poulantzas' observations and providing clarifications for my own hypotheses, I think the moment is ripe to introduce what I believe to be an essential point: the military dictatorships of the new type, in spite of the myth of their stability, do not just constitute crisis forms of the State because they emerge from specific crises, but can also be considered as critical State forms because they are marked by a specific kind of instability. Understanding this instability requires the study of their intra-military dynamics. Finally, it is the examination of these dynamics that allows us to critique the hegemonic model of analysis of the post-1964 intra-military conflicts. Within this model, the military world is understood through the lens of a dualistic and dichotomous hypothesis based on the notion of an opposition between two fundamental camps: a "liberal", "moderate" or "legalist" sector, bearer of an internationalist economic orientation, and a wide arena of "hard-liners", "ultras" and "radicals", spokespersons for military nationalism. The clash between these two camps is seen as defining the regime's intra-military dynamics. However, a critique of this perspective would take us beyond the scope of this article.

References

Antunes, R. 1988. *A rebeldia do trabalho*. Campinas/São Paulo, Unicamp-Ensaio.

Bacchus, W. 1990. *Mission in Mufti*: Brazil's military regimes, 1964-1985. New York, Greenwood Press.

Borón, A. 1977. "El fascismo como categoria histórica: en torno al problema de las dictaduras en América Latina". *Revista Mexicana de Sociologia*, v. 39 n. 2, p. 481-528, abril-jun.

Campos Coelho, E. 1976. *Em busca da identidade*: o exército e a política na sociedade brasileira. São Paulo, Forense-Universitária.

Cardoso, F. H. 1975a. "Estado e sociedade no Brasil". In _____. *Autoritarismo e democratização*. Rio de Janeiro, Paz e Terra.

Cardoso, F. H. 1975b. "A questão do Estado no Brasil". In _____. *Autoritarismo e democratização*. Rio de Janeiro, Paz e Terra.

Cardoso, F. H. 1979. *O modelo político brasileiro*. São Paulo, Difel.

Cardoso, F. H. 1982. "Da caracterização dos regimes autoritários na América Latina". In D. Collier (ed.) *O novo autoritarismo na América Latina*. Rio de Janeiro, Paz e Terra.

Cardoso, F. H. 1984. "A democracia na América Latina", *Novos Estudos*, v. 10, p. 45-56, out.

Carvalho, J. M. de. 1983. "Forças Armadas e política, 1930-1945". In Vários Autores, *A revolução de 30*: seminário internacional. Brasília, Ed. da UnB.

Collier, D. 1982a. "Resumo do modelo autoritário democrático". In D. Collier, *O novo autoritarismo na América Latina*. Rio de Janeiro, Paz e Terra.

Druckman, D. and Vario, E. 1983. "Regimes and Selection of Military Leaders: Brazilian Cabinet Ministries and Generals", *Journal of Political and Military Sociology*, v. 11, p. 301-324, Fall.

Feit, E. 1973. "Pen, Sword and People: Military Regimes in the Formation of Political Institutions", *World Politics*, v. 25 n. 2, p. 251-73, January.

Fiechter, G.-A. 1975. *Brazil since 1964*: modernization under a military regime. New York/Toronto, John Wiley and Sons.

Guimarães, C. 1988. "Domínio burguês incompleto: a teoria do autoritarismo em Marx". In N. V. de Carvalho (ed.), *Trilogia do terror*. São Paulo, Vértice.

Huntington, S. 1968. *Political Order in Changing Societies*. New York/London, Yale University Press.

Jaguaribe, H. 1968. "Brasil: estabilidad social por el colonial-fascismo?". In Furtado, C. *et alii*, *Brasil Hoy*. México, Siglo XXI.

Linz, J. 1970. "An Authoritarian Regime: Spain". In E. Allardt e S. Rokkan (eds.), *Mass Politics*: studies in political sociology. New York, Free Press.

Linz, J. 1973. "The Future of an Authoritarian Situation or the Institutionalization of an Authoritarian Regime: the Case of Brazil". In A. Stepan, *Authoritarian Brazil*: Origins, Policies and Future. New Haven, Yale University Press.

Linz, J. 1978. *Crisis, Breakdown and Reequilibration*. Baltimore/London, Johns Hopkins University Press.

Martins, C. E. 1977. *Capitalismo de Estado e modelo político no Brasil*. Rio de Janeiro, Graal.

Mendes, C. 1966. "Sistemas políticos e modelos de poder no Brasil". *Dados*, v. 1 n. 1, p. 7-41.

Mendes, C. 1967. "O governo Castelo Branco: paradigma e prognose". *Dados*, v. 1 n. 2/3, p. 63-111.

O'Donnell, G. 1973. *Modernization and Bureaucratic-Authoritarianism* – Studies in South American Politics. Berkeley, University of California Press.

O'Donnell, G. 1977. "Corporatism and the Question of the State". In J. Malloy (ed.), *Authoritarianism and Corporatism in Latin America*. Pittsburgh, University of Pittsburgh Press.

O'Donnell, G. 1980. "Desenvolvimento político ou mudança política?". In Paulo Sérgio Pinheiro (ed.) *O Estado autoritário e movimentos populares*. Rio de Janeiro, Paz e Terra.

O'Donnell, G. 1982. "Reply to Remmer and Merkx". *Latin American Research Review*, v. 17 n. 2, p. 41-50.

O'Donnell, G. 1986a. "Modernization and Military Coups: Theory, Comparisons and the Argentine Case". In A.Lowenthal e S. Fitch (eds.), *Armies and Politics in Latin America*. Revised ed. New York, Holmes and Meies.

O'Donnell, G. 1986b. "Tensões no estado burocrático-autoritário e a questão da democracia". In _____. *Contrapontos: autoritarismo e democratização*. São Paulo, Vértice.

O'Donnell, G. 1987. *Reflexões sobre os Estados burocráticos-autoritários*. Sao Paulo, Vértice.

O'Donnell, G. 1988. *Bureaucratic-Authoritarianism*: Argentina, 1966-73. Comparative Perspectives. Berkeley/Los Angeles, University of California Press.

Oliveira, E. R. de. 1978. *As forças armadas*: política e ideologia no Brasil 1964-69. 2a. ed. Petrópolis, Vozes.

Peixoto, A. C. 1991. "O Clube Militar e os confrontos no seio das Forças Armadas 1945-1964)". In A. Rouquié (ed.) *Os partidos militares no Brasil*. Rio de Janeiro, Record.

Perlmutter, A. 1969. "The Praetorian State and the Praetorian Army", *Comparative Politics*, v. 1 n. 3, p. 382-404, April.

Poulantzas, N. 1977. *Poder político e classes sociais*. São Paulo, Martins Fontes.

Poulantzas, N. 1978. *A crise das ditaduras*: Espanha, Portugal, Grécia. 2ª ed. Rio de Janeiro, Paz e Terra.

Poulantzas, N. 1978a. *Fascismo e ditadura*. São Paulo, Martins Fontes.

Poulantzas, N e Miliband, R. 1982. "O problema do Estado burguês". In Blackburn, R. (ed.), *Ideologia na Ciência Social*. Rio de Janeiro, Paz e Terra.

Quartim, J. 1971. "La nature de classe de l'État brésilien". *Les Temps Moderns*, Paris, v. 304/305, p. 651-675 and p. 853-78, nov./dec.

Quartim, J. 1985. "Alfred Stepan e o mito do poder moderador". *Filosofia Política*, v. 2, p. 163-199.

Remmer, K. and Merkx, G. 1982. "Bureaucratic-Authoritarianism Revisited", *Latin American Research Review*, v. 17 n. 2, p. 3-40.

Roett, R. 1973. "Un ejercito pretoriano en politica: el cambio de rol de los militares brasileños", *Revista Paraguaya de Sociologia*, v. 26 n. 26, p. 79-119, enero-abril.

Rouquié, A. 1978. *Pouvoir militaire et société politique en Republique Argentine*. Paris, Fondation Nationale des Sciences Politiques.

Rouquié, A. 1984. *O Estado militar na América Latina*. São Paulo, Alfa-Omega.

Rouquié, A. 1991. "Os processos políticos nos partidos militares do Brasil". In A. Rouquié (ed.) *Os partidos militares no Brasil*. Rio de Janeiro, Record.

Rowe, J. W. 1966. “The ‘Revolution’ and the ‘System’: Notes on Brazilian Politics”. *American Universities Field Staff Reports*, East Coast South America Series, v. 12, May-Aug.

Saes, D. 1982. “O conceito de Estado burguês: direito, burocratismo e representação popular”. *Cadernos IFCH/Unicamp*, v. 1, dez.

Saes, D.. 1987. *Democracia.* São Paulo, Ática.

Schmitter, P.. 1973. “The Portugalization of Brazil?” In Stepan, A. *Authoritarian Brazil*: Origins, Policies and Future. New Haven, Yale University Press.

Schmitter, P. 1974. “Still the Century of Corporatism?” *The Review of Politics,* v. 36 n. 1, p. 85-131, jan.

Schneider, R. 1971. *The Political System of Brazil*, New York and London, Columbia University Press.

Serra, J. 1982. “As desventuras do economicismo: três teses equivocadas sobre a conexão entre o autoritarismo e desenvolvimento”. In D. Collier (ed.) *O novo autoritarismo na América Latina.* Rio de Janeiro, Paz e Terra.

Skidmore, T. 1988. *Brasil*: de Castelo a Tancredo. Rio de Janeiro, Paz e Terra.

Stepan, A. 1973. *Authoritarian Brazil*: Origins, Policies and Future. New Haven, Yale University Press.

Stepan, A. 1973a. “The New Professionalism of Internal Warfare and Military Role Expansion”. In _____ (ed.). *Authoritarian Brazil*: Origins, Policies and Future. New Haven, Yale University Press.

Stepan, A. 1974. *The Military in Politics* – Changing Patterns in Brazil. Princeton, Princeton University Press.

Varas, A. 1982. “Fuerzas Armadas y gobierno militar: corporativización y politización castrense”. *Revista Mexicana de Sociología*, v. 44 n. 2, p. 397-411, abr.-jun.

Velasco e Cruz, S. and Martins, C. E. 1984. “De Castelo a Figueiredo: uma incursão na pré-história da abertura”. In Sorj, B. e Almeida, M. H.T. de (eds.). *Sociedade e política no Brasil pós-64*. São Paulo, Brasiliense.

Werneck Sodré, N. 1979. *A história militar do Brasil.* 3a ed. Rio de Janeiro, Civilização Brasileira.

Zirker, D. 1986. “Civilianization and authoritarian nationalism in Brazil: ideological opposition within a military dictatorship”. *Journal of Political and Military Sociology*, v. 14, p. 263-274, Fall.

In: Economics, Politics and Social Issues in Latin America ISBN 1-60021-182-8
Editor: Mary P. Lassiter, pp. 29-53

Chapter 3

BRAZILIAN TRADE POLICY AND THE UNITED STATES*

J. F. Hornbeck

ABSTRACT

As the largest and one of the most influential countries in Latin America, Brazil has emerged as a leading voice for developing countries in setting regional and multilateral trade agendas. The United States and Brazil have cultivated a constructive relationship in pursuit of their respective efforts to promote trade liberalization, including attempting to broker a compromise with the European Union in the World Trade Organization (WTO) Doha Round and forming bilateral working groups on trade (and other) issues. Still, they approach trade policy quite differently, are at odds over how to proceed regionally with the Free Trade Area of the Americas (FTAA), and share concerns over specific trade policies and practices.

Brazil's trade strategy can be explained only in part by economic incentives. Its "trade preferences" also reflect deeply embedded macroeconomic, industrial, and foreign policies. Whereas U.S. trade strategy emphasizes the negotiation of comprehensive trade agreements on multiple fronts, Brazil is focused primarily on market access issues as they pertain to its economic dominance in South America. Brazil exercises this priority in all trade arenas, such as pursuing changes to agricultural policies in the WTO, expanding the Southern Common Market (Mercosul) in South America, and resisting the FTAA for lack of a balance conducive to Brazilian interests.

Brazil has a modern, diversified economy in which services account for 53% of GDP, followed by industry and manufacturing at 37%, and agriculture at 9%. Agribusiness (commodity and processed goods) account for some 30% of GDP, explaining Brazil's emphasis on agricultural policies in trade negotiations. Brazil is the world's largest producer of sugar cane, oranges, and coffee, and the second largest of soybean, beef, poultry, and corn. It is also a major producer of steel, aircraft, automobiles, and auto parts, yet surprisingly, a relatively small trader by world standards. The United States is Brazil's largest single-country trading partner.

Brazil is critical of U.S. trade policies such as the Byrd Amendment (repealed, but program in effect until October 1, 2007), which directs duties from trade remedy cases to

* Excerpted from CRS Report RL33258 dated February 3, 2006.

affected industries, the administration of trade remedy rules, and what it considers to be discriminatory treatment in the U.S. expansion of free trade agreements in Latin America. It also objects to product-specific barriers such as tariff rate quotas on sugar, orange juice, ethanol, and tobacco; subsidies for cotton, ethanol, and soybeans; and prolonged antidumping orders on steel and orange juice. U.S. concerns focus on Brazil's comparatively high tariff structure, especially on industrial goods, Mercosul's common external tariff program, and Brazil's refusal to address issues of critical importance to the United States such as services trade, intellectual property rights, government procurement, and investment.

Despite these differences, both countries recognize the potential for important gains to be had from mutually acceptable trade liberalization at all levels. As a developing country with an opportunity for considerable growth in both exports and imports, however, Brazil may have the most to gain from addressing both foreign barriers to its trade, and unilaterally opening its economy further.

As the largest and one of the most influential countries in Latin America (see Figure 1), Brazil has emerged in recent years as a leading voice for developing countries, particularly in setting regional and multilateral trade agendas. Brazil led in the creation of the Southern Common Market (Mercado Común do Sul — Mercosul), is a co-chair with the United States of the Free Trade Area of the Americas (FTAA) negotiations, was a founding member of the Group of 20 (G-20) coalition that represents developing country interests in the Doha Development Round of the World Trade Organization (WTO) negotiations, and meets bilaterally in working sessions with the United States on trade (and other) issues, in part because of its influence in all these groups.[1]

Brazil is the 15th largest U.S. export market, but a distant second to Mexico as the United States' top trading partner in Latin America. For economies of their size, Brazil and the United States actually trade rather little with each other. Trade and investment between the two is growing, however, and the potential for deeper economic relations was a prominent theme in the two meetings that Presidents George W. Bush and Luiz Inácio Lula da Silva have held. During President Bush's visit to Brasilia in November 2005, the two presidents issued a joint communique reinforcing the importance of: 1) building on the many bilateral working groups already established; 2) increasing cooperation on trade matters at the WTO; and 3) taking advantage of the potential to double bilateral trade by 2010.[2]

The United States and Brazil have purposely cultivated a constructive relationship in pursuit of their respective efforts to promote trade liberalization. This is important because as a developing country, Brazil's trade priorities can vary from those of the United States, and the two are often at odds over specific trade practices. This has ranged from disagreements that have halted progress on the FTAA, to ongoing trade disputes before the WTO. For the United States, this means that maintaining a strong working relationship with Brazil is important for making progress with its own trade agenda. To assist Congress in understanding Brazil's stance on regional and global trade matters, this report analyzes Brazil's foreign trade policy and

---

1 Mercosul is the Portuguese variation of the more widely seen Spanish acronym Mercosur. It includes Brazil, Argentina, Uruguay, and Paraguay, with six other South American countries affiliated as associate members. The FTAA is a proposed free trade area that would encompass 34 countries of the Western Hemisphere (all except Cuba).

2 Joint Statement on the Occasion of the Visit by President George W. Bush to Brazil. November 5-6, 2005.

how it affects its trade relations with the world and the United States. It will be updated periodically.

Source: Map Resources. Adapted by CRS (K. Yancey 11/28/05)

Figure 1. Map of Brazil.

BRAZILIAN FOREIGN TRADE STRATEGY

David Ricardo postulated the rationale for free trade some 200 years ago when he argued that countries could improve their national welfare if they exploited their comparative advantage by exporting those goods at which they were relatively more efficient at producing and importing the rest. Later arguments for trade pointed to the benefits arising from intra-industry trade (and investment) in which specialized production along with scale economies could lead to even more efficient exchange and innovation-driven productivity increases. These foundational ideas, which recognize the value of both imports and exports, remain valid today for explaining why countries generally wish to pursue freer trade and why trade liberalization has been at the center of the economic reform debate in much of Latin America.

In practice, however, few countries have opted unilaterally to throw open their borders to unfettered free trade, and the call to maintain trade barriers is common even if it is understood that they come with a cost to society as a whole. There are many reasons for this. Perhaps most transparent is resistence by firms and workers who stand to bear most of the adjustment costs of freer trade, even if national welfare is ultimately enhanced through lower priced goods and services, a greater selection of choices from imports, and overall efficiency gains that can lead to higher national income. Less obvious is that countries adopt diverse trade policies based on historically, socially, and politically determined "trade preferences" that cannot be explained solely by a calculus of economic costs and benefits.

The "trade preference" framework helps explain Brazil's trade strategy. It pegs Brazil as a "regional leader" based on its leadership in pressing for South American economic integration, its conditional support of multilateral negotiations, and its reticence to consummate separate trade deals with developed countries.[3] Brazil's trade preferences in order of priority are: 1) expand and strengthen Mercosul, where Brazil is the undisputed industrial hub and political leader; 2) advocate developing country interests in the Doha Round, especially on agricultural issues, and; 3) resist what it views as a welfare reducing, U. S.-designed FTAA, and to a lesser extent, also a preferential trade arrangement with the European Union unless it serves as a counter influence to the FTAA.[4]

Brazil and the United States approach trade liberalization from different perspectives. U.S. trade strategy has been characterized as "competitive liberalization,"[5] where simultaneously negotiating comprehensive multilateral, regional, and bilateral pacts allows gains to be achieved where parties can agree. It is competitive in that gains at one level of negotiation (e.g. bilateral or regional) can create new incentives or pressures to make breakthroughs at other levels (e.g. regional or multilateral). It is comprehensive by its inclusion of issues that go beyond market access such as services trade, intellectual property rights, government procurement, and investment.

---

[3] The "trade preference" framework is developed in Aggarwal, Vinod K. and Ralph Espach. Diverging Trade Strategies in Latin America: A Framework for Analysis. In: Aggarwal, Vinod K., Ralph Espach, and Joseph S. Tulchin, eds. *The Strategic Dynamics of Latin American Trade.* Woodrow Wilson Center Press. Washington, D.C. 2004. p. 4-5. By comparison, Chile with its unilateral reduction in trade barriers and multiple trade agreements would be a "multilateral trader," and Argentina would be a "regional partner" based on its supportive role for regional integration. See pp. 11-12.

[4] Da Motta Veiga, Pedro. Regional and Transregional Dimensions of Brazilian Trade Policy. In: Aggarwal, Vinod K., Ralph Espach, and Joseph S. Tulchin, eds. *The Strategic Dynamics of Latin American Trade.* Woodrow Wilson Center Press. Washington, D.C. 2004. pp. 180-183 and multiple interviews by the author with Brazilian trade officials.

[5] Although this concept is widely associated with Robert Zoellick, first USTR in the George W. Bush administration, it has an intellectual antecedent in: Bergsten, C. Fred. Globalizing Free Trade. *Foreign Afairs.* May/June 1996. pp. 105-106.

Brazil has a narrower and more cautious tack, restricted largely to market access and dominance in regional trade, where it feels most ready to compete. The perceived benefits of Brazil's strategy include attaining greater bargaining power through the Mercosul coalition, slowing the multilateral trade liberalization process to allow more time for economic adjustment, and enhancing its national influence in the world by protecting domestic economic (industrial) capacity. These "trade preferences" are not randomly determined, but are deeply embedded in the country's industrial, foreign, and macroeconomic policies, discussed below.

Trade and Industrial Policy

The "regional leader" category captures well the influence Brazil's economic development strategy has had on its trade preferences and policy. Brazil adopted its own version of the import substitution industrialization (ISI) model employed throughout much of Latin America in the 20th century. To promote industrial development, Brazil created, and protected from foreign competition, important government sponsored enterprises that still operate today, although some are now privatized. These include the National Steel Company (CSN) founded in 1942; Petrobras, the national petroleum company, established in the 1 950s; the National Economic and Social Development Bank (BNDES), created in 1952; and Embraer, a leading manufacturer of regional jets, incorporated in 1969.[6] BNDES was at the heart of this policy, providing financing for public infrastructure and strategic industries. It continues today as a necessary major source of long-term business financing given the unique structure of Brazil's financial system.

Brazil's industrial policy achieved notable results for decades, but with predictable tradeoffs. The inward orientation of the ISI model shielded domestic industry from global competition, diminishing market incentives to innovate and become more efficient. Trade policy was essentially administered protectionism.[7]

The large state bureaucracy also contributed to inefficiency and the high cost of doing business in Brazil. Although privatization efforts in the 1990s have improved the competitive landscape in Brazil, the so-called Brazil cost or "Custo Brasil" endures, which is one way of saying there are numerous microeconomic distortions introduced by excessive taxation, high interest rates, cumbersome regulations, and corruption.[8] The large untaxed informal economy combined with Brazil's big government, for example, mean that formal businesses pay up to

---

6 Gordon, Lincoln. *Brazil's Second Chance: En Route toward the First World.* Brookings Institution Press, Washington, D.C. 2001. pp. 35 and 44.

7 This policy was overseen by the Carteira de Comércio Exterior do Banco do Brasil (CACEX), created during the military dictatorship (1964-1985). Trade policy today is set by the President with the Foreign Ministry as the lead agency. The Foreign Trade Board (Câmara de Comércio Exterior — CAMEX), created in 1995, acts as an advisory agency for all government departments. Cross-sectoral business interests are voiced by the Brazilian. Business Coalition (Coalizao Empresarial Brasiliera — CEB), established in 1996. NGOs, trade unions, and other independent groups are represented in coalition groups, such as the Brazilian Network for the Integration of People (Rede Brasileira pela Integracao dos Povos — REBRIP). Marconini, Mario. *Trade Policy-Making Process in Brazil.* Mimeo. March 2005. pp. 2-3 and 8-9, and author's interviews with Brazilian trade officials.

8 Globally, Brazil ranks at the bottom for the number of regulations and time it takes to start a new business, and is also known for its cumbersome labor force regulations. See The World Bank. *Doing Business in 2005: Removing Obstacles to Growth.* Washington, D.C. 2005. pp. 19, 28, and 89-97.

85% of the tax burden, more than twice that of the United States.[9] These issues directly diminish Brazilian productivity and indirectly deter trade liberalization. Yet, continuing to protect this regulatory regime and Brazil's "national production structure" remains an important aspect of the national trade strategy, a priority Brazil pursues unilaterally and through Mercosul.[10]

Trade and Foreign Policy

As with all countries, Brazil's foreign policy shapes its trade preferences, but compared to the United States it plays a more prominent role. Unlike the United States where trade policy is constitutionally defined as the responsibility of Congress and carried out in a separate cabinet-level agency (the United States Trade Representative — USTR), in Brazil it is undertaken by the executive branch under the purview of the Ministry of Foreign Relations. The most important aspects of trade policy, therefore, are driven less by commercial interests and often are subordinated to a larger foreign policy imperative, primarily, enhancing Brazil's influence in Latin America and the world. In the Western Hemisphere, this implies taking on the United States. In the words of one Brazilian expert, "Brazil's foreign policy over the past four decades is characterized by competition with the United States, and the objective of developing the nation's industrial capacity as a key condition for independent activities within the international system."[11]

Economically, there are two sides to this policy: offensively, it seeks to integrate South America; defensively, it seeks to deter encroaching U.S. economic influence in the region. Brazil's government has taken steps recently to realize this agenda, by establishing in 2004 the South America Community of Nations as a loosely interwoven example of political and economic integration and by limiting progress on the U.S. version of the FTAA. Although intentions may not be overtly adversarial, these two policies do present a challenge to the U.S trade agenda. By extension, Brazil's leadership in the region is played out at the WTO where it is an unyielding force in pushing for reductions in agricultural barriers in the Doha Round.

The foreign policy aspect of trade policy may also be seen in the emphasis on deepening developing country trade relations. In addition to negotiating for developing country interests in multilateral and regional trade talks, Brazil has also consummated an agreement with the Andean countries, India, and South Africa, and deepened relations with Portuguese-speaking African countries, by concluding various commitments on trade. Progress in the Doha Round, FTAA, and EU negotiations has proven harder to achieve.[12]

Trade and Macroeconomic Issues

Macroeconomic challenges have and continue to constrain Brazil's trade policy options. Brazil, for example, is known for its historical accommodation to inflation, having employed

---

[9] Lewis, William W. The Power of Productivity: Wealth, Poverty, and the Threat to Global Stability. University of Chicago Press, Chicago, 2004. pp. 140-41.

[10] Pedro Da Motta Veiga, Regional and Transregional Dimensions of Brazilian Trade Policy, p. 183.

[11] Ibid., p. 177.

[12] Mario Marconini, Trade Policy-Making in Brazil, p. 5.

for decades a comprehensive system of wage, price, and interest rate indexation as part of its macroeconomic management. Inflation ran at "manageably" high rates for years and was fought, albeit unsuccessfully, with a number of stabilization plans. By the 1970s, however, it eventually spiraled out of control following the oil price shocks. This led Brazil to the 1980s debt crisis along with much of Latin America.[13] By the 1990s, the economy was defined by its growing deficits and debt, failed efforts at stabilization, slow growth (averaging only 2.3% from 1980 to 2004), and reluctance to embrace reforms. An important factor in Brazil's sluggish economic performance was poor productivity growth due to microeconomic policy distortions discussed above, macroeconomic problems, and to some degree, also its closed trade policy.[14]

Brazilian trade policy also had to adjust to encroaching globalization in the 1 990s, including multilateral efforts (the conclusion of the Uruguay Round), new regional talks (the FTAA), and U.S. subregional initiatives (the North American Free Trade Agreement — NAFTA). Brazil responded with some unilateral liberalization, the formation of Mercosul in 1991 with Argentina, Uruguay, and Paraguay to consolidate its trade positions in South America, and the adoption of a government-assisted export promotion policy to help address its large and growing external debt. The average tariff in Brazil fell from 51% in 1988 to 14% in 1994, but the selective preferences given under Mercosul belied the liberalization message as Brazil continued to limit trade outside the regional pact, allowing it to manage carefully the degree to which foreign competition would be accepted.[15]

Brazil's trade policy shifted again in 1994 to accommodate the *Real* Plan, a price stabilization policy imposed by then-Finance Minister (and later-President) Fernando Henrique Cardoso. It was named for a new currency that was pegged to the U.S. dollar to serve as an anchor to bring down hyperinflation. The plan actually worked where others had not, but in pegging the *real* to the dollar, the differences in inflation between the two countries caused a large real appreciation of the Brazilian currency, as price levels between the two countries diverged. This resulted in a sudden turn to trade deficits in 1995 (see Figure 2), an economic consequence that ran counter to the political priority given to running trade surpluses. To offset the exchange rate effect on the balance of payments, Brazil raised interest rates and redoubled its protectionist policies.[16]

The macroeconomic story was further complicated by a major financial crisis in 1998 that resulted in a currency devaluation and return to a floating exchange rate in 1999, Argentina's financial collapse in 2001, and a financial panic in 2002 exaggerated by the impending

---

[13] In the 1970s, Brazil was a maj or importer of oil, but the government delayed passing on the full price increase to the public, financing the difference with debt. By 1982, this subsidy proved unsustainable and when eliminated, the higher price doubled the annual inflation rate to nearly 100%. Because of indexation, the oil price increase was passed on to wages, which then showed up as more price inflation. Suddenly, it seemed, Brazil was swamped by debt and spiraling hyperinflation, and so began the lost decade of the 1980s. For a good discussion of the economic points, see Dornbusch, Rudiger. Brazil's Incomplete Stabilization and Reform. *Brookings Papers on Economic Activity.* William C. Brainard and George L. Perry, editors. Washington, D.C. 1997. pp. 37 1-374.

[14] Blyde, Juan S and Eduardo Fernnadez-Arias. *Economic Growth in the Southern Cone.* Economic and Social Study Series. RE1-04-004. Inter-American Development Bank. Washington, D.C. April 2004. pp. 1-3, 10, and Lewis, *The Power of Productivity,* p. 138.

[15] Costa Vaz, Alcides. Trade Strategies in the Context of Economic Regionalism: The Case of MERCOSUR. In: Aggarwal, Vinod K., Ralph Espach, and Joseph S. Tulchin, eds. *The Strategic Dynamics of Latin American Trade.* Woodrow Wilson Center Press. Washington, D.C. 2004. pp. 235 and 255-57.

[16] Pedro Da Motta Veiga, Regional and Transregional Dimensions of Brazilian Trade Policy, p. 178.

presidential election of longtime Worker's Party leader Luiz Inácio Lula da Silva. Today Brazil's macroeconomic priorities still constrain trade and other policy choices. The economy is stable, but growing at inadequate levels to bring about desired development goals. To control inflation, the Lula Administration has had to maintain very high real interest rates, while Brazil's large debt service obligation has required a large primary budget surplus, approaching 5% of GDP in 2005, and a trade surplus.[17]

The cost of this development strategy has been accepting the microeconomic distortions discussed above and inadequate social spending, which raises the prospect for future social and political unrest given the already very high levels of income inequality and poverty. Subordinating trade liberalization to debt reduction and other goals also diminishes Brazil's growth prospects, a key variable in reducing poverty. Therefore, as may be seen, Brazil's "trade preferences," which point to a cautious (some would say protective) and carefully managed approach to trade liberalization, reflect a combination of industrial, foreign, and macroeconomic policy priorities that often outweigh purely trade-related economic arguments, and deters progress in Brazil's long-term development. These points bear remembering when considering specific trade negotiation stances and disputes, discussed later.

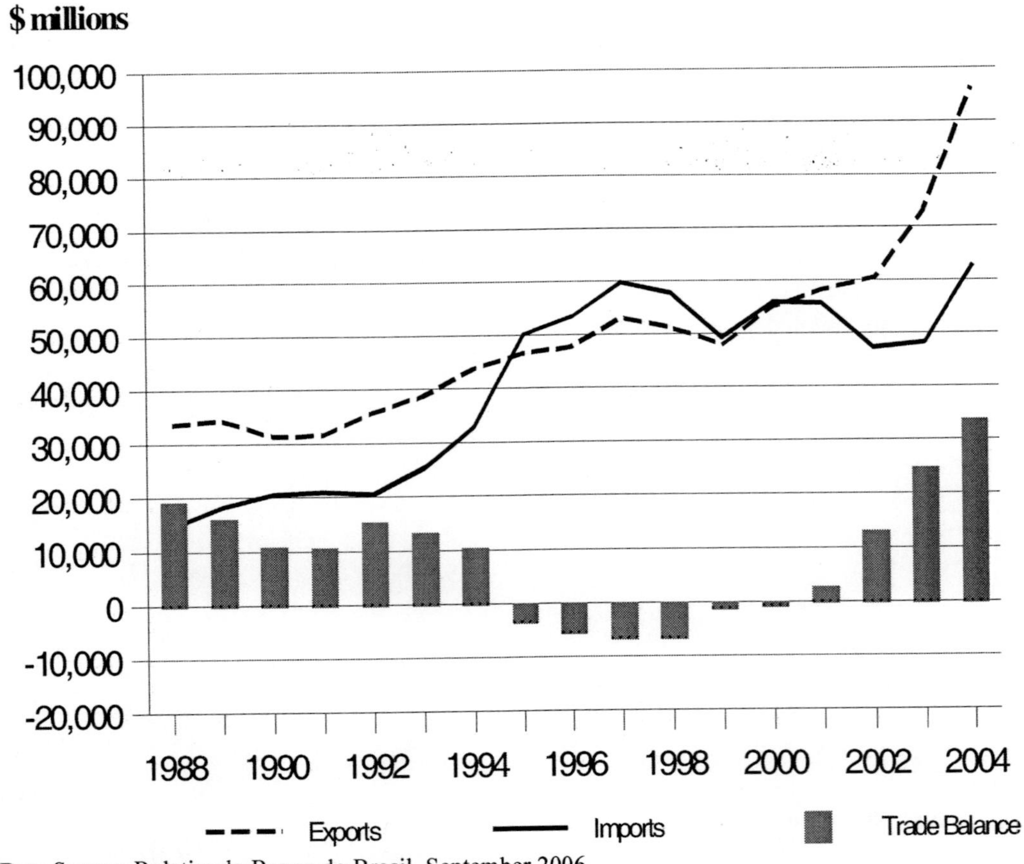

Data Source: Boletim do Banco do Brasil, September 2006

[17] The primary surplus is the fiscal surplus not including interest payments, and theoretically represents the amount available for debt service. Real interest rates (adjusted for inflation) in Brazil have hovered around 10% for years, making them among the highest in the world.

Figure 2. Brazil's Balance of Merchandise Trade, 1988-2004 $ millions.

BRAZILIAN TRADE WITH THE WORLD

Brazil has a modern, diversified economy, with services accounting for 53% of GDP, followed by industry and manufacturing at 37%, and agriculture at 9%. Depending on how agribusiness is measured, it contributes to some 30% of GDP. Brazil is the number one producer of raw sugar, oranges, and coffee in the world, and the second largest producer of soybean, beef, poultry, and corn.[18] It is also a major producer of steel, aircraft, automobiles, and auto parts. By comparative standards, however, Brazil is actually a small trader, with total trade accounting for only 26% of GDP in 2004, up from 14% a decade earlier, but still a relatively small amount compared to the rest of Latin America. Brazil represents only 0.9% of world trade, a number that has not grown, suggesting that Brazil's trade liberalization efforts have not resulted in any change in its trade openness relative to the rest of the world.

Brazil's global trade is diversified (see Figure 3), with 25% of exports going to the European Union, 21% to the United States, 20% to Latin America, and 15% to Asia. Brazil's imports mostly from the European Union (25%), Asia (20%), the United States (18%), and Latin America (16%). Brazil's top three trading partners are the United States, Argentina, and Germany. Together they account for over one-third of Brazil's world trade and each, interestingly, is the dominant trading partner of a different region or trade group (NAFTA, Mercosul, and the European Union).

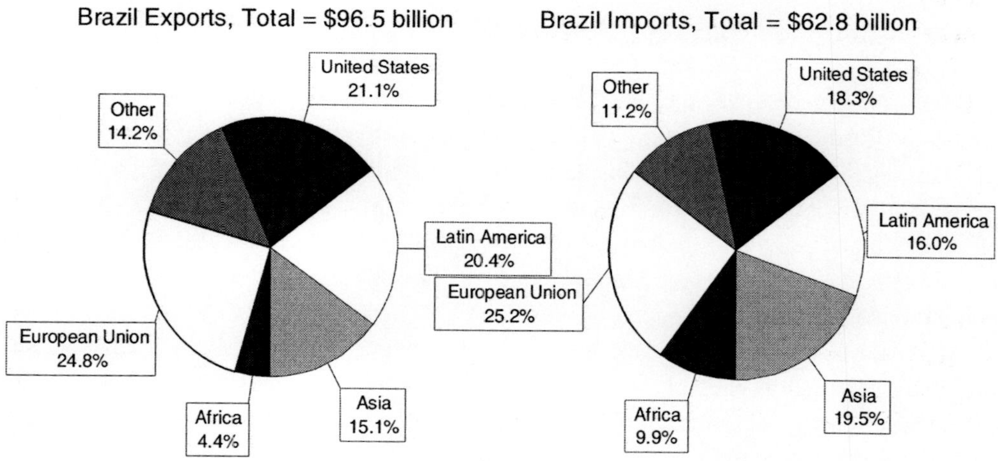

Figure 3. Brazil's Direction of Trade, 2004

Some 30% of Brazil's merchandise exports are primary products, 14% semi-manufactured goods, and 56% manufactured goods (see Appendix 1). Importantly, natural resource-based goods dominate in all categories. For example, together all steel and aluminum based products, fabricated to varying levels of completion, represent 10% of total exports. Agricultural products, including raw sugar and other products, as well as,

[18] Data from Brazilian Institute of Geography and Statistics and Brazilian Embassy, *Highlights of Brazilian Agriculture,* September 2004.

manufactured goods like orange juice and refined sugar, and semi-manufactured sugar and soybean products, account for at least 3 0-40% of exports. Soybean and soybean products alone amount to 10% of exports, more than automobile and related parts (8%) and aircraft (3%).[19] These numbers provide some insight into why Brazil places such a strong emphasis on further opening developed country markets to its agricultural products.

Brazilian imports fall into five categories: capital goods (17.6%); consumer goods (10.8%); durable consumer goods (4.9%), fuels (16.4%); and intermediate goods (50.3%). Brazil imports capital and intermediate goods in support of its own industrial and agricultural growth, development, and export. These goods range from aircraft engines to chemicals and pharmaceuticals that are used in processing other goods. Raw materials for farming, foodstuffs, and nondurable consumer goods round out the major imports.

Brazil's trade priorities cannot be derived entirely from a calculation of the trade-weighted importance of trade partners. The United States is Brazil's largest single-country trading partner, yet Brazil has resisted increasing trade liberalization with the large U.S. market via the FTAA because the U.S. model of liberalization is viewed as insufficiently balanced to meet Brazilian needs. To appreciate Brazil's approach to the United States and the world with respect to trade negotiations, it is critical to see how its "trade preferences," discussed above, take form in actual negotiations. Mercosul is most important to the economic and political life of Brazil and has taken on perhaps even greater priority under the Lula administration. It is discussed first followed by Brazil's approach to the FTAA and WTO, which will allow for a better understanding of U.S.-Brazil trade relations, as a whole.

Southern Common Market (Mercosul)

Mercosul was created in 1991, the outgrowth of Brazil-Argentine bilateral efforts in the late 1 980s to address longstanding political and security concerns. By including Uruguay and Paraguay, and defining the partnership along economic lines, Mercosul was expected to help the region improve its chances for mutual economic growth and development, and thereby stabilize regional political relations as well. Mercosul has succeeded on the political side and also developed as a credible collective voice in the WTO and the FTAA. Its success at economic integration is more questionable.

Mercosul began as a free trade area, but was designed to evolve into a customs union, defined by a common external tariff (CET), and eventually, a common market with the free movement of goods, investment, and labor. To date, Mercosul remains an incomplete customs union with many exceptions to the CET. Early successes were measured by the doubling of intra-Mercosul trade by 1995, as tariffs came down according to schedule, and cooperation remained largely positive. This trend reversed course in the late 1 990s because of financial crises in Argentina and Brazil, and the absence of macroeconomic coordination and other policy problems. Brazilian trade within Mercosul expanded by only 13% from 1999 to 2004, with Brazil's trade balance shifting from a nearly balanced position to an uncomfortably large surplus of $2.5 billion by 2004, as imports from all three Mercosul partners stagnated or

[19] Data from *Boletim do Banco Central do Brasil.* September 2005 and Jales, Mario. *Brazilian Agribusiness in International Trade and WTO Negotiations.* Presentation made June 12, 2006. Available at [http://www.Iconebrasil.org.br].

declined. Argentina responded with quotas and higher tariffs on certain Brazilian exports and calling for more equitable bilateral trade flows.

In reality, the trade rationale for Mercosul was always limited and fraught with challenges. After 15 years, Mercosul accounts for only 9% of Brazil's exports. The United States and Europe remain the dominant markets for Brazilian manufactures and agricultural goods, respectively, as well as, the major suppliers of capital goods. Argentina and Brazil have both resorted to raising trade barriers against each other in response to sectoral and macroeconomic problems, and Brazil stands alone as the industrial center, so Mercosul offers little competition in technological and innovative-based industries that can bring deeper gains from trade.

The increased intra-dependence fostered by a successful Mercosul also carries certain risks, as seen in the compression of trade and economic growth in Paraguay and Uruguay following financial crises and currency devaluations in Brazil (1999 and 2001) and Argentina (2002). These setbacks merely confirmed what has been widely understood, that Mercosul was really launched as a "political project carried out in the economic and commercial realms."[20] Deeper economic integration, under these circumstances, has proved elusive.

In response, Mercosul turned to broadening its membership rather than deepening the arrangement. Chile and Bolivia acceded to Mercosul in 1996 as associate members (not subject to the CET and other provisions), and after years of negotiation, the Andean Community of Nations (Ecuador, Bolivia, Venezuela, Peru, Colombia) was added in October 2004. Brazil took a further step in organizing the South American Community of Nations in December 2004, which is a very loose arrangement of the twelve major South American countries.[21] In December 2005, Venezuela agreed to become a full member of Mercosul, and has been promised full membership status, except for voting, despite its inability to adopt the CET and other policies. A similar proposal has been suggested for Bolivia following the presidential election of leftist Evo Morales in December 2005. These decisions suggest that Mercosul continues to operate based primarily on political incentives.

Mercosul has been negotiating with the European Union for an FTA for many years. These talks, once considered promising, have bogged down on market access and other issues that have similarly hindered progress on the FTAA. Brazil wants better access for agricultural goods, while the EU wants Brazil to lower tariffs on industrial goods. Brazil is unwilling to make such a commitment until the EU also addresses its agricultural subsidy program. Currently, the talks are stalled, with little expectation of significant movement in the near future, a prospect, as with the FTAA, that may hinge on developments in the Doha negotiations.

Despite the undisputed expansion in Mercosul affiliation, growth in trade has stagnated and after 15 years, by most accounts, the pact still lacks institutional strength and coordination, providing little evidence of enhanced trade-related productivity gains.[22] Still,

---

[20] Costa Vaz, Trade Strategies in the Context of Economic Regionalism, pp. 234-235 and Weintraub, Sidney. Development and Democracy in the Southern Cone: Imperatives for U.S. Policy in South America. Center for Strategic and International Studies. Washington, D.C. February 2000. pp. 12-13.

[21] Details on the various Latin American integration efforts may be found in: CRS Report RL33 162, *Trade Integration in the Americas,* by M. Angeles Villarreal.

[22] The limits of Brazil's trade-related productivity gains from Mercosul are analyzed in: Lopez-Cordova, Ernesto and Mauricio Mesquita Moreira. Regional Integration and Productivity: The Experiences of Brazil and Mexico. In: Estevadeordal, Antoni, Dani Rodrik, Alan M. Taylor, and Andrés Velasco, eds. *Integrating the Americas: FTAA and Beyond.* Harvard University Press, Cambridge, 2004. pp. 573-609.

support for the pact is strong despite its troubles. The smaller economies benefit from preferential access to the large Brazilian market, and Brazil sees a unified Mercosul as being the definitive counterbalance to the United States in FTAA negotiations, where the FTAA is viewed as a complement to, not a substitute for, Mercosul. The technical distinction between a free trade agreement and a customs unions becomes important here. A customs union with a CET implies that its members will negotiate trade agreements collectively with the outside world, or the union becomes largely meaningless.[23]

For these many reasons, Mercosul remains at the heart of Brazil's trade strategy. Brazil relies on the customs union to strengthen its regional economic leadership, and by extension, its trade negotiating position outside of Mercosul. Conversely, Brazil's strength would be undermined if any members of Mercosul opted for FTA status or chose to go their own way with extra-regional negotiations, a position Uruguay flirted with in January 2006, although apparently with no real conviction. Mercosul also serves Brazil's trade strategy precisely because Brazil can set the levels of deepening to ensure a balance between maintaining its industrial policy and co-opting regional voices in approaching the EU, WTO, or FTAA. Finally, Brazil uses Mercosul as a way to ease its transition to trade liberalization in the global economy because it has a ready-made regional comparative advantage in manufacturing.

Free Trade Area of the Americas (FTAA)

The FTAA is a proposed free trade area that would include 34 nations (all except Cuba) of the Western Hemisphere. It has been under consideration for a decade, but talks effectively stalled in late 2003. Problems arose over differences between Brazil and the United States, which as the co-chairs of the Trade Negotiations Committee (TNC), hold the key to consummating the agreement. At the heart of the disagreement are their diametrically opposing positions that reflect not only differences in sectoral and industry issues, but in broader trade preferences as well. The United States remains committed to an agreement that includes negotiating investment, services, intellectual property rights, and government procurement, among other issues. Brazil has not deviated from its more limited support of dealing mostly with market access, and its refusal to engage on these other issues unless the United States concedes to address agricultural subsidies and trade remedy issues.[24]

This impasse resulted in a compromise unveiled at the 2003 FTAA Ministerial meeting in Miami calling for a two-tier agreement under which countries could assume different levels of commitment. The proposed framework, viewed by the United States as an accommodation to Brazil, would include a common set of rights and obligations for all countries along with optional obligations that could be entered into on a plurilateral basis. Defining these various commitments so far has proven unworkable, and the breadth of an emerging resistence to the FTAA became clearer at the fourth Summit of the Americas held on November 4-5, 2005, in Mar del Plata, Argentina. Amid dramatic and sometimes violent public demonstrations against President George W. Bush and the FTAA, it was evident that Latin America was

[23] Weintraub, Development and Democracy in the Southern Cone, pp. 6-7.

[24] See CRS Report RS20864, A Free Trade Area of the Americas: Major Policy Issues and Status of Negotiations, by J. F. Hornbeck. pp. 5-6.

divided over how to proceed. A total of 29 countries supported renewing negotiations, and the United States pushed to set a specific date in 2006.

Brazil, Argentina, Uruguay, and Paraguay (the Mercosul countries) rejected this idea, arguing that the conditions for achieving a balanced and equitable agreement did not yet exist. Taking a more extreme position, Venezuela lobbied to end any further effort on the FTAA and for unified resistence against U.S. policies and presence in Latin America. The Summit declaration called for a time to explore problems in the FTAA process, while awaiting the outcome of the upcoming World Trade Organization (WTO) ministerial, indicating that at this juncture, there is no unified vision on how to proceed with the proposed FTAA. Brazil continues to offer to negotiate market access talks between the Mercosul countries and the United States (the so-called "4+1" option), an overture the USTR has repeatedly declined.

Brazil sees little advantage to an FTAA at this point in time, particularly one that does not address its interests, and so appears content with the status quo for the indefinite future. The United States, by contrast, has been frustrated by an inability to advance a NAFTA-like region-wide agreement. Therefore, it appears that Brazil will continue to reinforce support for Mercosul, while biding its time on the FTAA and attempting to make headway with agricultural issues in the WTO.

Mercosul negotiates the FTAA as a bloc, which may gather strength if Venezuela joins as a full member.[25] Interestingly, most analyses of the economic effects of joining the FTAA point to differences in costs and benefits between Brazil and the other three smaller members. The gains for Mercosul as a whole would come from its comparative advantage in agriculture vis-a-vis the United States, provided barriers to trade in this sector are meaningfully lowered. For Brazil, opening up the U.S. market to agricultural products is critical, but the United States is also its major market for many value-added manufactured exports (frozen orange juice concentrate, steel, aircraft, petroleum). There is, it seems, the potential for considerable commercial gains for Brazil should a far-reaching FTAA be completed.[26]

The cost and benefit calculus, however, is more complicated. For the smaller Mercosul countries, an FTAA means giving up preferential access to the large Brazilian market, which could mean a net loss in welfare for some sectors. The FTAA would also mean greater access to the U.S. and other Latin American markets, and reduced costs for capital goods and other imports that no longer face a high Mercosul CET (e.g. 35% in the case of automobiles). The smaller economies might also consider the effects of any future economic setbacks from potential macroeconomic problems in Brazil or Argentina. Brazil also is reticent to push for an FTAA precisely because with Mercosul (and more so with a functioning South America Community of Nations), it is the hub and industrial center of a major preferential trade arrangement, which would certainly change in importance if the FTAA comes to be.

With an FTAA, Brazilian manufacturing industries that compete directly with more efficient U.S. firms (e.g. machinery and chemicals) could lose in the short run. Combined

---

[25] It has been noted that the addition of Venezuela as a full member of Mercosul consolidates in one bloc all the countries resisting the FTAA, setting up the potential for a maj or political standoff with the United States on this issue. *Latin American Brazil and Southern Cone Report,* December 2005, p. 7.

[26] Weintraub, *Development and Democracy in the Southern Cone,* p. 12, Laens Silvia and Inés Terra. Integration in the Americas: Welfare Effects and options for the MERCOSUR. In Lorenzo, Fernando and Marcel Vaillant, eds. *MERCOSUR and the Creation of the Free Trade Area of the Americas.* Woodrow Wilson International Center for Scholars, Washington, D.C. 2005. p. 107, and Masi, Fernando and Carol Wise. Negotiating the FTAA between the Main Players: USA and MERCOSUR. In: Lorenzo and Vaillant, *MERCOSUR and the Creation of the Free Trade Area of the Americas,* p. 323.

with possible trade restructuring that other Mercosul countries might face, Brazil's comparative advantage might shift, to some degree, from industrial products in a regional economic union to more agricultural goods in a hemispheric one. Given the economic and political strength of the United States, the FTAA might alter the balance of power in the region, to the possible detriment of Brazil's regional leadership. The potential for these relative changes, compounded by Brazil's concerns over its ability to conform to provisions covering enforceable intellectual property rights, services trade, and investor protection, point to why Brazil remains reluctant to advance an FTAA, particularly if U.S. agricultural protection remains relatively untouched. Stated more succinctly, although an FTAA could provide commercial (and certainly consumer) gains to Brazil, it may come at a cost to industrial and foreign policy priorities.[27]

For the United States, even a two-tier FTAA may make sense, particularly if the alternative is an FTAA without Brazil. With a two-tier FTAA, most of the hemisphere would be integrated, including Brazil, at least nominally. It may be viewed as a way to co-opt Brazilian reticence, or at least diminish the stalemate approach that can also extend to other Mercosul countries. Given Brazil's deeply held concerns that reflect its "trade preferences," however, the status quo (impasse) seems to be Brazil's preferred position between moving ahead with the FTAA negotiations or killing them outright.[28]

World Trade Organization (WTO)

Brazil has also been a vocal leader of the G-20 that represents developing country interests in the WTO. Even prior to forming the G-20 group, Brazil stood up for including matters critical to developing countries in the WTO including the most pressing issue, barriers to agricultural trade, as well as, the treatment of rules covering antidumping and pharmaceutical data protection, among others.[29] In particular, Brazil has insisted on addressing the reduction of barriers to agricultural trade, particularly export and production subsidies. The United States is working in the WTO negotiations with Brazil to find a way to reduce agricultural subsidies, resists addressing antidumping rules, but is generally sympathetic to finding a solution to developing country concerns over providing drugs for HIV/AIDS and other emergencies.[30]

The implication for Brazil-U.S. trade relations is that the WTO is an arena where the two countries can find areas of both commonality and disagreement. For many issues, the United States has indicated that the multilateral forum is the preferred or only venue for issue resolution (domestic agricultural subsidies) and so progress in addressing Brazilian concerns in the FTAA are contingent, at a minimum, upon success at the WTO. Brazil has taken similar

---

[27] Lorenzo and Vaillant, eds., *Mercosur and the Creation of the Free Trade Area of the Americas,* various chapters, pp. 4, 38, 152, and 324.

[28] The future of the FTAA remains unclear from the Brazilian perspective. At the conclusion of the WTO Hong Kong Ministerial in December 2005, Ambassador Adhemar Bahadian, Brazil's FTAA co-chair representative, suggested that the FTAA may be put off for at least another year. He was, however, replaced soon thereafter as the co-chair, and Brazil has signaled that it is still interested in negotiating with the United States in 2006.

[29] Fishlow, Albert. Brazil: FTA or FTAA or WTO? In: Schott, Jeffrey J., ed. *Free Trade Agreements: US Strategies and Priorities.* Institute for International Economics. Washington, D.C. 2004. pp. 285-287.

[30] For a comprehensive discussion of WTO issues, see CRS Report RL33 176, *The World Trade Organization: The Hong Kong Ministerial,* coordinated by Ian F. Fergusson.

stands with respect to services trade, intellectual property rights, and other issues. Hence, it is important to integrate the various factors that drive Brazilian trade priorities at the different levels of negotiation to be able to interpret Brazil's underlying intent and perhaps offer some understanding of why U.S. negotiators have been frustrated in their attempts to move forward on some critical U.S. trade policy initiatives, especially the FTAA.

At the latest WTO ministerial in Hong Kong, Brazil played a leading role in continuing to represent developing country interests in the Doha Round. It's voice was prominent in becoming a member of the latest group of would-be brokers of a Doha Round agreement known as the Group of Six (EU, U.S., Japan, Australia, Brazil, and India). The WTO remains an important forum for Brazil, which could be a major winner if barriers to agricultural trade are significantly reduced. In the post-Hong Kong period, Brazil has expressed a readiness to offer reductions in barriers to trade in industrial goods and services, if the United States can convince the European Union to move forward on agricultural barriers. The current level of cooperation between Brazil and the United States bodes well for making headway in multilateral talks that could "trickle down" to regional and bilateral accommodations. This outcome, however, is far from assured.

U.S.-Brazil Trade Relations

Brazil and the United States are two independent political and economic leaders in the Western Hemisphere, and is reflected in their trade relationship. First, unlike much of Latin America, Brazil does not have a preferential trade arrangement with the United States such as NAFTA, the CBI, or the Andean Trade Preference Act, although it is protective of its U.S. preferences provided under the Generalized

System of Preferences (GSP). Second, although there is consistent effort to maintain constructive engagement between the two countries at all levels of negotiation, much attention turns to areas of disagreement. Indeed, progress on the FTAA has crept to a halt, bilateral disputes have left some interests dissatisfied, including those represented in the U.S. Congress, and key issues in the multilateral realm remain largely unresolved. A look at U.S.-Brazil trade and the issues that confront the two countries help explain this situation.

U.S.-Brazil Trade Trends

Brazil is the 15th largest U.S. export market, but a distant second to Mexico as the United States' largest trading partner in Latin America. For economies of their size, Brazil and the United States actually trade rather little with each other. Total merchandise trade (trade turnover) in 2004 between the United States and Brazil was $35 billion, or 8.2% of U.S. trade with Latin America. The United States purchased 21% of Brazil's exports and supplied 18% of its imports. The ebb and flow of U.S. bilateral trade with Brazil reflects a number of factors including their respective macroeconomic growth trends, Brazil's 1999 and 2001 devaluations (note rise in U.S. imports and fall in U.S. exports in Figure 4 — data presented in Appendix 2), and after 2002, Brazil's enhanced export promotion policy.

Brazil and the United States are far from achieving their full bilateral trade potential. It is clear that over nearly two decades, beginning before either NAFTA or Mercosul came into being, that the growth in U.S.-Brazil trade has lagged compared to U.S. trade with Latin America and especially Mexico, a close trader with the United States. As seen in Table 1, in 1987 Brazil accounted for 1.8% of total U.S. trade, compared to 5.3% for Mexico and 12.4% for Latin America as a whole. U.S.-Brazilian trade grew by 195% from 1987 to 2004, a meager amount compared to the 422% growth in U.S.-Latin American trade and the 665% growth in U.S.-Mexican trade. By 2004, Brazil had lost ground, making up only 1.5% of total U.S. trade compared to Mexico's 11.7% and Latin America's 18.7%.

Nonetheless, the United States is still Brazil's largest single-country trading partner, rivaling total trade with the European Union (EU) and exceeding Brazil's trade with Latin America. A simple analysis of Brazil's trade with the world suggests that the United States could play a more important role. This point is supported by more sophisticated estimates as well. One study using a gravity model simulation suggested that Brazil's trade with the United States in 1999 was only 44% of what the model estimated it should have been.[31]

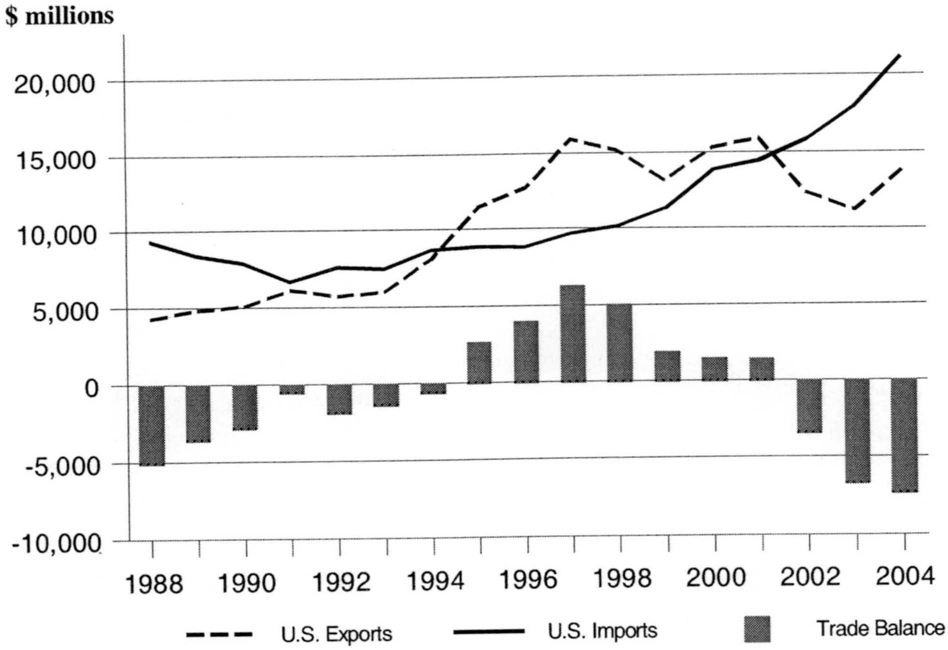

Data Source: Boletim do Banco do Brasil, September 2005.

Figure 4. U.S.-Brazil Merchandise Trade, 1988-2004.

Table 1. U.S. Trade with Brazil, Mexico, and Latin America

	% of Total U.S. Trade 1987	% of Total U.S. Trade 2004	Total U.S. Trade 2004 ($ millions)	% Growth in Trade 1987-2004
Brazil	1.8	1.5	35,057	195

[31] This point is developed in Schott, Jeffrey. J. *U.S.-Brazil Trade Relations in a New Era. Inst itute for International Economics.* November 2003. pp. 4-5. [http://www.iie.com]

Mexico	5.3	11.7	266,737	665
Latin America	12.4	18.7	426,849	422

Source: CRS computations from U.S. Department of Commerce data

The United States exports mostly capital goods to Brazil; the top three categories composing over half of U.S. exports are:

- *machinery* (gas turbines used in the manufacture of Brazilian aircraft, computers, office machinery and engine parts);
- *electrical machinery* (integrated circuits, radio, television, and telephone parts); and,
- *organic materials* (such as industrial chemicals).

The United States is also the largest market for Brazilian manufactured goods, which are included in the top three U.S. import categories and compose nearly one-third of U.S. imports from Brazil. These include:

- aircraft (regional jet airplanes);
- electrical machinery (cell phones, radio, and other transmission apparatus); and,
- machinery (automobile engine parts).

Other important U.S. import categories include mineral fuel, iron and steel, automobiles, and footwear (see Appendix 3 for bilateral services trade data, not discussed in this report). Treatment of Brazilian agricultural products, conspicuously absent from top categories of U.S. imports, are among Brazil's major bilateral issues.

U.S.-Brazil Foreign Investment

Trade liberalization is also important because it tends to encourage increased foreign direct investment (FDI). Permanent and predictable trade rules induce FDI because the flow of trade will be less likely to be interrupted by government actions. If a trade agreement also includes an investment chapter, which typically assures foreign investors that they will receive national treatment and have recourse to an impartial dispute settlement process, there is further inducement for FDI. This an important issue because the United States does not have a Bilateral Investment Treaty (BIT) with Brazil, another way to secure U.S. investor rights with developing countries.

The stock of U.S. FDI in Brazil was $33.3 billion in 2004 (see Appendix 4). This figure actually declined from a peak of $37.8 billion in 1998. U.S. investment in Brazil, the largest economy in Latin America next to Mexico, is relatively small, representing only 1.6% of U.S. FDI in the world and only 10.2% of U.S. FDI in Latin America (Mexico has twice this amount). In addition, Brazil invests little in the United States, with the stock of FDI amounting to $1.3 billion in 2004. Although this is double the previous year's level, it accounts for less then one-tenth of one percent of FDI in the United States. Brazilian investment is growing, however, concentrated in industries of strategic interest to its economy that face formidable U.S. barriers to entry, such as citrus and steel.

U.S.-Brazil Bilateral Trade Issues and Disputes

Brazil and the United States have a number of specific trade issues that are taken up at all levels of trade negotiations. As with all countries, the United States and Brazil practice some form of protection, although they are very different. The United States is most concerned over Brazil's high average tariffs, particularly on industrial goods, and multiple non-market access issues including intellectual property rights (IPR) enforcement, services trade, government procurement, and investment rules. The United States Trade Representative (USTR) considers the common external tariff (CET) a major barrier to U.S. agricultural exports, distilled spirits, and computer equipment.[32]

Brazil has raised its major concerns over broad U.S. policies such as the Byrd Amendment, which directs duties from trade remedy (antidumping) cases to affected industries, the calculation of antidumping margins, and what it considers to be discriminatory treatment inherent in U.S. expansion of preferential trade agreements in Latin America (NAFTA, Chile, CAFTA-DR). The Byrd Amendment was found to be in violation of WTO rules. Although repealed by Congress on February 1, 2006, the program remains in effect until October 1, 2007. The other two complaints face no challenge in the WTO. Brazil also objects to product-specific barriers that include restrictive tariff rate quotas (TRQs — sugar, orange juice, ethanol, and tobacco), subsidies (cotton, ethanol, and soybeans), and trade remedy cases (steel and orange juice). The U.S. 2002 Farm Bill that effectively increased agricultural subsidies further aggravated the situation. As of January 1, 2006, there were 17 U.S. antidumping and countervailing duty orders in place against Brazil.

Tariffs Structures

One significant difference between Brazil and the United States is their tariff structure. As shown in Table 2, Brazil has comparatively high average tariffs. Although the difference in average agricultural tariff is small, Brazil's average tariff on industrial products is three times that of the United States, the major product category of U.S. exports to Brazil. It follows that market access discussions between the two countries usually find the United States focusing on reduction of industrial tariffs, whereas Brazil emphasizes U.S. peak tariffs on agricultural imports subject to TRQs. The high out-of-quota tariffs are meant to deter imports to protect U.S. producers, which are, for example, 350% for tobacco and 78% for sugar, and reflected in the comparatively large standard deviation in U.S. agricultural tariffs. Brazil notes that the U.S. average agricultural tariff can mask the high cost Brazil faces from out-of-quota peak U.S tariffs.[33]

---

32 United States Trade Representative. *2005 National Trade Estimate Report on Foreign Trade Barriers.* Washington, D.C. March 2005, p. 30.

33 Brazil's positions in this section are summarized from: Embassy of Brazil. *U.S. Barriers to Brazilian Goods, Services, and Investment.* October 2002 and the summary update of the same publication printed in March 2005.

Table 2. U.S. and Brazil Avera^g^e Tariff Rates

Country	All Products		Agricultural Products		Industrial Products	
	Avg. Tariff*	Standard Deviation#	Avg. Tariff*	Standard Deviation#	Avg. Tariff*	Standard Deviation
United States	4.3%	11.3	8.5%	30.2	3.7%	5.1
Brazil	10.9%	6.8	10.2%	6.0	11.0%	6.8

Data source: Inter-American Development Bank via personal correspondence. * Simple average tariff for calender year 2004.

Standard deviation as measure of how much tariffs can vary from average

Brazilian Complaints against the United States

Brazil's major product-specific complaints are summarized briefly below.

Sugar. As part of U.S. support for the domestic sugar growing and processing industry, quotas are set under U.S. commitments made under WTO rules to restrict the amount of sugar imports that may enter the country. The purpose is to maintain the domestic price of sugar above a set minimal level. The United States Department of Agriculture (USDA) allocates quotas among eligible countries, with Brazil receiving approximately 13% of the world total. In-quota imports are subject to a very low duty. Amounts entering above the quota are subject to a tariff computed by the USITC to be 78% ad valorem in 2003.[34] Brazil has expressed concern over the small increases in quotas given to the Central American countries under the CAFTADR, suggesting it bodes poorly for future negotiations with the United States, given that Brazil is the world's largest producer of raw and refined sugar.

Cotton. Cotton is a protected crop in the United States, benefitting from direct payments, counter-cyclical payments, subsidized loans and other federal programs. Subsidies averaged $1.7 billion per year for fiscal years 1991 to 2004.[35] Brazil successfully challenged portions of the U.S. cotton program under WTO dispute settlement rules, requiring the United States to change or withdraw these prohibited support programs. Although the United States missed the deadlines to correct these programs, Brazil, unlike some other countries, did not take retaliatory measures. Congress repealed two of the offending programs as part of the FY2006 budget reconciliation conference bill on February 1, 2006, but Brazil remains critical of remaining cotton support programs.[36]

Steel. The steel industry files more antidumping and countervailing duty cases than any other U.S. industry, the subject of repeated complaints by Brazil.[37] As of January 1, 2006, there were 16 such orders in place against Brazil, some dating back to 1986. The steel issue was further exacerbated in 2002 when the United States imposed special safeguard duties of up to 30% on various steel imports, until successfully challenged in the WTO and withdrawn. Brazil estimates that the total cost of these measures exceeds $2 billion in lost sales, and with

---

[34] For details of the sugar program, see CRS Issue Brief IB95 117, *Sugar Policy Issues,* by Remy Jurenas. Brazil calculates a much higher ad valorem equivalent of 221% for 2004.

[35] See CRS Report RL3257 1, Background on the U.S.-Brazil WTO Cotton Subsidy Dispute, by Randy Schnepf.p. 1.

[36] International Trade Reporter. House Approves Budget Measure Containing Byrd Amendment Repeal. February 1, 2006.

[37] CRS Report RL32333, *Steel: Price and Availability Issues,* by Stephen Cooney. pp. 8 and 29.

the United States as one of its most important export markets, is eager to see restrictions reduced, if not eliminated.

Ethanol (corn). For years, both Brazil and the United States subsidized heavily the development of ethanol production from sugar and corn, respectively. Currently, Brazil's subsidy program has ended and it maintains a highly efficient ethanol production process. Brazil's exports of ethanol face two barriers to the U.S. market. First, U.S. corn production is subsidized by various U.S. programs, and some 13% of total corn production is used for ethanol. Second, there is a U.S. import duty on ethanol plus an additional 54 cents per gallon designed to offset a tax reduction all ethanol receives to offset the federal gasoline excise tax levied at the pump on all fuels.[38] Brazil continues to press for changes in both programs.

Orange Juice. Brazil argues that the U.S. tariff on orange juice concentrate is equivalent to 65% on an ad valorem basis and 18.4% on non-concentrated juice. In addition, the most recent U.S. antidumping order against Brazil was placed on orange juice on January 1, 2005. In January 2006, the U.S. Department of Commerce made a preliminary finding of dumping against Brazilian frozen concentrated orange juice, which Brazil has vowed to fight in the WTO.

Tobacco. Also subject to tariff rate quotas and very high over-quota tariffs, Brazil would like to see the U.S. market open more to greater imports of the product from Brazil. Tobacco represents only 1% of total U.S. imports from Brazil on a dollar value basis.

Soybeans. Brazil, the second largest producer of soybeans in the world, must compete against U.S. subsidies on soybeans ranging from $1.5 to $3.2 billion annually between 2004 and 2006. Brazil is evaluating whether to challenge these subsidies in the WTO, as it did with cotton.

Shrimp. On January 27, 2005, the United States imposed an antidumping duty order on frozen or canned shrimp, and prawns from Brazil, decreasing imports from shrimp farmed in the poorer northeast portion of the country.

Beef and Chicken. U.S. sanitary certification for Brazilian chicken has not been approved, and for beef was only approved in 2005, subject to a TRQ.

U.S. Complaints Against Brazil[39]

The USTR lists a number of complaints against Brazil, ranging from cumbersome import administrative procedures to outright restrictions on certain imports. Of equal importance is the inability to make more progress in areas where the United States is most competitive such as protection of intellectual property rights and services trade.

High Tariffs. Between Brazil's higher average tariffs (especially on industrial goods) and Mercosul's CET (exacerbated by a surcharge from 1997 to 2004), Brazil's tariff regime hurts U.S. exports of agricultural products, distilled spirits, computer and telecommunications equipment.

Prohibited Imports. Restrictions apply to various consumer goods, with a safeguard measure currently issued against certain toys.

Intellectual Property Rights. Although Brazil has numerous IPR laws on the books, the USTR is critical of many and notes that enforcement issues are a serious problem.[40] There is a

---

[38] CRS Report RL30369, *Fuel Ethanol: Background and Public Policy Issues,* by Brent D. Yacobucci and Jasper Womach. pp. 2-3 and 17.

[39] For Brazil's trade barriers, see United States Trade Representative. *2005 National Trade Estimate Report on Foreign Trade Barriers.* Washington, D.C. March 2005. pp. 30-37.

5-6 year backlog in processing patent applications, and data confidentiality protection for pharmaceuticals is not covered by law. Brazil lacks copyright enforcement leading to significant piracy losses for U.S. businesses (particularly video and audio cassettes). Despite Brazilian attempts to rectify the problem with a new task force and other initiatives, it lacks the resources to tackle the problem fully at this point in time. Brazil, therefore, is reluctant to sign on to an FTA that contains enforceable IPR provisions. The United States held up review of Brazil's eligibility for benefits under the Generalized System of Preferences (GSP) because of concerns over piracy issues, but the United States decided against taking action in recognition of Brazil's attempts to address piracy. Still, Brazil acknowledges its piracy problem, realizing the implications for its own producers and tax revenues as well. The Brazilian Congress conducted a study on the issue in 2004, which noted that piracy constituted nearly 60% of music sales and that Brazil had failed to close legal loopholes and counteract the problem more effectively, including its lack of organizational capacity and resources.[41]

Onerous Licensing and Regulatory Requirements. Importers complain of the high costs associated with meeting business registration and other requirements in Brazil.

Sanitary and Phytosanitary (SPS) Barriers. The USTR argues that SPS restrictions, including those that apply to beef, the prohibition of poultry imports (also a reciprocity issue), and certain types of wheats from various U.S. states are unfounded.

Government Procurement. Brazil is not a signatory to the WTO Agreement on Government Procurement and there are multiple preferences given to local businesses.

Export and Financing Subsidies. Through various programs at the National Social and Economic Development Bank (BNDES), Brazil promotes the purchase of domestic equipment and machinery and helps finance export activities.

Services Trade and Investment. There are restrictions on industries such as audio visual, telecommunications, financial (insurance), and express delivery services. Brazil has expressed concern over investor-state provisions, standard language in U.S. free trade agreements, and possible U.S. reaction to some of its subsidized financing programs conducted under BNDES. Brazil has not signed a bilateral investment treaty with the United States.

OUTLOOK

Brazil trades relatively little for an economy of its size and diversity and would benefit from trading more. It has embraced export promotion, which generates foreign exchange and can contribute to growth in economic output, but has shied away from deeper commitments to lowering barriers to imports, which are key to gains in productivity, per capita income, and development. This strategy is consistent with Brazil's short-term financing needs and its trade preferences, which are driven by a combination of macroeconomic, industrial, and foreign policy priorities.

For the United States, this presents a delicate policy conundrum because economic reciprocity may not be the only key to successful trade negotiations with Brazil. For example, even if significant progress could be made on agricultural issues in the Doha round, and

[40] USTR, 2005 National Trade Estimate Report on Foreign Trade Barriers, pp. 33-37.

[41] Federative Republic of Brazil. Chamber of Deputies. *Legislative Investigation Committee on Piracy (CPI) Report.* Brasilia, 2004. pp.127 and 267-269.

Brazilian trade complaints could be ameliorated in bilateral working groups with the United States, Brazil may still choose not to liberalize areas where either it cannot easily fulfill the provisions of an FTA (enforcing protection of IPR), or where the United States has a distinct comparative advantage or particular interest (industrial goods, services, investment). This has been made clear in statements by Brazilian officials and by formal trade negotiation positions.

To illustrate, in speaking on the FTAA, a former Brazilian Ambassador to the United States and noted trade expert wrote:

> The Brazilian position is not merely a tactical reaction to the U.S. negotiating strategy regarding the so-called systemic issues. In fact, Brazil has a clear interest in preventing hemispheric disciplines on topics such as investment, intellectual property, government procurement, and services from curtailing its ability to formulate and implement public policies that are in its highest national interest.[42]

This attitude is reinforced by evidence questioning the economic logic of Brazil's anti-FTAA position based on the U.S. preference for addressing subsidies in the WTO. For example, studies point out that ending agricultural subsidies would increase FTAA agricultural trade little compared to a far bigger gain for Brazil from eliminating tariffs.[43] Brazil seems to realize this on some level or it would not continue to offer the "4+ 1" market access talks as an alternative to the FTAA.

As such, U.S. trade negotiators may be frustrated because there is perhaps little they can do to nudge Brazil off its course of continuing to advance Mercosul, where the marginal gains from expansion are likely small, and pursuing selective priorities in the WTO, while leaving the FTAA to flounder indefinitely. Brazil may actually have more to lose, however, because as much as both countries could improve their economic well-being from greater trade liberalization, as a developing country, Brazil seems to have the most to gain from not only reducing foreign barriers to its exports, but unilaterally opening its economy further, particularly as part of completing its ongoing economic reform agenda.

---

[42] Barbosa, Rubens Antonio. The Free Trade Area of the Americas. *Fordham International Law Journal.* February 2004. p. 1021.

[43] Salazar-Xirinachs, José M. Development Issues Posed by the FTAA. In Weintraub, Sidney, Alan M. Rugman, and Gavin Boyd, eds. *Free Trade in the Americas: Economic and Political Issues for Governments and Firms.* Cheltenham, Edward Elgar Publishing, Inc. 2004. p. 238. A similar conclusion is drawn for global agricultural trade as well, where some 80-90% of trade-distorting cost is attributed to tariffs rather than subsidies. Congressional Budget Office. *The Efects of Liberalizing World Agricultural Trade: A Survey.* Washington, D.C. December 2005.

APPENDIX 1
BRAZIL: TOP 15 EXPORTS AND IMPORTS

(Calendar Year 2004, $ Millions)

Export Product	$ Value	Import Product	$ Value
1. Soybeans	5,395	1. Fuels and lubricants	10,317
2. Iron ore	4,759	2. Chem./Phar. Intermed. Goods	9,638
3. Motor vehicles	3,352	3. Intermediate parts	5,589
4. Soybean oil cake	3,271	4. Mineral products	5,068
5. Airplanes	3,269	5. Accessories for trans. equip.	4,905
6. Meat, chicken	2,494	6. Non-durable consumer goods	3,673
7. Iron/Steel semi finish	2,115	7. Farming, raw materials	3,473
8. Flat-rolled iron/steel	2,007	8. Industrial machinery	3,278
9. Motor vehicle engines	1,972	9. Office/Science equipment	2,679
10. Meat, bovine	1,963	10. Fixed equipment	2,528
11. Motor vehicle parts	1,961	11. Inedible farm products	2,213
12. Footwear	1,899	12. Parts, industrial capital goods	1,518
13. Coffee	1,750	13. Foodstuffs, intermediate	1,517
14. Cane sugar, raw	1,511	14. Pharmaceutical products	1,454
15. Tobacco	1,380	15. Accessories for indust. Mach.	1,065
Subtotal	39,098	Subtotal	58,915
% of Total Exports	40.5%	% of Total Imports	93.8%

Data Source: Boletim do Banco do Brasil, September, 2005

APPENDIX 2
U.S.-BRAZIL MERCHANDISE TRADE

($ millions)

Year	U.S. Exports	U.S. Imports	U.S.Trade Balance	Trade Turnover	% Growth in U.S. Exports	% Growth in U.S. Imports
1992	5,751	7,609	-1,858	13,360		
1993	6,058	7,479	-1,421	13,537	5.3%	-1.7%
1994	8,102	8,683	-581	16,785	33.7%	16.1%
1995	11,439	8,833	2,606	20,272	41.2%	1.7%
1996	12,718	8,773	3,945	21,491	11.2%	-0.7%
1997	15,915	9,625	6,290	25,540	25.1%	9.7%
1998	15,142	10,102	5,040	25,244	-4.9%	5.0%
1999	13,203	11,314	1,889	24,517	-12.8%	12.0%
2000	15,320	13,853	1,467	29,173	16.0%	22.4%
2001	15,880	14,467	1,413	30,347	3.7%	4.4%
2002	12,376	15,781	-3,405	28,157	-22.1%	9.1%
2003	11,211	17,910	-6,699	29,121	-9.4%	13.5%
2004	13,837	21,160	-7,323	34,997	23.4%	18.1%

Data source: U.S. Department of Commerce

APPENDIX 3
U.S.-BRAZIL SERVICES TRADE

($ millions)

Year	U.S. Exports	U.S. Imports	Trade Balance	*Trade Turnover	% Growth in U.S.Exports	% Growth in U.S. Imports	% of Total U.S. Trade
1992	2,500	688	1,812	3,188	na	na	1.2%
1993	2,944	744	2,200	3,688	17.8%	8.1%	1.3%
1994	3,732	917	2,815	4,649	26.8%	23.3%	1.5%
1995	4,994	1,176	3,818	6,170	33.8%	28.2%	1.9%
1996	5,208	1,403	3,805	6,611	4.3%	19.3%	1.8%
1997	6,408	1,775	4,633	8,183	23.0%	26.5%	2.1%
1998	6,620	1,962	4,658	8,582	3.3%	10.5%	2.1%
1999	5,641	1,726	3,915	7,367	-14.8%	-12.0%	1.6%
2000	6,309	1,953	4,356	8,262	11.8%	13.2%	1.7%
2001	5,826	1,856	3,970	7,682	-7.7%	-5.0%	1.7%
2002	5,005	1,723	3,282	6,728	-14.1%	-7.2%	1.4%
2003	4,795	1,841	2,954	6,636	-4.2%	6.8%	1.3%
2004	4,997	1,913	3,084	6,910	4.2%	3.9%	1.4%

Data Source: U.S. Department of Commerce. Bureau of Economic Analysis (BEA). * Trade turnover = total trade or exports plus imports

APPENDIX 4
U.S.-BRAZIL FOREIGN DIRECT INVESTMENT

(in millions of U.S. dollars, historical cost basis)

Year	U.S. FDI in Brazil	% Change	Brazil FDI in U.S.	% Change
1993	16,772	—	726	—
1994	18,400	9.7%	712	-1.9%
1995	23,706	28.8%	864	21.3%
1996	28,699	21.1%	689	-20.3%
1997	35,727	24.5%	698	1.3%
1998	37,802	5.8%	609	-12.8%
1999	37,184	-1.6%	735	20.7%
2000	36,717	-1.3%	882	20.0%
2001	32,027	-12.8%	596	-32.4%
2002	27,598	-13.8%	997	67.3%
2003	31,741	15.0%	667	-33.1%
2004	33,267	4.8%	1,286	92.8%

Source: U.S. Department of Commerce. Bureau of Economic Analysis (BEA)

Note: historical cost data measures the stock of FDI reflecting prices at the time of the investment

In: Economics, Politics and Social Issues in Latin America ISBN 1-60021-182-8
Editor: Mary P. Lassiter, pp. 53-73

Chapter 4

The Economic Impact of Unions and Collective Bargaining: Lessons from the International Experience

Amit Dar and Francisco Galrão Carneiro
World Bank

I. Introduction

The international debate on labor standards has focused on a set of internationally agreed upon "core labor standards" including: (1) the freedom of association (consisting of the right to unionize and the right to collective bargaining); (2) the elimination of all forms of forced labor; (3) the effective abolition of child labor; and (4) the elimination of discrimination in employment and occupation.

These core labor standards have been defined in a number of ILO conventions dating from 1930 on. However, not all countries have ratified them and even where ratification has taken place, sometimes implementation and enforcement have been problematic. In June 1998, the ILO adopted the *Declaration on Fundamental Principles and Rights at Work* in order to revive interest in adopting and ratifying these conventions and to signal a strategic shift towards more flexible implementation and a greater emphasis on technical assistance. The Declaration includes an obligation on the part of ILO members to promote and realize the four core labor standards identified above. It recognizes the obligation of the ILO to assist its member countries to attain the objectives of the Declaration. It also encourages other international organizations to support these efforts by offering technical assistance and by helping member countries to create a climate for economic and social development. The intent of the Declaration is to ensure that the trend towards globalization is accompanied by social justice. However, it acknowledges that the comparative advantage of low-wage countries should not be called into question.

Debate on core labor standards has also become more prominent in the international arena and remains controversial. For example, some (largely developed) countries have expressed the view that if these standards were linked to trade regulations through the WTO, this would represent a powerful incentive for members to improve labor conditions. By contrast, many developing and some developed member states have maintained that the introduction of labor standards in trade negotiations would amount to protectionism and would undermine the comparative advantage of lower-wage trading partners.

This paper focuses on one of these standards by shedding light on the economic facets of the freedom of association. While the human rights argument in support of freedom of association and the right to collective bargaining is compelling, the question from an economic point of view is to what extent these standards contribute to economic development and performance. Answering this question would, in principle, require a comparison between countries with and without unions. This is, however, impossible as in virtually all countries – even those which suppress labor – unions and employers' organizations play a (sometimes important) role in industrial relations.

In this chapter, we consider two related questions that *indirectly* can help us disentangle the economic effects associated with freedom of association and the right to collective bargaining. These questions are: (a) what are the microeconomic effects of unions and employers' organizations (unionism); and (b) how do different institutional approaches to collective bargaining affect macroeconomic performance?

The majority of the evidence that addresses various aspects of these questions comes from OECD countries, though available evidence from developing countries will also be presented. This evidence will inform us about the economic consequences of different types of unionism as well as the interaction between unionism and the economic, political and institutional environment in which collective bargaining takes place. The aim of this review is to summarize the empirical evidence and draw some lessons of experience.

The chapter is organized in the following sections: (a) presenting some data on unionism; (b) providing a brief theoretical overview of unionism and collective bargaining; (c) reviewing evidence derived from microeconometric analysis of the economic impact of unions; (d) reviewing evidence derived from econometric studies focusing on the relationship between different systems of collective bargaining and macroeconomic performance; and (e) conclusion and lessons. The evidence presented in this paper draws heavily on a recent comprehensive study of the issues *Core Labor Standards and the Freedom of Association: Economic Aspects* by Aidt and Tzannatos (2001).

II. Unionization and Collective Bargaining: Some Statistics

A recent development in the economics of the labor market was the appearance during the 1980s of a wide range of studies on the behavior of trade unions and their impact on the process of wage and employment determination. In the specific case of wage determination, it has been now widely suggested that wage moderation is usually associated with a more coordinated bargaining structure, or what has been termed corporatist arrangements. On the other extreme, however, explosive wage demands have been usually associated both with a lack of coordination and with synchronization in wage bargaining.

The discussion on the role of institutions and wage bargaining structures in determining wage moderation cannot be dissociated from the debate on labor market flexibility. In the competitive model of the labor market, for example, the balance of supply and demand in the whole market dictates wages. Hicks's Theory of Wages (1932) was the starting point for this argument, but even Hicks himself became skeptical about the overall applicability of the competitive model, as he made clear in the preface to Hicks (1963). There has been much debate whether wages can be considered as fixed by non-competitive pressures. A common argument often used is that in most cases, wages are determined by collective bargaining and also that other non-competitive factors might be important (e.g., efficiency wage and rent-sharing theories).

Table 4.1. Union Density and Bargaining Coverage

Country	Union density			Bargaining Coverage	
	1970	1980	1994	1990	1994
OECD					
Australia	50	48	41	80	80
Austria	62	56	42	98	98
Canada	31	36	38	38	38
Denmark	60	76	76	69	69
Finland	51	70	81	95	95
France	22	18	9	92	95
Germany	33	36	29	90	92
Italy	36	49	39	83	82
Japan	35	31	24	23	21
Netherlands	38	35	26	71	81
New Zealand	n.a.	56	30	67	31
Spain	27	19	19	76	78
Sweden	68	80	91	86	89
Switzerland	30	31	27	53	50
UK	45	50	34	47	47
US	23	22	16	18	18
Latin America and Caribbean					
Argentina	n.a.	49	25	n.a.	73
Brazil	n.a.	n.a.	32	n.a.	n.a.
Chile	n.a.	12	16	n.a.	13
Colombia	n.a.	11	7	n.a.	n.a.
Costa Rica	n.a.	23	13	n.a.	n.a.
Guatemala	n.a.	8	4	n.a.	n.a.
Guyana	n.a.	n.a.	25	n.a.	27
Mexico	n.a.	54	31	n.a.	n.a.
Peru	n.a.	n.a.	8	n.a.	n.a.
Uruguay	n.a.	20	12	n.a.	22
Venezuela	n.a.	26	15	n.a.	n.a.

Two indicators are often used to measure the extent of unionization in a country. These are (a) union density; and (b) bargaining coverage. Union density is defined as the number of workers who are members of a union, as a percentage of all workers (unionized and non-unionized). Bargaining coverage is defined as the number of workers, unionized or not, who have their pay and employment conditions determined by a collective agreement, as a percentage of all workers, unionized and non-unionized.

Box 4.1 - Trade Unions and Collective Bargaining in Brazil

The labor market in Brazil has developed wage setting institutions which allow its classification as an intermediate-centralized economy in terms of international comparisons.

Prior to 1964, collective wage adjustments were defined as part of a collective labor contract between workers' and employers' unions. For each professional category represented by a local union, negotiations took effect on a different day of the year, called "base date". Trade unions were defined in terms of industry affiliation and geographical location. After the 1964 military coup, collective bargaining was more or less replaced by centralized state wage indexation, and this situation prevailed until the 1980s. The State wage indexation system in operation between 1964 and 1985 provided for a state minimum wage to be annually indexed based on the average real wage of the previous 24 months (shortened to 12 months in 1975). This system represented a compulsory incomes policy, and for certain periods between 1964 and 1979 due to systematic underindexation it was moderately successful in lowering inflation.

By the end of the 1970s, inflation was growing rapidly in Brazil and this provoked the upsurge of strike activities in the most organized sectors of the economy. The consequences of the increased labor mobilization were two-fold: (i) an immediate reduction in the period between salary adjustments from 12 months, until 1979, to six months thereafter; and (ii) the return of direct negotiations between unions and employers, which opened the door for wage adjustments above the past rate of inflation.

The re-emergence of political democracy in the 1980s combined with labor dissatisfaction with the State wage policy led to the development of a new unionism. Unions have slowly increased their role in the wage determination process and have experienced an enhancement in their bargaining ability at both the regional and industrial levels. Union density is quite high - it is estimated to be over 30 percent. In terms of degree of bargaining centralization, what has emerged is an intermediate level of collective bargaining.

In the late 1980s and early 1990s, control of inflation became much more problematic in Brazil. One consequence of the generally unsuccessful counter-inflationary policy shocks was an increased defensiveness on the part of labor unions, keen to protect real wage levels in the face of deflationary shocks. This contributed to the breakdown in coordination and synchronization of wage determination, and the development of a structure for collective bargaining much more akin to that prevailing in western Europe

Source: Carneiro (1998, 1999); Carneiro and Henley (1998)

Table 4.1 shows union density and bargaining coverage for some non-Latin American OECD countries in the 1970s, 1980s and 1990s and for some Latin American countries where data is available for the latter two decades. Average union density in the OECD countries declined during the 1980s (47%) to 40 percent in the 1990s. The average movement, however, hides a lot of variation. Some countries, such as the US, the UK, Japan, and the Netherlands, have experienced a significant reduction in union density. Other countries, such as Finland and Sweden, have experienced a significant increase in union density over the three decades. Also, the cross-country variation is significant. Countries such as France, the

US, and Spain have very low union density rates (less than 30 percent). On the other hand, the Scandinavian countries have very high rates (all above 50 percent, some around 80 percent).

Some of the same trends are true for Latin American countries as shown in Table 4.1 – union density seems to have decreased sharply in the 1990s. While it is still high in some countries (e.g. Brazil 32%, Argentina 25%, Guyana 25%), in many countries union density is below 10%. Another interesting aspect is that union density is significantly lower, on average, in Latin America than it is in many non Latin OECD countries.

Bargaining coverage is on average much higher than union density in the OECD (and in the few Latin American countries for which this data is available). While high union density leads to high coverage of collective bargaining, the converse is not true. Countries such as Spain and France have very low union density, yet the coverage of collective agreements is very high. The difference between union density and coverage of collective bargaining is largely attributed to mandatory extensions of collective agreements to non-unionized sectors (OECD, 1994). Brazil's collective bargaining system can be characterized as an intermediate level of collective bargaining. Union density is over 30 percent – among the highest in Latin America (Box 4.1).

III. A THEORETICAL REVIEW OF UNIONISM AND COLLECTIVE BARGAINING

What Unions Do

Economists have traditionally argued that unions want to increase wages and "share rents" with employers while preserving employment of their membership. To the extent that rent is available for sharing, however, unions can force firms to give up some profits only if they can *monopolize* labor supply. This is because firms are willing to give up some of their profits to avoid industrial conflict. However, if nonunion workers can readily replace union workers, the union's bargaining position is substantially weakened. Hence the success of unions depends significantly on the economic environment, as measured by competitive pressure from product markets and nonunion labor markets in which they operate. If unions are successful in getting a wage mark-up, they impose a number of (external) costs on the rest of the society, known as the *monopoly cost* of unions (Medoff and Freeman, 1984). These could include firms trying to pass costs onto the consumer or the fact that more senior union members, who typically have a disproportional influence on the decisions of the union, may institutionalize a seniority principle in relation to layoffs and other aspects of deployment such as promotion, recall and training. This can create insider/outsider dynamics that can lead to persistently high levels of unemployment.

However, these costs are based on the assumption that the labor market would be competitive in the absence of unionism. The reality facing policy makers is far less clear cut than this for several reasons. First, the 'removal' of unions may not expose an underlying perfectly competitive situation in the labor market: instead it may reveal market imperfections on the labor demand side in the form of monopsony.[1] Second, when job-specific skills are important (or turnover costs are otherwise high), individual workers have sufficient bargaining power to get a wage mark-up, even in the absence of unions. Finally, it is possible that unions and firms can bargain over wages *and* employment and enter an efficient contract. This can reduce transaction costs which would be involved in dealing with individual employees.[2]

Another viewpoint focuses on the economic (*participatory*) benefit of unions. Unions facilitate worker-participation and worker-manager cooperation at the workplace. This can have efficiency-enhancing effects to the benefit of workers and management. These benefits can arise from a number of sources: (a) unions can play an important and beneficial role in communicating the preferences of workers directly to the management, plus participating in the establishment of work rules and seniority provisions in the internal labor market; (b) unions facilitate procedural arrangements and other agency services that help reduce the likelihood of costly disputes about wage and employment conditions; and (c) unions can increase productivity by providing a channel through which labor can draw to management's attention changes in working methods or production techniques that may be beneficial to both parties.

Bargaining Coordination

Some economists argue that the capacity of unions to determine wages increased over time because unemployment insurance and other labor market institutions which favor welfare-state measures led to reduced wage pressure from the unemployed. Thus, a higher rate of unemployment would be required if a noninflationary path of economic development were to be achieved. The effect of unemployment on the behavior of unions as regards wage determination generally depends on the objective function of the union, which may be strongly influenced by the size and composition of the labor force share a union represents. Two effects of the extent of representation on collective bargaining can be broadly identified: (i) with increasing comprehensiveness, unions gain market power that may be used to push up wages and working standards. At the same time, however, (ii) as organizations encompass larger groups, the negative effects of wage bargaining become endogenous, as suggested by Olson (1982)[3].

The economic effects of unions depend on the way collective bargaining is organized. Of particular interest is the degree of bargaining coordination. Here we outline from a theoretical

---

[1]Employer can derive monopsony power from the fact that it is costly for a worker to leave the firm (because of the firm-specific human capital they have accumulated) and move to another city to get a new similar job. Therefore, once a worker is hired, he or she would be reluctant to quit and the employer can exploit that.

[2] This outcome is based on the so-called "efficient bargain" model which is termed efficient by assuming that neither the union nor the firm will be made better off without making the other worse off, should a change in the agreed contract be effected; i.e., bargained levels of wages and employment will be on the contract curve and the outcome will be Pareto efficient.

[3] As argued by Mancur Olson (1982), special interest groups are most damaging once they have gained a certain amount of power, but little responsibility.

perspective three aspects of bargaining coordination, namely, centralization, concentration and informal coordination.[4]

Centralization of collective bargaining refers to the capacity of the peak union confederation and employers organization to influence wage levels/patterns across the economy. This capacity depends on two aspects. First, at what level bargaining takes place, that is, plant, industry or national level. Second, whether or not the peak organization(s) can control the behavior of their constituent organizations.

To see the implications of this, we need to take a closer look at what is likely to happen when, say, a company union demands a higher wage. Clearly, to avoid an increase in the product wage, the firm will try to pass on the wage demand as a higher product price. This reaction has two implications. First, a higher product price reduces the real consumption wage of all workers (the externality effect) including those who hold membership of the union. Second, a higher product price leads to a reduction in the demand for goods produced by the firm and a reduction in employment among unionized workers (the competitive pressure effect). The union, of course, dislikes both of these effects. Accordingly, it moderates its wage demands to the extent that they do not pay off in terms of a higher real consumption wage for the membership or/and to the extent that they put the jobs of too many union members at stake. In other words, if a union and an individual firm bargain over wages, the trade-off between a wage increase and employment greatly depends on the price elasticity of demand for the firm's product, and in the extreme, the power of unions at the company level will be limited by competition in the product market.

On the other hand, for unions whose utility function comprises the entire labor force, as in the case of centralized national unions, all external effects of the union's action enter directly into the union's utility function and, therefore, the negative effects of its actions become endogenous to these unions. As examples of this internalization mechanism, in an entirely centralized system, if workers lose their jobs and become dependent on benefits, these benefits will be financed by members of the union; thus, excessively high wage increases directly affect the member's net wage. Similarly, if wage increases induce inflation, the real wage of the union's members will be directly affected.

Such considerations of political science arguments have led some economists to suggest that wage bargaining at the company level (decentralized) or at the national level (centralized), leads to favorable macroeconomic outcomes, such as low unemployment, low inflation and high employment rates. Economies with an intermediate-centralized level of wage bargaining, however, suffer from union power that does not internalize negative effects and are, therefore, expected to experience less favorable macroeconomic outcomes (Calmfors and Driffill, 1988).

In general, the relationship between centralization of collective bargaining and economic performance is determined by the interaction between the externality effect and the competitive pressure effect. If the externality effect is important even at the industry level and the competitive pressure effect is unimportant, then the relationship is monotonic, i.e., a more centralized bargaining system produces better economic outcomes. However, if the externality effect is unimportant at the industry level and the competitive pressure effect is important, the relationship may be U-shaped, i.e., national and firm level bargaining produces

[4] The relevant, theoretical literature has been surveyed in great detail by Calmfors (1993), Moene and Wallerstein (1993a), Layard et al. (1991, ch. 2) and Henley and Tsakalotos (1993).

better outcomes than industry-based collective bargaining. In addition to openness to international trade, the relationship between bargaining centralization and economic performance also depends on competition from nonunion labor markets. The general point is that the nature of the relationship depends significantly on the context in which collective bargaining takes place.[5]

Union concentration refers to the number and type of unions at the relevant level of bargaining. An industrial relations system based on *multi-unionism* and *closed unions* is usually characterized by low concentration because of rivalry between unions that results in less coordinated wage bargaining. *Multi-unionism* refers to a situation in which many unions offer to organize the same workers. A *closed* union refers to the situation when workers can only join a particular union of his or her craft/profession/education/job. In contrast, *an open union* can have members with different education and from different trades. It is not, *a priori*, clear that bargaining coordination in the form of a concentrated union movement based on single-unionism and open unions leads to more desirable economic outcomes. This will depend on several factors such as whether workers in closed unions are complements or substitutes in production, individual preferences of union members etc..

Bargaining coordination needs not be embodied in the formal institutional framework of collective bargaining. It can be informal. *Informal coordination*, typically, takes two forms. The first form is *internal* coordination among employers and/or the employees. At the employer side this involves coordination between industry-based employers' organizations or individual firms. This plays an important role in Japan, Austria, and Switzerland (Soskice, 1990; OECD, 1994). At the employee side, internal coordination, typically, involves coordination between company- and industry-based unions. The second form of informal coordination is pattern bargaining. Here, a dominate industry or company enters a collective agreement that is followed by other firms and industries. This has been important in, e.g., Germany, where the metal industry, traditionally, has acted as the leader.

IV. Empirical Evidence from Micro Data

This section reviews a large body of empirical evidence about the economic effects of unions derived from microeconomic data on individual workers and establishments. A significant portion of the evidence relates to OECD countries (mainly the U.S. and the U.K) but there is also some evidence from some developing countries.

This section is organized as follows. First, evidence is presented on the union-nonunion wage mark-up. This aspect of union behavior is, by far, the most well researched aspect with over 200 studies in the US alone. Cross-country differences in the average wage mark-up as well as the variation in the wage mark-up across skills, gender, occupation, ethnicity as well as with respect to the underlying economic and institutional environment are examined. This is followed by a review of the effect of unions on other economic variables such as

---

[5] Freeman (1988) argues for care on this issue as centralized corporatist labor markets are primarily found in small countries while decentralized markets characterize larger economies. In this context, any policy recommendation should not concentrate only on a particular set of institutions which work better but rather try to identify specific policies which can succeed in particular environments.

employment growth, hours worked, productivity, job mobility, implementation of new technology etc.

Union Non-Union Wage Mark-Up

The union-nonunion wage mark-up (the "wage mark-up") is defined as the difference between the average (nominal) wage of unionized and nonunionized workers with similar individual and workplace characteristics divided by the average wage of a nonunionized worker.[6] The estimation of the wage mark-up can be based on data related to wages of individual workers or average sector-wide or occupational wage rates (for example, average wages in different industries or broad sectors – such as manufacturing versus services or manual versus nonmanual workers). As it is generally agreed that the mark-up calculated using sector-wide data are biased upwards, we focus below on studies that have used individual cross-section data.

A major econometric problem involved in estimating the wage mark-up is to control for all other factors, besides unionization, that affect wages. These factors have typically been proxied by variables such as education, work experience, gender, family status, hours worked, firm size, industry, occupation and so on. However, some of these variables may be highly correlated with union status. For example, the fact that a unionized worker works longer hours may be the result of union negotiated overtime or, to take another example, working in a particular industry may be a critical factor for belonging to a union (such as in the mining sector). Another problem is union-status selectivity. This problem arises because the union-status selection process is not random. For example, workers with high productivity can decide not to join a union or decide to work in the nonunion sector because they hope to get a higher wage than collectively agreed. This phenomenon gives rise to selectivity bias and reduces the reliability of the estimated mark-up.[7] Bearing these remarks in mind, we present below a summary of country-specific studies on the wage mark-up as well as cross-country comparisons.[8]

In all countries where the wage mark-up has been estimated, it has been found to be non-negative. There is, however, significant cross-country variation as well as variation of estimates within countries. There is also some evidence, albeit weak, that the wage mark-up is, on average, lower in high-income countries than in low- and middle-income ones.

More specifically, Table 4.2 presents summary estimates of the wage mark-up for six high-income economies (the US, the UK, Japan, Canada, Australia and West Germany), six middle-income economies (South Korea, Malaysia, South Africa, Brazil and Mexico), and

---

[6] In principle, we are interested in comparing the union wage with the wage that would have prevailed in the absence of unions (this is called the "wage gain"). However, the wage gain is unobservable and the literature has typically focused on the wage mark-up.

[7] One way to deal with the union-status selectivity problem is to estimate the wage equation and a union-status selection equation simultaneously. Another is to use a panel data set that contains time series of cross-sections for the same set of workers. This makes it possible to control for unobserved heterogeneity. For example, if unobserved characteristics of workers stay constant over time, they can be taken into account by comparing the wage of each worker at one date with that at a later date.

[8] Extensive discussion on methodological issues on the estimation of the wage mark-up can be found in Lewis (1986), Booth (1995) or Pencavel (1991).

one low-income economy (Ghana). These estimates are based on averages of regression analysis estimates in various studies.

The evidence is sparser for other OECD countries but some generalizations are possible. The wage mark-up for Australia has been estimated to vary between 7 percent and 17. Similarly, the Canadian wage mark-up has been estimated to be in the range of 10 to 20 percent, though most estimates seem to fall in the 10-15 percentage range. In Germany, where most unions are industry unions and work and pay conditions contained in collective agreements are largely extended to nonunionized workers, the wage-mark-up is found to be small, especially for male workers. Similarly, a study on Japan has found a small average wage mark-up of about 5 percent.

Table 4.2. Union-Nonunion Wage Mark-Up for Selected Countries

Country	Period/Year	Wage mark-up(%)
USA	1963-95	15
UK	1969-95	10
Japan		5
Canada	1969-86	10-20
Australia	1984-87	7-17
West Germany	1985-87	0-6
South Korea	1988	2-4
Malaysia	1988	15-20
South Africa	1993-95	10-24
Mexico	1989	10
Brazil	1992-95	7-11
Ghana	1992-94	21-28

There is much less evidence for developing economies. The mark-up in South Africa has been estimated in three studies from anywhere between 10-24% (Moll, 1993; Dabalen, 1998; and Rouse, 1999). Standing (1992) estimates the wage mark-up for Malaysia to be in the range between 15 and 20 percent, depending on the type of union. These effects are somewhat larger than in most industrialized countries. Standing attributes the high mark-up to the fact that Malaysia non-unionized workers can, in the absence of minimum wage legislation, be vulnerable to very low wages. He concludes that the mark-up can reasonably be in the estimated range despite the fact that the political and economic environment in Malaysia is difficult for unions.

For Ghana, estimates using three surveys of manufacturing firms in 1992, 1993 and 1994, find that the wage mark-up varies between 21-28%. Again, these estimates are significantly higher than those from the industrialized countries. For Mexico, Panagides and Patrinos (1994) find a 10 percent membership wage mark-up after having controlled for an large number of income generating characteristics in a cross-section sample of unionized and non-unionized non-agricultural workers in 1989. They attribute the relative low wage mark-up to the fact that the 1980s were a particular difficult time for unions in Mexico due to recession coupled with government austerity measures. It is, however, unclear if this can explain the result. First, recession and austerity measures should affect unionized sections and nonunionized sectors alike. Second, one could argue that unions would be in a better position than nonunionized workers to resist downwards pressure on wages, thereby increasing the wage mark-up.

Evidence for the case of Brazil is presented by Arbache and Carneiro (1999), based on household surveys for 1992 and 1995. Their results are suggestive that trade unions do have an important role in wage determination, as they found union wage mark-up that varied from 6.7% to 11.3%. Furthermore, these authors have found that a share of between 18.8% and 29.6% of the raw wage differentials between unionized and nonunionized workers were not explained by differences in observable productive endowments, occupation and other variables. This suggests that if a worker changes his/her union membership status from nonunion to union s/he is liable to perceive a wage increase in Brazil.

Gender wage gaps. Unions are one among many determinants of the gender wage gap. In his survey of the U.S. literature, Lewis (1986) concludes that there is very little, if any, difference between the mark-up for female and male workers. This has been further confirmed by more recent studies and the same result emerges from Australian studies (Christie, 1992; Mulvey, 1986). The evidence from other OECD and middle-income countries, however, unambiguously supports the view that the wage mark-up is greater for women. Nakumura et al. (1988), in their study of Japan, find a wage mark-up of 10% for women but fails to find any for men. Likewise, Schmidt (1995) shows that the small average wage mark-up in West German is mainly due to a wage mark-up among unionized female workers. The findings for Mexico suggest that the mark-up for women is 9.8 percentage points higher than that of men with similar characteristics. Similarly, in South Africa, the wage mark-up among black blue-collar workers in the mid 1980's was about 11 percentage points higher for women than for men. A comparison of the wage ratio of male and female workers in non-unionized and unionized firms in Malaysia suggest that the presence of a union reduces the ratio of male to female wages, leading to the conclusion that women gain more than proportionately from unionization (Standing, 1992).

Skill wage gaps. Collective bargaining can insert a wedge between worker productivity and wages. Though this can be desirable as part of avoiding wage inequality from a societal point of view, it can also distort the relative wage of skilled and unskilled workers or the relative rewards to different types of jobs. There is some evidence to back up this claim. In the U.S. and the U.K, evidence shows that manual workers get a larger mark-up than non-manual workers. In South Africa, the wage mark-up to workers with different skills varies between different ethnic groups. For example, the average wage mark-up for unskilled *non-white* workers is 19 percent, while the wage mark-up to skilled workers is practically zero. On the other hand, semi-skilled and skilled *white* workers got a wage mark-up of 13 percent in 1985 (Moll, 1993) implying that black unions tended to compress wages by skill level. Though Dabalen (1998) finds estimates that are somewhat smaller, his study confirms the general pattern found by Moll (1993). In Malaysia, unions reduce the intra-firm wage differential between skilled and unskilled workers. In particular, industry unions tend to reduce the differential between workers with different skills more than company unions do (Standing, 1992).

Collective bargaining characteristics. Some studies have also tried to estimate the wage mark-up in a cross-country context. These studies have used comparable individual data to estimate the wage differential for a set of OECD countries. These analysis, for the most part, come up with similar results to the ones stated above. Using these data, analysis which has tried to correlate the wage mark-up across countries with characteristics of collective bargaining[9] come up with interesting findings. This analysis shows that there is a tendency for countries with centralized/coordinated or decentralized/uncoordinated bargaining systems to have a higher mark-up than countries with semi-coordinated systems. Union density appears to be largely uncorrelated with to the wage mark-up (correlation coefficient 0.02) while bargaining coverage is negatively correlated with the mark-up (correlation coefficient -0.58). This seems to point to the conclusion that the more workers become unionized/covered by collective agreements, the lower the mark-up they can secure.[10] This may be so because the labor supply in the non-covered sector decreases when more workers become covered, thereby pushing the nonunion wage up. Somewhat related, using a time-series comparison, this analysis also shows that the wage markup seems to be lower for countries where the density rates have been increasing or constant between 1970-1993 (an average mark-up of 4.5%) as compared to mark-ups in countries where the union density rates have declined over the same time period (an average mark-up of 11.8%).

Other Union Effects

This section reviews the evidence on the impact of unions on employment growth, productivity, technology and profitability.

Employment Growth. Available evidence from the US, the UK, Canada, Malaysia and Jamaica suggests that employment *generally* grows more slowly in unionized firms than in nonunionized firms. Studies from the U.S., the UK and Canada typically find a *growth* differential in the range of 3-5 percentage points per year in favor of nonunionized firms.[11] The evidence on the employment growth differential is mixed in Malaysia. The employment growth differential is about 5 percentage points per year in firms that bargain with industrial unions but insignificant in firms that deal with a company union (Standing, 1992). Rama (1998) estimates the employment differential between sectors with high and low union membership rates for Jamaica over the period 1986-93 to be 2-5 percentage points per year. Rama (1998) provides a number of *potential* explanations for the observed employment growth differential including – (a) it takes time and effort to organize a union. As a consequence, at a given point in time, old firms are more likely to be covered by unions than young firms are. If young firms expand faster than old firms, we would expect to observe higher employment growth in the young, nonunionized firms; (b) unions are more likely to be concentrated in sectors that enjoy larger rents. If these sectors are less dynamic and their activities limited by the size of the domestic market, employment would tend to grow slower in these sectors; and (c) labor costs grow faster and productivity slower in unionized firms than in nonunionized firms.

---

9 These Characteristics Are – Degree Of Centralization/Coordination Of Collective Bargaining, Union Density, And Bargaining Coverage.

10 As Argued By Arbache And Carneiro (1999), The Case Of Brazil Seems To Contradict The International Evidence, As In The Brazilian Context, The More Workers Become Unionized The Larger Is The Mark-Up They Can Secure.

11 Boal and Pencavel (1994), however, find, in their study of coal-mining data from West Virginia over the period 1897-1938, that the employment growth differential is approximately zero if the variation in working days is explicitly taken into account. Machin and Wadhwani (1991) find, using UK data, that employment grows faster in unionized establishments in the 1970s. Blanchflower and Burgess (1996) find a negative effect of unions in the UK, but not in Australia.

Voluntary turnovers, tenure and layoffs. Evidence from the U.K, the U.S., Japan, Australia, and Malaysia unanimously shows that voluntary turnovers (measured by the quit rate) are lower and that job tenure is longer in unionized firms than in nonunionized ones. Freeman and Medoff (1984) estimate the welfare gain associated with a reduction in labor turnover to be by equivalent to a 0.2-0.3 percent increase in GDP in the U.S. in the 1980s. They base their estimate on a calculation of the how much the reduction in exit is worth to firms and to workers. For unionized firms, they estimate the gain to be equivalent to a 1-2 percent reduction in costs. While voluntary turnover tends to be lower in unionized firms than elsewhere, unions *increase* the use of layoffs, in particular temporary layoffs. Unions also significantly alter the firm's choice between layoffs, wage and hours adjustment in response to the business cycle fluctuations. Unionized firms adjust through temporary layoffs rather than reductions in weekly hours (work sharing) or wages.[12] In particular, unionized (blue-collar) workers are 50 to 60 percent more likely to be laid off temporarily than nonunionized workers. An explanation for this relates to the fact that junior workers can be more easily laid off. Senior workers typically have more influence on the union's policy than junior workers. Faced with the choice between a reduction in their earnings or temporary layoff of junior workers, unions are likely to prefer layoffs. Another explanation, especially in OECD economies, with well-developed income support schemes for the unemployed, is that the cost of temporary layoffs can be shifted on to the unemployment benefit system. As long as there is less than 100 percent experience rating, i.e., as long as firms contribute to unemployment benefits an amount less than the costs of the unemployment they generate, those firms with above-average layoffs are subsidized at the expense of firms with below-average layoffs.

Profitability. It is a commonly held view that unions reduce profitability of firms because they appropriate part of the rent that would otherwise have been available to shareholders. The fact that unions are able to get a wage mark-up supports this view. It is, however unwise to deduce the effect of unions on profitability by looking at the wage mark-up alone. By increasing moral and job-satisfaction among workers and facilitate worker-employer cooperation, unions can contribute positively to profitability. Therefore, instead of trying to capture a given rent, unions may help create profits from which they can achieve wage gains. The impact of unions on profitability has been estimated in a large number of studies. Bellman (1992) surveys 14 studies from the U.S.. All studies find that unions have a negative impact on profitability. The impact tends to be larger in industries or firms that have some monopoly power in the product market. Booth (1995) surveys seven British studies. While a few studies find that unionism has no impact on profitability, the general impression is that unions have a negative, often significant, impact on profitability in manufacturing firms. The adverse impact is larger when firms have product market power. A study on Japan (Brunello, 1992) finds that unions reduce the rate of return on equity by 20-25 percent and the ratio of profits to sales by about 40 percent.

Technology. The available empirical evidence suggests that new technology is adopted as fast in unionized firms as in nonunionized ones and that unions have little impact either way on technological innovations in firms. Keefe (1992) surveys research on the relationship between unions and technological change in the U.S., U.K. and Canada in the 1980s. He concludes that unions have no effect on firm's use of advanced manufacturing and

---

[12]Temporary layoffs refer to a situation in which a worker is laid-off for a shorter period of time (less than a mouth) and is recalled or rehired by the same firm.

microelectronic technologies and that "in most cases unions welcome technological modernization. Betcherman (1991) reaches a similar conclusion in his study of the impact of unions on technological change in Canada in 1980-85 but adds the observation that unions do have an impact on the *way* technological change is being implemented. In particular, he finds that unionized firms were more likely to introduce technological changes that nonunionized firms for of cost-cutting or production control reasons. Likewise, Machin and Wadhwani (1991) and Latreille (1992) find a small positive impact of unions on the introduction of new microelectronic equipment in U.K. firms in the mid-1980s. Finally, Standing (1992) in his study of industrial relations in Malaysia concludes that unions actually stimulate capital, product, and labor process innovations.

V. Empirical Evidence from Macro Data

In this section, we review studies that aim at capturing the *macroeconomic* impact of *the institutional framework of collective bargaining.* While there are differences in bargaining institutions across sectors and changes do take place in the long-term within a given economy, the institutional framework is, by and large, unchanged in the short- and medium run. To investigate the impact of collective bargaining on macroeconomic performance, it is, therefore, necessary to take a comparative approach and look at cross-country evidence. Though there is scattered evidence from developing countries, most of the reviewed studies focus on the group of OECD countries.

Union Density and Bargaining Coverage

The relationship between union density and bargaining coverage and a variety of economic performance indicators has been examined extensively, especially for OECD countries. From a theoretical perspective, the impact of *union density* on economic performance is unclear. Union density determines the number of (unionized) workers that can be call upon to strike and thereby it is a proxy of the bargaining power of unions. In countries with high union density, unions are more likely to succeed in pushing (union) wages up, leading to less employment, more unemployment and inflation. The negative impact of unionization on economic performance may, however, be reduced to the extent that unions participate in productivity-enhancing activities (by giving voice to dissatisfied workers) at the firm level.

Table 4.3 summarizes the findings of the studies from OECD countries that have investigated the relationship between union density and economic performance. Union density *per se* (i.e., for given bargaining coverage and for given level of bargaining coordination) appears to have little or no impact on comparative labor market performance measured by the unemployment rate, inflation, the employment rate, real earnings growth, the level of compensation, labor supply, adjustment speed to wage shocks, real wage rigidity, labor and total factor productivity.[13]

[13] Blanchflower (1996), who uses country-specific microeconomic data to analyze OECD countries, find similar results.

There is, however, one significant exception to the general result that the association between union density and economic performance is weak: Union density compresses the wage distribution and reduces earnings inequality.[14] This confirms the evidence from micro data discussed earlier.

Table 4.3. Union Density and Economic Performance in the OECD Countries

Study and years	Performance indicator	Result
OECD (1997) 1980-94	Unemployment rate Inflation Employment rate Real earnings growth Earnings inequality	Union density increases the employment rate but has no effect on the unemployment rate inflation and real earnings growth Union density reduces earnings inequality
OECD (1997) 1980-94	Unemployment rate Inflation Employment rate Real earnings growth Earnings inequality	Union density reduces earnings inequality in 1990 and 1994. Weak indication of a positive relationship between union density and the employment rate and a negative relationship between union density and real earnings growth in 1980 but not in other years.
Freeman (1988) 1979-85.	Unemployment rate Employment rate Compensation	Union density has no effect on the unemployment rate the employment rate, and compensation.
Scarpetta (1996) 1983-93	Unemployment rate	Union density increases unemployment in particular youth and long-term unemployment but no control for bargaining coverage is made.
Nickell and Layard (1997) and Nickell (1997), 1983-88, 1989-94	Unemployment Labor supply Productivity growth	Union density increases total unemployment but has no separate effect on short- and long-term unemployment. Union density has no effect on labor supply and productivity growth
Bean et al. (1986) 1956-85	Adjustment speed Real wage rigidity	Union density has no effect on either adjustment speed (to wage shocks), or on real wage rigidity.
Layard et al. (1991) 1980-94	Real wage rigidity	Union density has no effect on real wage rigidity.
Scarpetta (1996) 1970-93	Hysteresis in unemployment	Union density increases unemployment persistence but no control for bargaining coverage is made.

The picture looks quite different when we consider the association between union density and economic performance in developing countries. Evidence (Rama, 1995; McGuire, 1996; Fields and Wan, 1989) from developing countries in Latin America, the Caribbean, and South East Asia suggests that union density has a *negative* impact on output and employment growth. Rama (1997a) argues that the difference between the impact of union density in developing and OECD countries is caused by differences in the general economic and political environment.That is, the adverse effect of unions in developing countries may be caused not so much by what unions do but rather because of the context in which they are doing it. Hence, if unions operate in an environment of generally ill designed labor and product market regulation in which rent-seeking is a profitable business (also for unions), it is no wonder that the correlation between union density and economic performance is negative. Likewise, if unions operate in the context of an unstable political environment, the incentive

[14] Freeman (1988) also shows that wage dispersion tends to be lower in corporatist economies as opposed to economies with a decentralized labor market.

to "invest" in real wage restraint in exchange for (expected) future returns is low and union militancy comes at no surprise.

While union density relates to the number of unionized workers, bargaining coverage relates to the total number of workers that have their wage and employment conditions determined by collective agreements. In Table 4.4 we review the studies that have investigated the association between bargaining coverage and macroeconomic performance.

Table 4.4. Bargaining Coverage And Economic Performance: A Summary of the Relevant Studies

Study and years	Performance indicator	Result
Henley and Tsakalotos (1993)	Unemployment rate Inflation Real earnings growth Earnings inequality	The performance of highly centralized or "corporatist" economies, such as Sweden and Austria have in the past been superior to those of the EC members.
Appelbaum and Schettkat (1996)	Unemployment rate Inflation Employment rate	Finds evidence of a u-shaped relation between the degree of centralization of wage bargaining and labor market performance Countries with intermediate degrees of centralization performed worse than those at the extremes.
OECD (1997) 1980-94	Unemployment rate Inflation Employment rate Real earnings growth Earnings inequality	Bargaining coverage increases unemployment inflation and real earnings growth and reduces the employment rate and earnings inequality
OECD (1997) 1980-94	Unemployment rate Inflation Employment rate Real earnings growth Earnings inequality	Bargaining coverage increases unemployment only in 1994, reduces the employment rate in only 1990 and 1994 and earnings inequality in 1994. Otherwise it has no impact on economic performance
Siebert (1997)	Unemployment rate Inflation Employment rate Real earnings growth	Shows the adverse impact on employment creation of institutional rigidities, centralized collective bargaining high coverage rates, and generous benefits and protection.
Jackman (1993) 1983-88.	Unemployment rate	Bargaining coverage increases unemployment
Nickell and Layard (1997), Nickell (1997) 1989-94	Unemployment rate Labor supply Productivity growth	Bargaining coverage increases both short- and long-term unemployment and labor supply but has no effect on productivity growth

After controlling for union density and bargaining coordination, countries with high bargaining coverage (such as Austria, France and Finland), *ceteris paribus*, experience higher unemployment rates, lower employment rates, and more inflation than countries with low bargaining coverage (such as USA, Japan and Canada).

Moreover, high bargaining coverage seems to increase the supply of labor but has no effect on labor and total factor productivity (Nickell and Layard, 1997). Finally, high bargaining coverage is associated with higher real earnings growth and a reduction in earnings inequality.

These findings suggest that an increase in coverage at a given level of union density has a greater impact than an increase in density at a given level of coverage (at least in OECD countries). One explanation of this result is as follows. In those parts of the economy to which bargaining results are extended, only the monopoly effect of unions is present. The economic effects of the wage mark-up is, therefore, not compensated by worker/management cooperation or other institutional factors that could lead to productivity gains. On average, bargaining coverage can, therefore, affect unemployment, employment and inflation adversely, while the impact of unionization *per se* can be less significant. However, there is little evidence available on this issue from developing countries.

Bargaining Coordination and Comparative Economic Performance

Aidt and Tzannatos (2001) have reviewed 26 studies[15] that have examined the relationship between bargaining coordination and economic outcomes in a cross-country context since 1970 – again most of this evidence is from OECD countries. The empirical literature on bargaining coordination and economic performance has focused on two hypotheses: (a) Coordinated collective bargaining leads to better economic outcomes compared to semi-coordinated collective bargaining which, in turn, performs better than uncoordinated collective bargaining; and (b) The hump hypothesis - Semi-coordinated collective bargaining leads to worse economic outcomes than both coordinated and uncoordinated collective bargaining.

According to their findings: (i) countries with coordinated collective bargaining systems tend, *ceteris paribus*, to have lower unemployment rates than other countries. Studies that use composite measures of unemployment (such as Okun's index, which controls for inflation, and the open economy index, which controls for current account deficits) show the same tendency; (ii) countries with a high level of bargaining coordination tend to have a more compressed wage distribution. This seems to be the most robust result. It can be attributed to a number of causes, including egalitarian bargaining; a reflection of the fact that centralized bargaining reduces the scope for firm- and/or industry-specific factors to enter the wage bargaining; or a reflection of a concern for social insurance.

The hump hypothesis has been tested, explicitly, in a number of studies - accounting for nearly half of the sub-studies. The evidence in favor of the hump hypothesis is weak. Overall, only 21 out of the reviewed sub-studies (around 20%) statistically "confirm" the hump hypothesis. To test whether this may just be an artifact of the differences in the underlying econometric methodology and test procedure, Aidt and Tzannatos have tested whether the estimation approach used affects the results. Though there are some differences, the main conclusions remain: irrespective of the test used, most sub-studies do not provide statistical evidence of the hump hypothesis.

Bargaining Coordination and Labor Market Flexibility. Studies have also attempted to examine the relationship of bargaining coordination with labor market flexibility (e.g. real wage rigidity, adjustment to wage shocks etc.). Most of the evidence in this regard comes

[15] These 26 studies have been broken up into 125 sub-studies which define a relationship between a specific indicator of bargaining coordination *vis-à-vis* a specific economic indicator.

from OECD countries (Aidt and Tzannatos, 2001) and seems to support the relationship that the higher the level of bargaining coordination, the less flexible are the real wages.

Hysteresis (or persistence) in unemployment, arises when high unemployment in the current period tends to cause high unemployment in the future. Persistence can arise because of union membership (insider-induced hysteresis)[16] or due to loss of skills or because capital depreciated during recession takes a long time to recover (outsider-induced hysteresis). Layard *et. al* (1991) find that higher level of worker coordination increases persistence while higher level of employer coordination reduced persistence. Further research has also shown that the employer effect is greater. In addition, evidence tends to show that countries with a high or low level of coordination are associated with low persistence, while those with semi-coordinated systems have higher persistence.

Carneiro (1999) characterizes the Brazilian bargaining structure as semi-coordinated (intermediate-centralized). Carneiro's analysis of wage determination in Brazil between 1985-1993, conforms with the insider-outsider hypothesis in that high levels of current employment lead to subsequent wage moderation – evidence of insider induced hysteresis. His results seem to show that unions may be more interested in protecting the incumbent workforce rather than defending the interests of the unemployed and favorable demand shocks are likely to be converted into wage gains rather than employment gains. Furthermore his results show a positive "catch-up" effect – suggesting that strong trade unions have the capacity to use their bargaining power to appropriate rents.

VI. Conclusions

This chapter has attempted to layout the evidence on the economic aspects of freedom of association by reviewing the international evidence derived from the microeconometric analysis of the economic impact of unions as well as evidence focusing on the relationship between different systems of collective bargaining and macroeconomic and overall labor market performance. Most of the evidence presented is from OECD countries, though there is some analysis of these issues for developing countries too.

The microeconomic impact of unionism consistently points towards the existence of wage mark-ups. This evidence also points towards the existence of wage compression – the male-female wage gap is usually lower when unions are present – implying less discrimination, but at the same time, the wage gap between unskilled and skilled workers is lower – implying a distortion in relative wages. While employment growth and profitability is usually lower in unionized firms, they are also associated with more rapid adoption of technological innovations. Based on the evidence, it is clear that the impacts are context-specific and no general conclusions about the *net* costs of unionism can be reached. Depending on the economic, institutional and political environment in which unions and employers interact, unionism can contribute negatively or positively to economic performance.

---

16 Only the group of insiders (e.g. union members and employed workers) counts in the wage bargaining. When the insiders are reduced in number (e.g., after layoffs in a recession), they can push for higher wages in the next bargaining round and cause unemployment to remain persistently high (insider-induced hysteresis).

Similarly, the macroeconomic impact of collective bargaining is hard to disentangle. In OECD countries, evidence points to union density having little or no impact on indicators of comparative labor market performance – other than wage distribution. Increased bargaining coverage, on the other hand, seem to affect unemployment and employment adversely. However in developing countries, evidence suggests a negative relationship between union density and employment growth – it is possible that these results could be more due to the environment that unions operate within rather than what unions do.

With respect to bargaining coordination – most evidence from OECD countries seems to show that countries with a high or low level of coordination are associated with low persistence in unemployment, while those with semi-coordinated systems have higher persistence (hysteresis). Evidence presented from Brazil on this issue give evidence of insider-induced hysteresis (e.g. due to union membership). These results seem to show that unions may be more interested in protecting the incumbent workforce rather than supporting interests of the unemployed. Similar to the micro argument, the macro argument shows that the impact of collective bargaining on various aspects of economic performance depends on the economic and political environment in which collective bargaining takes place.

REFERENCES

Aidt, T. and Z. Tzannatos (2001 forthcoming). *Core Labor Standards and the Freedom of Association: Economic Aspects.* Working Paper. The World Bank.

Appelbaum, E. and R. Schettkat (1996). *The Importance of Wage-Bargaining Institutions for Employment Performance*, in: G. Shmid, J. O'Reilly, and K. Schömann (eds.), *International Handbook of Labour Market Policy and Evaluation*, Chelteham: Edward Elgar.

Arbache, J. and F.G. Carneiro (1999). *Unions and Interindustry Wage Differentials. World Development* vol.(27), pp. 1875-83.

Bean, C. , P. Layard and S. Nickell (1986). *The Rise in Unemployment: a Multi-Country Study. Economica* vol. (53), pp. 1-22.

Bellman, D., 1992, *Unions, the Quality Of Labor Relations, and Firm Performance*, in: L. Mishel and P. B. Voos (eds.), *Unions and Economic Competitiveness.* New York: M. E. Sharpe.

Betcherman, G. (1991). *The Effect of Unions on the Innovative Behavior of Firms in Canada. Industrial Relations Journal* vol. 22(2), pp. 142-151.

Blanchflower, D. (1996). *Product Market Competition, Wages And Productivity: International Evidence From Establishment Level Data. Annals d'Economie et de Statistique* vol. 41/42, pp. 219-254.

Blanchflower, D. (1997). *Changes Over Time In Union Relative Wage Effects In Great Britain and the United States.* Working Paper no. 6100, NBER, Cambridge, MA.

Blanchflower, D.G., and S. Burgess, 1996, *New Technology and Jobs: Comparative Evidence From a Two Country Study*, in: B. Hall, M. Doms, and F. Kramarz (eds.) *Economics of Innovation and New Technology.* National Academy Press.

Booth, A. (1995). *The Economics of the Trade Union.* Cambridge University Press, Cambridge, U.K.

Brunello, G., 1992, *The Effect of Unions on Firms In Japanese Manufacturing. Industrial and Labor Relations Review* vol. 45, pp. 471-487.

Calmfors, L. (1993). *Centralization of Wage Bargaining and Macroeconomics Performance: A Survey.* Seminar Paper No. 536, Institute for International Economic Studies, Stockholm University.

Calmfors, L. and J. Driffill (1988). *Bargaining Structure, Corporatism and Macroeconomic Performance. Economic Policy*, vol. 9, pp. 14-61.

Carneiro, F. (1998). *Productivity Effects in Brazilian Wage Determination. World Development* vol. 26(1), pp. 139-153.

Carneiro, F. and A. Henley (1998). *Wage Determination in Brazil: The Growth of Union Bargaining Power and Informal Employment. The Journal of Development Studies* vol. 34(4), pp. 117-138.

Carneiro, F. (1999). *Insider Power in Wage Determination: Evidence from Brazilian Data. Review of Development Economics* vol 3(2), pp. 55-169.

Christie, V., 1992, *Union Wage Effects and the Probability of Union Membership. Economic Record* vol. 68(200), pp. 43-56.

Dabalen, A. (1998). *The Effect of Unions on Wages in South Africa: Repeated Cross-Section Estimates.* Working Paper, The University of California, Berkeley.

Daniels, W. (1987). *Workplace Industrial Relations and Technological Change.* Frances Printer, London.

Fields, G., and H. Wan, Jr. (1989). *Wage-Setting Institutions and Economic Growth. World Development* vol. (17), pp. 1471-1483.

Freeman, R. and J. Medoff (1984). *What Do Unions Do?* Basic Books, New York.

Freeman, R. (1988). *Labor Market Institutions and Economic Performance. Economic Policy* vol. (3), pp. 64-78.

Henley, A., and Euclid Tsakalotos (1993). *Corporatism and Economic Performance.* Edward Elgar, U.K.

Hicks, R. (1963), *The Theory of Wages*, (1st edn. 1932), London: Macmillan.

Jackman, R. (1993). *Mass Unemployment: International Experience and Lessons for Policy.* CEPR, LSE, Discussion Paper no. 152.

Keefe, J. (1992). *Do Unions Hinder Technological Change?* in: L. Mishel and P. Voos (eds.), *Unions and Economic Competitiveness*. M. E. Sharpe, New York.

Layard, R., S. Nickell, and R. Jackman (1991). *Unemployment.* Oxford University Press.

Latreille, P. (1992). Unions and the Inter-Establishment Adoption of New Microelectronic Technologies in the British Private Manufacturing Sector. *Oxford Bulletin of Economics and Statistics* vol. 54(1), pp. 31-51.

Lewis, H. (1986). *Union Relative Wage Effects: A Survey.* University of Chicago Press.

Machin, S., and S. Wadhwani (1991). The Effect of Unions on Organizational Change and Employment. *Economic Journal* vol. (101), pp. 835-54.

Moene, K.O., M. Wallerstein (1993). Technical Progress, Wage Compression and the Centralization of Collective Bargaining. Unpublished paper, University of California, Los Angeles.

Mulvey, C. (1986). *Wage Levels: Do Unions Make a Difference?* In J. Niland, (eds.) *Wage Fixation in Australia.* Allen and Urwin Press, Sydney.

Moll, P. (1993). *Black, South African Unions: Relative Wage Effects In International Perspective. Industrial and Labor Relations Review* vol. 46(2), pp. 245-262.

Nakumura, K, Sato, H. and Kamiya, T. (1988). *Do Labor Unions Really Have a Useful Role?* Tokyo: Sago Rodo Kenkyujo.

Nickell, S. (1997). *Unemployment and Labor Market Rigidities: Europe versus North America. Journal of Economic Perspectives* vol. 11(3), pp. 55-74.

Nickell, S., and R. Layard (1997). *Labor Market Institutions and Economic Performance.* Center for Economic Performance, Discussion paper series no. 23, Oxford University.

O' Connell, L. (1999). *Collective Bargaining Systems in Six Latin American Countries: Degrees of Autonomy and Decentralization.* Working Paper, Inter-American Development Bank.

OECD (1994). *Employment Outlook.* Paris.

OECD (1997). *Employment Outlook.* Paris.

Olson, M. (1982). *The Rise and Decline of Nations. Economic Growth, Stagflation, and Social Rigidities*. New Haven/London: Yale University Press.

Panagides, A., and Patrinos, H. (1994). *Union-Nonunion Wage Differentials In the Developing World: A Case Study of Mexico.* Policy Research Working Paper 1269, The World Bank, Washington D.C..

Pencavel, J. (1991). *The Origins of Trade Union Power.* Oxford University Press.

Rama, M. (1995). *Do Labor Market Policies and Institutions Matter? The Adjustment Experience in Latin America and the Caribbean. Labour*, special issue, pp. 243-268.

Rama, M., 1997a, *Trade Unions and Economic Performance: East Asia And Latin America*, in J. McGuire, (ed.), *Rethinking Development In East Asia and Latin America.* Center for International Studies, University of Southern California.

Rama, M. (1998). *Unions and Employment Growth: Evidence From Jamaica.* Working Paper, World Bank, Washington D.C..

Sapsford, D. and Z. Tzannatos (1993). *The Economics of the Labour Market.* MacMillan Books, London.

Scarpetta, S. (1996). *Assessing the Role of Labor Market Policies and Institutional Settings on Unemployment: A Cross-Country Study. OECD Economic Studies*, vol. (26), pp. 43-98.

Schmidt, C. (1995). *Relative Wage Effects of German Unions*. Memo, Selapo, University of Munch.

Siebert, H. (1997). *Labor Rigidities: At the Root of Unemployment in Europe. Journal of Economic Perspectives*, vol. 11(3), pp. 37-54.

Soskice, D. (1990). *Wage determination: The Changing Role of Institutions in Advanced Industrialized Countries. Oxford Review of Economic Policy* Vol. 6 (4), pp. 36-61.

Standing, G. (1992). Do Unions Impede or Accelerate Structural Adjustment? Industrial Versus Company Unions In an Industrializing Labour Market. *Cambridge Journal of Economics* vol. 16, pp. 327-354.

In: Economics, Politics and Social Issues in Latin America ISBN 1-60021-182-8
Editor: Mary P. Lassiter, pp. 75-96

Chapter 5

ECONOMIC DEVELOPMENT AND THE DETERMINANTS OF SPATIAL INTEGRATION IN AGRICULTURAL MARKETS

Gloria González-Rivera and Steven M. Helfand*
University of California, Riverside

ABSTRACT

Surprisingly absent from the literature on spatial market integration are studies that seek to identify factors that increase the degree of market integration. In this paper, we provide a conceptual framework for analyzing these determinants. We argue that the degree of integration is principally a function of the transactions costs related to the spatial flow of goods and information. For the Brazilian rice market, we find that the degree of market integration is positively associated with spatial differences in physical capital, human capital, and the level of development. These are among the most important factors identified as contributing to lower transactions costs. Our empirical analysis is the first to provide a link between spatial integration of agricultural markets, human capital, and the level of development.

Key Words: Market integration, economic development, agriculture, rice, Brazil.
JEL Classification: O13, O18.

1. INTRODUCTION

Most of the literature on spatial market integration in the 1990s focused on the question of whether or not prices in distinct locations are cointegrated. Many papers also addressed the question of how quickly prices adjust between pairs of locations. Surprisingly absent from this literature are studies that seek to identify the factors that increase market integration. In a

* Contact information: Steven M. Helfand ,Department of Economics, University of California, Riverside, Riverside, CA 92521-0427 USA. Phone: (909) 787-5037x1572. FAX: (909) 787-5685. shelfand@mail.ucr.edu

comprehensive survey of more than 60 empirical papers, for example, Fackler and Goodwin (2001) only identified 4 studies that addressed this issue.[1] The objective of this paper is to begin the process of filling this gap in the literature by providing a conceptual framework for analyzing the determinants of market integration, and by offering an empirical application with data from Brazil. As we demonstrate below, this is a research agenda with rich policy implications and important lessons for economic development.

In contrast to the dichotomous approach that is common in this literature, whereby markets are either deemed integrated or not, we believe that the question of market integration is most usefully posed in terms of a continuum of degrees of integration (González-Rivera and Helfand, 2001). The basic idea is that given a set of locations, not all of them belong to the same economic market, and among those that do belong to the market, some will be more integrated than others. Reflecting this view, our methodology consists of three stages. In a first stage, we seek to determine the *extent*, or geographical boundaries, of the market. Next, we establish a ranking from less to more integrated among the locations that were found to belong to the same economic market. This is what we call the *degree* of integration. In a final stage, which is the principal focus of this paper, we explore the determinants of the degree of integration.

Higher degrees of market integration can have important implications for economic development. The process of increasing the degree of integration of isolated markets, or of locations that are only weakly integrated into a national market, can bring significant benefits for local residents. It can raise the incomes of producers by permitting increased specialization and trade, and it can improve the welfare of risk averse consumers by reducing the variability of prices for goods that were previously non-tradable. To the extent that rapidly adjusting and well functioning microeconomic markets are an important ingredient for macroeconomic growth, increased market integration can bring wider benefits as well. Thus, it is pertinent to inquire what the necessary conditions are to increase the degree of integration. Some of these conditions may relate to public investments in physical and human capital, such as roads or schools, thus making increased market integration one of the externalities associated with their provision.

To this end, we provide a taxonomy of determinants of the degree of integration. In contrast to the papers by Goletti and co-authors (1993, 1995, 1995), which privilege the physical determinants of market integration (distance, infrastructure, and production), we provide a more general framework related to transactions costs. Our principal hypothesis is that the smaller the transactions costs that separate locations, the higher the degree of integration. Thus, in the same way that high transactions costs in rural areas of developing countries create imperfections in the markets for credit, insurance, labor or land (Hoff, Braverman, and Stiglitz, 1993), our study seeks to investigate these effects in the spatial context of a product market.

There are numerous factors that can lower transactions costs and increase the degree of integration. These should be distinguished according to their impact on the transactions costs that affect trade flows versus those that influence information flows. In addition to physical capital, market characteristics, and policies, we argue that human capital has an important role to play. Although this point has not been addressed in the literature on market integration, it is a natural extension of research in other areas on the importance of human capital. In the

[1] See Goodwin and Schroeder (1991), Goletti (1993), Goletti and Christina-Tsigas (1995), and Goletti et al. (1995).

literature on agricultural productivity, for example, human capital has been shown to increase productivity, the probability of technological adoption, and the profitability of newly adopted technologies (Lockheed et al., 1980). Similarly, in the growth literature, human capital is treated not only as an input, but also as a potential source of increasing returns to scale (Bardhan 1995, Barro and Sala-i-Martin, 1995). With regard to market integration, higher levels of human capital should increase the productivity of activities related to the marketing of goods, and should facilitate the speed and accuracy of information flows within the market. Both effects serve to lower transactions costs.

The remainder of the paper is organized as follows. In section 2 we present a taxonomy of determinants of the degree of integration. Section 3 describes the methodology used to estimate our dependent variable, the degree of market integration. We then briefly review the construction of principal components, which will be applied to the explanatory variables. To the extent possible, we incorporate a wide range of variables to capture the multiple determinants of the degree of integration. We are aware that some of these variables are proxies, many are highly correlated, and all are subject to measurement error. We adopt a principal components approach, as in Adelman and Morris (1995), to overcome substantial multicolinearity and to mitigate the problems of measurement error. We apply the methodology to the Brazilian rice market in section 4. Section 5 provides conclusions.

2. Determinants of the Degree of Integration: Conceptual Framework

In Section 3 we provide a formal definition of the extent of the market, and of the degree of integration. For our purposes here, it is sufficient to provide an intuitive explanation. In our view, a market is integrated if a) all locations are connected directly or indirectly by trade, and b) there is sufficient arbitrage to ensure that the prices in all locations share the same long run information. Within an integrated market, some pairs of locations are more integrated than others. We call this the *degree* of integration, and measure it by the length of time it takes prices to return to equilibrium after experiencing a shock.[2] Thus, pairs of locations that return to their long run equilibrium quickly are considered more integrated than pairs for which disequilibria have greater persistence. In this context, our analysis of the determinants of integration focuses on the factors that increase the speed of price adjustment. It presupposes that these locations belong to the same market, i.e., that they are linked by trade and have cointegrated prices.

There are multiple factors that can increase the degree of spatial integration in a market. In general, these factors operate by lowering the transactions costs (TC) that affect the flow of goods and information between locations. In a spatial context, TC capture the economic distance between locations. They tend to rise with physical distance, the time required to transfer goods and information, and other factors that impede the flows between locations.[3]

[2] Because impulse response functions are not unique, we use persistence profiles. Their construction is explained in Section 3.

[3] The relationship between TC and time could be reversed in the case of a product that were transported by more than one mode, such as truck and airplane. In such a case, higher TC might reflect the costs of increased speed. With most agricultural commodities this is not likely to be a serious problem. In the Brazilian agricultural sector, for example, almost all inter-state trade is done by truck.

Higher TC increase the probability that goods markets will be segmented because it becomes more likely that a region will have its own local supply and demand intersect within the price band generated by TC (and thus choose not to engage in trade). Yet even when a region is integrated with the rest of the market, the fact that it is more expensive to transfer goods and information to or from this location implies that price adjustments to supply and demand shocks are likely to take more time. Consequently, our principal hypothesis is that the smaller the transactions costs, the higher the degree of integration.

The issue of how to fully and accurately measure the TC associated with the flow of goods and information is by no means trivial.[4] TC should be conceived of quite broadly as including commissions related to product search and transfer, legal and other costs stemming from contract negotiation and enforcement, financial costs, taxes, transportation costs, and the opportunity cost of time allocated to searching for information. In what follows we discuss the ways in which the TC of moving goods and information across locations can be influenced by a) physical capital, b) human capital, c) supply, demand, and trade, d) policies, and e) other factors. When appropriate, we identify how these variables relate differentially to the farm, local, and inter-regional levels of a market.

Physical Capital

Distance increases the TC associated with the flow of goods, and to a lesser extent, information. Increasing the quantity of different forms of physical capital is probably the most direct way to lower these costs. Table 1 provides examples of several of the most important types of capital that can facilitate both types of flows. Since the marketing of agricultural products begins on the farm, infrastructure that eases access to, and loading of, goods on the farm provides the first building block of the system. Many agricultural goods are stored off of the farm in rural areas, and thus local roads, storage, and marketing infrastructure are also important components of the physical capital that permits goods to flow. Finally, the quantity and quality of the infrastructure that connects one region to another--generally highways--is also an important component of the system. Because many types of physical capital, such as roads, are provided by local, state, and federal governments, there is an important role for policy that we will return to.

Physical capital is also essential to reduce the costs and increase the speed of information flows. While information circulates by word of mouth and through informal channels in the rural areas of developing countries, the importance of radios, televisions, and telephones is increasingly important. In part due to high illiteracy rates, rural radio and television programs are two of the most important mechanisms for farmers to obtain information about agricultural markets. Telephones, in contrast, are much less common among farm households, but are essential for traders located in rural areas to coordinate the flow of goods and to share information with traders located in other regions. Again, there are substantial investments in infrastructure, related to electricity and telephones, that can create an entry point for policy.

[4] See Lin and Nugent (1995) for a general discussion of TC and economic development, Barrett (1999) for a discussion of transactions costs in the context of agricultural markets, and *Companhia de Financiamento da Produção* (1983) for a snapshot of transfer costs in Brazil in the early 1980s.

Table 1. Determinants of the Degree of Market Integration

Type	Examples / Comments
Trade Flows	
1a. Physical capital	• Farm: infrastructure that eases access to products • Local: roads, storage and marketing infrastructure • Inter-regional: quantity and quality of highways
1b. Human capital	• Can increase the productivity of marketing activities at the farm, local, and inter-regional levels
1c. Supply, demand, and trade	• Relative size or openness of the trading locations • Supply shocks (small vs. large)
1d. Policy	• Investments in physical and human capital • Taxes can impede flows • Credit for marketing can facilitate inter-regional flows • Heterogeneity of policies such as support prices can impede flows • Uncertainty and/or volatility of policies such as purchases/sales of stocks can impede inter-regional flows
1e. Other	• Structure and competitiveness of the marketing sector • Shocks such as strikes or floods • Social capital: trust can lower monitoring and enforcement transactions costs
Information flows	
2a. Physical capital	• Radios, televisions, telephones, computers
2b. Human capital	• Increases the ability to accurately and efficiently process information
2c. Supply, demand, and trade	• Relative size or openness of the trading locations • Direct vs. indirect trade links
2d. Policy	• Investments in physical and human capital • Direct: agricultural extension • Targeted: rural public radio and television programs • Impersonal: stimulate commodity and futures markets
2e. Other	• Structure and competitiveness of the marketing sector • Social capital: formal and informal organizations, as well as networks of individuals, can facilitate the flow of information and lower transactions costs

Human Capital

Human capital has played a prominent role in many fields of economics. Public and private investments in education (used as a proxy for human capital) are often estimated to have extremely high returns (Psacharopoulos, 1994), human capital intensive development strategies have been shown to be associated with more equitable development outcomes (Griffin, 1989), and human capital is seen as contributing to long term growth both because it is an input and a potential source of increasing returns to scale (Bardhan 1995, Barro and Sala-i-Martin, 1995). In this section we contend that a strong argument can be made for extending the literature on human capital to the topic of market integration.

In the agricultural sectors of developing and developed countries, education levels have been widely and strongly associated with higher levels of productivity and with faster rates of adoption of new technologies. In a survey of studies spanning 37 farm level data sets from 13 countries, for example, Lockheed et al. (1980) conclude that education had a positive effect on the productivity of farmers in 31 of the 37 cases. The authors also refer to numerous studies using aggregate county and state level data that have reached similar conclusions. The relationship between education and agricultural productivity is complex. Alternative types of education (formal, non-formal, and informal) are thought to influence productivity directly through a "worker" effect and indirectly through an "allocative" effect.[5] Important components of the allocative effect are the ability to absorb new information and to adopt new technologies. Higher levels of education not only increase the probability of adopting new technologies, but are also necessary for the success of the technologies once adopted. The positive effects of farmer education on productivity should not be limited to agriculture alone, but should carry over to the other activities that farmers are involved in.

Based on the broad consensus in the literature about the positive effects of human capital on productivity and on the ability to process information, we hypothesize that higher levels of human capital should contribute to increasing the productivity of the agents who are responsible for the flow of goods, and to increasing the accuracy and speed with which information flows across space. Both effects should lower TC. To the extent that farmers are involved in the initial phases of marketing, then higher levels of human capital on farms should be associated with both higher agricultural productivity and higher productivity in marketing. To the extent that the flow of goods is coordinated through intermediaries, cooperatives, or directly by industry, then differences in human capital across these groups should generate differential levels of productivity in the marketing of agricultural goods.

Trade, Supply, and Demand

There are a number of factors related to supply, demand, and trade that are likely to influence the degree of integration. We limit ourselves here to briefly discuss several of these. First, a larger volume of inter-regional trade should lead to a higher degree of integration because it contributes to reducing TC. The work by Barros and Filho (1990) on marketing

[5] These terms come from Welch (1970). Our discussion draws from Cotlear (1990). Formal education consists primarily of schooling, informal education includes activities such as apprenticeships and contacts with extension agents, and non-formal education—learning-by-doing—encompasses a wide variety of forms through which individuals learn, such as direct experience and indirect exposure.

margins for agricultural products in Brazil, for example, demonstrates that per unit transportation costs ($/ton/km) are an inverse function of volume. There are quantity discounts due to factors such as the use of larger trucks, lower per unit costs of loading and unloading larger quantities, and reduced logistical costs.[6] Second, the magnitude of supply or demand within a state could also contribute to reducing TC for the same reasons that this occurs with inter-regional trade. Third, Goletti et al. (1995) hypothesized that pairs of importers and exporters should be more integrated than pairs of locations with the same trade status. While it is true that dissimilar pairs should have a higher propensity to trade, trade is not synonymous with the degree of integration. Our previous work on the Brazilian rice market revealed a considerable amount of interdependence among groups of exporting locations and groups of importing locations. Thus, it is possible that proximity, or the volume of trade, matter more than trade status for the flow of information and price adjustment. This is an issue that should be explored empirically.

Policy

Table 1 lists many of the policies that could influence the degree of integration. Their relative importance should vary considerably across products and countries. Because many of the types of physical and human capital that we have been discussing contain elements of public goods, sometimes with strong positive externalities, public investments in them are an important component of a strategy to increase the spatial flow of goods and information. These investments contribute to increasing market integration, and this should be viewed as part of the process of economic development.

In terms of goods flows, tax policy that discriminates against inter-regional trade, such as state level sales taxes in Brazil that are higher for out of state goods, can reduce the degree of integration. Credit for the marketing of agricultural goods, in contrast, can provide liquidity that contributes to inter-regional flows. Goletti et al. (1995) hypothesized that the volatility and unpredictability of government stock policies contributed to reducing market integration in Bangladesh. There is evidence of similar complaints in the Brazilian literature concerning the disincentives to production and storage created by erratic agricultural policies (Lopes, 1979). However, many of these policies are national in scope and it is not clear how they would differentially affect certain regions. Policies that vary across regions, such as the predominance of public storage in one region and private storage in another, are more likely to have a differentiated effect on the degree of integration across locations.

With regard to the flow of information, extension agents are often an important source of market information for agricultural producers. However, extension agents are relatively expensive, and their principal focus relates to the flow of technical information. Governments that desire to disseminate market information in rural areas can do so much more cost effectively through daily or weekly radio and television programs. Governments can also stimulate the development of commodity and futures markets as a mechanism for providing information, liquidity, and insurance to market participants. The Brazilian government has been pursuing this approach in recent years. It is possible that futures markets may gain

---

[6] The authors also show that per unit costs fall with distance, largely because loading and unloading a truck can be thought of as a fixed cost that is spread over the length of the journey.

importance for traders and large agricultural producers. They are, however, likely to be inaccessible and too complicated for the majority of agricultural producers in most developing countries.

Other Factors

The structure and competitiveness of the marketing sector are additional factors that are likely to influence the degree of integration. Inter-regional marketing activities, for example, can take place through traders, cooperatives, industry, or the government. While it is not clear which of these should achieve the lowest trade and information costs, it is possible that regional differences in the predominance of one or another of these agents could reduce the degree of integration. Similarly, it is not obvious what the effect of a lack of competition should be on the degree of integration. On the one hand, a more concentrated marketing structure might achieve certain economies of scale in trade and information that could lead to lower costs. On the other hand, less competitive markets could restrict flows in order to raise prices and profits. Goodwin and Schroeder (1991) examined this question in the context of U.S. regional cattle markets in the 1980s. They found that increasing cointegration of these markets coincided with increasing concentration of the cattle slaughtering industry. More empirical research on these issues is clearly warranted.

A final factor that is worth exploring is social capital. There is a burgeoning literature on the importance of social capital for economic development.[7] Social capital relates to trust and networks that allow people to cooperate. It is sometimes viewed as a factor of production (like physical or human capital), and sometimes as a factor that can lower the transactions costs of information flows, monitoring, and enforcement. Measured with a variety of proxies, it has been shown to have a positive effect on the growth rate of county level per capita income in the U.S. (Rupasingha et al., 2000), to have a positive effect on the incomes of households in rural villages of Tanzania (Narayan and Pritchett, 1999), and to have a positive effect on the productivity and flows of technical information of entrepreneurs in the Ghanaian manufacturing sector (Barr, 2000). To the extent that social capital in the form of networks can increase information flows and productivity, or in the form of trust can lower transactions costs and facilitate trade flows, then it is relevant to a study of the degree of market integration.

3. Methodology for Constructing the Dependent and Independent Variables

The Dependent Variable: Persistence Profiles and the Degree of Integration

The objective of this paper is to study how the degree of integration varies across locations that belong to the same economic market. To do this, first we define explicitly what we mean by market integration. Next, we explain the construction of our dependent variable,

[7] See Woolcock and Narayan (2000), Paldam (2000), and Paldam and Svendsen (2000) for interesting reviews of this literature.

the degree of integration, following the methodology proposed by González-Rivera and Helfand (2001).

Our definition of market integration relies on two related dimensions: trade and information. For a market to be called integrated, we require that the set of locations share both the same traded commodity and the same long run information. Formally, a market with *n* geographically distinct locations will be considered integrated if the following two conditions are satisfied:

(1) There must be physical flows of goods connecting all *n* locations either directly or indirectly.

(2) The *n* locations must have a corresponding vector of prices $P_t = \{p_{1t}, p_{2t} \ldots . p_{nt}\}$ that can be decomposed as $p_{it} = a_i f_t + \widetilde{p}_{it}$, i = 1...n, and $a_i \neq 0$, where f_t is the integrating factor that characterizes the permanent (long run) component of the price, and $\widetilde{p}_{it}$ is the transitory (short run) component for each location.

The basic elements of this definition are the existence of trade and that f_t is common to all series of prices. The physical flow of goods, by itself, does not guarantee integration because there may exist markets with very thin or discontinuous trade patterns for which a common integrating factor for all *i* and *t* does not exist. Similarly, the existence of a single integrating factor, by itself, does not guarantee market integration because there may exist isolated markets that exhibit co-movements of prices due to seasonal patterns or economic policies.

The advantage of our definition is that it provides an operational framework to search for the geographical boundaries of an integrated market. First, we identify the set of locations that is connected either directly or indirectly through continuous unidirectional trade. Based on estimated trade flows for each location, we exclude locations that have experienced trade reversals (exporters that have become importers, and vice versa) and we identify locations that are close to self-sufficiency and are candidates for experiencing discontinuous trade. By only focusing on locations that experience continuous unidirectional trade, we avoid having to use a switching regime model and ensure that cointegration is an appropriate methodology. Once we determine which locations are connected either directly or indirectly through trade, we search for those locations that share the same long run information. In a cointegration framework, this condition is equivalent to requiring the existence of one and only one integrating factor that is common to all series of prices. Since cointegrating vectors and integrating factors are intimately related, the existence of *one and only one* integrating factor for all prices implies that (i) prices must be cointegrated, and (ii) there must be *n*-1 cointegrating vectors.[8] Condition (2) in our definition is the common factor representation of a multivariate cointegrated system of prices with *n*-1 cointegrating vectors. Searching for just one common factor is equivalent to searching for *n*-1 cointegrating vectors. This is a key point of our methodology. In our approach, the *economic market* is not given a priori by the set of locations where a good is produced and/or consumed. Nor is the existence of cointegrated prices sufficient to find the market. It needs to be found through a multivariate

[8] If transactions costs are non-stationary, then *n*-1 cointegrating vectors must be found when prices are measured net of transactions costs.

search for a single common factor. In the case of the Brazilian rice market, we have 19 locations but we show that only 15 belong to the same economic market.

The search for the largest set of locations that share n-1 cointegrating vectors is conducted in a multivariate framework: the reduced rank VAR proposed by Johansen (1988, 1991). According to the Granger representation theorem, a cointegrated system can be written as a Vector Error Correction (VEC) model

$$\Delta P_t = \mu + \Pi P_{t-1} + \Gamma_1 \Delta P_{t-1} + \Gamma_2 \Delta P_{t-2} + \ldots + \Gamma_{p-1} \Delta P_{t-p+1} + \varepsilon_t \tag{1}$$

where Γ_i and Π are n x n matrices and, if there are n-1 cointegrating vectors, Π has reduced rank equal to n -1. The matrix Π can be written as $\Pi = \alpha\beta'$, where α is an n x (n-1) matrix of coefficients, and β is an n x (n-1) matrix of cointegrating vectors. Using this expression for Π, we have $\Pi P_{t-1} = \alpha\beta' P_{t-1} = \alpha Z_{t-1}$. The error correction term, also known as short run disequilibrium, is $Z_{t-1} = \beta' P_{t-1}$, and α is the matrix of adjustment coefficients. The elements of the matrix β cancel the common unit roots in P_t and, in the long run, link the movements of the elements of P_t.

Johansen's test for the number of cointegrating vectors focuses on testing the rank of Π. The process of testing for the rank of Π occurs jointly with the estimation of the cointegrating vectors and the associated vector error correction model. Our goal is to find those locations for which the rank of Π is n-1. To determine which locations belong to the same market, we start with the maximum set of locations, n, and test for n-1 cointegrating vectors. We do this by performing Johansen's likelihood ratio test based on the trace statistic. If the number of cointegrating vectors is less than n-1, we need to identify those locations that should be removed from the system. In order to do so we implement a sequential procedure. We start with a core of m locations ($m < n$) that we believe are most likely to belong to the market and test for the number of cointegrating vectors. If the number is m - 1 we add an additional location. With m + 1 locations, either the new one shares a common trend with the previous m locations or it does not. In the first case, we should find m cointegrating vectors, while in the second, we should continue to find m - 1, thus adding a second common trend to the m + 1 locations. If we find one common trend, we repeat the procedure by adding locations one at a time. If not, we exclude the location that added a second trend and repeat the procedure until the number of locations is exhausted.[9]

When the extent of the market has been found, we enter into the second stage of the analysis which consists of assessing the degree of integration of each location. We define the degree of integration between locations that belong to the same market as the reaction time to remove disequilibria. Impulse response functions have been used extensively for this purpose. An important drawback of these functions is that they are not uniquely identifiable when shocks to the system are correlated. In a study of spatial prices it is unreasonable to expect uncorrelated errors because the time series of prices are highly correlated. The solution adopted in the literature has been to orthogonalize the shocks with a Cholesky decomposition,

[9] In our empirical analysis, we experimented with different orders and with different initial cores of locations. We concluded that the exclusion of locations is invariant to the order in which they have been analyzed.

which imposes a recursive ordering of the variables in the system. However, the impulse response functions are not invariant to the ordering, and consequently, for every order, we have a different impulse response function. We use a different measure called a persistence profile (Pesaran and Shin, 1996) that is robust to any ordering of the variables in the system. A persistence profile characterizes the response of a cointegrating relation $Z_t = \beta' P_t$ to a system-wide, rather than to an individual, shock.

For *n*-1 cointegrating vectors, the long run equilibrium among prices can be written as

$$p_{it} = \beta_{0i} + \beta_{1i} p_{nt} + z_{it} \quad i = 1,2,....n-1 \tag{2}$$

where z_{it} is the short-run disequilibrium of the *i*-th cointegrating relation, transitory in nature, and $(1, -\beta_{1i})$ is the cointegrating vector. In equilibrium, we expect z_{it}=0. A shock to any variable or set of variables produces a short term disequilibrium $|z_{it}|>0$. Since z_{it} is stationary, the effect of the shock will be transitory and the long run equilibrium relation will eventually be restored. We define the degree of integration as the reaction time for each of the long run equilibrium relations to absorb a system-wide shock. This depends on all of the estimated coefficients of the α, β, and Γ matrices. By analyzing the joint impact of these coefficients, it is possible to construct a consistent ranking of markets based on reaction times.

A persistence profile measures the reaction time of each long run equilibrium relation to absorb a system-wide shock, where the response is measured in units of variance. A system-wide shock is understood as a draw from the multivariate distribution of the vector ε_t in the underlying VAR system. The advantage of considering a system-wide shock is that the persistence profiles are unique functions and there is no need to orthogonalize individual shocks. At time *t*, the variance-covariance matrix of the shock ε_t is Ω. We study the propagation through time (*t*+1, *t*+2. ...) of the variance of the shock, conditioning on information up to time *t*-1. Thus, with an initial shock to the economy at time *t*, and considering the information up to time *t*-1, the persistence profile focuses on the *incremental* variance of the disequilibrium error at time *t*+*k*, as the time horizon increases by one period. In stationary systems, a shock will eventually die out. This implies that its incremental variance becomes smaller as time passes and approaches zero as time goes to infinity. Pesaran and Shin (1996) define the (unscaled) persistence profile as

$$H_z(k) = Var\left(Z_{t+k} \middle| \psi_{t-1}\right) - Var\left(Z_{t+k-1} \middle| \psi_{t-1}\right) \qquad k = 0, 1, 2 \tag{3}$$

where ψ_{t-1} is the information set containing information up to time *t*-1, $Var\left(Z_{t+k} \middle| \psi_{t-1}\right)$ is the variance of Z_{t+k} conditional on the information set, and k is the time horizon. To compare the persistence profiles, expression (3) is scaled by a diagonal matrix G that contains the inverse of the square root of the diagonal elements of $H_Z(0)$. The scaled persistence profile is defined as $h_z(k) = GH_Z(k)G = \{h_{ij}(k)\} \quad k = 0,1,2...$, such that upon impact k=0, $h_{ii}(0)=1$ for i=1,2….n-1.

The construction of persistence profiles permits us to establish a consistent ranking of locations based on their reaction times. Our dependent variable in the analysis of the determinants of market integration is the median persistence profile for each pair of locations. It is defined as the number of periods necessary for 50% of the adjustment towards the long run equilibrium to take place.

SUMMARIZING THE EXPLANATORY VARIABLES: PRINCIPAL COMPONENTS

In section 2 we describe a set of socio-economic variables as potential factors to explain the degree of integration. In practice, these variables are highly correlated and, consequently, multicollinearity will be a problem that will impede the discovery of those factors that are associated with a high degree of integration. For this reason, we turn to the use of principal components as a multivariate technique that permits translating a large set of correlated variables into a smaller set of uncorrelated variables that contains the same amount of information as the original variables (Jolliffe, 1986).

A principal component is defined as a linear combination of the original variables such that its variance is maximized subject to certain constraints. Formally, let x be a vector of p variables whose variance-covariance matrix is Σ. The j-th principal component of Σ is defined as

$$y_j = \sum_{i=1}^{p} \alpha_{ji} x_i = \alpha'_j x \qquad j = 1,2...p$$

where the vector α_j is such that the variance of y_j, $\mathrm{var}(y_j) = \alpha'_j \Sigma \alpha_j$, is maximized subject to the following constraints

$$\text{(i) } \alpha'_j \alpha_j = 1, \qquad \text{(ii) } \alpha'_j \alpha_k = 0 \qquad k \neq j$$

Constraint (ii) imposes orthogonality among the p principal components. This constrained maximization involves solving for the eigenvalues and eigenvectors of Σ. We need to solve $(\Sigma - \lambda_j I_p)\alpha_j = 0$, where λ_j is an eigenvalue of Σ and α_j is the corresponding eigenvector. The maximum value of the variance is $\mathrm{var}(\alpha'_j x) = \alpha'_j \Sigma \alpha_j = \alpha'_j \alpha_j \lambda_j = \lambda_j$, where λ_j is the *largest* eigenvalue of Σ and α_j the corresponding eigenvector.

The principal components are ranked such that the first accounts for the largest variance, and the last principal component accounts for the smallest variance, that is, $\lambda_1 > \lambda_2 > ... > \lambda_p$. The sum of the variances of the p principal components is equal to the sum of the variances of the original variables. Principal components can also be calculated from the correlation matrix of the variables x. The use of the principal components of the correlation matrix is advisable when the original variables have very different variances. Otherwise, the variables with the largest variance tend to dominate in the initial principal components. In the following sections we find the principal components of the correlation matrix. In this case, the original variables are standardized and $\sum_{j=1}^{p} \lambda_j = p$.

When analyzing the principal components, it is helpful to know the correlation of each original variable with each principal component. A high correlation of a variable with a particular principal component gives a meaningful interpretation to that component. The correlations of the variables with the *j*-th principal component are called "loadings." It can be shown that the loadings are calculated as $\sqrt{\lambda_j}\alpha_j$. It is easy to see that the eigenvector α_j and the loadings convey the same information. In the following section we report the loadings.

4. The Determinants of Spatial Integration in the Brazilian Rice Market

Description of the Dependent and Independent Variables

The methodology described in Section 3 was applied to monthly rice prices from 19 states in Brazil for the period 1970:1-1997:8. Regarding the extent of the market, we concluded that only 15 of the 19 states belonged to the same economic market for rice.[10] With these states, we then calculated the degree of integration (persistence profiles) between all 105 pairs of the 15 states in the market. In order to calculate 105 persistence profiles, we estimated 15 vector error correction models, where for each model we used a different state to normalize the cointegrating vectors. Several examples are provided to illustrate the interpretation of the persistence profiles.

When there is a shock that affects the long run equilibrium between São Paulo and Minas Gerais, for example, 45 percent of the adjustments necessary to absorb the shock and return to the long run equilibrium take place in the first month, and nearly 80 percent within three months. Disequilibria between Goiás and São Paulo are removed a bit slower, with only 68 percent of the adjustment occurring within three months. Maranhão actually overshoots at first, and after three months only 30 percent of the disequilibrium with São Paulo is removed.

In order to summarize the entire path of adjustment for a given pair of states, we calculated the median persistence, or half-life, of the effect of the shock for each pair of states. The median profile measures the number of months necessary for 50 percent of the adjustments to take place. This information is summarized in Table 2. Considering all 105 pairs, on average it takes 2.45 months to remove half of the effect of a shock to the equilibrium price relations in the Brazilian rice market. There is, however, considerable variation. Mato Grosso and Goiás, two exporting states in the Center-West of the country, were the pair with the smallest median profile (0.73 months).

[10] For a detailed discussion of the estimated trade flows and Johansen rank tests that led to this conclusion, see González-Rivera and Helfand (2001).

Table 2. Descriptive Statistics

Variable	Units	Mean	Min	Max	Correlation with Median Profile	SD
Median Profile	(months)	2,45	0,73	4,96	---	0,57
Linear distance btwn. capitals	(km)	1454	251	3205	0,47	739
Transportation costs	(R$/km)	0,48	0,31	0,59	0,31	0,08
Federal highways (national share)	(%)	5,01	0,56	15,92	-0,12	3,79
Federal highways density	(km/100km^2)	1,46	0,22	3,52	-0,16	0,83
Phone terminal density	(per 100)	4,86	1,33	10,47	-0,19	2,56
Phone calls density	(per person)	14,26	5,81	22,69	-0,38	5,48
Value of transportation density	(index)	0,87	0,03	1,89	-0,23	0,58
Rice production (national share)	(%)	6,25	0,17	30,65	0,09	7,82
Population (national share)	(%)	5,72	0,98	20,59	-0,07	5,14
Rice trade (national share)	(%)	6,34	0,32	24,57	0,07	6,91
Rice Yields	(mt/ha)	2,65	1,11	4,70	-0,23	1,25
Rural schooling	(years)	5,68	4,03	7,44	-0,19	1,00
Illiteracy density	(%)	20,12	8,84	34,44	0,31	9,30
Illiteracy (national share)	(%)	5,28	0,67	12,98	0,08	4,00
Agricultural GDP per capita	(index)	1,23	0,38	3,35	-0,28	0,82
Agricultural GDP (state share)	(%)	18,78	1,63	33,94	0,21	8,70
GDP per capita	(index)	0,89	0,29	2,00	-0,26	0,46

Notes:

1) Median profile: number of months required to remove 50% of a desequilibria in rice prices.
2) Linear distance between the counties where the capital cities are located. AEB 1996, IBGE.
3) Transport costs: 1970-95 average in $R of 12/95. Source: FGV.
4) Federal Highways in 1980: share of national total. Source: AEB, IBGE
5) Federal Highways in 1980: density within each state. Source: AEB, IBGE.
6) Phone terminals: 1970-94 average / average population. Source: AEB, IBGE.
7) Phone call density: 1993-95 inter-city calls / 1991 population. Source: AEB 1996, IBGE
8) Value of transport: 1994 revenue of highway freight transport firms/state GDP. AEB 1996, IBGE
9) Share of production: Average of 1970-95 rice production. Source: IBGE.
10) Share of population: Average of 1970, 1980, and 1991. Source: IBGE
11) Share of trade: absolute value of average 1970-95 share of domestic rice trade. Authors' estimates.
12) Rice yields: average of 1993 and 1994. AEB 1996, IBGE.
13) Average years of schooling in rural areas for people 18-49 years old in 1990 and 1995 . IBGE
14) Illiteracy rate: state average for 1970, 80, and 91. 10 years and older. Source: IBGE.
15) Illiteracy: share of national total; average of 1970, 80, and 91. 10 years and older. Source: IBGE
16) Agricultural GDP per capita. Average of 1970, 80, 91 indices relative to national average. IBGE.
17) Agricultural share of GDP. Average of 1970, 80, 91. Source: IBGE.
18) GDP per capita: Average of 1970, 80, 91 indices relative to national average. Source: IBGE

Maranhão and Pernambuco, an exporter and an importer that are both located in the Northeast, were the pair with the largest median profile (4.96). One state, Minas Gerais, had median profiles smaller than 2 months in relation to 10 of the 14 remaining states. The median profiles for Maranhão, in contrast, were larger than 4 months in 9 cases. These are the differences that we seek to explain below.

Table 2 also provides descriptive statistics for the 17 explanatory variables that are included in the analysis. With reference to Section 2, we have included state level data related to physical capital, human capital, and supply, demand, and trade. The narrowing of our focus reflects, in part, the difficulties that we faced in finding relevant data. It also reflects the view that these are the structural determinants of the spatial differences in the degree of integration, whereas the other factors either vary less across space or were only relevant for sub-periods of our sample. Credit policy, for example, was an important instrument from the mid-1970s through the mid-1980s, but much less central before and after this period (Helfand, 2001). Similarly, support price policy was used extensively in the 1980s, but less so in the 1970s and 1990s (Helfand and Rezende, 2001). Given that the profiles reflect the average behavior of a 27 year period, to the extent possible we have attempted to measure the explanatory variables in a way that would be broadly representative of the same period. In many cases this meant taking an average of census data from 1970, 1980, and 1991. The precise definitions and data sources are listed in the footnotes to the Table.

The first group of variables in Table 2 relates directly to the costs of moving goods and information across states. *Linear distance* between capital cities is a proxy for inter-state transportation costs. Because we are working at a rather high level of aggregation, with state level data, this variable will contain a considerable amount of measurement error. This is especially true for states that are close to each other because intra-state distances could dominate the distance between capital cities. We attempt to reduce the severity of this problem by introducing a dummy variable for states that are neighbors. It reflects the fact that locations that share a border are likely to be proximate in ways that average linear distance does not capture. The next variable measures average *transportation costs* paid by farmers for agricultural goods within each state. This variable provides an indication of the quality of the infrastructure within each state. *Federal highways*, which are almost all paved, are intended to capture the quality of inter-state infrastructure. For intra-state infrastructure, the density of roads (km of roads/km^2 of area) is probably a better measure than the extension (km). For inter-state infrastructure, this is not as clear. Large states might be well connected to other regions with one or two good highways, even though the density is quite low. For this reason, we use the national share of federal highways as well as the density within each state. Per capita *phone terminals*, as well as per capita long distance *phone calls*, are two proxies for physical capital related to the flow of information across states. Finally, we have included an index (relative to the national average) for the *value of transportation* within each state. This measures the revenue of highway transportation firms relative to the GDP of each state. The idea was to capture the density of the marketing sector. Increased marketing activity in a given state, even if it is not specifically related to rice, should be associated with lower transactions costs.

The simple correlations of the variables in this first group with the median profiles all have the expected sign. The final column of Table 2 shows that distance and transport costs are positively correlated with the median profiles, implying slower adjustment and a lower degree of integration. Highways, telephones, and transport density all have negative correlations, implying that they are associated with faster adjustment and a higher degree of integration.

The next group of variables in Table 2 relates to rice production, consumption, and trade. *Rice production, population* (as a proxy for rice consumption), and *rice trade* are all measured as a share of their respective national totals. These are intended to capture the potential cost reductions in the flow of goods and information associated with scale. These variables are only weakly correlated with the median profiles.

The third group of variables seeks to capture human capital at alternative levels of the market. *Rice yields* reflect the average level of production technology used in each state. Based on the large body of international research demonstrating a strong positive relationship between human capital and productivity, it is likely that yields are highly correlated with the level of human capital of the farmers involved in rice production. While this is clearly not an ideal measure, it is the only rice specific proxy that the data permit us to construct. *Rural schooling* measures the average years of schooling of adults in rural areas, and the density and the national share of *illiteracy* measure the rate and mass of the illiterate population in each state. Again, all correlations are of the expected sign, with the mass of illiterates exhibiting a notably weaker correlation with the median profiles than the other variables.

The final three variables in Table 2, *agricultural GDP per capita, agricultural GDP* as a share of the GDP in each state, and *GDP per capita*, provide alternative ways of measuring the level of development in each state. These are intended to capture residual differences in the quantity and quality of the marketing infrastructure in each state that could lower transactions costs and increase the degree of integration. As expected, higher levels of income per capita, and lower shares of agriculture in GDP, are correlated with higher degrees of integration.

Because each observation on the dependent variable refers to a relationship between a pair of states, the explanatory variables must be defined in a similar fashion. Thus, in the analysis that follows, for each of the 105 pair-wise combinations we have summed the explanatory variables from the corresponding states.

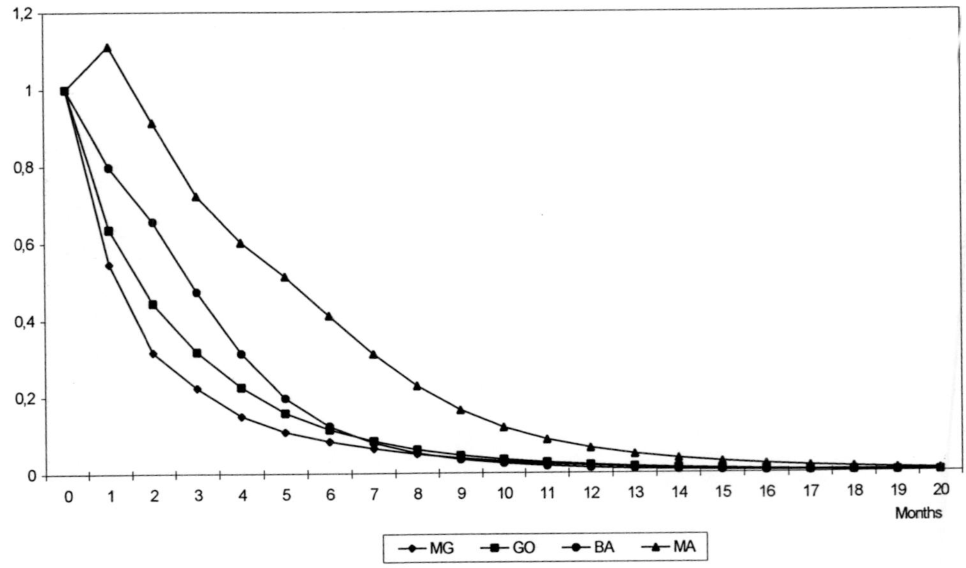

Figure 1. Persistence Profiles in Relation to São Paulo (1970-97)

Principal Components and Their Relationship to the Degree of Integration

The upper portion of Table 3 shows the loadings in the first 10 principal components (PCs) that were constructed from the 17 explanatory variables. The proportion of the variance in the original set of variables that is explained by each PC is shown toward the bottom of the Table. The bottom row of the Table shows the estimated coefficients from a regression of the median profiles on the PCs.

The first principal component, PC1, by itself explains 36% of the variance contained in the original variables. PC2 explains an additional 15%, and together the first five PCs explain 85%. If our goal were simply to summarize the 17 variables, rather than to explain the median profiles, then it might be adequate to use only the first five PCs. However, there might be a set of variables that only accounts for a small fraction of the variance in the original 17 variables, but that is an important determinant of the degree of integration. For this reason, we chose to retain the first 10 PCs. Together they explain 99% of the variance of the original variables.

The analysis of the PCs is simplified by keeping several facts in mind. First, the loadings can be interpreted as correlations. Second, by identifying the maximum loading in each row, one can determine the PC with which a particular variable is most closely associated. We have done this and placed a border around the variables mostly closely associated with each of the first five principal components. We have parsimoniously placed broken borders around the variables most closely associated with the remaining 5 PCs. Third, the relative magnitude of the loadings determines the relative importance of the variables within each PC. As a general practice, we will restrict our attention to loadings that are at least half the size of the largest loading in a PC.

The first PC represents the level of development. In addition to GDP per capita and agricultural GDP per capita, the most important variables in this PC are high levels of human capital (as expressed through low rates of illiteracy and high levels of rural schooling), high levels of physical capital related to information flows (the density of telephones and long distance phone calls), and high densities of transportation activities. The loadings for three additional variables are also high, even though they are more closely associated with other PCs. Thus, higher levels of development are also associated with low shares of agriculture in GDP, large populations (which is also a proxy for rice demand), and large volumes of rice trade.

The bottom row of the Table reports the results of a linear regression of the median profiles on the 10 PCs. The adjusted R^2 from this regression is 0.49, indicating that our determinants explain a substantial portion of the state level differences in the degree of market integration. The coefficient on PC1 is negative and significant at the 1% level. The interpretation is that higher levels of development are strongly associated with smaller median profiles and, thus, higher degrees of integration. Because our study of determinants is cross-sectional, we prefer to talk about "association" rather than "causality." Increasing the degree of spatial market integration is an important component of the process of development. In some cases market integration might lead other dimensions of economic development, and in other cases it could follow.

Table 3. First 10 Principal Components (PCs) and Regression of Median Profiles on PCs

	PC1	PC2	PC3	PC4	PC5	PC6	PC7	PC8	PC9	PC10
1. GDP per capita	,94	,17	,00	-,15	,18	,01	-,01	,09	,07	,02
2. Illiteracy (density)	-,94	,21	,12	,04	,09	-,14	-,1	-,05	,08	,03
3. Rural schooling (years)	,91	-,26	-,11	,15	,02	,01	,07	-,10	-,17	,08
4. Phone terminals (density)	,83	,26	,09	-,30	,24	-,03	-,06	,13	-,13	,13
5. Agricultural GDP per capita	,69	-,44	,30	-,13	,10	,10	-,13	,13	,41	,01
6. L.D. phone calls (density)	,68	-,47	,12	-,45	,02	,22	,08	,01	-,08	-,18
7. Value of transport (density	,65	-,06	-,26	,28	-,39	,30	-,03	-,41	,03	,06
8. Illiteracy (national share)	-,09	,78	,55	,14	-,09	,18	,01	-,10	,11	,00
9. Ag. GDP (state share)	-,48	-,78	,29	,13	-,03	,07	,05	,06	,07	,21
10. Population (national share)	,59	,64	,46	,02	,08	,06	-,06	-,06	,01	,08
11. Rice yields (kg/ha)	,30	,12	-,82	,34	-,08	-,13	-,14	-,03	,24	-,04
12. Fed. highways (density)	,14	,40	-,73	-,01	-,32	,15	,13	,37	-,01	,08
13. Rice production (national share)	,35	-,31	,11	,84	,06	-,17	,11	,05	-,08	,00
14. Rice trade (national share)	.60[a]	,13	,19	.59[a]	,38	-,27	,04	,06	,02	-,07
15. Fed. highways (national share)	,00	,03	,52	,47	-,61	,23	,07	,26	-,03	-,07
16. Transportation costs	-,37	,13	-,21	,16	,59	,36	,54	-,03	,09	,00
17. Distance	-,34	-,06	-,17	,38	,47	,45	-,51	,10	-,12	-,02
Variance explained by PCs										
Proportion	,36	,15	,14	,12	,09	,04	,04	,03	,02	,01
Cumulative	,36	,51	,65	,77	,85	,90	,94	,96	,98	,99

Regression of Median Profiles on PCs

Adj. R2 = 0.49	Intercept	Neighbors	PC1	PC2	PC3	PC4	PC5	PC6	PC7	PC8	PC9	PC10
Coefficient	2.61***	-.77***	-.30***	,05	.14*	.20**	.31***	,06	-,02	-,06	-.20**	.36***

Notes: * = statistically significant at 10% level; ** = statistically significant at 5% level; *** = statistically significant at 1% level.

a) Because the loadings for the variable rice trade were not significantly different in PCs 1 and 4, the choice of location was somewhat arbitrary.

The fact that the level of development is highly correlated with the degree of integration would be even more significant if we could show that this were true after controlling for the factors most commonly thought to determine market integration--distance and transportation costs. These are precisely the variables that are mostly closely associated with PC5. The regression coefficient on PC5 is positive and significant at the 1% level, indicating that an increase in this PC is associated with slower adjustment and a lower degree of integration. Thus, as we would expect, larger distances, higher transactions costs, and fewer highways are all associated with slower adjustment. Along these lines, lower densities of highways and of transportation activities also have relatively large loadings in this PC. The dummy for states that are neighbors is also statistically significant at the 1% level, providing an additional control for proximity and transportation costs.

The second principal component can be identified with large rice consuming states. They are characterized by large populations, a large number of people with low levels of human capital (illiteracy), and low shares of agriculture in GDP. This PC does not have a significant statistical relationship with the degree of integration.

The most important variables in the third PC are the level of productivity in rice production (used as a proxy for human capital) and the density of highways. This PC is also associated with large populations that contain a large mass of illiterates. The coefficient on this PC is positive and statistically significant at the 10% level. Thus, in addition to PC1, this provides further support for the view that human capital matters for the degree of integration. Increasing the level of human capital in production, and reducing the size of the illiterate population, could both contribute to increasing the degree of integration.

PC4 has a very clear interpretation. It relates to large producing states that also engage in a substantial amount of trade. Secondarily, these states are characterized by low levels of communications infrastructure, large distances from other states, and perhaps for this reason, high shares (though not densities) of federal highways. PC4 has a positive and statistically significant relationship with the degree of integration. Contrary to what we hypothesized, larger volumes of production and trade are associated with lower degrees of integration.

The most important loadings in PC6, PC7, and PC8 relate to the variables distance, transportation costs, highways, and value of transportation. These repeat much of what was already captured in PC1 through PC5, and none of these PCs are statistically significant. The last two PCs are statistically significant and provide additional support for the view that states with wealthier agricultural sectors and higher levels of human capital in production are more integrated (PC9), and states with a higher share of agriculture in GDP are less integrated (PC10).

5. Conclusions

The objective of this paper was to argue for a shift in the focus of the literature on market integration. We believe that research in this area should move beyond the determination of which locations belong to a unified economic market and the estimation of how quickly these locations transmit prices and adjust to shocks. These are important steps, but there is much more that can be done. If, as appears to be the case, there is a consensus that market integration is associated with desirable development outcomes, then the challenge is to identify the factors that contribute to increased integration. We proposed a conceptual framework for analyzing these factors, and explored their importance in the context of the Brazilian rice market.

There are two principal lessons of our study. The first relates to the multiple determinants of the degree of integration, and the second to the relationship between economic development and market integration. With regard to the first issue, we argued that the degree of integration is principally a function of the transactions costs related to the flows of goods and information. Physical capital, such as roads and telephones, is necessary to reduce transactions costs, but by itself is unlikely to be sufficient for achieving a high degree of market integration. Among the other determinants of integration, we emphasized human capital. Higher levels of human capital should increase the productivity of the agents who are responsible for the flow of goods at all levels of the market, and should increase the speed and accuracy of the flow of information. Our empirical analysis provided support for this view. More research is called for to understand the ways in which human capital, physical capital, and other factors jointly determine transactions costs and market integration.

With regard to economic development and market integration, we found that a principal component representing the level of development was strongly associated with the degree of integration in the rice market. In addition to income per capita, this component was highly correlated with measures of human capital (illiteracy and rural schooling), variables related to communications infrastructure, and the relative size of the transportation sector. Thus, in the same way that less developed regions have been shown to have greater imperfections in their factor markets, our study provides evidence of similar effects in a product market. More developed states in Brazil had more integrated rice markets. An important question that remains for future research relates to the direction of causality between market integration and economic development. In some cases a higher degree of market integration might contribute to economic development, while in others cases it could be a by-product of the development process.

REFERENCES

Adelman, I., and C.T. Morris. “A Factor Analysis of the Interrelationship Between Social and Political Variables and Per Capita Gross National Product.” Chapter 6 in *Institutions and Development Strategies: The Selected Essays of Irma Adelman, Vol. I.* Brookfield, VT.: Edward Elgar, 1995.

Alexander, Carol, and John Wyeth, "Cointegration and Market Integration: An Application to the Indonesian Rice Market." *Journal of Development Studies.* 30,2(January 1994):303-28.

Bardhan, P. “The Contributions of Endogenous Growth Theory to the Analysis of Development Problems: An Assessment.” Chapter 46 in *Handbook of Development Economics, Vol. IIIB.* Behrman, J. and T.N. Srinivasan (eds.). Amsterdam: Elsevier, 1995.

Barr, A. “Social Capital and Technical Information Flows in the Ghanaian Manufacturing Sector.” *Oxford Economic Papers.* 52(2000):539-59.

Barrett, C.B. "Market Analysis Methods: Are Our Enriched Toolkits Well Suited to Enlivened Markets?" *Amer. J. Agr. Econ.* 78(August 1996):825-29.

-----."Measuring Integration and Efficiency in International Agricultural Markets." Mimeo, Department of Ag., Res., and Man. Economics, Cornell University, December 1999.

Barro, R.J., and X. Sala-i-Martin. *Economic Growth.* New York: McGraw-Hill, 1995.

Barros, G.S.C., and J.G.M. Filho. "Transmissão de Preços e Margens de Comercialização de Produtos Agrícolas." *Agricultura e Políticas Públicas.* Delgado, G.C., Gasques, J.G., and Verde, C.M.V (eds.), pp. 515-65. (IPEA Série 127.) Brasília: IPEA, 1990.

Baulch, Bob, "Testing for Food Market Integration Revisited." *Journal of Development Studies.* 33,4(1997):512-534.

Companhia de Financiamento da Produção (CFP). *Análise das Distorções dos Preços Domésticos en Relação aos Preços de Fronteira: Um Estudo Preliminar.* (Coleção Análise e Pesquisa, 30.) Brásilia: CFP, 1983.

Cotlear, D. "The Effects of Education on Farm Productivity," in *Human Development and an International Development Strategy for the 1990s.* Griffin, K., and Knight, J. (eds.). London: Macmillan, 1990.

Dercon, Stefan, "On Market Integration and Liberalisation: Method and Application to Ethiopia." *Journal of Development Studies.* 32,1(October, 1995):112-43.

Fundação Getulio Vargas (FGV). *Agropecuária: Índices e Preços Médios de Arrendamentos, Vendas de Terras, Salários, Empreitadas, e Transportes.* Centro de Estudos Agrícolas, Instituto Brasileiro de Economia, Rio de Janeiro: Fundação Getúlio Vargas, 1988.

Fackler, P.L. and B.K. Goodwin. "Spatial Price Analysis," Chapter 17 in *Handbook of Agricultural Economics, Volume 1B.* Gardner, B. and G. Rausser (eds.), Elsevier Science: The Netherlands, 2001, pp. 971-1024.

Goletti, F., and E. Christina-Tsigas. "Analyzing Market Integration," in *Prices, Products, and People: Analyzing Agricultural Markets in Developing Countries.* Scott, G.J. (ed.). Boulder: Lynne Rienner, 1995.

Goletti, F., R. Ahmed, and N. Farid. "Structural Determinants of Market Integration: The Case of Rice Markets in Bangladesh." *The Developing* Economies. 33,2(1995):185-202.

Goletti, F. "The Effects of Supply Shocks on Market Integration: An Application to Bangladesh Rice Markets." Mimeo, Washington, D.C., IFPRI, 1993.

González-Rivera, G. and S.M. Helfand. "The Extent, Pattern, and Degree of Market Integration: A Multivariate Approach for the Brazilian Rice Market." *Amer. J. Agr. Econ.* 83,3(August 2001):576-592.

Goodwin, B.K., and T.C. Schroeder. "Cointegration Tests and Spatial Price Linkages in Regional Cattle Markets." *Amer. J. Agr. Econ.* 73,2(May 1991):452-64.

Griffin, K. *Alternative Strategies for Economic Development.* Houndmills, Basingstoke, Hampshire: Macmillan in association with the OECD Development Centre, 1989.

Helfand, S.M. "The Distribution of Subsidized Agricultural Credit in Brazil: Do Interest Groups Matter?" *Development and Change.* 32,3(June 2001):465-90.

Helfand, S.M. and G.C. Rezende. "Brazilian Agriculture in the 1990s: Impact of the Policy Reforms." Texto Para Discussão 785, IPEA, April 2001.

Hoff, K., A. Braverman, and J.E. Stiglitz (eds.), *The Economics of Rural Organization: Theory, Practice, and Policy.* New York: Oxford University Press for the World Bank, 1993.

Instituto Brasileiro de Geografia e Estatística (IBGE). *Anuário Estatístico do Brasil*. Rio de Janeiro: IBGE, various years.

-----, *Produção Agrícola Municipal*. Rio de Janeiro: IBGE, various years, and www.ibge.gov.br.

Jamison, D.T. and P.R. Moock. "Farmer Education and Farm Efficiency in Nepal: The Role of Schooling, Extension Services, and Cognitive Skills." *World Development* 12,1(1984):67-86.

Johansen, S. "Statistical Analysis of Cointegration Vectors." *J. Econ. Dyn. and Control* 12(June/September 1988):231-54.

-----. "Estimation and Hypothesis Testing of Cointegration Vectors in Gaussian Vector Autoregressive Models" *Econometrica*. 59(November 1991):1551-80.

Jolliffe, I.T. *Principal Component Analysis*. New York: Springer-Verlag, 1986.

Lin, J. Y., and J.B. Nugent. "Institutions and Economic Development." Chapter 38 in *Handbook of Development Economics Volume IIIA*. Amsterdam: Elsevier, 1995.

Lockheed, M.E., D.T. Jamison, and L.J. Lau. "Farmer Education and Farm Efficiency: A Survey." *Economic Development and Cultural Change* 29,1(Oct. 1980): 37-76.

Lopes, M.R., "A Redução dos Efeitos da Incerteza de Médio Prazo: O Papel de um Preço Mínimo Plurianual," in M.R. Lopes (ed.), *A Política de Preços Mínimos: Estudos Técnicos 1949/1978; Coletânea de Artigos Técnicos Acerca da Política de Garantia de Preços Mínimos*. Brasília: Comissão de Financiamento da Produção, 1979.

Narayan, D., and L. Pritchett. "Cents and Sociability: Household Income and Social Capital in Rural Tanzania." *Economic Development and Cultural Change*. 47,4(July 1999):871-97.

Paldam, M. "Social Capital: One or Many? Definition and Measurement." *Journal of Economics Surveys* 14,5(2000):629-53.

Paldam, M., and G.T. Svendsen. "An Essay on Social Capital: Looking for the Fire Behind the Smoke." *European Journal of Political Economy*. 16(2000):339-66.

Pesaran M.H. and Y. Shin. "Cointegration and Speed of Convergence to Equilibrium. *J. Econometrics*. 71(March 1996):117-43.

Psacharopoulos, G. "Returns to Investment in Education: A Global Update." *World Development*. 22,9(1994):1325-43.

Rupasingha, A., S.J. Goetz, and D. Freshwater. "Social Capital and Economic Growth: A County-Level Analysis." *Journal of Agricultural and Applied Economics*. 32,3(December 2000):565-72.

Welch, F. "Education in Production." *Journal of Political Economy*. 78,1(Jan.-Feb. 1970):35-59.

Woolcock, M., and D. Narayan. "Social Capital: Implications for Development Theory, Research, and Policy." *The World Bank Research Observer*. 15,2(August 2000):225-49.

In: Economics, Politics and Social Issues in Latin America ISBN 1-60021-182-8
Editor: Mary P. Lassiter, pp. 97-128

Chapter 6

UNIONS AND THE LABOR MARKET IN BRAZIL

Jorge Saba Arbache
Universidade de Brasilia, Brazil

I. INTRODUCTION

Although labor unions are considered one of the most important institutions of modern capitalism (Freeman, 2000), the literature shows that their mode of operation and impact on the economy vary from country to country. Although there is a wide variety of systems, institutions, and union action strategies in the different countries, an important stylized fact in the literature is that labor unions reduce wage dispersion through collective bargaining processes. This has led Metcalf et al. (2000) to refer to them as a "sword of justice." According to Freeman (2000), this phenomenon is actually more widespread than the more thoroughly researched effect of unions on wages, namely their ability to raise the relative wages of their members. The literature shows that: (i) the distribution of wages among unionized workers and/or those covered by collective bargaining is more concentrated than the wage distribution for other workers, even when demographic and productive characteristics are controlled for in the corresponding regressions; and (ii) collective bargaining diminishes the importance of merit in wage formation, thereby narrowing the wage spread between jobs (Freeman, 1980, 1992; Hirsch 1982; Card, 1992; DiNardo et al., 1995; Gosling and Machin, 1995; Blau and Kahn, 1996; DiNardo et al. 1997; Metcalf et al., 2000, among others).

Estimates of the impact of unions on the labor market in Brazil are still very preliminary. The few results available include those obtained by Arbache (1999), who investigates the wage and income-distribution effects of unions among male manufacturing workers; Arbache and Carneiro (1999), who examine the importance and effects of unions on collective bargaining; Arbache (2000), who studies the effects of trade liberalization on unions and collective bargaining; Menezes-Filho et al. (2002) who assesses the impact of trade unions on the economic performance of Brazilian establishments; and Amorim (2000), who analyzes the relationship between unions and indirect pay. Little is known about the effect of unions on employment, productivity or labor market rigidity, and especially on wages and income distribution. Knowledge of the impact of unions on pay dispersion is particularly important for Brazil, given its highly unequal income distribution. If the legal framework that regulates labor relations is a decisive factor in the functioning of unions and collective bargaining processes, then knowing this could help us to understand the effects of unions on the overall economy.

This chapter seeks to answer the following questions: (i) How do employment and union laws affect collective bargaining processes? (ii) Do unions affect wage formation and income distribution? (iii) Do unions increase the rigidity of the labor market? We conclude by making some suggestions for enhancing collective bargaining and unions in Brazil.

The chapter is organized as follows: Section 2 describes labor laws and union legislation in Brazil. Section 3 describes the characteristics of unionized and non-union workers, union density, and the determinants of unionization. Section 4 investigates the effects of unions on wages and income distribution. Section 5 discusses the results obtained and seeks to demonstrate the effects of employment and union laws on collective bargaining processes and union behavior. Section 6 offers some recommendations for improving labor relations in Brazil.

II. Labor Laws, Union Legislation, and Collective Bargaining Processes

The institutions that regulate labor relations in Brazil have a huge impact on collective bargaining, given the way they are involved in employment contracts, labor disputes and union activity, and the intensity of that involvement. This section provides a historical overview and describes the characteristics of the main institutions governing the country's labor relations. As we shall see, such institutions contribute to adversarial labor relations and curb the development of collective bargaining. We also show that the nature and functioning of those institutions have potential effects on income distribution and on macroeconomic stability.

Labor Laws and Labor Courts

Relations between workers and employers in Brazil are governed by the Consolidated Labor Laws [*Consolidação das Leis do Trabalho*] (CLT). The CLT law is extremely wide ranging and detailed, regulating the most varied aspects of labor relations. The CLT was first introduced in 1943, during the administration of Getúlio Vargas, in order to consolidate the labor laws existing at that time. One of its main aims was to create a system to protect workers from exploitation by employers, and to harmonize labor relations with a view to avoiding direct disputes between the parties. Camargo (2001) points out that the CLT was premised on the existence of asymmetric power relations between capital and labor, and that the role of the law was to protect and regulate workers' interests. The all-embracing and paternalistic nature of the law created an atmosphere that was not conducive to the development of collective bargaining. The CLT also created unstable labor relations, generating disequilibrium by providing excessive protection for workers. The law requires disputes to be settled in labor tribunals rather than in the companies involved, so little space is left for direct negotiations between employers and employees; and it discourages the development of a cooperative relationship between the two parties.

As Camargo (2001) shows, an important feature of Brazil's labor legislation is the coexistence of individual and collective employment contracts. Individual contracts (i.e. contracts involving employment record cards) are agreed into between the company and the worker and deal with issues such as working conditions and wages. Collective contracts, on the other hand, are agreed between the employer and the workers' union, or between the employers' association and the union, and cover minimum working conditions and minimum wages, among other issues. Workers without an individual contract *are not* covered by collective contracts in their job category. Legally, the results of collective bargaining processes are extended to all workers and companies in that occupation or industry, respectively, even if the workers or companies involved are not members of the respective unions negotiating the agreement. This provision attributes great importance to unions in labor relations.

In Brazil, the justice system is required to rule on disputes related to compliance with labor laws, and on those relating to individual and collective employment contracts. It is also called upon to promote conciliation and arbitration in collective bargaining processes. If negotiations between workers and employers break down, the labor court is required to rule on the dispute. If the impasse is the result of a failure to comply with the legislation, the court will merely apply the law in reaching its decision. But if the impasse stems from a lack of agreement on other issues, the tribunal may decide according to the judges' point of view, possibly even using political criteria (Camargo, 2001). The decision of the labor court *must* be complied with by the parties. Accordingly, labor courts have regulatory authority that affords them great power within the collective bargaining and labor relations framework in Brazil. The courts offer many incentives for free-rider behavior by workers, since employers are the ones who bear the onus of the proof. Thus, the paternalism of the law, together with the tremendous power and involvement of the justice system in labor disputes, act as obstacles to the modernization of labor relations by inhibiting cooperation between the parties and fostering disputes between workers and employers.

Union Organization and Collective Bargaining

Under the CLT, labor unions are organized by occupational category, but employer associations are organized by economic sector. Job categories and economic sectors are defined by the Ministry of Labor, on the basis of similar characteristics. Up to 1988, different occupations and economic categories were prohibited from grouping together in a single union. This restriction was lifted in the 1988 Constitution, when the formation of nationwide unions and union confederations was authorized.

In order to control the unions, the law instituted monopoly of representation and the union levy, together with *mandatory extension* of the results of collective bargaining processes to all workers, including non-union members. Once the union has been recognized by the Ministry of Labor, it then has a monopoly in its predefined geographic jurisdiction. The smallest regional base is the municipality, but unions can also have regional, state, or even national jurisdiction. All collective bargaining processes in a given category have to be carried out with participation from the union holding the monopoly representation in the geographic area concerned.

Although union membership is not compulsory, workers and employers *are required* to collect a union levy each year; 60 percent of this is passed on to the respective union by the Ministry of Labor, which is the body responsible for collecting it. The remaining funds are divided between the Ministry of Labor and the federation and confederation for the occupational or economic category concerned. By law, funds transferred to labor unions must be used exclusively for purposes such as recreation, social assistance, education, and consumer cooperatives, but *never* to finance political activities, collective bargaining processes, or strike funds. Only funds obtained through *voluntary* contributions can be used for such purposes.[1]

Collective bargaining is compulsory and must take place once a year, during the "base-date" period, in which the workers' union and the employer's organization or individual company negotiate wages and other employment issues. Base dates vary between occupations and categories, and this results in negotiations being spread throughout the year. It is possible, however, for different occupations to sign agreements on the same day in the same company or economic category, thereby resulting in a collective agreement covering a large proportion of the workers in a given industry. In bargaining processes between employer organizations and worker unions, the result is known as a collective contract *(convenção coletiva)*; if bargaining takes place between the workers' union and a single company, the outcome is known as a collective agreement *(acordo coletivo).*

Monopoly representation, the union levy, and the extension of collective bargaining results to all workers gave great power to union leaders, but fostered a lack of responsibility among them with respect to workers' interests and situations. There were two reasons for this: firstly, union finances are guaranteed by an assured income from the union levy, which means union leaders do not have to attract members to finance union activities. Secondly, mandatory union participation in collective bargaining processes in their area of jurisdiction, together with compulsory extension of the results to all workers, gives union leaders great power in labor relations, whether union density is high or low. Consequently, as history shows, union leaders have not always been concerned with attracting and maintaining workers affiliated to their unions, or with working on behalf of the most obvious interests in their category. In many cases, union legislation has spawned bureaucrats that have little interest in workers' situations, but who maintain close relations with the Government in order to maintain their power in the unions. Moreover, the monopolistic nature of unions has resulted in collective bargaining taking place on a fragmented basis with no inter-union coordination across the different occupations and economic categories.

When the military dictatorship took power in 1964, amendments were made to the laws governing union organization and pay-setting processes. One of the most important changes was the introduction of a hardline law on strikes, aimed at regulating the right to strike and creating new criteria for strikes to be considered legal. Highly restrictive rules inhibited the outbreak of strikes and restricted union action; in practice, the changes were intended to repress movements in support of claims of any type. These and other measures, such as prison for union leaders, caused the union movement to stagnate until the late 1970s.

[1] Up to 1988, the Ministry of Labor could intervene in labor unions for reasons such as misuse of the union levy, or for calling unauthorized strikes or lock-outs.

In the 1960s, a law on wage adjustments was also introduced with the aim of centralizing and regulating the wage-setting process. This gave the Government power to determine the minimum rate of increase for all wages in the economy. The formula and frequency of pay raises changed several times between the mid-1960s when the law was introduced and the end of the 1980s, but it tended to set pay increases below the rate of inflation and even below productivity gains. The lag in pay raises also tended to generate wage erosion because of the accelerating inflation of that period. The law on pay increases was created as an economic policy tool, with wages in practice being used as adjustment variables in stabilization policies. Any pay increases above those stipulated by law had to be negotiated individually between the company and its workers. Given the weakness of labor unions and the centralization of pay-setting processes, the law not only operated as an instrument of wage control, but also inhibited collective bargaining from the 1960s until the mid-1990s, when it was shelved.[2]

A key feature of the period in which the wage law was in force was that, while wages could theoretically be negotiated between workers and employers, in practice the latter would invoke "collective disagreement" during the bargaining process, which meant referring the dispute to the labor tribunal for settlement. As wages were set by law, the courts did no more than applying the corresponding legislation, overriding any attempt to negotiate increases above the correction set by the Government. Thus, although wages were supposed to be negotiable, pay raises in practice adhered to the rates of increase set by the Government, leaving little or no space for collective bargaining over pay. As a result, the tremendous sway of the Government over wage setting for more than twenty years seriously undermined the development and modernization of collective bargaining processes in the country.

Control of wages and repression of the union movement prompted major wage claims in the late 1970s, and gave rise to a new phase in the organization of the union movement. Workers sought greater autonomy, freedom of action, and changes in wage policy. The reorganization of the movement was particularly significant in the wealthiest and most industrialized areas of São Paulo, where many multinationals and large local companies are based. The perception held by workers that companies in the region were extracting monopoly rents possibly contributed to the emergence of this movement. As shown by Booth (1995) and Nickell et al. (1994), unions tend to demand pay raises where there are *quasi-rents* to be shared out. In such a context, the law on wage increases placed a straitjacket on pay in the most developed regions and most dynamic sectors of the economy, where wage increases above the law were supposedly possible; this led to demonstrations that later culminated in the "new unionism" movement (see Camargo, 2001; and Amadeo and Camargo, 1989).

With this additional flexibility, collective bargaining became more important, and the wage adjustment rates determined by law became the floor and no longer the ceiling for pay raises, as it was now possible to negotiate over productivity.[3] Unions now started to bargain over wage increases above the floor set by the law, through negotiations at the company level. Success in bargaining, however, depended on industry characteristics, occupational category, and region. Unions in companies or industries with greater market power, or those that were more concentrated, had stronger bargaining power. Unions in more competitive sectors had

[2] See Carneiro and Henley (1998) for a description of the main features of the wage determination process in Brazil over this period.

[3] Carneiro (1998) provides evidence of the presence of productivity effects in the Brazilian wage determination process during the 1980s and 1990s.

little chance of bargaining over productivity, however, and contracts were negotiated in a more individual and less collective fashion.

In practice, as pointed out by Camargo (2001), the bargaining system was hybrid: on the one hand it was partly centralized, since unions in some sectors negotiated wages collectively; on the other hand, the weakness of unions elsewhere meant that wages were bargained in a decentralized fashion, with actual pay raises tending to match the adjustments set by law. This system of labor relations and collective bargaining led to scant cooperation between unions, as bargaining power between them varied widely. Unions in companies or sectors that were more inclined to grant pay increases had little interest in the possibility of centralized negotiations.

Promulgation of the new Constitution led to the overhaul of legislation on collective bargaining, wages, strikes, and unions. Collective bargaining began to be encouraged, the concept of "illegal strike" ceased to exist, prohibition of worker organization at national level was lifted, and unionization of civil servants was allowed, along with other changes making union organization more democratic. Nonetheless, these changes were insufficient to reduce the greatest obstacles to implementing collective bargaining processes in Brazil, since the basic rules governing employment contracts, the powers of labor tribunals, and union organization remained virtually intact.

III. Characteristics of Unionized Workers and Union Density

This section discusses some of the main socioeconomic characteristics of unionized workers and their non-union counterparts. The aim is to determine who the union members are, and where they are located, along with information on union density and whether there is a correlation between socioeconomic profile and union membership.

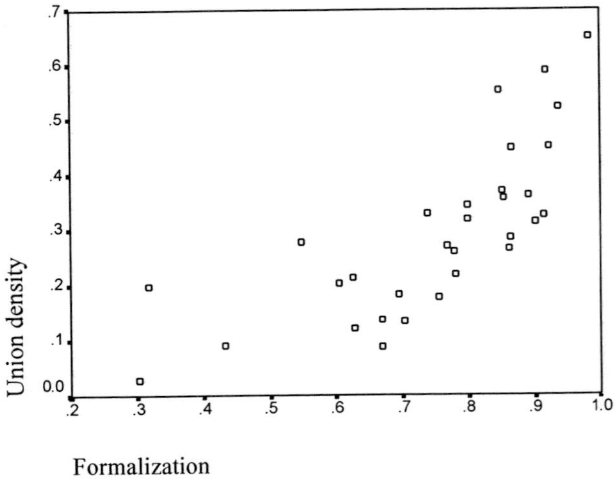

Figure 6.1. Union Density vs. Formalization, 1999

Our research on unions draws on data from the National Household Sample Survey (PNAD) conducted by the Brazilian Institute of Geography and Statistics (IBGE) for 1986, 1992, 1993, and 1995 to 1999, years for which the "unionization" variable is available. Unions are analyzed by industry at the two-digit level, which covers economic activities ranging from agriculture and manufacturing industry to services and public administration.

The data have been filtered for individuals of 18 to 65 years of age, economically active, and earning a positive wage. We took pay earned in the individual's main activity, and transformed this into a real hourly wage. Although PNAD data are acknowledged to be of high quality, 0.1 percent of cases were suppressed from each end of the real wage distribution as a precaution to avoid outliers arising from measurement errors. As a result of the filter, we have at least 100,000 individuals for each year, about 20 percent of whom are union members.

Characteristics of Unionized Workers

Table 6.1 shows that the vast majority of unionized workers hold an employment record card (*carteira de trabalho assinada*). While almost 90 percent of unionized workers benefit from the guarantees afforded by a formal work contract, only about 54 percent of non-union workers have this card. As only formal workers are covered by collective bargaining, one might expect that all unionized workers would have a formal contract. The shortfall could arise from measurement error, or unionized workers migrating from formal to informal jobs for some reason. The figures suggest that: (i) workers holding an employment record card have a greater incentive to unionize; (ii) unions are active in guaranteeing workers' rights, thereby reducing the level of informal contracting in the industries where they are strongest; and (iii) unions tend to be concentrated in industries where there is a higher percentage of formal contracting.

These three hypotheses help to explain the higher level of formalization among unionized workers. It is reasonable to assume that formal workers have a greater incentive to join unions, because the costs of union membership for them are less than the benefits. Informal workers do not have incentives to join unions, however, as they do not benefit from the results of collective bargaining.

Figure 6.1 shows a positive relation between union density and the degree of formalization in the labor force at the industry level, thereby supporting hypotheses (ii) and (iii). It remains to be seen whether there is a causal relationship between the two variables and if so in what direction: i.e. whether greater union activism produces a high level of formalization, or whether greater formalization facilitates union activism.

There seems to be a correlation between union membership and status in the family. About 62 percent of unionized workers are heads of households, compared to just 52 percent of non-unionists. These figures suggest that union membership is a characteristic of more mature workers, and that young people participate in unions less.

Also, there seems to be a correlation between union membership and race: about 61 percent of unionized workers are white, compared to 52 percent of non-union members. In addition, the proportion of men among unionized workers is higher than among non-union members. It can therefore be concluded that either: (i) minorities have fewer incentives to join unions; or (ii) unions are concentrated in sectors or regions where these groups are under-represented.

The distribution of education among unionized and non-union workers is the variable that most clearly distinguishes the two groups. While at least 60 percent of non-union workers are in the first three education brackets (ranging from no education at all to some primary education), at least 50 percent of union members are in the three highest education brackets – covering primary school completed to higher education. This result seems even more remarkable when we analyze the distribution of workers with higher education. Whereas at least 13.7 percent of unionized workers have completed a higher education course, no more than 5.4 percent of non-union workers have done so. If we group the two higher education brackets together (i.e. secondary and tertiary education both completed) we see that in 1999, for example, 47 percent of unionized workers had this level of schooling, compared to just 26.6 percent of their non-union counterparts. Thus, unlike the situation in developed countries (Freeman, 1982; Booth, 1995; Metcalf, 2000), education is a key characteristic of unionized workers in Brazil.

The distribution of workers by size of establishment (a variable not shown in Table 4.1) shows that nearly 85 percent of unionized workers are in establishments with more than 11 employees, while 58 percent of non-union members work in establishments with 11 employees or less.[4]

Table 6.2 shows the distribution of unionized workers by region and job category. The proportion of unionized workers in rural and urban areas is quite similar, while unionization is greater in metropolitan than in non-metropolitan areas. The regional distribution shows that the proportion of unionized workers in the southeast – where most of the country's industry and financial center are located – is similar to that in other regions. The proportions of unionized workers in the North, Northeast, and Central-Western regions, are in all cases less than in the other regions combined. In contrast, the level of unionization in the south is considerably higher than in the rest of the country, which suggests that the union movement in this area is relatively more active and enjoys greater bargaining power.

The lower panel of Table 6.2 shows the distribution of unionized workers by occupational category. Unionization is a clear characteristic of managers, skilled production workers, office workers, and, in particular, professionals. Levels of union membership are substantially above the average in each of these job categories. Among professionals, a group that encompasses all higher-level staff, at least 42 percent are union members; this is much more than the average for other occupations. One possible explanation for this is the regulation and legal control maintained over the practice of higher-level professions through Regional Councils (for example, the *Conselho Regional de Economia*, *Ordem dos Advogados*, *Conselho Regional de Medicina*, etc.), supported by compulsory membership of such bodies as a precondition for professional practice. Often, these bodies operate in traditional areas of union activity, for example regulating fees and establishing wage floors.

[4] For this calculation, we used the PNAD variable that classifies the size of establishments in which individuals work as "up to 11 employees" and "over 11 employees".

Table 6.1. Characteristics of Unionized and Non-Union Workers

(Percentages)

	1986		1992		1993		1995		1996		1997		1998		1999	
	Union	Non-union	Union	Non-union	Union	Non-union	Union	Non-union	Union	Non-union	Union	Non-union	Union	Non-union	Union	Non-union
General characteristics																
Employment record card	82.3	57.5	91.3	55.2	91.0	54.1	91.4	53.5	90.4	53.8	90.4	53.4	90.5	53.3	89.7	52.4
Head of household	66.8	48.6	64.3	50.7	64.5	50.9	62.8	50.2	62.0	49.7	61.6	50.0	61.3	50.2	61.2	50.2
White	61.5	51.0	61.5	52.0	60.9	51.8	61.1	51.8	62.1	52.5	60.5	51.8	61.2	51.5	59.9	51.7
Male	75.6	63.9	70.5	62.3	69.5	62.4	68.1	61.0	66.7	61.0	66.6	61.5	65.3	61.1	65.2	60.6
Experience (absolute value)	22.9	22.1	22.4	21.8	22.3	21.9	22.6	21.9	22.5	21.7	22.5	21.7	22.6	21.7	22.9	21.7
Age (absolute value)	36.0	33.8	37.0	34.6	37.2	34.7	37.7	34.8	37.9	35.0	38.0	35.0	38.3	35.2	38.5	35.3
Illiterate	11.7	17.0	9.8	15.3	9.1	14.1	7.9	13.0	7.2	12.5	7.7	11.9	6.9	11.1	7.5	10.6
Some elementary education	13.7	19.8	11.5	17.3	10.9	17.0	10.3	16.5	9.2	15.0	9.1	15.4	8.5	14.8	8.4	14.3
Elementary or some primary education	26.4	32.7	26.2	33.0	25.5	33.6	25.4	33.9	23.6	32.7	22.9	32.7	22.3	32.3	21.8	32.0
Primary or some secondary education	13.2	13.1	14.0	14.1	13.7	14.4	13.9	14.7	15.3	16.3	14.8	15.7	14.7	16.3	15.0	16.5
Secondary or some higher education	21.4	13.9	25.0	16.0	25.9	16.5	26.8	17.3	28.1	18.6	28.4	19.2	29.8	20.2	29.6	21.2
Higher education	13.7	3.4	13.6	4.4	15.0	4.4	15.7	4.6	16.6	4.9	17.0	5.1	17.9	5.3	17.7	5.4
Years of schooling (absolute value)	7.2	5.2	7.7	5.7	7.9	5.8	8.1	6.0	8.4	6.2	8.4	6.3	8.7	6.4	8.6	6.6

Table 6.2. Proportion of Unionized Workers by Region and Occupation

(Percentages)

	1986	1992	1993	1995	1996	1997	1998	1999
Geographic region								
Urban	22.1	20.2	20.0	19.1	18.7	18.2	17.8	17.4
Rural	22.1	20.0	19.6	17.8	17.7	17.1	16.5	17.2
Metropolitan region	24.2	22.0	22.1	21.2	20.9	20.3	20.0	18.8
Non-metropolitan	20.6	18.8	18.4	17.3	16.8	16.4	15.9	16.4
South-east	22.9	19.1	18.4	17.9	18.6	17.9	17.4	16.7
Other regions	21.7	20.8	20.8	19.5	18.5	18.1	17.7	17.7
North	22.3	16.4	16.2	14.6	15.5	15.4	14.3	14.7
Other regions	22.2	20.4	20.2	19.3	18.8	18.2	17.9	17.6
North-east	19.1	20.8	20.2	18.4	16.6	16.7	16.6	17.2
Other regions	23.4	18.6	19.2	19.2	19.3	18.5	18.0	17.5
Central-western	16.9	17.8	18.7	15.7	16.6	15.2	15.1	15.0
Other regions	23.0	20.5	20.1	19.4	18.8	18.4	18.0	17.7
South	29.8	27.4	26.4	25.5	23.6	23.1	25.5	21.6
Other regions	20.7	18.5	18.5	17.5	17.4	16.9	16.6	16.5
Managers	40.2	34.5	36.0	34.7	33.4	32.2	31.4	30.2
Other occupations	21.6	19.7	19.5	18.5	18.1	17.6	17.3	17.0
Higher-level professionals	52.5	44.8	45.2	45.0	42.3	42.4	43.0	42.2
Other occupations	20.1	19.1	18.8	17.7	17.4	16.8	16.4	16.1
Technical workers	25.2	27.9	29.9	28.4	28.5	28.8	27.4	27.7
Other occupations	22.0	19.7	19.3	18.3	17.9	17.3	17.0	16.7
Office staff	30.8	31.6	32.7	31.1	29.7	29.1	28.7	27.7
Other occupations	21.3	19.2	18.9	18.0	17.7	17.2	16.8	16.6
Sales staff	12.9	8.9	10.1	9.7	10.3	10.0	10.2	9.6
Other occupations	23.8	11.3	21.8	20.8	20.2	19.6	19.2	19.0
Skilled production workers	29.3	19.5	28.3	26.8	26.0	25.3	24.9	24.8
Other occupations	20.6	18.5	18.5	17.6	17.3	16.8	16.5	16.2
Unskilled production workers	15.3	13.9	16.3	12.9	12.3	11.9	11.5	11.4
Other occupations	27.2	25.0	24.9	23.6	23.4	22.8	22.6	22.2

Table 6.3. Probability of Union Membership

Marginal effects (%)	1986	1992	1993	1995	1996	1997	1998	1999
Some elementary education	18.59	24.27	21.23	26.43	31.21	15.04	16.07	8.81
Elementary or some primary education	62.60	76.04	71.74	81.50	85.27	64.87	68.87	60.22
Primary or some secondary education	149.75	161.31	157.50	174.43	186.89	162.11	164.81	165.31
Secondary or some higher education	287.43	308.45	304.18	327.67	354.47	291.27	312.00	292.32
Higher education	835.15	624.02	680.75	721.92	760.35	633.53	691.90	671.78
Experience	1.38	1.97	1.92	2.25	2.31	2.32	2.44	2.62
Male	24.50	21.91	15.68	18.20	14.74	17.68	12.99	15.82
Head of household	89.43	47.36	51.98	41.20	41.79	39.31	37.09	34.10
Urban region	-13.86	-15.51	-12.41	-9.24	-12.99	-11.87	-9.92	-10.70
Metropolitan region	9.87	12.41	16.32	17.39	21.64	21.87	21.89	12.01
South-east	11.06	-10.12	-19.28	-19.08	*1.89*	*-2.94*	-6.76	-13.45
North	19.83	-18.75	-20.74	-27.73	-7.39	-10.23	-16.57	-20.56
Central-western	-20.55	-7.89	-9.23	-21.91	*-1.69*	-14.45	-13.77	-18.28
South	58.77	45.90	31.47	28.31	37.63	33.18	28.36	15.88
Agriculture	84.91	92.94	119.83	109.82	114.95	107.71	106.25	125.68
Manufacturing	121.24	164.18	178.35	193.99	151.76	134.72	120.43	130.49
Civil construction	-30.66	-19.09	-16.82	-14.54	-26.05	-28.75	-30.20	-33.23
Other industrial activities	187.18	343.72	369.61	442.29	355.15	304.29	310.65	317.70
Services	-48.39	-37.48	-37.16	-38.46	-33.12	-35.44	-37.32	-32.21
Other services	30.16	44.84	44.97	30.16	33.34	31.52	29.09	29.59
Transport and communication services	133.32	255.47	286.31	253.98	244.85	201.06	190.42	218.62

Table 6.3. Probability of Union Membership (Continued)

Social services	32.26	108.21	141.79	155.10	133.87	150.52	129.10	150.60
Public administration	-12.02	28.39	49.39	74.81	53.48	75.89	66.99	93.66
Other activities	164.23	284.65	328.61	330.09	229.34	237.05	166.07	183.97
N	99 305	104 154	106 285	114 377	111 358	118 135	117 045	120 685

Note: All coefficients are significant at the 5% level, except those shown in *italics*.

Reference categories are: illiterate, north east region, and commerce.

The models were estimated by logistic regression. The standard errors of the estimators are robust

Nonetheless, it is not uncommon to find unions operating in the same location as the these professional councils, and this facilitates and publicizes union activities, promotes union membership, and encourages integration between the two bodies, leading even to some unification of agendas.

About one-third of managers, technical staff, qualified production workers, and office staff are union members, compared to just 12 percent of unskilled production and manual workers – a group covering over half of the entire workforce. Unionization is even lower among sales staff, at around 10 percent[1] This distribution of union membership by occupational group is surprising, as the literature portrays union membership as a characteristic of low-skilled and production-line workers; moreover, workers with higher qualifications presumably have incentives to demand wages related to productivity, rather than based on pre-established pay scales. The occupational distribution of unionized workers in Brazil suggests that unions have the strongest presence in industries that concentrate highly skilled workers, including executives and office staff.

Table 6.1 and Table 6.2 therefore suggest that unionization in Brazil is a characteristic of more educated workers, holding the best jobs and working in large establishments; they also tend to be white, male, and heads of households; in addition union members are likely to be in metropolitan regions and to hold an employment record card. This profile suggests that the typical union member is very different from the average Brazilian worker, whose most common characteristic is a low skill level.

Bearing in mind the different characteristics between unionized workers and their non-union counterparts, it is reasonable to assume that socioeconomic variables affect the probability of union membership. To investigate this issue, we have estimated models that identify the contribution of individual characteristics to the likelihood of a unionized worker. Binomial logistic regressions were estimated using the union-membership indicator as the dependent variable. The model's explanatory variables were education, experience, experience squared, gender, head of household, urban/rural, metropolitan region, geographic region, and industry classification at the IBGE 1-digit level. The results appear in Table 6.3 and show the following:

- The likelihood of union membership rises substantially with schooling; in 1999 for example, an individual who had completed a higher education course was 672 percent more likely than an illiterate worker to be a union member;
- Experience raises the probability of union membership; in 1999 this increased by 2.6 percent with each additional year of experience;
- Men are more likely to be union members than women;
- Heads of households are more likely to be members of unions than other family members;
- Workers in urban areas are less likely to be unionized than those from rural areas;
- Workers in metropolitan areas are more likely to be union members;
- Workers from the south-east, north, and central-western regions are less likely to be union members than workers from the north-east; only workers from the southern region are more likely to be union members than those in the north-east;

[1] Not surprisingly, the distribution of occupations between unionized and non-union workers matches the distribution of education.

- Economic activity seems to have a major influence on the probability of union membership, as the estimates vary substantially between sectors. Workers in manufacturing industry, other industrial activities, transport and communication services, and even agriculture show high probabilities of union membership; while workers in civil construction and services are unlikely to be unionized.

Union Density

Table 6.4 (bottom line) shows the proportion of unionized workers weighted by the share of each industry in total employment. The figures indicate that union density fell uniformly from 22.2 percent to 17.4 percent between 1986 and 1999, declining by 27 percent during the period. This decline in unionization may be associated with the changes that have taken place in the economy and in the labor market over the last two decades, and particularly in the 1990s when trade liberalization policies were introduced. Other potential explanatory factors include market deregulation, including the labor market, and the privatization of state-owned companies (a sector where unionization was traditionally active), compounded by deep recession in 1990-1992 and a consequent rise in the open unemployment rate. These changes increased competition, undermined profits, and forced companies to adopt cost-cutting measures, potentially affecting workers through a decrease in both the number of jobs and the *quasi-rents* available to be shared out. A drop in union density was an expected consequence of this situation, resulting from higher unemployment and less chance of success in wage claims. Hay (2001) shows that while trade liberalization led to an increase in productivity, the profits of Brazilian companies declined. Arbache (2000) shows that trade liberalization eroded the union wage premium, especially in sectors most affected by imports.

In order to analyze the level of unionization in Brazil, union density was compared with that of other countries for 1994.[2] Blau and Kahn (1999) report that average union density in a group of developed countries excluding the United States was 42 percent that year, whereas the figure in Brazil was 19.5 percent. Density in Brazil only exceeded the figures for the United States (16 percent) and France (9 percent). Differences in union density among countries may be a reflection of the institutions governing unions and collective bargaining processes. In Brazil, legal extension of the results of collective bargaining to all formal workers in the category, even non-union members, must partly explain the relatively low rate of unionization, because it encourages a free-rider behavior. In fact, Nickell and Layard (1999) show that union density is relatively low in countries where the results of collective bargaining are extended to non-union workers, as in France, Spain and Holland.[3]

Table 6.5 shows union density at the two-digit industry level. Industries are classified into three union-density groups, using the following procedure: the average density of industry *i* in the period 1986-1999 was compared with the average density economy-wide during the same period, namely 19.2 percent. On the basis of this comparison, the union

---

[2] As there was no PNAD for 1994, we use the average union density for 1993 and 1995 to compare with density in developed countries.

[3] Gosling and Maching (1995) and Fortin and Lemieux (1997) show that the decline in union density in the United Kingdom and the United States caused a decrease in union bargaining power, and this helps to explain the observed increase in wage inequality.

density distribution at the industry level was constructed, and this was then split into three groups as follows:

- Up to one standard deviation – average or low union density;
- Between one and two standard deviations – high union density;
- Three or more standard deviations – very high union density.

Table 6.4. Union Density

(Percentages)

Industry	1986	1992	1993	1995	1996	1997	1998	1999	Mean
Agriculture	23.6	20.6	20.7	18.5	18.9	18.4	18.1	18.9	19.7
Mining	30.1	22.0	19.6	24.2	15.9	17.0	16.6	16.5	20.2
Oil, gas, and coal	68.3	67.1	71.8	71.7	49.3	64.8	61.1	66.7	65.1
Non-met. products	22.1	19.0	17.5	19.5	17.2	20.1	16.2	15.1	18.3
Metallurgical products	41.0	35.5	38.8	34.9	36.4	30.3	29.7	29.2	34.5
Mechanical products	43.5	40.1	41.7	40.2	31.1	36.6	31.7	31.3	37.0
Elect. and electronic products	47.6	42.4	36.1	38.2	33.6	33.3	33.0	27.1	36.4
Vehicles and autoparts	43.3	47.2	46.5	48.9	46.8	43.2	41.8	42.5	45.0
Wood and furniture	18.2	15.0	10.2	11.2	11.0	9.1	11.2	10.0	12.0
Paper and publishing	36.1	35.1	32.9	32.9	36.0	27.1	27.4	27.2	31.8
Rubber	30.2	28.2	42.9	40.8	28.9	24.6	34.2	31.0	32.6
Chemicals	35.3	30.3	31.1	30.5	31.2	28.2	29.3	34.4	31.3
Oil refining	53.4	63.8	48.7	57.7	49.7	54.6	40.9	48.7	52.2
Perfumes and pharmac.	31.8	23.9	29.0	27.2	26.7	24.0	23.9	26.4	26.6
Plastic products	32.3	28.7	28.4	27.7	31.2	29.4	24.1	27.0	28.6
Textiles	33.1	40.7	38.9	43.3	31.7	33.6	35.3	30.5	35.9
Clothing	8.9	9.4	9.4	9.5	8.2	8.0	8.4	8.7	8.8
Footwear	32.1	30.4	31.5	27.9	22.8	24.2	18.4	21.0	26.0
Foodstuff	26.2	24.1	22.9	22.6	20.9	20.3	20.0	18.1	21.9
Other manufact. products	22.6	16.9	14.6	21.6	20.1	16.2	17.3	13.5	17.9
Industrial services	50.6	66.2	63.3	65.3	60.6	56.6	55.0	54.2	59.0
Civil construction	11.9	10.2	9.5	9.2	8.2	8.0	7.6	6.9	8.9
Commerce	17.9	14.3	13.2	12.2	12.7	12.6	12.7	11.7	13.4
Transport services	34.9	37.1	36.1	32.4	33.1	30.3	29.8	29.4	32.9
Communication	43.3	45.9	52.1	52.2	45.6	41.3	38.9	38.5	44.7
Financial institutions	54.1	60.8	58.7	61.8	53.8	53.8	48.9	49.9	55.2
Social services	14.1	13.9	13.7	12.8	14.0	13.2	13.5	13.0	13.5
Business services	32.1	28.0	28.0	26.1	26.9	25.1	25.4	24.8	27.1
Public administration	24.4	21.1	25.1	19.7	18.0	22.3	20.5	20.2	21.4
Rental and leasing	23.9	26.0	27.9	29.0	28.1	29.5	28.8	29.9	27.9
Other services	4.0	2.7	2.7	2.7	2.8	2.8	2.9	2.7	2.9
Total	22.2	20.2	20.0	19.0	18.6	18.1	17.7	17.4	19.2

Table 6.5. Union Density By Group

(Percentages)

Group	Mean
1. Medium or low-density (up to one standard deviation)	
Other services	2.9
Clothing	8.8
Civil construction	8.9
Wood and furniture	12.0
Commerce	13.4
Social services	13.5
Other manufactured products	17.9
Non-metallic products	18.3
Agriculture	19.7
Mining	20.2
Public administration	21.4
Foodstuff	21.9
Footwear	26.0
Perfumes and pharmaceuticals	26.6
Other industrial services	27.1
Rental and leasing	27.9
Plastic products	28.6
Chemicals	31.3
Paper and publishing	31.8
Rubber	32.6
Transport services	32.9
2. High-density (up to two standard deviations)	
Metallurgical products	34.5
Textiles	35.9
Electric and electronic products	36.4
Mechanical products	37.0
Communications	44.7
Vehicles and autoparts	45.0
3. Very high-density (three or more standard deviations)	
Oil refining	52.2
Financial institutions	55.2
Industrial services	59.0
Oil, gas, and coal	65.1

Notes: Standard deviation = 15%; overall mean density = 19.2%; mean values between 1986 and 1999.

Industries with densities less than or equal to the economy average include civil construction, commerce, agriculture and clothing, among industries traditionally characterized by low levels of technology and capital and low market concentration.

Industries with union densities between 19.2 percent and 33 percent, include those with a high technology level, such as the pharmaceutical and chemical industries, together with various activities in the service sector. This interval also includes public administration, where union density is slightly above the average for the economy as a whole.

The medium or low union-density group included industries with unionization coefficients ranging from 3 percent to 33 percent; so dispersion in that group is very wide. The high density category includes industries with unionization rates of between 34.5 percent and 45 percent. Industries in this group are characterized by high levels of technology, capital, and market concentration, and they operate in large establishments. The very high density group contains industries with unionization rates above 52.2 percent, including the financial sector, oil drilling and other fuel mineral extraction industries, together with oil refining. These sectors are essentially dominated by the State oil company, Petrobrás, and by large multinationals.

The distribution of employment by union-density group is highly unequal. In 1999, 93.88 percent of workers were employed in medium or low union-density industries, while 66.47 percent were in industries with densities below the economy average; 4.05 percent of workers were employed in industries in the high density group, while just 2.07 percent of the workforce were in very high union-density industries.[4] The very unequal distribution of workers by union-density group is likely to have significant effects on union behavior at the industry level, and hence on the distribution of the rents extracted by them.

IV. Unions and Wages

How do unions affect wages and the distribution of income in Brazil? Is union bargaining behavior influenced by the institutions that regulate labor relations? How is income distribution affected by the concentration of unions in more sophisticated industries and higher unionization rates among skilled workers? This section seeks to answer these questions.

Union Wage Premium[5]

One of the best-known effects of unions in the economy is their ability to raise wages through collective bargaining. The literature shows that unionized workers with the same characteristics as their non-union counterparts enjoy a wage premium thanks to the action of their unions in pay negotiations. Booth (1995), Abowd and Lemieux (1993), and Nickell et al. (1994) all claim that the success of union activism in raising rates of pay is directly related to the market power of the company and the degree of concentration of the industry concerned. Highly competitive companies or industries cannot pay wages over the odds, for fear of going out of business. A union wage premium will only be seen in companies or industries that generate monopoly rents.

[4] The distribution of employment by union-density group in other years is quite similar.

[5] We use the terms "union wage premium", "union premium", "union mark-up" and "union wage differential" synonymously.

To analyze the wage spread between unionized and non-union workers, we have calculated the difference between the logarithm of the real hourly wage of the two groups. The results shown in Table 6.6 indicate an average wage differential of 58 percent.

Given that union members have a very different socioeconomic profile compared to non-members, the wage differential should next be calculated controlling for individual characteristics. This has been estimated by three methods, namely ordinary least squares (OLS), the Booth method, (1995, p.164), and the Oaxaca-Blinder decomposition.

Table 6.6. Differential of Log. Of Real Hourly Wages

(Percentages)

1986	55.8
1992	59.1
1993	63.0
1995	57.5
1996	57.0
1997	57.7
1998	57.8
1999	54.2

The results in Table 6.7 suggest substantially lower union wage premiums than those indicated in Table 6.6, confirming that individual socioeconomic characteristics are a major factor in explaining the wage gap between unionized and non-union workers. Given that the mean wage differential shown in Table 6.6 is 58 percent, while the average premium estimated by OLS is just 17.9 percent, we can conclude that nearly 70 percent of the uncontrolled wage differential is explained by differences in worker characteristics.

Table 6.7. Union Wage Mark-Up

Year	Union dummy (OLS)	Booth method*	Oaxaca-Blinder method**
1986	0.1670	0.1365	0.1281 - 0.1662
1992	0.1772	0.1381	0.1203 - 0.2057
1993	0.2008	0.1682	0.1516 - 0.2316
1995	0.1855	0.1698	0.1581 - 0.2190
1996	0.1813	0.1596	0.1469 - 0.2135
1997	0.1881	0.1702	0.1606 - 0.2134
1998	0.1774	0.1580	0.1479 - 0.2040
1999	0.1574	0.1228	0.1106 - 0.1778

Notes: The explanatory variables in the wage equation model are: education, experience, experience squared, employment record card, urban region, metropolitan region, head of household, race, gender, five geographic regions, and 31 industries.

* Booth (1995).

** Results vary according to the means vector used in the calculations, of non-union and unionized workers, respectively

Average values for the union wage premium are calculated as 17.9 percent, 15.3 percent and 17.2 percent, using ordinary least squares, the Booth method, and the Oaxaca-Blinder method, respectively. The salary differential is greater in Brazil than in several continental European countries, where the premium is around 7 percent, but quite similar to the 18 percent differential seen in the United States (Blanchflower and Freeman, 1992).[6] Although the figures for Brazil and the United States are similar, the determinants of the premium in the two countries are not the same, as the labor market and collective bargaining processes operate very differently in the two countries.

The high union wage premium in Brazil contrasts with generally low union density. One plausible explanation for this is that union mark-ups are very significant in industries of high and very high union density (see Table 6.5), and this raises the average union wage premium for the economy as a whole. This hypothesis is borne out by the high correlation between union density and the inter-industry wage premium (0.798, significant at the 1 percent level), and the results obtained by Arbache and Menezes-Filho (2000) showing evidence of rent sharing in industries that generate greatest value-added and highest return.

Unions and Wage Dispersion

According to Freeman (2000), the most universal stylized fact in the literature on unions is that wage dispersion among unionized workers is less than that among non-union members. The reasons for this are as follows: (i) unions depart from the principle that there should be a rate of pay for the job, and wages should have little or nothing to do with performance or individual characteristics; (ii) unions defend the existence of rigid job and wage structures, with promotion criteria based on seniority and occupation, and a narrow wage spread over the job hierarchy; and (iii) unions strive to ensure their members do not earn less than the minimum wage for their category or for the overall economy, if one exists, thereby truncating the wage distribution and making it more compact. Consequently, individual characteristics that normally contribute to wage formation, especially human capital variables, have scant influence on rates of pay for unionized workers. The marginal return on schooling, experience and training, for example, will therefore be lower for unionized workers than for their non-union counterparts; and discrimination based on gender, race, age, and so forth, also tends to be less among union members.

The reasons why unions seek rigid pay scales and a narrower wage spread between occupations are as follows: (i) to define clear objectives for collective bargaining processes; (ii) to eliminate competition among worker through wage disputes; (iii) to engender a feeling of solidarity among workers in the search for equal treatment by the employer; and (iv) the power of the median voter, which tends to favor redistribution in favor of the lower paid whenever the median wage rate is below the mean. The most important consequence of union action is that there will be less wage inequality *throughout* the economy, despite union members enjoying a wage premium (Freeman, 2000; Metcalf et al. 2000).

Table 6.8 shows the dispersion of the logarithm of real hourly wages for unionized and non-union workers. The spread is always *greater* among the former. Figure 6.2 and Figure 6.3

[6] Blanchflower and Freeman estimated wage models using OLS, with very similar specifications to the model estimated in this paper.

illustrate wage dispersion in 1999, showing that the distribution for non-union workers is a good deal more leptokurtic, with strong positive asymmetry. These results are strange, since they are contrary to the stylized fact that wage dispersion is lower among unionized workers than among non-union members. The most plausible explanation for this is that unions in Brazil do *not* attempt to standardize wages.

Table 6.8. Wage Dispersion Among Unionized And Non-Union Workers

	Standard deviation of log. of real hourly wage		
Year	Unionized	Non-union	Total
1986	0.9740	0.8914	0.9397
1992	0.9412	0.9076	0.9448
1993	0.9910	0.9229	0.9702
1995	0.9631	0.8936	0.9349
1996	0.9629	0.8949	0.9352
1997	0.9667	0.8926	0.9332
1998	0.9620	0.8751	0.9181
1999	0.9485	0.8636	0.9028

Source: National Household Surveys (PNADs), several years.

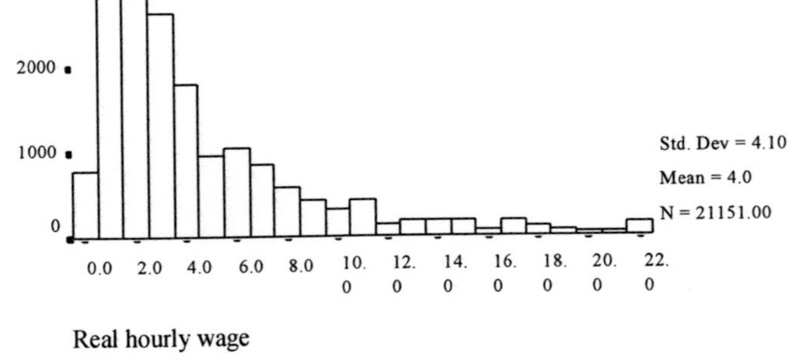

Figure 6.2. Distribution of Real Hourly Wages – Union Members, 1999

One potential effect of the high wage dispersion among unionized workers is greater wage inequality throughout the economy.[7] This effect will be greater the higher the wage dispersion between unionized and non-union workers, and/or the higher the level of union density. To examine the impact of unions on wage inequality, we use counterfactual analysis

[7] Blau and Kahn (1996) show that one of the reasons for greater wage dispersion in the United States compared to other developed countries is the high level of wage dispersion among unionized workers, although this is no greater than dispersion among non-union members in that country.

to simulate what would happen to inequality if the pay of non-unionists adhered to the wage policy in force for unionized workers.[8] If we find that wage formation for unionized workers increases wage dispersion among non-unionists, we will have evidence that unions increase inequality in the overall economy. To confirm the result of the simulation, we examine what would happen with the distribution if unionized workers were to earn the same as their non-union counterparts.

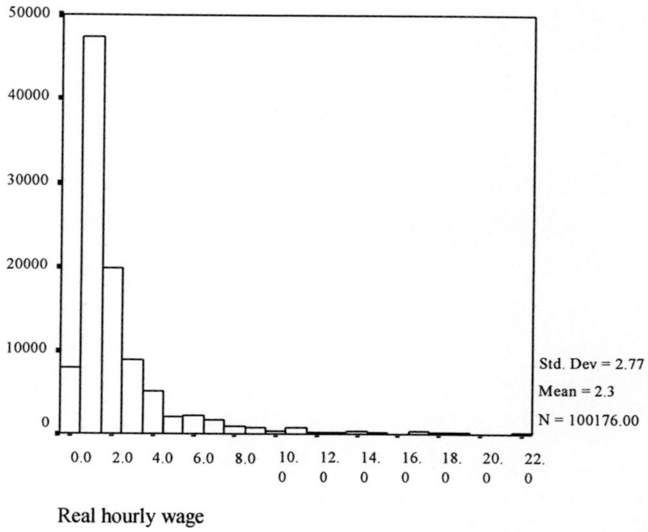

Figure 6.3. Distribution of Real Hourly Wage – Non-union Members, 1999

The counterfactual for non-unionized workers was implemented as follows:

$$\ln y_i^{ns} = y_i^* + \hat{u}_i^{ns}\left(\frac{\sigma^{s}}{\sigma^{ns}}\right)$$

Where y_i^* is the simulation of the logarithm of the real hourly wage of the *i*th non-union worker (the simulation is performed using the βs estimated in the unionized workers wage model); $\hat{u}_i^{ns}$ is the residual from the non-union wage model; σ^s is the standard deviation of the residual from the unionized workers wage model; and σ^{ns} is the standard deviation of the residuals from the non-union wage model.[9]

Table 4.9 summarizes the effects of unions on the standard deviation of non-union wages, calculated in two stages. Firstly, the standard deviation of the wages of non-union and unionized workers was simulated on the basis of coefficients estimated in the unionized and non-union wage models, respectively. Secondly, we calculated the ratio between the

[8] This could happen if, in order to avoid unionization, companies decided to follow the unionized workers wage policy.

simulated standard deviation and the original standard deviation (calculated without simulation).

The results presented in line 1 of Table 6.9 show that, apart from 1995, if the unionized worker wage policy was used to set the pay of non-union members, wage inequality would increase by between 5.1 percent and 37.3 percent, depending on the year. This result is unequivocal evidence that unions increase wage inequality in the Brazilian economy, rather than reduce it. Line 2 reports the reverse exercise, using the wage policy for non-union members to set unionized workers' pay. This produces a reduction in wage dispersion of 12.7 percent to 18.7 percent, thereby corroborating the previous evidence. Thus, the effects of unions on wage dispersion in Brazil are precisely the opposite of those reported in the international literature.

Table 6.9. Simulation Of Standard Deviation Of Unionized And Non-Union Workers' Wages

(simulated value/original value %)

	1986	1992	1993	1995	1996	1997	1998	1999
Non-union	13.57	5.08	20.82	-4.64	14.43	11.88	15.79	37.33
Unionized	-13.45	-13.77	-17.45	-12.66	-14.05	-11.97	-14.99	-18.75

Notes: The figures shown in the table represent the ratio of the simulated standard deviation divided by the original standard deviation, expressed as a percentage. The values shown for non-union members refer to the simulated standard deviation obtained using coefficients estimated from the unionized workers wage model. The values for unionized workers refer to the simulated standard deviation obtained with coefficients estimated from the non-union workers wage model.

A very strong factor that may explain the wider dispersion of unionized wages is that merit plays a greater role in setting union members' pay. If so, the coefficients estimated for the productive variables in the unionized wage models ought to be higher than those estimated in the models for non-union members. To investigate this hypothesis, we compared the schooling and experience coefficients in the unionized and non-union wage models.

The results in Table 6.10 show that the marginal returns on human capital variables in the unionized worker models are always higher than those obtained in the non-union models, which suggests that unions magnify rather than diminish the effects of personal characteristics on wages.[10] These results are counterintuitive and contrary to the literature; they also contradict the idea that unions are sources of wage equalization and standardization.

There are at least three possible explanations for this result. The first relates to dispersion in unionized and non-union workers' characteristics. This could add to inequality insofar as wages are determined by productivity differences. The larger the variance of characteristics within a given group, the higher will be the variance of wages in that group, and vice versa. To test this hypothesis, Arbache (1999) decomposes the variance of unionized workers' wages conditional on the variance of non-union workers' characteristics. The result indicates that 37 percent of wage dispersion among unionized workers is caused by the difference in the dispersion of characteristics between union and non-union members. In fact, on the one hand, unionization is highly concentrated in certain industries that account for a small

[9] The equation for unionized workers is the same, with the *ns* superscripts replaced by *s* and vice versa.

[10] The results reported correspond to 1999; qualitative results for other years are similar.

proportion of employment, and in certain occupational categories, notably those requiring higher qualifications, which are in short supply in the economy. On the other hand, unionization is substantially lower in traditional industries and among the low-skilled workers who make up the vast majority of the workforce. Thus, the dispersion of characteristics among unionized workers is likely to be large.

Table 6.10. Returns To Human Capital Variables In Unionized and Non-Union Workers Wage equations, 1999

Variable	Unionized	Non-union
Experience	0.0347	0.0331
Experience squared	-0.0004	-0.0005
Some elementary education	0.1573	0.1151
Elementary or some primary education	0.3678	0.2888
Primary or some secondary education	0.6414	0.5288
Secondary or some higher education	1.0850	0.9380
Higher education	1.8080	1.7260

Note: All coefficients are significant at the 1% level

The second explanation relates to the median voter theorem. As more highly qualified workers are over-represented in union membership, they wield significant power in defining policies that favor returns to human capital, thereby increasing wage inequality. If unions place a higher value on merit, then more highly skilled workers will seek jobs in sectors where unions have greatest influence in pay-setting processes. Thus, the market would respond to higher wages among unionized workers by allocating the best workers to industries where unions are most active.[11]

The third explanation relates to the scant or non-existent coordination and centralization of collective bargaining processes.[12] This point is discussed below.

Dispersion of characteristics and pay among unionized workers, together with the relatively greater importance of skill in wage formation, suggest that the returns to human capital variables will differ significantly *among* unionized workers throughout the distribution. In other words, the marginal return on education is higher among workers further towards the right-hand tail of the distribution. To examine this hypothesis, we compared the marginal returns on schooling in the unionized and non-union wage models, estimated by quantile regression.

The results, shown in Table 6.11, reveal three phenomena. Firstly, marginal returns on education rise throughout the wage distribution. A worker in the 90th percentile obtains a greater return from a higher education course than a worker attaining the same level of schooling in any lower income percentile. Secondly, the returns to education are always higher for unionized workers. Thirdly, marginal returns among unionized workers grow proportionately more as the level of schooling rises. These results are evidence that unions

[11] This would create a potential sample selection problem. At the limit, selection would tend to reduce wage dispersion as workers would have increasingly similar characteristics.

[12] By "centralization" we refer to the level at which collective bargaining takes place, namely plant, company, industry or economy.

contribute to greater wage inequality, by providing greater relative benefits to workers further to the right in the distribution, as well as workers with more years of schooling.

Table 6.11. Schooling Coefficients Among Unionized and Non-Union Workers, 1999

Percentile	0.1		0.25		0.50		0.75		0.9	
	Union	Non-union	Union	Non-union	Union	Non-union	Union	Non-union	Union	Non-union
Some elementary education	0.0589	0.0394	0.0961	0.0416	0.1055	0.0465	0.1591	0.0703	0.1560	0.1017
Elementary or some primary education	0.1625	0.1211	0.2180	0.1146	0.2488	0.1175	0.2781	0.1340	0.2656	0.1709
Primary or some secondary education	0.2976	0.2060	0.3428	0.1915	0.3731	0.2244	0.4411	0.2756	0.4790	0.3498
Secondary or some higher education	0.5479	0.4123	0.6510	0.4581	0.7549	0.5674	0.8901	0.7118	0.9513	0.8657
Higher education	1.3916	1.1577	1.5364	1.3185	1.6765	1.5176	1.7903	1.6751	1.7487	1.7513

Notes: Models were estimated by quantile regression. All coefficients are significant at the 1% level. Standard errors were estimated by the bootstrap method. The models' explanatory variables are gender, urban region, metropolitan region, 5 geographic regions, 31 industries, head of household, employment record card, and schooling.

Unions and Collective Bargaining

One important aspect of collective bargaining processes is their potential economic effect, which goes beyond wage distribution. In the most centralized and coordinated bargaining systems, wage determination tends to be more sensitive to the general conditions of the labor market (Layard et al., 1991) and income distribution tends to be more equal. At the other end of the scale, fragmented bargaining systems that operate at the establishment level tend to be more sensitive to the economic conditions facing the company. In both cases, union demands are tempered by disincentives arising from the effects of inconsistent demands on the workers themselves, such as unemployment, inflation, or a lack of formalization of the employment contract. Discussion on this topic initially analyzed the effects of the crises of the 1970s on the macroeconomic performance of rich countries, and showed that the institutions that regulate collective bargaining play a decisive role in macroeconomic performance (Bruno and Sachs, 1985; Freeman, 1988).

Calmfors and Driffill (1988) show that collective bargaining organized at the industry level, as in Brazil, is the worst possible structure, because workers have few incentives to incorporate into their objective functions the conditions facing the economy and companies, or the external effects on themselves of potentially inconsistent demands. Moreover, the absence of coordination and synchronization among collective bargaining processes in Brazil means that unions are permanently creating pockets of instability, by holding out for wage increases that are inconsistent with macroeconomic balance. This feature of collective bargaining in Brazil has been empirically addressed by Carneiro (1999) and Carneiro and Henley (2000) who argue that the semi-coordinated (intermediate-centralized) bargaining structure currently in place in the country conforms with the insider-outsider hypotheis.[13]

The literature indicates that the most important consequence of coordinated and centralized collective bargaining processes is low wage dispersion. The empirical literature shows that wage differentials are narrower in countries with centralized bargaining processes than where they are more fragmented (Kahn, 1998). Blau and Khan (1996) find, for a set of developed countries, that wage dispersion is lower where collective bargaining is more centralized. Metcalf et al. (2000) discuss and show that the retreat of collective bargaining coverage in the United Kingdom since the 1980s was accompanied by greater wage inequality. Rowthorn (1992) uses the centralization criterion proposed by Calmfors and Driffill (1988) and finds a negative relation between centralization and inter-industry wage dispersion. Thus, the greater the coordination and centralization of bargaining processes, and/or the higher the proportion of workers covered by collective bargaining, the lower the wage dispersion in the economy will be.[14]

The structure of labor relations and union organization in Brazil is highly unfavorable to the strengthening, centralization, and coordination of collective bargaining processes. Unions from the most organized and sophisticated industries are encouraged to adopt individualistic behavior to exploit bargaining power associated with the conditions facing the company or industry. As a result, inter-industry wage differentials may be wider among unionized than among non-union workers. As the rate and composition of unemployment varies from region to region, unions from a single industry but in different localities will have different degrees of bargaining power, leading to potentially greater inequality in the wages of unionized workers.

The effects of the structure of collective bargaining processes in Brazil are particularly important, given the country's highly unequal income distribution and the severe macroeconomic instability it has been experiencing for at least two decades. Negotiations at the industry level and by geographic area mean that unions have less incentive to internalize the effects of the trade off between wage/employment and wage/formal employment contract. Consequently, there will be: (i) high dispersion of inter-industry wages – this will rise with the heterogeneity of technology and market power between industries, and the heterogeneity of bargaining power between unions; (ii) a prolongation of and/or increase in the costs of stabilization processes and/or coordination of macroeconomic policies, with potential effects on unemployment and inflation.

To investigate the effects of the collective bargaining structure on inequality, we compared the standard deviation of the inter-industry wage differential between unionized and non-union workers. Inter-industry wage differentials relate to that part of wages not explained by human capital, demographic characteristics, regional variables, etc., but

[13] That is, larger employment today leads to subsequent wage moderation.

[14] It should be borne in mind that wages agreed upon in more centralized collective bargaining systems affect the vast majority of workers, including non-union members, either because the result of the bargaining process is legally extended to everyone, or because companies take the negotiated wage rate as a benchmark for constructing their own pay scale. In either situation, wage dispersion among workers covered by the bargaining process should be less than among those who are not covered.

associated with the industry to which the worker is attached. Thus, the higher the industry wage premium, the higher will be the wage received by the individual in that industry *vis-à-vis* the representative worker. Insofar as industry wage premiums and profits are positively related (Arbache and Menezes-Filho, 2000), it is reasonable to expect a positive relation between union activism and the industry wage premium, because unions negotiate where there are monopoly rents to be shared out. As collective bargaining processes usually occur at the industry level, union pressure for higher pay could lead to greater inter-industry wage dispersion.

We estimated inter-industry wage premiums and calculated the respective standard deviation using the Haisken-DeNew and Schmidt (1997) procedure. Table 6.12 shows that the dispersion of industry wage premiums among unionized workers is greater than among non-union members. This confirms that union bargaining power at the industry level is quite heterogeneous, a situation that tends to be boosted by fragmentation and a lack of synchronization among collective bargaining processes. Little cooperation between unions can therefore be expected on wages and coordination in collective bargaining processes is unlikely.

Table 6.12. Standard Deviation of the Inter-Industry Wage Differential

Year	Unionized	Non-union	Total
1986	0.2491	0.1827	0.2023
1992	0.2640	0.1713	0.2061
1993	0.2741	0.1619	0.2002
1995	0.2631	0.1614	0.1934
1996	0.2456	0.1652	0.1892
1997	0.2375	0.1685	0.1898
1998	0.2310	0.1605	0.1796
1999	0.2313	0.1625	0.1818

Notes: (1) The inter-industry wage differential and standard deviation were estimated by the Haisken-DeNew and Schmidt (1997) method. (2) The models' explanatory variables are: education, gender, experience, experience squared, employment record card, head of household, urban region, metropolitan region, regions, and 31 industries (IBGE two-digit level).

V. DISCUSSION

This chapter has addressed the following questions: (i) How do labor and union laws affect collective bargaining processes? (ii) Do unions affect wage formation and income distribution? (iii) Do unions increase rigidity in the labor market? Upon reaching the end of the chapter, we realize we have not found unequivocal answers to these questions. The complexity of the topic and the limitations of relying on economics alone to provide answers may help explain the shortcomings of our findings. Nonetheless, the chapter offers several pieces of evidence that elucidate the issues addressed.

Possibly the most important lesson to be drawn from the study is that institutions are fundamental in explaining union actions, along with their effects on income distribution and macroeconomic stability, and on the current state of collective bargaining in Brazil. The answer to question (i) is closely linked to the institutional apparatus. As we have seen, labor and union legislation – particularly through the union levy, monopoly representation and labor courts – create disincentives for the development of collective bargaining and cause problems for macroeconomic coordination.

The mandatory union levy creates contract problems between the union and the worker. As the union thus has an assured income, the bureaucrat will not always need to obtain additional funds from voluntary affiliations to run the organization. This may result in the relaxation or even disappearance of the contractual relation between the two parties, in which the union member (the principal) would expect "contractual" attitudes and decisions from the union bureaucrat (the agent). Consequently, union leaders may perform their union activities with less commitment, and this may lead to a weakened relationship between the union and its workers. The assured income, which is often sizeable, gives enormous power to the union bureaucracy, and nurtures bitter disputes for leadership of the organization.

In the period prior to the 1988 Constitution, when the State was given great freedom to meddle in union affairs, the contractual relation between union leaders and workers was often tenuous, and union bureaucracy essentially strove to keep itself in power by forging ever closer relationships with Government. More recently, the distribution of funds by Government for unions to use in training and labor intermediation programs has fostered a further strengthening of relations between union leaders and government authorities.

The contract problem created by the union levy means that union leaders do not always feel committed to the most obvious interests of the worker; this inhibits a strengthening of the relationship between worker and union, thereby impairing the development of collective bargaining.

Monopoly representation is another institution that may interfere with the actions of unions in collective bargaining processes. The monopoly guarantees union bureaucracy enormous power in its geographical jurisdiction, giving it major prerogatives such as mandatory participation in discussions on any issue relating to the interests of the category it represents. A problem of union involvement in all negotiations is that it tends to inhibit bargaining between employers and employees at the company level. In addition, excess power linked to the contract problem may also influence the behavior and actions of union leaders in bargaining processes.

The regulatory power of labor courts, together with the paternalistic character of labor legislation and in many cases the justice system itself, prevent workers and employers from entering into direct negotiations with one another. Employees, protected by legislation and the culture of appealing to the court, are encouraged to use to the justice system to resolve disagreements with employers. Employees frequently have appealed to the justice system even before proposing or presenting their allegations or claims to their employers. The latter, either as a way of delaying payments owed, exploiting the opportunity cost of the worker, or increasing the transaction cost of access to amounts supposedly owed, also has incentives to appeal to the courts rather than negotiating with the worker. Direct negotiations are thus replaced by the institutionalization of indirect negotiations through the labor court system.

With regard to question (ii), pertaining to the effects of unions on pay setting and the wage distribution, we find a variety of econometric evidence. Unions clearly contribute to wage formation, by establishing a wage premium that enables union members to earn more than their non-union counterparts with the same individual characteristics and industrial affiliation. In principle, the existence of the wage premium is unexpected, since the law requires the results of collective bargaining processes to be extended to all workers in the occupational category concerned. Thus, any pay raise negotiated by the union must be given to all workers in that category. Possible explanations for the empirical verification of union wage premiums include the following: (i) automatic extension of gains may not have taken place, meaning non-compliance with the law; (ii) wage negotiations may predominantly be carried out at the company rather than the industry level, as we investigated in this study, which would not require extension of bargained results to other workers in the industry; (iii) unions may essentially be negotiating pay floors rather than actual wage rates, thereby giving space for companies to negotiate wages above the floor; and (iv) there may be a wage differential between workers in a given category, but in different *municipios* or jurisdictions of unions or their federations. Unfortunately, shortcomings in union data prevent us from testing these hypotheses. Nonetheless, we would not be surprised if future calculations using company and/or municipal-level data produced lower union wage premiums.

We find evidence that unions do affect income distribution; but contrary to the view prevailing in the literature, unions in Brazil are associated with more rather than less wage inequality. Several factors appear to explain this. Firstly, higher-skilled workers and those in better jobs are proportionately more unionized than less skilled workers. This is counterintuitive, since better qualified workers would not have an incentive to be paid standardized wages. On the contrary, as they are more skilled they ought to prefer their pay to be performance-related rather than predetermined.

Our results suggest that the higher rates of unionization among more skilled workers encourage unions to adopt strategies favoring this group. This is consistent with the median voter theorem, the greater mobilization power of like-minded people, or insider power. The finding that marginal returns on human capital variables are higher among unionized workers and those to the right of the wage distribution, compared to non-union members, is remarkable. Given that the country is so lacking in skilled labor, unions would therefore seem to be exploiting labor scarcity to magnify the returns to skill, thus benefiting workers with more human capital and/or those holding better posts in the job hierarchy. This issue becomes even more important if unions are insensitive to the wage/employment and wage/informal sector trade-offs.

One possible explanation for the higher rate of unionization among highly skilled workers may be the regulation of higher-level professions by regional councils, which, to some extent, behave or end up behaving in a similar way to unions. As we showed above, an example of this is the publication of fee scales and the establishment of pay floors by these institutions. On the other hand, the unions in the respective categories, which often work in conjunction with and in the same place as the regional councils, can take advantage of externalities arising from the actions of these bodies, to promote and disseminate unionization among professional people and thereby increase union membership among them.

Secondly, the dispersion of characteristics among unionized workers is greater than among their non-union counterparts, resulting in higher wage dispersion among union members.

Thirdly, the resurgence of unionism at the end of the 1970s in the industrialized and wealthy areas of São Paulo, does not seem to be mere coincidence. Clearly, it is associated with the nature of the companies and industries in that region, which include multinationals and large domestic companies, mostly operating in concentrated, high technology industries. The conjunction of these two phenomena, namely the extraction of monopoly rents by companies in the region, and the strict law on pay increases, which limited wage hikes, would have encouraged workers to organize and lobby for greater flexibility to facilitate rent sharing. Thus, the reorganization of the union movement in the wealthiest part of the country and in industries using sophisticated technologies and moderately more qualified workers seems to have molded the "new unionism" as an activity associated with workers who are more rather than less qualified.[15]

Fourthly, the fact that occupational categories' base dates are spread throughout the year, compounded by the fragmentation of collective bargaining by region, reduces the chances of centralization and/or coordination of bargaining processes and encourages free-rider behavior. In this context, unions in sectors that extract monopoly rents have incentives to act in a decentralized fashion, exploiting circumstances that are favorable to them, in accordance with the characteristics of the industry and/or region in which they are located. On the other hand, the weakness of unions in more competitive sectors means they have less chance of bargaining success. As union density is higher in the more concentrated and sophisticated industries, we consequently find greater inter-industry wage inequality associated with unions.

Another major consequence of the fragmentation of bargaining processes is the difficulty this raises for macroeconomic coordination. A fragmented system of negotiations, with highly variable bargaining power between unions, encourages free riding and inconsistent wage demands, constantly generating potential pressure on prices. But the effects of fragmentation become even more acute as unions in more organized sectors show scant concern for the wage/employment and wage/informal sector trade-offs, provoking potentially negative consequences for the level and quality of employment, and harming outsiders in particular.

As for the relation between unions and labor market rigidity posed in question (iii), we find evidence that union action on wages tends to increase rigidity and segmentation in the labor market. The union wage premium, together with an over-valuation of human capital, raise labor costs, creating entry barriers for less skilled workers in certain industries and encouraging segmentation. *Broadly speaking*, this produces one group of industries with higher union density, higher wages, and more skilled workers; and another group of industries with lower union density, lower wages, and less skilled workers.

VI. RECOMMENDATIONS

In the light of the above discussion, we now make some recommendations for encouraging and strengthening collective bargaining processes, ideally turning them into the key instrument of labor relations in Brazil. We believe the following measures should be adopted: (i) abolish the union monopoly; (ii) abolish the mandatory union levy; (iii) abolish the regulatory power of the labor tribunal system; (iv) organize unions by economic activity rather than occupation; (v) strengthen representation at the workplace; and (vi) change collective bargaining base dates so as to reduce fragmentation and encourage centralization

[15] It should be noted that the concept of skill in a country with a high proportion of illiterate or functionally illiterate workers, such as Brazil, is different from that of a country with a higher average level of education. Thus, even an individual who has not completed second grade, for example, could be considered to have formal education well above the national average.

and/or cooperation between unions in bargaining processes. We believe these measures would enhance unions and give them greater independence; the measures would also strengthen them and elicit more committed engagement from them on issues pertaining to workers' interests. The current structure of collective bargaining in Brazil reflects and reveals scant consensus among the agents involved in improving and modernizing the country's labor relations.

Given the paucity of research on unions in Brazil, investigation of their impact on employment, productivity, profits, and working conditions, together with studies of the differences between unions in the public and private sectors, and at the company and regional level, would be particularly welcome in order to shed further light on the issues raised in this paper.

REFERENCES

Abowd, J.M. and Lemieux, T. (1993), 'The effects of product market competition on collective bargaining agreements: the case of foreign competition in Canada', *Quarterly Journal of Economics*, 108: 983-1014.

Amorim, B.M. (2000), Salários indiretos e sindicatos no Brasil, Campinas: *Anais do XXVIII Encontro Nacional de Economia.*

Arbache, J.S. (1999), 'Do unions always decrease wage dispersion? The case of Brazilian manufacturing', *Journal of Labor Research*, 20: 425-436.

Arbache, J.S. (2000), 'Does trade liberalization always decrease unions bargaining power?', *Proceedings of the 2000 EALE/SOLE World Conference*, Milão.

Arbache, J.S. and Carneiro, F.G. (1999), 'Unions and wage differentials', *World Development*, 27: 1875-1883.

Arbache, J.S. and Menezes-Filho, N., (2000), 'Rent-sharing in Brazil: Using trade liberalization as a natural experiment', Rio de Janeiro: *Annals of the V Annual Meeting of the Latin American and Caribbean Economic Association.*

Blanchflower, D.G. and Freeman, R.B. (1992), 'Unionism in the United States and other advanced OECD countries', *Industrial Relations*, 31: 57-79.

Blau, F.D. and Kahn, L.M. (1996), 'International differences in male wage inequality: institutions versus market forces', *Journal of Political Economy*, 104: 791-837.

Blau, F.D. and Kahn, L.M. (1999), 'Institutions and laws in the labor market', in O. Ashenfelter and D. Card (eds.), *Handbook of Labor Economics*, Amsterdam: Elsevier.

Booth, A. (1995), '*The economics of the trade unions*', Cambridge: Cambridge University Press.

Camargo, J.M. (2001), *'Sindicatos e justiça do trabalho no Brasil'*, mimeo, Departamento de Economia, PUC-Rio.

Calmfors, L. and Driffill, J. (1988), 'Centralization and wage bargaining, *Economic Policy*, 3: 14-61.

Card, D. (1992), '*The effect of unions on the distribution of wages: redistribution or relabelling?'*, NBER Working Paper 4195.

Carneiro, F. (1998). *Productivity Effects in Brazilian Wage Determination. World Development* vol. 26(1), pp. 139-153.

Carneiro, F. and A. Henley (1998). *Wage Determination in Brazil: The Growth of Union Bargaining Power and Informal Employment. The Journal of Development Studies* vol. 34(4), pp. 117-138.

Carneiro, F. (1999). *Insider Power in Wage Determination: Evidence from Brazilian Data. Review of Development Economics* vol 3(2), pp. 55-169.

Carneiro, F. and A. Henley (2000), *Real Wages and the Lucas Critique: Can the Government Tax Policy Influence Wage Growth in Brazil?, Brazilian Review of Econometrics*, Vol. 20(1):89-113.

DiNardo, J., Fortin, N.M. and Lemieux, T. (1995), 'Labor market institutions and the distribution of wages, 1973-1992: a semiparametric approach', NBER Working Paper 5093.

DiNardo, J., Hallock, K. and Pischke, J.S. (1997), 'Unions and managerial pay', NBER Working Paper 6318.

Fortin, N.M. and Lemieux T. (1997), 'Institutional changes and rising wage inequality: is there a linkage?', *Journal of Economic Perspectives*, 11: 75-96.

Freeman, R.B. (1980), 'Unionism and the dispersion of wages', *Industrial and Labor Relations Review*, 34: 3-23.

Freeman, R.B. (1982), 'Union wage practices and wage dispersion within establishments', *Industrial and Labor Relations Review*, 36: 3-21.

Freeman, R.B. (1988), 'Labor market institutions and economic performance', NBER Working Paper 2560.

Freeman, R.B. (1992), 'How much has de-unionization contributed to the rise in male earnings inequality?', in S. Danzinger and P. Gottschalk (eds.), *Uneven tides*, New York: Sage Press.

Freeman, R.B. (2000), 'Single peaked vs. diversified capitalism: the relation between economic institutions and outcomes', NBER Working Paper 7556.

Gosling, A. and Machin, S. (1995), 'Trade unions and the dispersion of earnings in British establishments, 1980-90', *Oxford Bulletin of Economics and Statistics*, 57: 167-184.

Green, F., Dickerson, A., and Arbache, J.S. (2001), 'A picture of wage inequality and the allocation of labor through a period of trade liberalization: the case of Brazil', *World Development*, 29:1923-39.

Haisken-DeNew, J.P. and Schmidt, C.M. (1997), 'Inter-industry and inter-region differentials: mechanics and interpretation', *Review of Economics and Statistics*, 79: 516-521.

Hay, D. (2001), 'The post 1990 Brazilian trade liberalization and the performance of large manufacturing firms: Productivity, market share and profits', *Economic Journal*, 473:620-641.

Hirsch, B.T. (1982), 'The interindustry structure of unionism, earnings and earnings dispersion', *Industrial and Labor Relations Review*, 36: 22-39.

Kahn, L.M. (1998), 'Collective bargaining and the interindustry wage structure: international evidence', *Economica*, 65: 507-534.

Menezes-Filho, N., H. Zylberstajn, J.P. Chahad, and E. Pazello (2002), '*Trade Unions and the Economic Performance of Brazilian Establishments*', Paper Presented at the 2002 Latin American Meeting of the Econometric Society, São Paulo, Brazil.

Metcalf, D., Hansen, K., and Charlwood, A. (2000), 'Unions and the sword of justice: unions and pay systems, pay inequality, pay discrimination and low pay', mimeo, Center for Economic Performance, London School of Economics.

Nickell, S.J., Vainiomaki, J. and Wadhwani, S. (1994), 'Wages, unions and product market power', *Economica*, 61: 457-474.

Nickell, S.J. and Layard, R. (1999), 'Labor market institutions and economic performance', in O. Ashenfelter and D. Card (eds.), *Handbook of Labor Economics*, Amsterdam: Elsevier.

Rowthorn, R.E. (1992), 'Centralization, employment and wage dispersion', *Economic Journal*, 102: 506-523.

In: Economics, Politics and Social Issues in Latin America ISBN 1-60021-182-8
Editor: Mary P. Lassiter, pp. 129-149

Chapter 7

LABOR MARKET INTEGRATION AND ECONOMIC ADJUSTMENT

***Norbert Fiess*[1], *Marco Fugazza*[2] *and William F. Maloney*[1]**
[1]World Bank
[2]Ecole Nationale des Ponts et Chausses, Paris, France

I. INTRODUCTION

Over the last two decades, most Latin American countries went through the experience of fiscal adjustment, stabilization and trade liberalization along the lines of the so-called Washington Consensus. Recently, growing attention has been devoted to assessing the role of the labor markets in the transmission process of such economic policies to the population's standards of living, in particular the poor (e.g., Horton and Mazumdar, 1994). One of the main conclusions of studies of this sort is that market imperfections prevent an efficient allocation of resources, and hence are likely to mitigate the success of such policies and a fair distribution of their potential benefits.

The predominant conceptual approach adopted in the existing labor market literature is based on the assumption that labor market institutions are always a source of distortion (Olson, 1982). A representative statement of this view sees the informal sector as the residual of a highly distorted formal sector labor market, where unions and/or government regulation keep wages above their equilibrium level, rationing workers into the informal sector where they are then left completely unprotected by labor legislation (e.g., Harris-Todaro, 1970). Participation in the non-regulated section of the economy is thus seen as non-voluntary, with workers regarding the regulated section always as the best alternative. The perceived reaction of a dualistic labor market to negative shocks is then also predetermined. As wages in the formal sector are downwardly rigid, wages in the informal sector will fall in response to the increase in informal labor supply. The outcome is a segmented labor market, where relative earnings and relative employment shares of the formal and informal sector move in opposite directions.

In Chapter 3, Maloney and Cunningham present empirical evidence that the labor market does not exclusively behave in a segmented fashion (e.g., Vijverberg, 1986, Yamada, 1996,

Maloney, 1998a, Aroca and Maloney, 1999, Carneiro and Henley, 2002). In particular, the observed increase in informality over the last decade in Latin America reflected prolonged episodes where — despite potentially distorting labor market regulations — participation rates in the formal and informal sector move up and down together, that is, formal and informal labor markets behave in an "integrated" rather than in a segmented or dualistic fashion (see Davila Capalleja, 1994, and Marquez, 1997). These studies have attempted to explain the integrated behavior of labor markets and present the alternative view that as a first approximation, the informal sector should be treated as an unregulated/unprotected entrepreneurial sector that may be desirable to many workers. In other words, the choice to participate in the informal sector is a rational one. This rationality could be linked to elements like the misalignment of implicit and explicit labor taxes with perceived benefits or the desire of workers to retain a degree of independence in their work[1].

But this is not all. This new approach also illustrates that the extent to which labor market rigidities are binding, viz., the degree of segmentation of labor markets, is not determined exclusively by labor legislation but varies depending on the macroeconomic stage that the economy is passing through. Accordingly, what we propose in this chapter is that the macroeconomic environment itself can affect the degree of segmentation in the labor market and consequently the impact of policy interventions. Viewed another way, the expected outcome of stabilization and adjustment policies varies whether the labor market behaves like an integrated or a segmented market. That is, we postulate an interdependence between labor market composition and macroeconomic environment.

The chapter also uses this approach to briefly contrast labor market functioning in three Latin American countries — Mexico, Colombia and Brazil — in order to draw policy lessons in specific settings. The result of the exercise is that Mexico appears to have had the most "flexible" or integrated labor markets until the mid-1990s, Colombia exhibits traits that can be better classified as segmented or dualistic, and Brazil appears to oscillate between these two forms during the 1990s. The case of Brazil is examined further in some detail and policy implications are drawn.

The remainder of the chapter is organized as follows. Section 2 provides the conceptual and empirical background of the study, and also presents additional evidence for other Latin American countries. Section 3 presents detailed empirical findings for the Brazilian economy and relates the Brazilian experience to conceptual insights. General and Brazil-specific policy implications are developed in section 4. Finally, section 5 summarizes the main results of the study and concludes.

II. Conceptual and Empirical Motivation[2]

There are different definitions of informality in the development economics literature[3] which rely on a variety of criteria such as establishment size, type of employment, technological or capital level, income level, legal status, type of goods produced, and type of

[1] See Maloney (1998b) for a comprehensive presentation of the arguments.
[2] The empirical results and the conceptual framework presented in this section are drawn from Fiess et al. (2001).
[3] See Peattie (1987), Turnham and Eröcal (1990), James (1992), Tokman (1992), Portes and Schauffler (1993) for comprehensive overviews.

transactions that are carried out.[4] The last criterion refers to the fact that activities being encompassed in the informal sector are unregulated. As discussed by Charmes (1990), some of these criteria overlap in practice.[5] The formal sector is then characterized by large firms producing essentially traded goods and complying with fiscal and labor legislations. Workers classified as belonging to the formal sector are those who benefit from labor unions influence in the wage formation process and labor protection.

Just as there are more than one criteria for an empirical delineation of the formal from the informal sector, there are different interpretations of why informality arises in the first place. These can be classified into two categories. The traditional "dualistic" view sees the informal sector as the residual of a highly distorted labor market in the formal sector. Unions and/or government regulation push wages above their equilibrium level, rationing workers into the informal sector where they are not protected by labor legislation. Participation in the non-regulated section of the economy is non-voluntary, the regulated section always offering a better alternative. Thus, distorting labor market regulations are the cause for a formal-informal segmentation of the labor market. As part of this segmentation, relative wages and relative employment shares of the formal and informal sector move in opposite directions.

A more recent line of thought presents the view that as a first approximation, the informal sector could be treated as an unregulated/unprotected entrepreneurial sector that offers work and working conditions that are desirable to many workers. In other words, the choice to participate in the informal sector is a rational and unforced one. This view also implies that there is voluntary movement of workers both to and from the formal sector. This rationality could be related to elements like the desire of independence and/or the misalignment of implicit and explicit labor taxes with perceived benefits. This "integrated labor markets" view stands in sharp contrast with the dualistic view.

This chapter argues that the two views are not necessarily incompatible with each other and should instead be seen as special cases of the same model. The informal sector may very well be a dynamic and entrepreneurial sector, but one which also contains unfortunate workers holding poor the degree of segmentation in the labor market which can vary depending on the shocks to the economy. And depending upon the general health of the economy, one of these phenomena may dominate the other. The main technical characteristics of the model are presented in Box 7.1 and Box 7.2.

Our conceptual approach offers a rich framework for policy analysis as it can nest both the dualistic and integrated views in a non-trivial way. Wage differentials across sectors are not due to rigidities exclusively and the removal of such rigidities would not lead to wage equalization even in a context of perfect mobility of factors of production. These features reflect a more realistic view of the economy and enrich the discussion of possible policy implications.

---

[4] We usually distinguish three major sectors in the labor market in developing countries: the rural sector, the informal sector and the formal sector. In this chapter we concentrate on urban areas where only the last two sectors are present.

[5] In this study, the informal sector is characterized by self-employed individuals or small privately owned enterprises (with no more than six workers) producing essentially services and non-traded goods and, not (fully) complying with government imposed taxes and regulations (mainly labor related). The reason why informal wage workers are excluded relies on the fact that the informal wage sector takes on the form of a transitory sector essentially populated by young people closely linked to self-employment activities (see Maloney, 1999). This is reinforced by our empirical investigation for Brazil which shows positive co-movements in relative earnings and labor force size of informal wage workers and self-employed.

To reiterate, the usefulness of our conceptual framework is twofold. First, it offers insights that can be used to qualify empirically a labor market:

- the market is segmented if earnings in the informal sector and the size of the latter, relative to their respective counter-part in the formal sector, move in opposite directions: relative earnings fall while participation in the informal sector increases;
- the pattern of relative earnings and participation inherent to segmentation can be observed only if there are effective downward wage rigidities in the formal sector (the labor legislation is binding);
- downward wage rigidities in the informal sector are of first order relevance in the event of a negative shock (technology and/or preferences) to the formal sector and of second order relevance in the event of a negative shock (technology and/or preferences) to the informal sector;
- any evidence of positive co-movements in relative earnings and participation allows to conclude in favor of an integrated labor market.

Second, accounting for the nature of the labor market (segmented versus integrated), and observing movements of macroeconomic indicators like the real exchange rate, enables the identification of the underlying macroeconomic environment. Put another way, our framework allows us to determine the likely impact of policy shocks, i.e., changes in the macroeconomic environment, on employment and earnings according to the nature of the labor market. We delve deeper into the analysis in the next section.

Box 7.1. Conceptual Framework

- The Core Model

- Open economy model based on Obstfeld and Rogoff (1996) and Lucas (1978):
- Agents in the economy:

- households: consume goods available in the economy, hold foreign traded bonds
- producers: firms of indeterminate size and self-employed

- Sectors of production:

- Formal sector: production of traded goods, wage work, compliance with regulations
- Informal sector: production of non-traded goods, self-employment, non compliance regulations, non perfect access to physical capital

- Characteristcs of production factors:

- Capital:

- mobile both internationally and across sectors
- not instantaneously: capital market is not perfect for informal producers (installation costs)

Box 7.1. Conceptual Framework - Continued

- Labor:
- constant total labor force
- workers are homogenous when salaried in the formal sector *but* differ in terms of their entrepreneurial capability when self-employed
- mobile across sectors
- not instantaneously because of capital market imperfections

Properties of the framework:

- interactions between macroeconomic variables and the labor market
- steady state analysis *and* transitional dynamics due to non instantaneous adjustment of both capital and labor

The Government

Government characteristics can be easily introduced in the core model and can include some or all of the following elements. The listing is obviously not exhaustive.

- Expenditures:

- Consumption of traded and/or non-traded goods
- Production of services that can be used as intermediate inputs
- Social security benefits and assistance
- Debt interests payments

- Revenues:

- Taxes: payroll, corporation and individuals income taxes, indirect taxes, tariffs (according to the above specification, none of these taxes are expected to be voluntary paid by individuals involved in informal activities)
- Other sources of revenues can consist of domestic and foreign credit and transfers from the central bank including seignorage and/or interest receipts on net foreign assets

The Labor Market

- Segmentation implies that the formal section of the labor market is characterized by downward rigidities in wages which can be related to the presence of unions and/or indexation practices and/or legal minimum wages.

Box 7.2. Fundamental Equilibrium Relations in the Core Model

We present steady state responses of the variables of interest to the various shocks that can possibly occur in our framework. The following equations are used to formulate Table 7.1. The relative price of non-traded goods in terms of traded goods is denoted by p that is, $p = \frac{P_N}{\varepsilon}$, where P_N denotes the price of non traded goods and ε the price of traded goods (the nominal exchange rate). In other words p stands for the inverse of the real exchange rate. Then, a real appreciation would correspond to a rise in p.

A T subscript refers to the traded goods sector and a N subscript to the non-traded goods sector. A L subscript refers to formal labor and a se subscript to self-employment. η refers to the share in the respective sector total earnings while φ refers to the share in total revenues. Then, φ_{LT} denotes the share of formal workers labor earnings in total revenue. Nse is the self-employed labor force, θ is the intra-temporal elasticity of substitution and γ is the share of individuals' revenue spent on traded goods. A stands for a technology shock. Average earnings are denoted by w. ε denotes the nominal exchange rate and r the real interest rate. Finally, variables with hats refer to rates of change ($\hat{x} = \frac{\Delta x}{x}$).

$$\hat{p} = \frac{\eta_{LN}}{\eta_{LT}}\left(\hat{A}_T + \hat{\varepsilon}\right) - \hat{A}_N + \left(1 - \frac{\eta_{LN}}{\eta_{LT}}\right)\hat{r} \tag{1}$$

If only technological shocks are considered, we obtain the standard Balassa -Samuelson result (Balassa, 1964).

$$\hat{N}_{se} = \Omega_1\left[\hat{A}_N\left(1 - \gamma(1-\theta)\right) - \hat{\gamma} - \frac{\hat{A}_T + \hat{\varepsilon} + \left(1 - \frac{\eta_{LT}}{\eta_{LN}}\right)\hat{r}}{\eta_{LT}}\left[1 - \varphi_{LT} - \varphi_{se} - (1-\alpha_N)(\gamma(1-\theta)\right.\right. \tag{2}$$

$$\hat{w}_T = \frac{1}{\eta_{LT}}\left[\hat{A}_T - (1 - \eta_{LT})\hat{r}\right] \tag{3}$$

$$\hat{w}_N = \frac{\hat{A}_T + \hat{\varepsilon}}{\eta_{LT}} + \left(\eta_{LT} - \frac{1}{\eta_{LN}}\right)\hat{r} + \left(\Psi - \frac{N^*_{se}}{1 - N^*_{se}}\right)\hat{N}_{se} \tag{4}$$

where $\Omega_1 = \left[(1 - \varphi_{se})\Psi + \varphi_{LT}\right]^{-1}$, $\Psi = \frac{2-\alpha_N}{1-\alpha_N}\left[\frac{\left(N^*_{se}\right)^{\frac{2-\alpha_N}{1-\alpha_N}}}{1 - \left(N^*_{se}\right)^{\frac{2-\alpha_N}{1-\alpha_N}}}\right]$ and N*se represents the initial steady state level self-employment.

III. The Empirical Evidence

In what follows we use modern econometric time series techniques[6] on quarterly data for the cases of Mexico, Brazil and Colombia to explore the nature of the long run relationship among relative earnings, relative sector size and the real exchange rate with the aim of establishing the degree of dualism in their labor markets. This exercise can give us a preliminary answer to the question of whether and to what degree are the labor markets in these three countries "flexible" in the broadest terms, viz., whether key earnings and employment indicators respond to macroeconomic shocks in a manner that is consistent with efficient functioning of markets. The empirical analysis is also used to extract some conclusions about the source of real appreciations in the three countries. These results are explored in more detail in the next section.

Figure 7.1 displays the time series of the three variables under consideration for the three countries respectively. The estimated results are presented in the appendix. In what follows, we limit ourselves to a qualitative presentation of the results and refer the reader to Fiess et al. (2001) for technical details. The period under consideration runs from 1985:Q1 to 1999:Q2 for Colombia, from 1987:Q1 to 1999:Q1 for Mexico and from 1992:Q1 to 2000:Q4 for Brazil. By looking first at the whole sample, we find that for Mexico the test of integrated markets can be strongly rejected while the test of segmentation cannot be rejected. For Brazil, the hypothesis of integration cannot be rejected and the hypothesis of segmentation is rejected at the 1% level. For Colombia, the hypothesis of segmentation cannot be rejected while the hypothesis of integration can be.

In all three cases, however, tests of the stability of the cointegration space suggest the possibility of different relationships in different sub-periods. This finding is consistent with the previous argument that rigidities in the formal sector may be binding in some periods and not in others, depending on the macroeconomic environment.

- For Mexico, the segmentation hypothesis is only accepted from 1995 onwards and the hypothesis of integration cannot be rejected prior to 1995. This suggests that the Mexican labor market behaves pretty much like a flexible market in the recovery period leading up to 1995.
- For Colombia, statistical tests support the hypothesis of a segmented labor market post 1995 onwards and never support the view of integration for any sub-sample. These findings are in accordance with the view that regulations in the Colombian labor market are binding strongly and that the dualistic view reflects relatively well its functioning.
- In Brazil, despite full sample evidence of integration, there is evidence of segmentation during the pre-Real plan period and in the post Asian crisis period (see Figure 7.2). These findings indicate that the labor market nature in Brazil is likely to have changed over the decade.

---

[6] The methodology involves the estimation of long run cointegration vectors using the multivariate approach proposed by Johansen (1988).

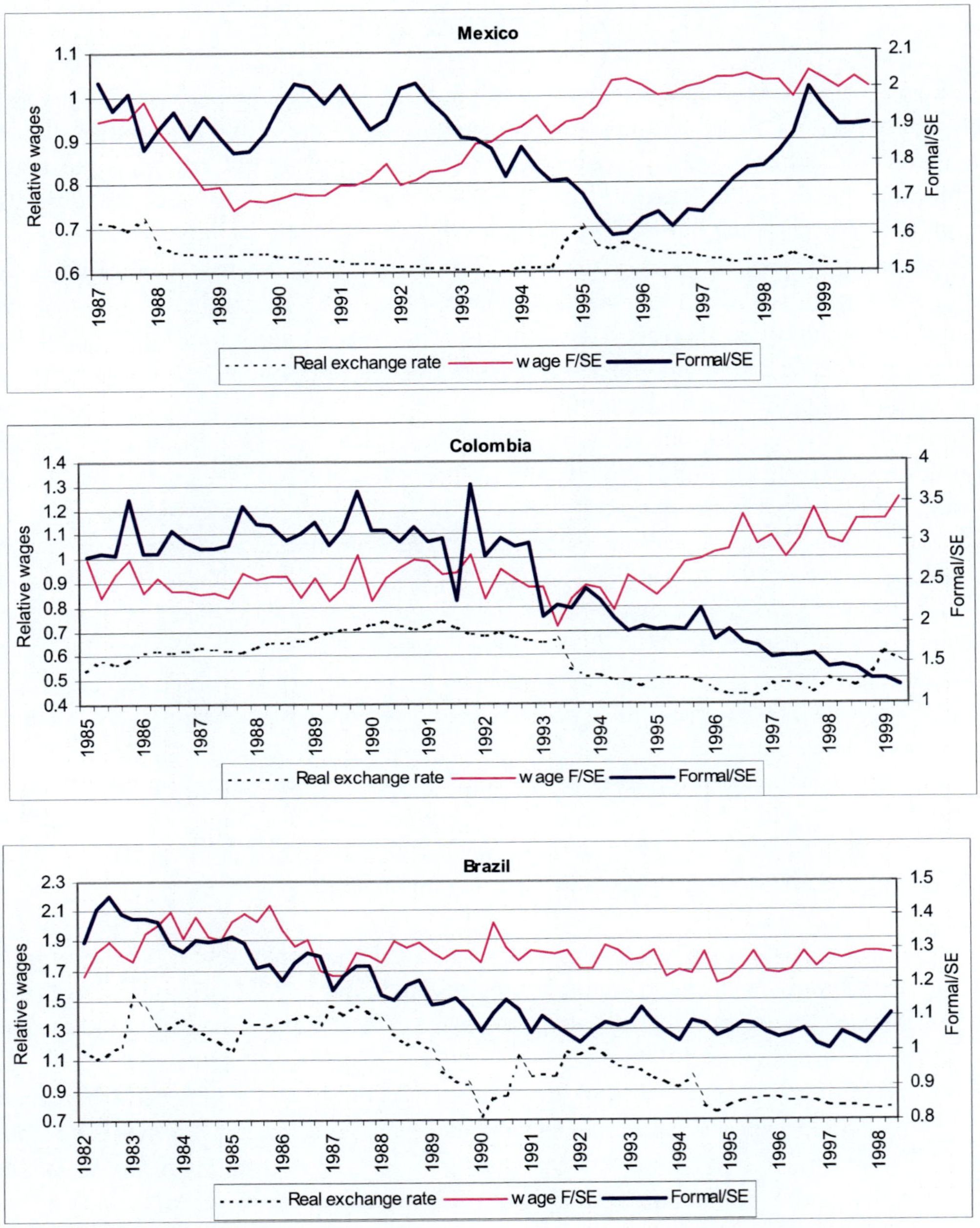

Source: Fiess, Fugazza and Maloney (2001)

Figure 7.1. Real Effective Exchange Rate, Relative Wage and Share of Informal Workers

IV. THE BRAZILIAN CASE

Brazil represents an interesting case as periods of evidence in favor of segmentation and periods of evidence in favor of integration alternate. Accordingly, in what follows we focus on the case of Brazil. While the cointegration approach in the last section allowed the identification of segmentation and integration based on negative and positive co-movements of relative wages and sector sizes, in this section we make use of a different technique to identify segmented and integrated labor market episodes based on the sensitivity of employment and real wages with respect to output based on Okun coefficients. As we would expect, quantities adjust more than prices in a segmented market and the reverse holds in an integrated market.

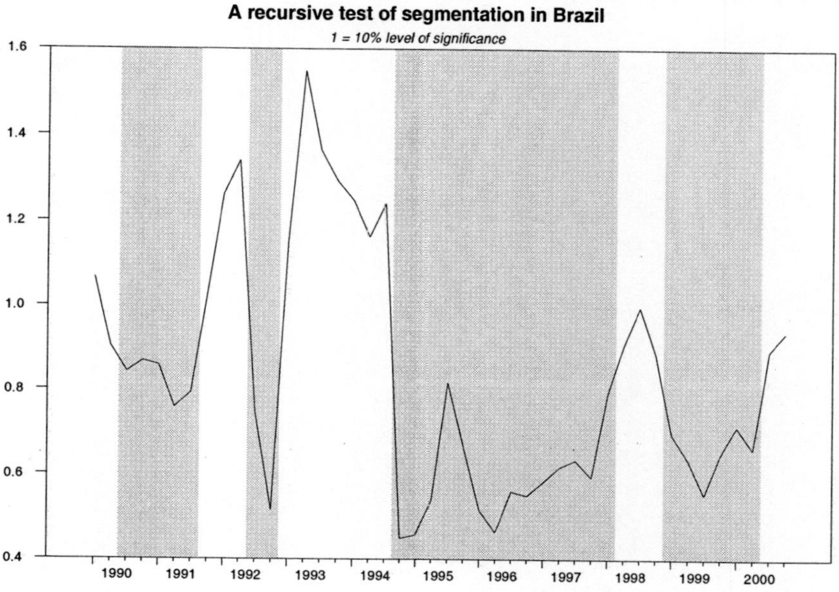

Note: Figure 7.2 shows a recursive test of the hypothesis of segmentation in the Brazilian labor market. The hypothesis of segmentation cannot be rejected for test statistics below 1 and the shaded areas are thus indicative for segmentation. Starting with an original sample from 1982:01 to 1989:04, the estimation period is increased by one observation at a time and the corresponding test statistic is calculated. It is important to realize that the periods where the hypothesis is rejected do not indicate exact break points. Much rather, they reveal what a researcher would find if she had only access to data stretching from 1982:01 to the specific point in time where the test statistic is calculated.

Figure 7.2. Some Evidence for Segmentation in Brazil

To investigate the sensitivity of real wages and employment with respect to output we estimate rolling Okun coefficients for total employment and real wages for 1982 to 2001.[7] The advantage of a rolling regression approach is that as the estimation procedure moves through the sample, new observations are picked up and changes in the Okun coefficients can be attributed to changed circumstances in the latest incorporated period. The resulting period-specific wage and employment Okun coefficients are graphed in Figure 7.3.

[7] As Okun's law was developed for total employment and overall GDP, we do not distinguish between the formal and informal sector.

As already mentioned, we expect quantities to adjust more to macroeconomic shocks than prices in a segmented market. This appears to be the case for the years 1991 and 1992. Even though wage reaction is not monotonic, it roughly remains less pronounced than employment reaction during these two years. The Collor Plan failed to rein in inflation and the economy was on a recessive path with increasing fears of the effects of a rapid and incisive opening of the economy. The return of hyperinflation without perfect indexation of workers' wages allowed firms to adjust through prices rather than quantities in 1993 and in the first half of 1994. In that period the labor market behaved in an integrated manner, and the economy recovered from a period of negative growth.

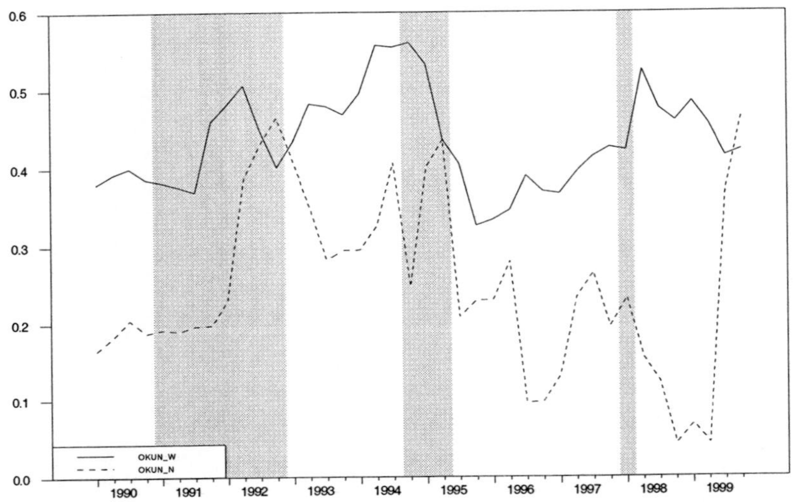

Note: Shaded areas indicate segmentation, i.e. situations where employment Okun coefficients react stronger than wage Okun coefficients.

Figure 7.3. Wage and Employment Okun Coefficients: 1989Q1 to 1999Q4

In July 1994, as the Real Plan was implemented, inflation fell sharply and indexation practices were stopped. As a consequence firms were less able to erode real wages and adjustment occurred increasingly through quantities. This corresponds to the second shaded area in Figure 7.3. In the last quarter of 1994 and the first quarter of 1995, the labor market behaved in a segmented manner until the economy adapted to the low-inflation environment, reverting then to an integrated market. With the Asian crisis, once again, adjustment through quantities picked up while wage reactions were more muted. This corresponds to the third shaded area covering the last quarter of 1997 and beginning of 1998. The labor market again behaved more like an integrated market in the rest of 1998. Generally speaking, therefore, the Real Plan period was characterized by a roughly integrated labor market, with the exception of the period that follows the Asian crisis. However, since the devaluation in January 1999, the labor market has been showing an increased tendency to adjust more through quantities than prices, a phenomenon that corresponds to increased segmentation.

A Conceptual and Factual Assessment

We concentrate on three variables, namely the informal workers' earnings relative to formal workers' wage, the size of the informal sector relative to that of the formal sector and the real exchange rate (price of non-traded goods over price of traded goods). The behavior of these three variables in the 1990s are reported in Figure 7.4.

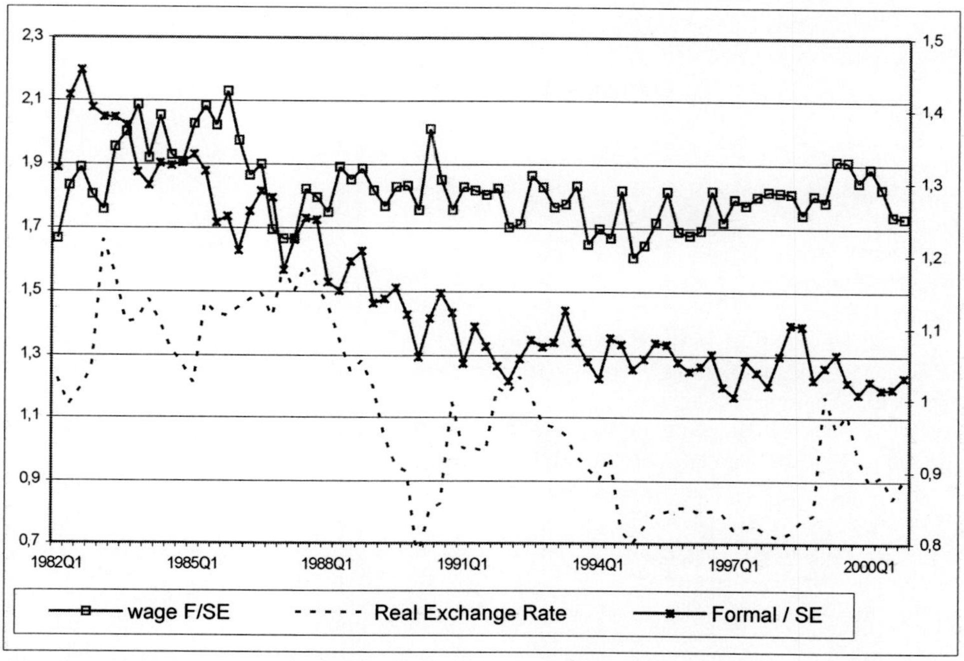

Note: Real Exchange Rate and wage F/SE are scaled to left-hand axis.

Figure 7.4. Real Effective Exchange Rate, Relative Wage and Share of Informality in Brazil

It might be argued that the real interest rate should not be treated as an exogenous variable as it is the case in our framework. Nevertheless, as far as Brazil is concerned, we have found that the real interest rate does not form part of the cointegration relationship and can thus be treated as an exogenous variable[8].

Our conceptual framework offers a wide spectrum of causes of real exchange rate movements which correspond to a specific macroeconomic environment and labor market behavior. We have:

- a real depreciation (non-traded goods become less expensive relative to traded goods) with evidence of segmentation could be the outcome of either a negative shock to the traded-goods sector, or a shift in preferences towards traded-goods, or a rise in the real interest rate
- a real appreciation with evidence of segmentation could only be the outcome of a negative shock to the non-traded goods sector

[8] Indeed, a joint test of long-run exclusion and weak-exogeneity of the real interest rate could not be rejected (LR-test: $\chi^2(2)$=2.91, p-value=0.23).

- a real depreciation with evidence of integration could be the outcome either of a positive shock to the non-traded goods sector, or of a negative shock to the traded goods sector, or a shift in preferences towards traded-goods, or of a rise in the real interest rate
- a real appreciation with evidence of integration could be the outcome of either a positive shock to the traded-goods sector, or a negative shock to the non-traded goods sector, or a shift in preferences towards non-traded goods or a fall in the real interest rate

Box 7.3. Empirical Estimation of Okun Coefficients

Okun coefficients reflect the sensitivity of real wages and employment to changes in output. We follow Gonzalez Anaya (1999) and estimate "rolling" Okun coefficients for 1982 to 2001. Rolling coefficients implies that these magnitudes are estimated for consecutive sub-periods. The advantage of a rolling regression approach is that as the estimation procedure moves through the sample, new observations are picked up and a change in the Okun coefficient can be attributed to an innovation in the latest period.

We make use of the Okun (1962) initial method which relates first differences of unemployment and output. Although Okun's initial approach has given way to more sophisticated methods, it still represents a simple and efficient tool.

We use quarterly data for real wage, total employment and seasonally adjusted GDP. The wage data is from PME and the output data from IBGE.

Since we deal with quarterly data, we introduce a lag structure to reflect the fact that a change in output might not fully adjust within one period and also to control for serial correlation. We find that real wages adjust in the same period to changes in output, while lagged changes in output up to the third lag impact contemporaneous changes in employment. This findings is not surprising as prices tend to react faster than quantities. The estimated equations are:

$$\Delta w_t = \alpha_w + \beta_w \Delta Y_t + \delta_w \Delta w_{t-1} + \varepsilon_{wt}$$

$$\Delta N_t = \alpha_N + \beta_N \Delta Y_t + \sum_{i=1}^{3} \eta_{iN} \Delta Y_{t-i} + \delta_N \Delta N_{t-1} + \varepsilon_{Nt}$$

where ΔN_t, Δw_t and ΔY_t are changes in total employment, real wages and output respectively.

The respective wage and employment Okun coefficients are calculated as follows:

$$Okun_w = \frac{\beta_{Nt}}{1-\delta_w} \quad \text{and} \quad Okun_N = \frac{\beta_{Nt} + \sum_{i=1}^{3} \eta_{iN}}{1-\delta_N}$$

Given the period-sensitivity of the computation of Okun coefficients we estimate 9-year rolling regressions (36 observations per regression). Operationally, the Okun coefficient for t is the result of a regression based on the last 36 quarters, i.e. the Okun coefficent for 1999Q1 is the results from a regression based on 1990Q1 to 1999Q1.

Data Based on Augmented Dickey Fuller tests we find real wages, output and employment are nonstationary (I(1)) in levels and stationary in first differences . Recursive cointegration tests (see appendix) indicate no evidence of cointegration between the labor market variables and output, thus eliminating the need to introduce an error correction mechanism.

These results are summarized in Table 7.1. Box 7.4 presents heuristically the effects of macroeconomic policies by referring the latter to the shocks considered previously.

Table 7.1. Sources of Real Exchange Rate Variations and Labor Market Behavior

	Real Appreciation		Real Depreciation	
	Segmentation	Integration	Segmentation	Integration
$\hat{A}_T, \hat{\varepsilon}$	_	>0	<0	<0
$\hat{A}_N$	<0	<0	_	>0
$\hat{\gamma}$	_	<0	>0	>0
$\hat{r}$	_	<0	>0	>0

The period between 1990-93, also known as the Collor period, is characterized by evidence of a segmented labor market. We also have that the price of non-traded relative to traded goods is falling dramatically. The real interest rate remains at very high levels. All these elements seem to indicate that through this period the formal sector was undergoing a negative shock or at least was behaving as if. The fact that the economy was opening progressively and in a credible manner makes this explanation quite plausible. The end of the Collor period brought back some positive growth prospects and the labor market appeared to be less segmented.

At the same time the real exchange rate path was reverted. As real interests rates remained very high, essentially because of the return of hyper-inflation, a possible explanation of the phenomenon could be a shift in preferences towards the non-traded goods sector.

The Real Plan implemented in 1998 has been a path-breaking economic event. After a relatively short period of adjustment, characterized by segmentation in the labor market due to a substantial rise in labor costs brought about by a fall in inflation which led to depreciation, we observe a sharp increase in the relative price of non-traded goods essentially driven by a surge in consumption. The latter was due to the fall in the cost of holding money, the relaxation of liquidity constraints and increased access to credit brought about by financial liberalization. There is no clear evidence of any positive shock to the traded goods sector. On the contrary, productivity improvements appear to have been the consequence of lower worker participation in that sector. The expansion of the informal sector together perhaps with a possible positive shock could have explained the fall, even though not a dramatic one, of the relative price of non-traded goods in the period leading up to the Asian crisis, the Russian crisis and the subsequent recessionary period that includes the devaluation of January 1999. Again labor regulations appear to have been binding beginning in late 1997. Even though the economy as a whole has been hit by these external shocks, the formal sector which was more exposed to foreign investments may have suffered the most.

The year of 1998 is characterized by negative growth rates, a falling relative price of non-traded goods in terms of traded goods, falling self-employed earnings relative to formal wages and an increasing participation in the informal sector. These elements corroborate evidence of a predominant negative shock to the formal sector which has led to a higher degree of segmentation in the labor market. The first signs of overall economic recovery are perceived in late 1998 and are strengthened by the devaluation that occurred at the beginning of 1999. There is some evidence of an industry-led recovery which explains the reverted tendency in the real exchange rate. We may also interpret the real appreciation as the outcome of a negative shock to the non-traded goods sector as there is still some evidence of a segmented labor market to date. The contribution to gross domestic product of the industrial sector has risen from 34.6 % in 1998 to 35.5 % in 1999 while that of the services sector has fallen from 62.3 % in 1998 to 61.1 in 1999. These tendencies were maintained in 2000. GDP growth has jumped to more than 4% and the relative size of the formal sector has increased in terms of the size of the informal sector. The degree of segmentation has fallen since 1999 and there is some evidence of the return of job creating growth after a mitigated decade.

Box 7.4. The Impact of Macroeconomic Policies in the Core Framework

Trade Liberalization

Production. If the traded goods sector is competing directly with imports then liberalizing trade corresponds to a negative shock to the formal sector in the short (medium) run. However, the sign of the shock is expected to be reverted in the longer run because of imported technological improvements. Input costs are also expected to fall a fortiori if trade liberalization is accompanied by financial liberalization and/or deepening. Then the cost of borrowing physical capital is expected to fall and borrowing constraints to be eased, possibly also in the informal sector.

Consumption. Consumption is expected to boom because of the fall in the price of traded goods. The inherent positive income effect also leads to a rise in the level of consumption of non-traded goods.

Government. If trade liberalization implies a conspicuous fall in government revenues because of lower tariffs proceedings, then other tax rates may have to be increased and/or expenditures reduced. Any rise in taxation could generate a bias towards informality. In general, if the government adjusts immediately for revenue losses, then the negative impact on formal production is likely to be more pronounced. If the government adjusts its expenditure level by reducing its consumption of non-traded goods then this would have the effect of a negative shock to the informal sector. The overall income effect is discussed in more detail in the fiscal adjustment section.

Exchange-Rate-Based Disinflation

Production. Exchange-rate-based disinflation has the effect of a negative shock to the traded-goods sector as it corresponds to a fall in the price of the traded good.

Consumption. A fall in the inflation rate leads to two contrasting effects. First, lower prices imply a higher consumption based real interest rate, which tends to lower the current level of consumption. Second, lower price levels reduce the opportunity cost of holding money (or equivalently it generates a positive real balances wealth effect), which tends to increase the current level of consumption. Then, the predominant effect has to be determined empirically.

Government. Lower inflation implies lower revenues from seignorage. Then, government may be willing to reduce expenses and/or increase tax rates to avoid fiscal crisis like in the case of trade liberalization.

Fiscal Adjustment

Both, a trade liberalization and an exchange-rate-based disinflation program are expected to be coupled with fiscal adjustment to offset losses in government revenues. Fiscal adjustment could consist either in an increase in taxation or a reduction in expenditures or both.

Higher taxation, besides having a negative impact on formal production, makes the informal sector more attractive as the latter is characterized by tax evasion. This is specially true if formal production (firms and/or workers earnings) is the target of higher tax rates. This would also be true, although to a lower extent, if indirect taxes are raised.

As to a reduction in the level of expenditures, its impact depends essentially on the consequent changes in expenditure composition. If reduction in consumption of non-traded goods is the main target then the informal sector is directly affected and this could increase the degree of segmentation in the labor market.

The purpose of fiscal adjustment can also be the reduction of government debt per se. In that case interest rates could be expected to fall consequently.

The 1990s have been characterized by a growing informal sector. This trend has not exclusively been the result of an increasing degree of segmentation in the labor market. Rather it has been the result of the conjunction of a series of economic events that hit negatively and predominantly the formal sector and of always threateningly binding labor legislation. In addition, a general shift of preferences in favor of non-traded goods also has contributed to this pattern in the composition of the economic activity.

Policy Implications

Empirical evidence presented in previous sections supports the view that neither a purely "dualistic" nor a purely "non-dualistic" approach can be applied to labor markets in less developed economies without referring to any further qualification. We argue that an approach able to encompass both views is rather desirable, specially in terms of policy implications. We argued previously that in the presence of a labor market that behaves like an integrated labor market, then, reforming labor regulations should not be the core of policy orientation as there is no evidence that the latter are either strongly binding and/or distorting. Rather, efficiency improvements should be eased in both formal and informal sectors. On the contrary, if there is evidence of segmentation in the labor market, then reforming the labor regulation is likely to generate efficiency and eventually equity gains. In the case of a labor market that behaves both like a segmented and an integrated market, then policy orientation should be defined according to both sets of characteristics. A rise in the degree of segmentation at some points in time underlines the necessity to reform labor market legislation in order to dampen the effects of activity downturns. Nevertheless, evidence of integration in other periods is the signal of a potentially efficient labor market and, policies aiming at reducing operational costs and at improving economic growth potential in all sectors of the economy are likely to be efficiency and equity enhancing. Again, labor-related policy orientations could not be disentangled from other macroeconomic objectives as the two are expected to interact.

Less Segmentation Versus More Integration

A higher degree of segmentation is the outcome of a negative shock to the economy in the presence of downward wage rigidities in the formal sector. Sources of downward rigidities include wage inertia due to indexation mechanisms (backward-looking contracts)[9], unions and government imposed wage floors. Then, we would expect the removal of these downward rigidities to generate strong efficiency gains as worker flows would be driven essentially by earnings differentials considerations.

It could be argued that the implementation of macroeconomic reforms can take advantage of a dramatic economic environment[10]. However, as far as labor institution reforms are concerned, the validity of this argument can be questioned. Recently, various authors presented the view that labor institution reforms have proved difficult to implement essentially because of political opposition[11]. Lora and Pagés (1996) argue that this is effectively the case in most of Latin American countries. Political opposition is mounted by formally employed workers as they constitute the labor cohort who benefit directly from labor market institutions. Indeed, the latter generate rents that take the form of high relative wages and high relative employment security. Moreover, in contrast to informal and unemployed workers, formal workers are usually strongly represented in the political decisional process despite the fact that they do not represent the largest cohort in the labor force. As a consequence, the interest of workers with formal work contracts would prevail, even though the inherent economic outcome proves to be suboptimal and often unfair.

The previous sections suggest that in a market that behaves like an integrated market, the informal sector and specially the self-employed, are likely to present the features of a dynamic and potentially highly productive sector. In this context, the main challenge for policy makers is to make the informal sector to act like the formal sector with respect to compliance with social security contributions and taxation. Indeed, when there is evidence of labor market integration, tax and social security contribution evasion should be a major concern for policy makers.

In the same way that rigidities in the formal sector represent rents to formal workers, tax evasion can be seen as a rent seeking activity for informal individuals that is detrimental for the economy. However, it is important to stress that tax evasion and non compliance with regulations are only a characteristic of the informal sector, not its very and only nature. Then, it could be counter-effective and harmful to impose on the informal sector compliance with taxes and regulations as long as other possible production impediments are not removed from that sector. Indeed, despite signals of a quasi well-functioning of the labor market, inefficiencies may still prevail in the informal sector. These inefficiencies result from the existence of costs not related to the very process of production. As such labor regulations for formal firms, weak judicial protection and high cost of capital can represent a bulk of "excessive" costs of production for informal producers[12].

Weak judicial protection, as well as weak political representation, are essentially due to the fact that activities in the informal sector are not fully legal. Therefore, producers can not exercise full property rights over their capital and product and contracts can not be enforced

[9] See Crowley (1997) for an extensive analysis.
[10] See Rodrik (1996) for a general discussion of the argument.
[11] See, for instance, Saint-Paul (2000) for a comprehensive theoretical analysis and further references.
[12] De Soto (1989) presents evidence of the phenomena for Peru.

through the judicial system. This translates into abnormally higher transaction and monitoring costs for the informal sector compared to the formal sector.

Capital accumulation is also severely affected by non fully enforceable contracts. Indeed, effective borrowing rates paid by informal producers are higher than those paid by their formal counterpart. A promotion of the efficiency of productive activities in the formal sector would contribute to lowering the cost of compliance with taxation and regulations to informal workers. This cost would be further reduced through a social security reform that strives to align the costs with the benefits of contributors.

In the light of the above discussion, we argue that pursuing in the first place higher integration rather than lower segmentation, leads eventually to lower segmentation. Higher labor market integration implies better production conditions and a higher ability to take advantage of government-provided services in the informal sector. Subsequently the informal sector becomes increasingly attractive to all workers, implying that opposition to labor institution reforms could be weakened because of lower rents attached to formal activity. Moreover, the political weight of informal workers can be expected to increase, which could further contrast formal workers opposition. This tendency would be made even stronger by social security reforms that would ensure compliance of the full labor force.

In a country like Brazil, where segmentation and integration periods alternate, working for higher integration of the labor market is likely to produce almost immediate results. In generic terms, the medium-to-long run policy objective is to fully align interests of participants in the formal sector with the interests of the participants in the informal sector, that is, to make sector-participation arbitrage rely exclusively on the skills and intrinsic ability of the individual. The policy intervention orientation in the short-to-medium-run depends on the one hand on the behavior of the labor market and on the other hand on decision-making efficiency of the political process.

Table 7.2. Policy Priorities During Alternative Macroeconomic Scenarios

	Trade Liberalization	Disinflation	Fiscal Adjustment
Pro-Integration	Lower cost of borrowing physical capital Strengthening property rights	Lower cost of borrowing physical capital Strengthening property rights	Social security reform
Anti-Segmentation	Training schemes Lower cost of borrowing physical capital Temporary and conditional subsidies	Collective bargaining reform Lower cost of borrowing physical capital Temporary and conditional subsidies	Severance payments reform Payroll tax reform

V. CONCLUSIONS

Since nearly 60 percent of the workforce in developing countries are employed in the informal sector, any analysis of labor markets in developing countries cannot ignore the importance of the labor market composition, i.e. the relative size of the formal and informal sectors. In this chapter, it has been argued that the labor market composition is not determined only by the existence of labor market rigidities per se, but that is also a function of the macroeconomic environment, which determines if labor market rigidities become binding or not. We have shown that labor market composition and macroeconomic environment are intimately linked and need to be analyzed jointly, as:

- the macroeconomic environment itself can affect the degree of segmentation in the labor market and consequently the impact of policy interventions;
- the expected outcome of macroeconomic policies such as stabilization and adjustment policies varies whether the labor market behaves like an integrated or a segmented market.

We have empirically tested the hypotheses of segmentation and integration using recursive cointegration techniques and rolling Okun coefficients. Within the first approach, evidence of integration or segmentation is nested within the hypothesis of a positive or negative co-movement of relative formal/informal real wages and participation rates. Regarding the latter approach, the hypothesis of segmentation is accepted if quantities react stronger than prices to changes in output, i.e. employment Okun coefficient are more sensitive than wage Okun coefficients.

Both approaches identify alternating periods of labor market integration and segmentation during the 1990. As the 1990 decade in Brazil has been characterized by a growing informal sector, this trend is not the exclusive result of an increasing degree of segmentation in the labor market. Rather, it appears to be the result of the conjunction of a series of economic events and of always threateningly binding labor legislation. In addition, a general shift of preferences in favor of the non-traded goods also contribute to the pattern of the economic activity composition.

In terms of policy implications, the following major points can be underlined:

- When a labor market behaves like an integrated market at some points in time, then trying to increase integration rather that to decrease segmentation proves to be a better policy orientation.
- In a political economy context, increasing integration may lead to lower segmentation.
- Higher integration contributes to ease compliance with social security contributions and taxation among informal individuals.
- Full integration cannot be observed as long as pure taxes features prevail in the economy.

REFERENCES

Aroca, P and W. F. Maloney (1999), *"Logit Analysis in a Rotating Panel Context and an Application to Self-Employment Decisions,"* IBRD Working Paper 2069. Latin America and Carribean Region, Poverty Reduction and Economic Management Unit, World Bank, Washington D.C. Processed.

Carneiro, F.G. and A. Henley (2002), *"Earnings and Choice of Formal versus Informal Employment in a Developing Economy Labour Market: Evidence for Brazil"*, University of Wales at Aberystwyth Working Paper, UK.

Crowley J., (1997), *"The Effects of Forward- Versus Backward-Looking Wage Indexation on Price Stabilization Programs"*, IMF WP/97/38.

Davila Capalleja, E., (1994), "Regulaciones Laborales y Mercado de Trabajo en Mexico", in Gustavo marquez ed., *Regulacion del Mercado de Trabajo en America Latina*, Centro Internacional para el Desarollo Economico, San Francisco.

De Soto H., (1989), *The Other Path*, Harper and Row, New York.

Fields, G. S., (1990), "Labor Market Modelling and the Urban Informal Sector: Theory and Evidence", in Turnham D., B. Salomé and A. Schwartz (eds.), *The Informal Sector Revisited*, OECD , Paris.

Fiess N., M. Fugazza and W. Maloney, (2001), *"Exchange Rate Appreciations, Labor Market Rigidities, and Informality"*, World Bank forthcoming WP.

Harris J. and M. P. Todaro, "Migration, Unemployment and Development: A Two-Sector Analysis", *American Economic Review*, 60, pp 126-43.

Horton S., R. Kanbur and D. Mazumdar, 1994, *Labor Markets in an Era of Adjustment*, The World Bank, Washington D.C.

Johansen, Soren, (1988), "Statistical Analysis of Cointegrating Vectors", *Journal of Economic Dynamics and Control*, 12:231-54 June-September 1988.

Lora, E. and C. Pagés, (1996), "La legislacion Laboral en el Proceso de Reformas Estructurales de America Latina e el Caribe", unpublished manuscript.

Loayaza N., (1996), "The Economics of the Informal Sector: A Simple Model and some Empirical Evidence from Latin America", *Carnergie-Rochester Conference Series on Public Policy*, 45, pp.

Maloney, W.F. (1998a), *"The Structure of Labor Markets in Developing Countries: Time Series Evidence on Competing Views,"* IBRD Working Paper 1940, Latin America and the Caribbean Region, Poverty Reduction and Economic Management Unit, World Bank, Washington, D.C. Processed.

___(1998b), *"Are Labor Markets in Developing Countries Dualistic ? "*, World Bank Policy Research WP 1941.

___ (1999), *"Self-Employment and Labor Turnover: Cross-Country Evidence. The Structure of Labor Markets in Developing Countries: Time Series Evidence on Competing Views,"* IBRD Working Paper 2102, Latin America and the Caribbean Region, Poverty Reduction and Economic Management Unit, World Bank, Washington, D.C. Processed.

Marquez, G., (1997), "Proteccion al Empleo y Funcionamiento del Mercado de Trabajo: una aproximacion comparativa", in Empleo, Flexibilidad Laboral y Proteccion Social, *Proccedings of the Second Technical Meeting*, Circulo de Montevideo, UNDP.

Olson, M. (1982), *The Rise and Decline of Nations. Economic Growth, Stagflation and Social Rigidities*. New Haven/London: Yale University Press.

Rodrik, D., (1996), "Understanding Economic Policy Reform", *Journal of Economic Literature, Vol 36.1*, pp 9-41.

Peattie, L., (1987), "An Idea in Good Currency and How It Grew: The Informal sector", *World Development*, 15, pp 851-860.

Portes R. and R. Schauffler (1993), "Competing Perspective on the Latin American Informal Sector", *Population and Development Review*, 19, 33-59.

Saint-Paul G., (2000), *The political economy of labour market institutions*", Oxford U. Press.

Thomas, J.J., (1992), Informal Economic Activity, *LES Hanbooks in Economics*, London.

Tokman, V.E, (1992), *Beyond Regulation, The Informal Economy in Latin America*, Lynne Rienner, Boulder.

Vijverberg, W. P. M., (1986), "Consistent Estimates of the Wage Equation when Individuals Choose among Income-Earnings Activities", *Southern Economic Journal*, 52, pp 1028-42.

Yamada, G., (1996), *"Urban Informal Employment and Self-Employment in Developing Countries: Theory and Evidence"*.

APPENDIX 1: RECURSIVE COINTEGRATION TESTS

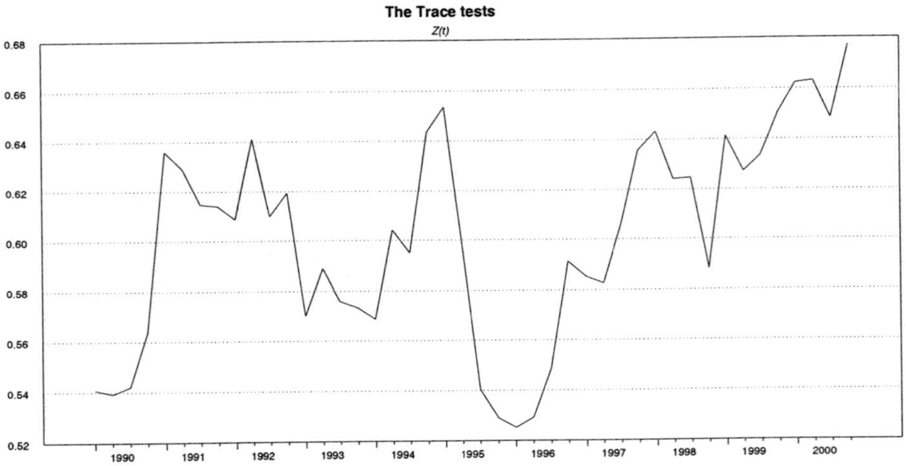

Figure 7.5. Recursive Cointegration Tests Between Real GDP and Employment

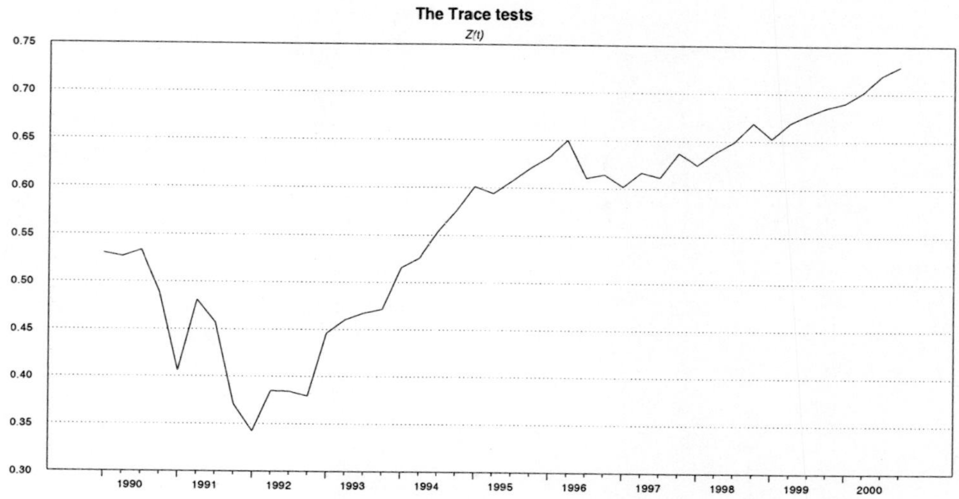

Figure 7.6. Recursive Cointegration Tests Between Real GDP and Real wages

APPENDIX 2: COINTEGRATION TESTS BETWEEN RELATIVE SIZE OF SELF-EMPLOYED TO INFORMAL, N_N/N_{IF}, AND RELATIVE WAGES OF SELF-EMPLOYED TO INFORMAL, W_N/W_{IF}

The VAR model is estimated over the sample from 1990Q1 to 2000Q1 and includes a constant in the cointegration space and 4 lags for W_N/W_{IF} and n_n/n_{if} and these specification proves sufficient to produce random errors. The λ_{trace} tests indicate one significant cointegrating vector in the model:

Null Hypothesis	Alternative Hypothesis	Lag: 4 With Constant	90%Critical Value
λ_{trace} test			
r = 0	r > 0	19.44*	17.79
r ≤ 1	r > 1	5.09	7.50

A hypothesis test of procyclical behaviour between the W_N/W_{IF} and n_n/n_{if} cannot be rejected. (The LR test, $\chi^2(1) = 0.35$, p-value = 0.55).

The resulting cointegrating vector, β, is:

	β
n_n/n_{if}	1.000
W_N/W_{IF}	-1.000
Constant	0.093

In: Economics, Politics and Social Issues in Latin America
Editor: Mary P. Lassiter, pp. 151-174
ISBN 1-60021-182-8

Chapter 8

THE POVERTY IMPLICATIONS OF MINIMUM WAGES IN DEVELOPING COUNTRIES

Wendy Cunningham
World Bank

I. INTRODUCTION

> Minimum wages do, of course, distort relative prices, and hence compromise economic efficiency, but so do all other attempts to redistribute income through tax-and-transfer systems. The important question is not whether minimum wages distort, but whether the benefits of any income redistribution they bring about are in some political sense sufficient to outweigh the efficiency costs. - Gramlich (1976)

A primary policy objective of minimum wage laws is to reduce poverty and inequality, but there is little empirical evidence that they meet this goal. Instead, much of the research examines the dis-employment and wage effects of an increase in the minimum wage and uses these results to draw conclusions about the poverty impacts. The imprecise nature of the exercise does not convincingly show that the minimum wage is meeting its intended objective, but the exercise also falls short, particularly in the context of developing countries, since it does not take into consideration coverage of minimum wage laws or resource pooling.

The poor often work in uncovered jobs so an understanding of the coverage of minimum wage laws is important to identify their impact on poverty. In most developing countries, more than 40 percent of the jobs are in the informal sector, i.e. not bound by legislation, including informal salaried employment, self-employment, unpaid work, and agricultural labor. Under the traditional dualism model, labor laws govern and are enforced in the formal sector, but not in the informal sector, so minimum wage legislation would not cover half of the labor force. More recent theories suggest that minimum wages may affect informal sector workers due to linkages between the formal and informal sectors in labor and product markets. This suggests that although only half of the labor force is covered, the whole labor force feels the employment and wage effects of minimum wage laws.

The concept of risk pooling is also important to understand the impact of minimum wages on the individual's welfare since a change in the worker's employment or wage status caused by an increase in the minimum wage is not likely to lead to an equivalent effect on his/her welfare. In industrialized countries, resources are pooled at two general levels: the household and society. Household risk sharing is somewhat complete, such that all members share incomes and costs. An income loss as a result of the unemployment effects of a higher minimum wage will not be born by the individual alone. Instead, he/she is likely to live in a household such that the earnings of others in the household are re-allocated to the newly jobless household member, thus greatly diminishing the potential individual welfare effects of the job loss.[1] Risk pooling may exist at the societal level, as well, where everyone contributes a portion of their income to a general pool that serves as insurance for those who may experience unemployment. This scheme leads to partial insurance such that the loss of income of the newly unemployed individual is partially offset by a transfer of income from those who maintained their jobs. The former method of pooling is used in all countries, but the latter is largely absent in developing countries due to underdeveloped social protection programs. Thus, to understand the impacts of minimum wage laws on poverty in developing countries, it is important to take into consideration how changes in the minimum wage (and associated income and employment changes) affect *household*, rather than *individual*, income.[2]

This chapter reviews the literature on the poverty effects of minimum wages to determine whether or not the minimum wage is an effective and efficient poverty alleviation tool. Lessons are drawn from developed and industrialized countries to build a picture of the impacts of minimum wages on employment, the wage distribution, household income level and inequality,[3] and fiscal balances. To capture the developing country model, particular focus is given to the structure of the labor market in terms of its implications for coverage of minimum wage laws and risk pooling at the household level.

The chapter is structured in 8 sections. After this Introduction, Section II discusses the conceptual framework used in the analysis of the poverty impact of minimum wages. Section III analyses different measures as regards the definition of the correct minimum wage level. The impacts of the minimum wage on the wage distribution, employment, poverty and fiscal balance are assessed in the remaining sections. Finally, Section VIII presents some conclusions.

---

[1] Various models of household dynamics suggest that income is not shared equally among household members. Unlike the Mincer (1962) and Becker (1976) models where the household head (the person with the most power in the household) is altruistic and ensures an equitable distribution of household resources, these alternative models assume a cooperative or even a non-cooperative bargaining game where the outcome is not necessarily Pareto Optimal. In other words, the person who has the most power in the household and makes resource allocation decisions will not necessarily distribute household income in a way such that everyone is equally well-off. See Haddad et. al. (1997) for a review of household bargaining models.

[2] The minimum wage may also contribute to non-economic well-being. For example, if an increase in the minimum wage leads to higher earnings of women, they may have more say in how household resources are spent and/or on the formation and dissolution of the household. The intra-household dynamics of minimum wages are not covered in this paper.

[3] Ideally, a causal relationship between minimum wages and household's poverty level would be established, but consumption data are needed for the exercise. Due to the scarcity of consumption data, there are no studies that empirically establish a connection.

II. Conceptual Framework

Several theories explain the impact of minimum wages on employment and earnings, but they do not consider poverty effects. This section discusses the standard theories of minimum wages, applies the theories to developing countries, and adds risk pooling and poverty discussions to the models.

Competitive Model

The competitive model is based on the theory of the supply and demand for labor. In its most simple form, the demand for labor is negatively correlated with the price (wage) and the supply is positively correlated. In a purely competitive market, the equilibrium price and quantity is determined by the intersection of these two schedules (Figure 8.1). When a minimum wage is set above the market clearing wage, individuals who are attracted by the higher wages will enter the labor force, but firms will also dismiss workers by substituting labor with capital, replacing current workers with more skilled workers (such that the wage again reflects the marginal product of labor), or going out of business. These two effects lead to an increase in the unemployment rate since the number of people willing to work exceeds the number of available jobs. The labor supply curve may shift back due to a discouraged worker effect, but the minimum wage remains above the market wage so the labor market does not clear. The increased wage reduces the poverty of those who keep their jobs, but it increases the poverty of those who become jobless. The net employment effect will depend on the elasticity of the demand and supply curves while the net poverty effect depends on the net change in household income as some household members' wages increase and others lose their jobs.

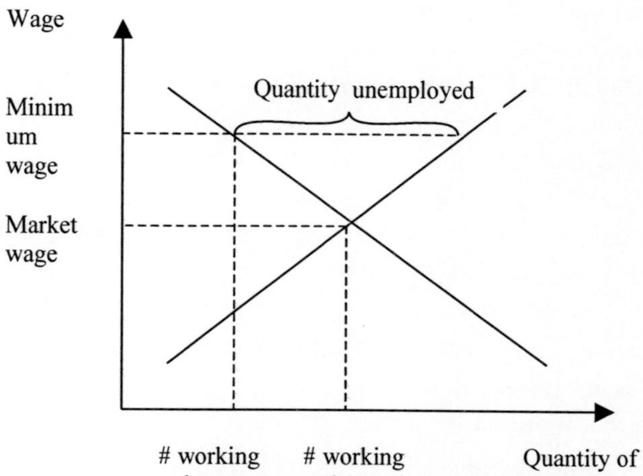

Figure 8.1. Minimum Wages and Unemployment

This model has several shortcomings. *First,* the model assumes that all workers are covered by minimum wage laws. In fact, in most developing countries, less than 60% of workers are covered, so a change in the minimum wage law will not necessarily affect employment of all low wage earners. *Second,* it does not predict the effects of a change in the minimum wage on the wage in the *uncovered* sector, so it is very incomplete in a developing country setting. *Third,* the model assumes that minimum wages are above the equilibrium wage, but this is not necessarily the case. Especially during periods of high inflation, minimum wages often erode to below market clearing wages. For such cases, a corollary to the model is needed that states that if minimum wages are set below the market wage, there is no effect on employment, wages, or poverty. *Fourth,* an increase in the minimum wage may simply align wages with marginal productivity, not leading to any disemployment effects. *Fifth,* workers do not have full information about wages, so legislative alterations in the minimum wage may not be transferred to the worker. Casual interviews, especially with the poor, reveal that they often do not know the minimum wage. Instead, labor contracts are negotiated on a case by case basis. *Finally,* it is not a good predictor of poverty since households pool resources, so a job loss by one family member may be dampened by the earnings of other working household members. Households may diversify their "labor portfolio" such that some members are in the covered sector, providing a stable income and benefits to the household while others are in the uncovered sector. If a member in the covered sector does lose his/her job due to an increase in the minimum wage, the increased earnings of other household members may compensate, or, at the very least, the poverty effects on the household would be dampened by the continued employment of household members in the uncovered sector.

Two Sector Model

Most development literature argues that a primary characteristic that differentiates developing country labor markets from those of developed countries is the simultaneous existence of two labor markets: the formal and informal sectors. The linkages between these range from a dualistic view (Harris-Todaro 1970, Mazumdar 1983, Stiglitz 1984) to an integration interpretation (see Chapter 2 by Fiess, Fugazza and Maloney). The impact of minimum wages on employment, wages, and poverty differs based on the model adopted.

The dualistic model assumes that segmentation is partly a result of minimum wages. The existence of the formal sector is attributed to institutional constraints that set wages above the market wage. Employers pay that wage either to increase the productivity of workers (Esfahani and Salehi-Isfahani 1989, Krebs and Maloney 2001), avoid payment of fines from non-compliance, or provide concessions to unions (Maloney and Ribeiro 1999). Those who are not fortunate enough to secure a formal sector job work in the informal sector while waiting for formal sector jobs to open.[4]

An increase in the minimum wage would create an even larger gap between the formal sector wage and the market wage as employers substitute skilled workers or capital for their existing labor force or even close their firms, thereby leading to a greater dislocation of workers from the formal sector. Those individuals who lose their jobs may enter unemployment to queue for formal sector jobs, enter the informal sector, or leave the labor

[4] Alternatively, individuals may choose to become unemployed rather than working in the informal sector, but the very low levels of unemployment in many developing countries suggest that this does not occur.

force if the market wage in the informal sector is below their reservation wage. As the supply of workers in the informal sector increases, the equilibrium informal sector market wage would fall for all workers. Poverty would increase for two reasons: 1) those who are laid off from the formal sector would lose all income as they enter unemployment or would take lower paying informal sector jobs and 2) the wages of all informal sector workers would fall.

Dualistic Model

This model falls short in six primary areas.

First, statistics do not support the assumption that the formal sector is superior to the informal sector, so workers are not necessarily forced into the informal sector. Instead, wages of informal sector workers may exceed those of formal sector workers with the same observable characteristics; this is particularly notable for those who are self-employed (Maloney 1998, 1999). Furthermore, even if informal sector wages are below formal sector wages, the jobs are not necessarily inferior since the time flexibility and independence of informal sector work is a valuable non-pecuniary benefit to informal sector work, especially for women with household responsibilities and retired men (Cunningham and Maloney 2001, Cunningham 2001). This explains the frequent voluntary movement between the formal and informal sectors observed in many countries.

Second, informal sector employment does not necessarily increase and informal sector wages do not necessarily decrease with a rise in wages. Recent work in Mexico shows that employment in the informal self-employment sector may be pro-cyclical, i.e. as the economy grew, the self-employment sector did as well (see the Chapter by Fiess, Fugazza and Maloney). The increase in the size of the informal sector in Brazil since 1994 has been accompanied by an increase in wages as well (Ministerio do Trabalho 2000).

Third, unemployment rates are rising in Latin America suggesting that the informal sector cannot absorb all excess labor. Studies in Argentina (Arias 1999) and Mexico (Arango and Maloney 2000) show that most unemployment comes from the informal sector, so it is not a reliable means of employing excess labor. This may be due to a lack of demand for informally produced goods when the economy slows down, since the informal sector is heavily comprised of services and construction, both of which may be easily substituted by own labor or deferred to better times. However, even if labor demand does not fall, all displaced labor may not choose to enter the informal sector since there are barriers to entry, especially for men (Geldstein 2001). Therefore, if minimum wages increase, the movement of people to the informal sector is likely to be more limited than the theory predicts, indicating that the fall in informal sector wages, and resulting poverty, is likely to be less than predicted.

Fourth, as in the competitive model, firms do not necessarily comply with regulations. Labor may not shift between sectors, but rather sectoral allocation would remain constant and non-compliance would increase. This is only possible if the enforcement of the new laws is incomplete.

Fifth, this model omits the consideration of risk pooling. If the household has a diversified labor portfolio, an increase in the minimum wage of a formal sector employee who does not lose her job may compensate for the lower wage of her husband who does lose his job and enter the informal sector. Thus, the model cannot predict the effects of an increase of the minimum wage on poverty.

Sixth, it ignores the product demand side of the story. If minimum wages increase, the demand for goods and services produced in the informal sector may increase, since the consumption of informal sector goods is positively correlated with income. The increased product demand would lead to higher demand for informal sector employees, thereby pushing up the informal sector wage, especially if unemployment rates are low (Fiszbein 1992)

Integration Model

In the integration model, the formal and informal sectors are assumed to be linked through product and labor markets such that changes in the minimum wage will indirectly affect the informal sector through many channels, not only through employment. In a closed economy, an increase in the minimum wage in the covered sector would increase the price of formal sector goods, causing the relative price of informal sector goods to decrease. The demand for informal sector goods would increase, so wages in the informal sector would increase as well to attract new workers to the jobs. Thus, an increase in the minimum wage would *increase* wages in the informal sector. In an open economy, an increase in the minimum wage could not be covered by higher prices, so firms shut-down, capital moves to the informal sector, and the demand (and price) for informal sector workers increases. Unemployment may increase, but all wages will as well, thereby having a dubious effect on poverty.

This model challenges the conventional belief that minimum wages cannot reduce the poverty of those who work in the uncovered sector (World Bank 1995, Inter-American Development Bank 2000). Instead, it suggests that the benefits of minimum wage legislation do reach the poorest, although the linkages are less direct. The model does fall short, though, since it ignores risk pooling.

III. The Correct Minimum Wage Level

The "correct" level of the minimum wage is difficult to determine. Comparisons of minimum wages across countries is not informative since productivity levels and the cost of living differs between countries and currency or PPP conversions introduce measurement error to the statistics. Alternatively, the ratio between the minimum wage and the industrial wage can be compared across countries since it omits the need to convert to a single currency and, since wages are a measure of productivity, the denominator serves as a way to “normalize” the productivity differences (Inter-American Development Bank 2000). For example, in Chapter 10 by Paes de Barros et alli, the authors use the ratio of the minimum wage to the industrial mean wage to calculate an international norm for the minimum wage. Drawing from countries as diverse as the United States, Botswana, Belgium, Hungary, and the Philippines, a ratio of 0.4 is identified as the international standard. The paper concludes that minimum wages in Brazil should be doubled to meet the same ratio.

The ratio of the minimum wage to the mean industrial wage may not be the best measure to calculate a target ratio. *First*, the median wage, rather than the mean wage is a better benchmark against which to measure the minimum wage. Wage distributions tend to have long right tails, so outliers may increase the size of the denominator. Table 8.1 shows that when using the mean wage as the statistic of comparison, of eight countries in LAC, only Colombia and Honduras meet the 40 percent criteria for the appropriate minimum wage.[5] The ratios range from 19 percent of mean wages (urban Uruguay) to 62 percent (Honduras) However, when using the median wage as the base, five of the nine countries meet the 40 percent criteria, including Brazil. The range of the ratios shifts upward, falling between 27 percent (Uruguay) and 90 percent (Honduras), showing that the relative minimum wage is much closer to the recommended 40 percent when omitting the high earners in the upper tails of the wage distribution.

Table 8.1. Ratio of the Minimum Wage (Mw) to Comparison Wages

	year	Mw/mean	Mw/median	Mw/10th percentile wage
Argentina (urban)	1998	0.26	0.33	0.67
Bolivia	1997	0.22	0.34	0.80
Brazil (all)	1998	0.24	0.43	1.00
Brazil (urban)	1998	0.22	0.37	1.00
Chile	1996	0.34	0.55	1.09
Colombia (urban)	1998	0.40	0.68	1.00
Honduras	1999	0.62	0.90	2.26
Mexico (urban)	1999	0.34	0.48	0.87
Uruguay (urban)	1998	0.19	0.27	0.64

Source: Maloney and Nuñez (2001)

Second, a target level is perhaps better calculated by a ratio between those with similar skill levels since the returns to the highly skilled manufacturing may not be purely due to productivity differences, especially when manufacturing wages are distorted by union pressures. Minimum wage earners tend to be in the lower tail of the wage distribution while industrial workers are in the upper tail. The last column of Table 8.1 attempts to control for productivity differences by calculating the ratio of the minimum wage to wages in the lower 10 percent of the distribution, which is where unskilled worker wages are clustered. The eight country sample shows that the minimum wage is at or above the wage at the 10th wage decile in four countries (Brazil, Chile, Colombia, Honduras). In Bolivia (80 percent) and Mexico (87 percent), the minimum wage is not far from the earnings of the low skilled.

Finally, since the minimum wage is determined by political, not economic standards, there is not an economic rule for the correct level. A problem with using any ratio to identify the correct level of the minimum wage is that it does not give a criteria for a "correct" level, especially if the objective of the minimum wage is to reduce poverty. Those who are earning the minimum wage are likely to be those whose productivity is equal to the wage, so in fact, they are earning the correct level of wages. The ratio is useful to show where minimum wage earners are relative to various segments of the working population, but it cannot be used to identify whether or not the minimum wage is set at a fair level.

---

[5] This is calculated for all wages, not only manufacturing wages, as Paes de Barros et alli suggest since the manufacturing wage was not available for the countries in the sample. Nevertheless, the argument will hold for manufacturing wages as well.

IV. Impact of The Minimum Wages on the Wage Distribution

A change in the minimum wage may affect the shape of the whole wage distribution. If an increase in the minimum wage causes firms to substitute more productive labor, the wages paid to these new, more skilled workers may exceed the new minimum wage. Alternatively, wages may adjust along the distribution as employers alter wages of workers who earn more than the new minimum to keep relative wages among employees differentiated (Card and Krueger 1995). A comparison of minimum wage studies in developed and developing countries shows that minimum wages affect the distribution of the entire wage distribution in developing countries but not in industrialized countries.

Is the Minimum Wage Binding?

The usefulness of the minimum wage as a tool to address poverty depends on whether or not it is binding. In industrialized countries, where most employers abide by labor laws, minimum wages tend to be binding, i.e. they do tend to set a lower bound (Card and Krueger 1995). The high proportion of informal sector workers in developing countries may suggest that the minimum wage is not binding since, by definition, this sector is outside of the sphere of the legal system. However, the relationship between the formal and informal sectors may be such that minimum wages in the covered sector spillover to the uncovered sector.

A series of studies in industrialized countries show that minimum wages are binding for youth. A comparison of the minimum wage to the average wage does not indicate whether or not the minimum wage is binding; instead, spikes in the wage distribution are more revealing.[6] In the United States, while two to four percent of adults earn the minimum wage in the period 1988-1996, twelve to nineteen percent of youth did (Brown 1999). Katz and Krueger (1992) show that an increase in the minimum wage in the period 1989-1991 shifts upward the earnings of those who were earning between the old and new minimum wages. In Europe, the minimum wage is even more binding (Machin and Manning 1997).

Surprisingly, the minimum wage tends to be more binding in the uncovered sector than the covered sector in many Latin American countries. In Brazil, Colombia, Chile, Mexico, Argentina, and Uruguay, there is a "spike" at the minimum wage for the informal sector wage distributions, while this spike is only evident in the formal sector wage distributions for Brazil, Chile, and Colombia (Maloney and Nuñez 2001). Additional work in Brazil (Neri, Gonzaga, and Camargo 2000) shows that there are spikes in the wage distribution not only at the minimum wage, but also at multiples of the minimum wage, indicating that the minimum rate binds wages that are above the legal minimum. These trends are seen in both the covered and uncovered sectors, indicating that there is a spillover effect of minimum wages to the unprotected sector. In the United States, a spillover from the covered to the uncovered sector

[6] This technique only works if the minimum wage is not a round number, in which people commonly denominate wages. For example, surveys often show that people will report wages in multiples of 10. If the minimum wage is a multiple of 10, it will be difficult to distinguish in cross-sectional data between a spike due to "rounding error" versus a spike due to the minimum wage.

is also statistically identifiable and the spike is higher in the uncovered sector wage distribution than in the covered sector wage distribution (Brown 1999 p. 2144).

How Does the Minimum Wage Affect the Wage Distribution?

A change in the minimum wage has little impact on the wage distribution in industrialized countries. In the United States, wages of workers who earn below or near the (new) minimum wage before the wage increase are positively affected by the new minimum wage (Neumark, Schweitzer and Wascher 2000), especially women (DiNardo, Fortin, and Lemieux 1996). However, these effects are neutralized when considering the lagged effects (Neumark 2000) such that only those earning below the minimum wage benefit in the long-run. Those who earn above the new minimum wage experience small increases in the period of the increased minimum wage (Grossman 1983, Neumark, Schweitzer and Wascher 2000) but negative changes in the long run as the supply of labor increases more than the demand for more skilled workers. Katz and Krueger (1992) find that an increase in the minimum wage increases wages of those earning in the bottom ten percent of the wage distribution, but they also find that any effects disappear at higher income levels. In the low wage (fast food) industry, an increase in the minimum wage leads to a corresponding increase in wages that were below the new minimum, but there are little effects further up the wage distribution (Katz and Krueger 1992, Card and Krueger 1995).

In Latin America, minimum wage laws positively affect formal sector wages throughout the whole wage distribution. In Colombia (Maloney and Nuñez 2001) and Brazil (Fajnzylber and Maloney 2001), a one percent increase in the minimum wage leads to wage increases along the formal sector wage distribution, with the greatest effects occurring *below* the minimum wage, and the effects diminishing across the wage distribution. Even those who are earning far above the minimum wage experience an increase in their wages.

A higher minimum wage spills-over to the informal wage sector, possibly due to "benchmarking", but evidence of spillover effects in the self-employment sector are mixed. Neri, Gonzaga, and Camargo (2000) find clear spikes at multiples of the minimum wage for the informal sector wage distribution in Brazil. They hypothesizes that these are due to a lighthouse effect, where the wages in the formal sector affect those in the other sectors. Maloney and Nuñez (2001) hypothesize that in Latin America, the lighthouse effect of minimum wage laws on uncovered wage work is due to the common usage of the minimum wage as a "benchmark" for fair remuneration. Although the minimum wage is often randomly set, it my be commonly taken to be a market-wide standard for wages. Even without formal enforcement, this wage indirectly affects the earnings of those (especially the poor) who are outside of the formal labor market. In the Maloney and Nuñez study (2001), this is corroborated by an absence of minimum wage effects on self-employment, a sector that is not paid by wages but rather by profits.[7]

[7] It is surprising that spikes in the earnings distribution of the self-employed in Brazil are also detected since their income is from profits, not from a set wage (Neri, Gonzaga, and Camargo 2000). This may reflect reporting bias in the data. This suspicion is supported by studies of the lighthouse effect on the self-employment earnings of Mexicans and Colombians where spikes are visible in the formal wage distribution but are absent in the self-employment earnings distribution.

V. IMPACT OF THE MINIMUM WAGE ON EMPLOYMENT

The theoretical implications for the employment effects of an increase in the minimum wage are clearly negative for the single labor market model and mixed for a dual labor market, but the empirical evidence show little if any dis-employment effects. Over the past twenty years, numerous studies in the United States and Europe find small and (marginally) negative employment effects in response to an increase in the minimum wage for those clustered near the minimum wage. There is less evidence in developing countries, but the neutral or slightly negative effects are also identified. The primary differential effect between developed and developing countries is that the dis-employment effects are felt further up the wage distribution for the former than they are for the latter.

Single Labor Market

Most empirical work finds a small negative impact or no influence of an increase in the minimum wage on employment (Appendix I). The research from the 1970s on the US and French labor markets finds that a 10 percent increase in minimum wages is associated with a one to three percent decline in youth employment (Brown 1999). The negative employment effect is stronger for girls than boys (Brown Gilroy and Kohen 1982, p. 504). The employment effects are even smaller among young adults in the United States (Brown 1999). A similar magnitude of disemployment effect is also found for Canada, Portugal, and Greece using data from the 1980s (Ghellab 1998). In the United Kingdom, though, employment effects have not been generally identified (Ghellab 1998, Machin and Manning 1996) but have been noted for specific industries (Machin and Manning 1994).

More recent studies in the United States and France, using longer time series and more careful analysis, find mixed results, but maintain that the employment effects are small. Contrary to earlier studies, analysis of the recent minimum wage increase in the fast food industry in the United States show that employment may actually *increase* as the minimum wage rises (since fast food jobs are undesirable so the labor shortage can only be allayed by a rise in wages) (Katz and Krueger 1992) while others find the standard disemployment effect of two percent (Neumark and Wascher 1998).

Less evidence exists in developing countries, but findings are similar to those in industrialized countries. Under the assumption of a single labor market, dis-employment effects range from 0 to 5 percent for a 10 percent increase in the minimum wage in Indonesia, Puerto Rico, Botswana, and the Czech Republic (Appendix I).[8]

Covered and Uncovered Sectors

In the covered sector, only explicitly examined for developing countries, an increase in the minimum wage by 10 percent leads to a fall of formal sector employment ranging from 5

[8] The estimates for Botswana and Kenya are not econometrically derived but instead are the result of manager interviews in these countries, with recall about the change in the firm's labor force when the minimum wage increased.

percent (Colombia) to 0 percent (Mexico). Bell (1997), who analyzes the impact of an increase in the minimum wage in both Mexico and Colombia, attributes the difference in the effects to the high level of the Colombian minimum wage, thus making it more binding, while the Mexican minimum wage is "too low" and easily paid by employers. An alternative estimate for Colombia (Maloney and Nuñez 2001) support Bell's findings, but find a lower elasticity of -1.9 percent to -3.5 percent for a 10 percent increase in the minimum wage. Interestingly, this study shows that the employment of those across the wage distribution, not only those who are earning at or near the minimum wage, is also negatively affected. Even smaller effects are found in Brazil, where the minimum wage is low (IPEA 2000b) but binding (Neri, Gonzaga, and Camargo 2000, Fajnzylber and Maloney 2001) - disemployment of 0.5 percent in response to a ten percent increase in the minimum wage.

Three papers that examine the effects of the minimum wage on employment in the informal sector have mixed conclusions. In Brazil, as the minimum wage increases by 10 percent, employment in the informal sector increases by 1.76 percent (Carneiro 2004). A similar finding is estimated for Ghana, where employment increases by 1.4 percent in the uncovered sector (Ghellab 1998). These employment effects can be attributed to the dual nature of the labor markets in these countries such that as minimum wages increase, formal employment decreases and the unemployed are forced into the informal sector. Or, under the integration hypothesis, the increased informal sector employment may be explained as a spillover effect between sectors such that the wage in the informal sector also increases and absorbs those who lost formal sector jobs while attracting new workers to the labor market. The evidence does not permit selection of one of these hypotheses. Conversely, in Colombia, an increase in the minimum wage has negative employment effects on the self-employment sector of the magnitude 0.6 percent to 2.2 percent (Maloney and Nuñez 2001).

VI. Poverty Impacts

The small but negative employment effects of the minimum wage found in the some countries in the covered and the uncovered sector may lead to a net increase in poverty. However, the ripple effects of an increase in the minimum wage may sufficiently boost wages such that, on average, people are better off. Given the distribution of minimum wage earners across the working population, though, it is not likely that all workers and households will equally share in the benefits and losses. Instead, the positive and negative effects of the minimum wage may affect people along the wealth distribution differently. There is a shortage of evidence on the poverty effects of minimum wages, so lessons will be drawn from the few existing studies that are summarized in Table 8.2. The general finding drawn from US data is that minimum wages do not reduce poverty, but they do reduce inequality by increasing household income of the poorest households. However, this conclusion may underestimate the impacts in Latin America since the minimum wage positively affects a larger portion of the labor force, in terms of higher wages, than in the United States while having similar disemployment effects.

Poverty Without Risk Pooling

Taking the individual as the unit of observation, the impact of a higher minimum wage on net average income is mixed in the five studies reviewed. Evidence is found in the United States that the unemployment effect dominates the wage effect since those who earn near the minimum wage experience a fall in net income of six percent for an 10 percent increase in the minimum wage (Neumark, Schweitzer, and Wascher 2000), but another study shows that poverty *decreases* by 3.5 percent for a 10 percent increase in the minimum wage (Addison and Blackburn 1999). Mixed results are also found in Brazil. One study finds no correlation between a higher minimum wage and the rate of poverty (IPEA 2000b) while another shows that the minimum wage does reduce poverty across the wage distribution due to indexing of the minimum wage.[9] Under the assumption of no dis-employment effects and no risk pooling, a one percent increase in the minimum wage in Brazil is associated with a decrease in poverty of 0.1 percent for those earning the minimum, but a fall of 0.14 percent for workers across the whole wage distribution (Neri, Gonzaga, and Camargo 2000). Similarly to Brazil, an increase in the minimum wage in Colombia is felt across the whole earnings distribution, not just at the minimum, but the change in net income (poverty) effects depends on where the individual was located in the distribution before the change. An increase in Colombia's minimum wage of 10 percent leads to an increase in poverty (net fall of average income) by two percent among those earning more than 1.3 minimum wages, but among the poor, poverty falls 5 percent to 18 percent among those earnings 0-1.3 minimum wages (Maloney and Nuñez 2001).

Who Earns the Minimum Wage?

A newer set of papers have examined the poverty impacts of the minimum wage by using the household as the unit of observation, which is perhaps more appropriate for developing countries due to risk pooling at the household level. As pointed out in the developed country literature (Neumark and Wascher 1997, Gramlich 1976, Card and Krueger 1995), poverty at the individual level is not synonymous with poverty at the household level. In the United States, it is found that 40 percent of minimum wage earners live in households with a total income more than three times the poverty line. Thus, to identify the poverty reduction effectiveness of the minimum wages, it is important to identify who earns the minimum wage and if they are the poor.

Using data from Mexico and Argentina, Table 8.3 shows that most minimum wage earners are not the primary income earner in the household. In Argentina, ten percent of household heads (male or female) earn at or below the minimum wage while four percent of Mexican households heads do. In contrast, 21 percent of Argentine children living with their parents and ten percent of Mexican children in their parents' home (age 12-17) earn the minimum wage. This is supported by the breakdown by age where 70 percent of working people age 12-17 earn the minimum wage or less in Argentina and 26 percent in Mexico, compared to 20 percent and 6 percent, respectively, of young working adults (18-24). The

[9] The conflicting results from studies in the same country that examine the poverty effects over the same period are due to different assumptions made by the authors and different estimation techniques.

proportions in the United States are similar to those in Mexico with 29.4 percent of those age 16-19 and 19.8 percent of those age 20-24 earning at or below the minimum (Card and Krueger 1995).

Table 8.2. Overview of the Impact of Minimum Wage on Poverty

Country (year of data)	Magnitudes of change in minimum wage and poverty rate	Source
Individual poverty (No risk pooling)		
Brazil (1997)	Increase in the minimum wage have insignificant effects on the level of poverty	IPEA (2000)
Brazil (1996)	A 10% increase in the minimum wage would bring 1% of poor minimum wage earners above the poverty line and 1.4% of all poor above the poverty line	Neri, Gonzaga, and Carmargo (2000)
United States (1983-1996)	10% increase in the minimum wage => decrease poverty an average of 3.6% for unskilled workers in the 1990s (no dis-employment effects); by 0%in the 1980s (with disemployment effects).	Addison and Blackburn (1999)
Colombia (1997-2000)	10% increase in the minimum wage => decrease individual poverty of those earning 0-1.3 m.w. by 5-18%; increase poverty of those earning more than 1.3 m.w. by 2%	Maloney and Nuñez
United States (1986-1992)	10 % increase in minimum wage => increase individual poverty of minimum wage earners by 6% because hours worked fell and wages increased very little; zero change for those earning above the minimum wage	Neumark, Schweitzer and Wascher (2000)
Family Poverty (Risk Pooling at the Household Level)		
Asia, Africa, LAC (1950-1980)	10% increase in m.w. => decrease in poverty rate 6-10%	Lustig and McLeod (1996)
Latin America (1981-1989)	An increase in the minimum wage is more correlated with a decrease in the poverty rate during periods of recession and a decrease in the poverty rate is more correlated with a decrease in the m.w. in periods of recovery	Morley (1995)
United States (1986-1995)	An increase in the minimum wage moves poor families into a non-poor status and moves non-poor families intopoverty, with a net increase in poverty, though this is not statistically significant. However, it does boost incomes of families who are below the poverty line both before and after the change in the minimum wage	Neumark and Wascher (1997)
United States (1990, 1992)	Increase in the minimum wage 1 percent => no effect on poverty rates or a decline of the poverty rate by 1.6 percentage points, but this measure cannot be fully attributed to an increased minimum wage rather than to other changes in the economy at the time.	Card and Krueger (1995)

Table 8.3 and Table 8.4 show that the poor are more likely to earn at or below the minimum wage, but households in *all* wealth quintiles include minimum wage earners in Argentina, Mexico, and the United States. In Argentina, 24.5 percent of the workers in the first wealth quintile (poorest) earn at or below the minimum wage while 5.6 percent of the top quintile do. In Mexico, there are fewer minimum wage earners across all wealth quintiles with 14.6 percent of those in the first wealth quintile and 4.1 percent of those in the fifth quintile

earning the minimum wage. The United States is similar with 28.8 percent of the lowest decile earning below the minimum wage but only 2.7 percent of the highest income decile. Minimum wages constitute 17 percent of poor household's income but two percent of wealthy household's income in Argentina and 30 percent in Mexico (Table 8.4) while in the US, they contribute to 51 percent of total family income (Card and Krueger 1995). Thus, in the two Latin American countries selected for the table, minimum wages are a less important source of income than in the United States. Although minimum wages constitute a larger portion of poor households' total income, nearly equal proportions of households have minimum wage earners in Argentina: 22 percent of poor households have at least one minimum wage earner while 18 percent of wealthy households do. This pattern is not reflected in Mexico, where the poor are three times as likely as the wealthy to have a minimum wage earner in the household.

Table 8.3. Wage Earners at or Below The Minimum Wage

	Argentina[1]	México[2]		Argentina	México
Role in household			**Sector**		
Head	10.1	4.2	Self-employment	23.7	13.9
Spouse	19.8	14.3	Informal wage	31.7	16.9
Child	20.9	9.9	Formal	4.7	0.5
Age			**Education**		
12-17	70	25.6	None	---	22.7
18-24	20.3	6.5	Primary	24.6	11.9
25-64	12.4	6.03	Secondary	12.9	6.5
65+	31.7	24.4	Higher	6.5	2.2
Sex			**Wealth quintile**		
Male	11.9	4.6	1	24.5	14.6
Female	19.9	13.2	2	16.4	10.3
			3	12.1	8.4
			4	10.5	6.9
			5	5.6	4.1

[1] The National Urban Employment Survey (Encuesta Nacional de Empleo Urbano) 1997, quarter two

[2] The Permanent Household Survey (Encuesta Permanante de Hogares) 1997, semester one

Table 8.4. Household Characteristics

	Argentina[1]	Mexico[2]
Percent of household income that is minimum wage		
All	0.084	0.14
Poor (wealth quintile 1)	0.17	0.30
Rich (wealth quintile 5)	0.02	0.17
Percent with a minimum wage earner		
All	22.59	8.94
Poor (wealth quintile 1)	21.95	16.56
Rich (wealth quintile 5)	18.09	5.89

[1] The National Urban Employment Survey (Encuesta Nacional de Empleo Urbano) 1997, quarter two

[2] The Pernanent Household Survey (Encuesta Permanante de Hogares) 1997, semester one

Table 8.3 also shows that those who are typically associated with lower wages tend to be minimum wage earners. Argentine women are nearly twice as likely as Argentine men to be minimum wage earners while Mexican women are three times as likely as Mexican men to earn at or below the minimum wage, despite working women's higher levels of education in both countries. These proportions are very similar to the percentage of spouses (who are likely to be women) who earn at or below the minimum wage. Less educated workers are also more likely to be minimum wage earners, with over 25 percent of those with less than primary education earning the minimum wage. However, 6.5 percent of Argentines with higher education and 2.2 percent of Mexican who have more than secondary school are minimum wage earners, showing that it is not confined to low skilled people. A very low percentage of formal sector workers earn the minimum wage, with a larger portion of self-employed (23 percent in Argentina, 14 percent in Mexico) and informal wage employees (32 percent and 17 percent in Argentina and Mexico, respectively) earning at or below the minimum.

Poverty and Inequality with Risk Pooling at the Household Level

Since those who earn the minimum wage do not tend to be the sole income earner, or even the primary income earner, in the household, and households do pool income, poverty rates at the individual level are not very meaningful. If the negative impact of the minimum wage is concentrated among those who live in households that are clustered around the poverty line while the benefits accrue to the non-poor, the average negative effects on individual poverty, discussed in the last section, may not lead to a reduction of poverty for poor households. Instead, it is more appropriate to simultaneously consider the net change in household income resulting from an increase in wages of working household members and dis-employment of others when the minimum wage increases.

The minimum wage and national poverty rates (measured at the household level) are negatively correlated. A study of the minimum wage in Asia, Africa and Latin America (Lustig and McLeod 1996) estimates that an increase in the minimum wage of 1 percent leads to a decrease in the poverty rate in developing countries of 0.6 to one percent. These estimates are robust across regions, urban and rural sectors, and business cycles. Morley (1995) and de Janvry (cited in Lustig and McLeod 1996) identify a negative correlation between minimum wages and poverty in Latin America, though their findings are not robust across the business cycle. Lustig and McLeod (1996) also find that an increase of the minimum wage leads to a fall in poverty among formal sector workers by 2.5 percent but a decrease of 2.9 percent among workers in self-employment and the informal wage sector (Lustig and McLeod 1996).

When considering the transition of families into or out of poverty, the negative correlation between minimum wages and poverty weakens or even disappears, suggesting that the minimum wage is not an effective poverty reduction strategy and that the national correlations may be due to other factors. Two papers, both for the United States, present the only micro evidence of the effect of minimum wages on poverty at the household level. Neumark and Wascher (1997) directly examine the poverty effects of a change in the minimum wage when there is risk pooling in the household. They show that an increase in the minimum wage causes an increase in incomes of the poor and near-poor such that 4.1 percent of rise out of poverty but 3.9 percent of those who are near-poor fall below the poverty line.

The 0.2 percent net decrease in poverty is not statistically significant, indicating that a real improvement in the poverty status cannot be clearly identified. Instead, the minimum wage redistributes income and jobs among households that are clustered around the poverty line rather than redistributing income from wealthy households to poor households. Card and Krueger (1995) conduct a similar experiment, finding that an increase in the minimum wage by one percent is correlated with a decline of the poverty rate by 1.6 percentage points, but this may be due to changes in the economy apart from the minimum wage. No studies were found to understand the impacts of the minimum wage on poverty in developing countries when there is risk pooling.

The evidence of the impacts of the minimum wage on family income inequality weakly suggests an inequality decreasing effect of the minimum wage. In the United States, an increased in wage inequality in the period 1973-1992 is attributed to a fall in the real value of the minimum wage, especially among women (di Nardo, Fortin, and Lemieux 1996, Horrigan and Mincy 1993), but these do not affect family income inequality (Horrigan and Mincy 1993, Neumark and Wascher 1998). Card and Krueger (1995) find that a 10 percent increase in the minimum wage leads to an increase in family income by an average of 2.3 percent for families in the lowest wealth decile and an increase in family income of 2.5 percent for families in the fifth (median) decile while no changes in family income are detected in the top wealth deciles. This suggests that income inequality falls, but the results are not strongly statistically identified. Machin and Manning (1997) also find an equalizing effect on income distribution for Europe. Card and Krueger (1995) report that in states where the minimum wage is binding, it is associated with a larger increase in the earnings of the poorest families relative to the poorest families in states where it is not binding, indicating that minimum wages do increase the earnings of those at the bottom of the family income distribution. Similar results are found in Colombia, where minimum wages are found to be very binding (Maloney 2000): cross-sectional data show that an increase in the minimum wage corresponds to a decrease in inequality, even during recessionary periods (Bell 1997).

VII. Fiscal Impacts of the Minimum Wage

The cost of an increase in the minimum wage is not confined to the individual or household level, but it may have implications for fiscal balances as well. Since the minimum wage has been used as a denominator for the wages of public servants, government social programs, indexation, and government revenues, a politically motivated increase in the minimum wage, which may gain votes (despite its minimal effect on the labor market or poverty) may have grave implications for fiscal imbalances. To name a few.

Public Sector

Many public sector workers earn at or below the minimum wage. In Brazil, it is estimated that an increase in the minimum wage of 7.5 percent would increase total government expenditures on the public sector by nearly 75 percent, with most of the increase occurring at the municipal level, which already has the largest wage bill (Foguel et al. 2001). A similar exercise in Ecuador suggested that a one percent increase in the minimum wage would increase the government's wage bill by 2.4 percent (World Bank 1996).

Government Transfers

Some government programs are tied to the minimum wage. For example, in Brazil, poor workers receive a "thirteenth wage" every year, which is a direct transfer that is equal to one monthly payment of their wages. Only formal sector workers are eligible, but all workers who earn at or below three minimum wages are eligible. An increase in the minimum wage would have two effects on the costs of the program: (a) increase the number of recipients since the threshold for eligibility has increased even though wages have not and (b) the value of the payout is higher since the maximum amount paid out has increased.

Another example is the unemployment insurance program in Brazil. The minimum payment to the unemployed is one minimum wage, regardless of the wage that he/she earned before becoming unemployed. As the minimum wage increases, the value of this payment increases as well. A similar lower bound is set for pensions in Brazil, as well (ILO 1995a). In Uruguay, social benefits such as pensions, family allowance, unemployment and illness benefits are multiples of the minimum wage (ILO 1995b). Additionally, a higher minimum wage may create disemployment, as seen in Section V. An increase in unemployment would increase the number of eligible for unemployment insurance programs or other means tested government programs that are based on income. This would increase government expenditures on those people who had been productive members of society before the increase.

Price or Wage Indexing

The minimum wage may be used as a denominator to which other measures, used for the provision of government services, are indexed. An increase in the minimum wage would increase the level of the indexed indicator and therefore indirectly affect government expenditures. For example, in the Brazilian state of Ceará, the poverty line is based on the minimum wage. If the minimum wage increases, the poverty line also rises, thus increasing the number of people who are eligible for various social protection programs. Or, in the case of Argentina, the *mopre* is a unit of measure that is indexed to the minimum wage. If the minimum wage increases, the *mopre* does, too, but this may actually decrease health expenditures in Argentina, for example, since formal sector workers earning less than three times the mopre (valued at approximately $80 monthly) are ineligible for government provided health benefits. This would decrease government expenditures but also lower benefits to the poor.

Government Revenues

Taxation may also be tied to the minimum wage. In México, for example, individuals who earn less than three times the minimum wage are exempt from income taxes and are even eligible for tax credits. An increase in the minimum would decrease the stock of individuals who are required to pay taxes, thus negatively affecting government revenues. Furthermore, they would also be eligible for tax credits, thus further draining government reserves.

Thus, the potential inequality reducing benefits of the minimum wage may be outweighed by an increased fiscal deficit in governments that use of the minimum wage as a denominator for social spending or revenues and for those that have social programs to support the unemployed. Any decision to increase the minimum wage need take into account the fiscal impacts as well.

VIII. Conclusions and Implications for Policy

The international evidence reviewed in this chapter showed that minimum wages have a bigger impact on the labor market in developing countries than in developed countries, despite the lower potential coverage. While an increase in the minimum wage only increases wages of those between the old and new minimum in the US, it positively influences wages across the distribution in Latin America. These effects are felt in both the covered (formal) and uncovered (informal) wage sectors. Similarly, the disemployment effects may be larger in Latin America, ranging from zero to five percent and affecting workers along the entire wage distribution, compared to the United States where only workers near the minimum wage are affected, if at all. Taking together the dis-employment and wage effects, in the three developing country studies (two countries) reviewed, the wage and employment effects either cancel each other out or the former dominates the latter, leading to a net improvement in the average individual's earnings. This contrasts with studies in the United States that find no effect.

Despite these finding, little can be concluded about the poverty impacts of the minimum wage, especially in a developing country context. Although cross-country comparisons shows a negative correlation between the minimum wage and poverty, studies for the US labor market suggest that the minimum wage causes a churning of those who are near the poverty line. Many of those who were below the poverty line retain their jobs and benefit from a higher wage when the minimum wage is increased, thereby rising above the poverty line, while others lose their jobs and sink below the line. These results perhaps cannot be extrapolated to developing countries since the wage and employment effects are further reaching than in industrialized countries, thereby affecting everyone, not only those near the poverty line.

This is not to say that the minimum wage does not or cannot improve the lot of the poor, in Latin America, though. In the United States, although an increase in the minimum wage only caused families just below and just above the poverty line to swap positions, the household income of those below the poverty line did increase, though not enough to pull them out of poverty. Since minimum wages affect the employment and wages of those along the wealth distribution, its increase may have larger effects than in the United States, however, to date, no evidence exists to support this. Furthermore, a higher minimum wage is correlated with a zero change or a decrease in income inequality measured at the household level, so it does have the effect of brining up the bottom of the distribution.

Minimum wages can be binding even in a labor market with a large uncovered sector. Whether due to an indexing effect or some other spill-over, policymakers should not assume that the minimum wage only affects the welfare of those in the formal sector. It is likely to have even larger effects on informal sector workers since it is more binding in that sector.

A final fact to point out is that the minimum wage may be a means of helping those who are most disadvantaged in the labor market. Although there is much leakage in the minimum wage, since even workers whose households rank in the top wealth quintile earn the minimum wage, those who are considered the least likely to succeed in the labor market tend to earn the minimum. Women, youth, informal sector workers, and the uneducated are more likely to be minimum wage earners than are those who have more skills or are more entrenched in the labor market. Thus, the minimum may make the labor make the labor market more attractive for these groups, though empirical evidence is absent.

Policy recommendations may be premature since the evidence of the poverty implications of the minimum wage are still largely unknown. At this preliminary stage, maintaining the minimum wage may be beneficial since it does decrease income inequality at both the household and individual level, it may be helpful to those who are typically low earners while not being too distortionary on the labor market, and it does impact those who are otherwise uncovered by labor legislation. However, if the minimum is set too high, as in Colombia, it may do more harm than good by causing the dis-employment effect to outweigh the positive wage effects.

Thus, if the minimum is to be maintained, governments need to clearly identify the criteria for the minimum, thus making it an economic rather than a political tool. The "correct" level of the minimum would be that amount that achieves the government's social objectives while not distorting the labor market to the extent of creating unemployment that is not counter-balanced by safety nets. This would require tying the minimum wage to economic factors, which may be a function of wages, as used in the Brazilian study to calculate a "correct" minimum wage, or may be tied to poverty indicators with some upper bound.

Any systematic development of a minimum wage need also consider the fiscal impacts. As discussed in the review, there is a great deal of leakage in the program since most minimum wage earners are not poor. If distortionary effects are created such that the poor lose their jobs, but the government plans to counter-balance this with social safety nets, the costs of a minimum wage policy are potentially high. Also, the propensity of governments to tie social protection eligibility and payouts to the minimum wage may lead to unnecessary fiscal imbalances. Since the minimum wage is largely a political, not an economic value, an increase based on political motives will increase the income of those who benefit from government transfers or wages tied to the minimum even though their needs have not increased. Linking eligibility and payouts of social protection to a poverty indicator would be more beneficial to the poor.

The foremost recommendation, though, is to better identify the poverty impacts and the cost to government of changes in the minimum wage. Only then can the usefulness of the minimu0m wage 1as a poverty alleviation tool be evaluated.

Table 8.5. Summary of the Literature on the Employment Effects of Minimum Wages

Country	Change in the employment rate due to a 10% increase in the minimum wage			Notes
	All	*Male*	*Female*	
Developed Countries				
US (1970s) [1]	-1% to - 3%			For time series estimates, the results are consistent. Cross section estimates have more variance, but still tend to be <0 for
US (after 1970s) [1]	No employment effects			Mixed effects, but may be due to econometric problems. Katz and Krueger (1992) find 18.5 to 26.4% increases in unemployment.
Canada (1980s) [1]	-1.4% to -5%			
UK (1980s) [1]	No employment effects			
France (1970s) [1]	-3.5% to -4.1%	-2.63% to -6.1%	Weakly negatively significant	
France (1980s) [1]	-1% to -3.5%	-1.3% to -6.24%	-1.88% to -3.6%	
Netherlands [1] (1980s)	No employment effects			
Portugal* (1980s) [2]		-0.1 to -0.8%	-0.3% to -4.7%	Negative effects for youth are larger
Greece* (1980s) [2]	-0.59% to -1.09%	-0.6% to -1.1%		
Indonesia (1998) [3]	0 to -5%			For a doubling of the minimum wage; the estimates are not statistically significant
Puerto Rico (1977) [4]	-0.5			
Brazil (1988 [5], 2000 [6])	-0.4%; -0.1% in the formal sector, 1.76% the informal sector;			Formal is defined as "com carteira" and informal is defined as "sem carteira"
Botswana (1988) [2]	Some disemployment effects			Not econometrically tested
Kenya (1988)*2	Dis-employment effects in the private sector, none in the public sector			Not econometrically tested
Czech Republic2	Disemployment effect on low-skilled workers			

Table 8.5. Summary of the Literature on the Employment Effects of Minimum Wages

(Continued)

Country	**Change in the employment rate due to a 10% increase in the minimum wage**			**Notes**
	All	***Male***	***Female***	
Developed Countries				
Mexico (1997)[7]	No employment effect			Formal sector manufacturing firms
Ghana (1970s-1980s)[2]	-1.2% (all); 1.4% (informal) sector;		0.06%-0.05%	Coefficients for the women are not significant
Colombia (1980s[7], 1997-2000[8])	Less than –5%;	-1.9% to -3.5% for salaried workers across the wage distribution; -0.6% to –2.2% for self-employed across the wage distribution		Formal sector manufacturing firms; only men

* results from one study only

1 from various studies, most summarized in Brown (1999)

2 as reported by Ghellab (1998)

3 Rama (forthcoming)

4 Freeman and Castillo (1991)

5 Camargo (1988)

6 Carneiro (2000)

7 Bell (1997)

8 Maloney and Núñez (2001)

REFERENCES

Addison, John T. and McKinley L. Blackburn (1999) "Minimum Wages and Poverty" *Industrial and Labor Relations Review* 52(3), 393-409.

Arango and Maloney (2000) "Reform and Income Insecurity in Argentina and Mexico" *draft* (World Bank: Washington, DC).

Arias, Omar (1999) "Marginalization of Men in Argentina: Evidence from Changes in Wage Distributions" *mimeo*, (World Bank: Washington, DC).

Becker, Gary (1976) "Altruism, Egoism, and Genetic Fitness: Economics and Sociobiology" *Journal of Economic Literature* 14(3).

Bell, Linda (1997) "The Impact of Minimum Wages in Mexico and Colombia" *Journal of Labor Economics* 15(3), S102-S135.

Brown, Charles, Gilroy, C. and A. Kohen (1982) "The Effect of Minimum Wage on Employment and Unemployment" *Journal of Economic Literature*, , June, 487-528.

Brown, Charles (1999). "Minimum Wages, Employment and the Distribution of Income" in Orley. Ashenfelter and David Card eds. *The Handbook of Labor Economics*, Volume 3b.

Card, David and Alan Krueger (1995) *Myth and Measurement: The Economics of the Minimum Wage* (Princeton University Press: Princeton, NJ).

Carneiro, Francisco (2004), Are Minimum Wages to Blame for Informality in the Labour Market?, Empirica, 31:295-306..

Cunningham, W. and W. Maloney (2001), "Heterogeneity in the Mexican Micro-enterprise Sector," *Economic Development and Cultural Change*, 5:131-156.

Cunningham, W. (2001) "Breadwinner versus Caregiver: Labor Force Participation and Sectoral choice over the Mexican Business Cycle," in Correia, Maria and Elizabeth Katz *The Economics of Gender in Mexico* (World Bank: Washington, DC).

Di Nardo, J.; Fortin, N. and T. Lemieux. (1996) "Labor Market Institutions and the Distribution of Wages 1973-1992: A Semiaparametric Approach" *Econometrica*, , September, 1001-1044.

Esfahani, H. and D. Salehi-Isfahani (1989), "Effort Observability and Worker Productivity: Towards and Explanation of Economic Dualism," *Economic Journal*, 99, 818-836.

Fajnzylber, Pablo and William F. Maloney (2001) "Minimum Wage Effects Throughout the Wage Distribution: Evidence from Brazil's Formal and Informal Sectors." *Universidade Federal de Minais Gerais, Department of Economics and CEDEPLAR*, Mimeo, March.

Fiszbein, Ariel (1992) *Do Workers in the Informal Sector Benefit from Cuts in the Minimum Wage?* Working Paper Series #826 (World Bank: Washington, DC).

Foguel, Miguel, Lauro Ramos and Francisco Carneiro "The Impacts of the Minimum Wage on the Labor Market, Poverty, and Fiscal Budget in Brazil", *mimeo* (IPEA: Rio de Janeiro).

Geldstein, Rosa (2001) "Non-Labor Market Coping Strategies in Argentina", LCSPG/World Bank, *draft*.

Ghellab, Y. (1998) "Minimum Wage and Youth Unemployment", *ILO*, Employment and Training Papers

Gramlich, Edward (1976) "Impact of Minimum Wages on Other Wages, Employment, and Family Incomes" *Brookings Paper on Economic Activity* 1, 409-451.

Grossman, J. (1983) "The Impact of Minimum Wage on Other Wages." *Journal of Human Resources*, Summer, 359-378.

Haddad, Lawrence, John Hoddinott, and Harold Alderman (1997) *Intrahousehold Resource Allocation in Developing Countries* (Johns Hopkins University Press: Baltimore).

Harris, J.R. and M. P. Todaro (1970), "Migration, Unemployment, and Development: A Two Sector Analysis, " *American Economic Review*, 60:1, 126-142.

Horrigan, M. and R. Mincy (1993) "Minimum Wage and Earnings and Income Inequality" in S. Danziger and P. Gottschalk eds. "Uneven Tides: Rising Inequality in America", *Russel Sage Foundation,* 251-275.

Inter-American Development Bank (2000) *Facing Up to Inequality* (Inter-American Development Bank: Washington, DC).

ILO (International Labor Organization) (1995a) *Minimum Wage Fixing in Brazil*, Briefing Note No. 9, http://www.ilo.org/public/english/dialogue/infocus/papers/minwages/brasil3.htm.

ILO (International Labor Organization) (1995b) *Minimum Wage Fixing in Uruguay*, Briefing Note No. 5, http://www.ilo.org/public/english/dialogue/infocus/papers/minwages/uruguay.htm.

IPEA (Instituto de Pesquisa Econômica Aplicada) (2000b) *Impactos do Salário Mínimo sobre a Folha de Pagamentos das Três Esferas de Governo* (IPEA: Rio de Janeiro).

IPEA (Instituto de Pesquisa Econômica Aplicada) (2000b) *Uma Análise da Eficacia das Políticas Públicas de Trábalo e Renda no Combate à Pobreza no Brasil* (IPEA: Rio de Janeiro).

Katz and Krueger (1992) "The Effect of the Minimum Wage on the Fast-Food Industry", *Industrial and Labor Relations Review* v46, n1 (October 1992): 6-21

Krebs, T and W.F. Maloney *"Quitting and Labor Turnover: Micro-economic Evidence and Macro-economic Consequences."* IBRD Working Paper 2068, Latin America and the Caribbean Region, Poverty Reduction and Economic Management Unit, World Bank. Wshington, D.C. Processed.

Lustig, Nora and Darryl McLeod (1996) "Minimum Wages and Poverty in Developing Countries: Some Empirical Evidence" *Brookings Discussion Papers in International Economics,* DP # 125, June.

Machin, S. and A. Manning (1994) "The Effects of Minimum wages on Wage Dispersion and Employment: Evidence from the U.K Wage Councils", Industrial and Labor Relations Review, January, pp. 319-29

Machin, Stephen and Alan Manning (1996) "Employment and the Introduction of a Minimum Wage in Britain" *The Economic Journal* 106(430), 650-656.

Machin, Stephen and Alan Manning (1997) "Minimum Wages and Economic Outcomes in Europe" *European Economic Review* 41, 733-742.

Maloney, William F. (1999). "Does Informality Imply Segmentation in Urban Labor Markets? Evidence from Sectoral Transitions in Mexico, *World Bank Economic Review*, 13: 275-302.

——— (1998). *"The Structure of Labor Markets in Developing Countries: Time Series Evidence on Competing Views."* Working Paper 1940. World Bank, Washington, D.C. Processed.

——— (2000) *Minimum Wages in Latin America*, mimeo, IBRD.

——— and E. Ribeiro (1999) *"Efficiency wage and Union Effects in labor Demand and Wage Structure in Mexico"* Working paper 2131, World Bank, Washington, D.C.

——— and J. Nuñez (2001) "Minimum Wages In Latin America" *The World Bank*, Mimeo, March.

Mazumdar, D. (1983). "Segmented Labor Markets in LDC's." *American Economic Review*, 73, 2 254-259.

Mincer, Jacob (1962) "Labor Force Participation of Married Women" in *Aspects of Labor Economics* H. Greg Lewis, ed., Universities NBER Conference Series no. 14 (Princeton Univ. Press: Princeton, New Jersey).

Ministerio de Trabalho. (2000) *Mercado de Trabalho: Conjuntura e Analise*, Number 12, February.

Morley, Samuel A. (1995) "Structural Adjustment and Determinants of Poverty in Latin America" in ed. Nora Lustig *Coping with Austerity: Poverty and Inequality in Latin America* (Brookings Institution: Washington, DC)

Neri, Marcelo, Gustavo Gonzaga and Jose Marcio Camargo (2000) *Efeitos Informais do Salário Mínimo e Pobreza*, Texto para Discussão #724 (IPEA: Rio de Janeiro)

Neumark, David and W. Wascher (1997). *Do Minimum Wages Fight Poverty,* NBER WP # 6127, August.

Neumark, D. and W. Wascher. (1998) *The Effects of Minimum Wages on the Distribution of Family Incomes: A Nonparametric Analysis*, NBER, WP # 6536.

Neumark, D. Schweitzer, M. and W. Wascher (2000) *The Effects of Minimum Wages Throughout the Wage Distribution*, NBER, WP # 7519.

Rama, Martin (forthcoming) "The Consequences of Doubling the Minimum Wage: The Case of Indonesia" *International Labor Relations Review.*

Stiglitz, Joseph. E., (1984) "Alternative Theories of Wage Determination and Unemployment in LDC's: The Labor Turnover Model," *Quarterly Journal of Economics*, 88:194-227.

World Bank (1995) *World Development Report* (World Bank: Washington, DC).

World Bank (1996) *Ecuador Poverty Report* (World Bank: Washington, DC).

In: Economics, Politics and Social Issues in Latin America ISBN 1-60021-182-8
Editor: Mary P. Lassiter, pp. 175-194

Chapter 9

RURAL DEVELOPMENT PROGRAMS IN ARGENTINA AND ITS INSTITUTIONS (IN THE CONTEXT OF NEOLIBERAL ACROECONOMIC ADJUSTMENT)*

Mabel Manzanal*

CONICET, Facultad de Filosofía y Letras, UBA, Argentina

ABSTRACT

Rural development begins in Argentina together with the restoration of democracy in the 1980s, but the first actions only started to be developed in the 1990s. Since then, different programs have followed and overlapped. These programs are precisely the purpose of our study.

This paper discusses the resultant rural strategies of the main rural development programs of Argentina in the context of the neoliberal macroeconomic adjustment. It identifies its institutions and analyses whether the actions that are being carried out are suitable or not, and if the assistance to help the rural poor (promoted by international financing organisms) is feasible in face of the negative impact of the neoliberal policy over the small and medium farmers. Besides, this paper looks into and develops questions about the suitability of local and provincial institutional structures for satisfying the institutional demands of rural development programs.

Our starting point is the macroeconomic transformation of the 1990s, which affected the agricultural activity and brought about permanent processes of re-structuring and de-structuring of the public and private institutions linked with rural development management.

---

* This paper is part of an ongoing research, under the direction of the author, related to Rural Development Programs in Argentina. The research is funded by the Consejo Nacional de Investigaciones Científicas y Tecnológicas –CONICET- and the Universidad de Buenos Aires –UBA-, Argentina.

* Researcher from CONICET, Facultad de Filosofía y Letras, UBA (Address: Rojas 575, 1405 Buenos Aires, Tel/Fax 54 11 4431-1257, e-mail: postmaster@manzan.ba.ar).

INTRODUCTION

In Argentina, during the mid-1970s, precisely in 1976, with the overthrow of the constitutional government of Isabel Perón, and the take-over of the military dictatorship, with Martínez de Hoz as Minister of Economy, a new economic model began to develop. This new model coincided with the onset of a neoliberal policy that would progressively replace the Keynesian model and the policy of the Welfare State that had been applied during the three previous decades. The advent of neoliberalism would bring about a policy of structural adjustment which, with differences, would go further than the succeeding governments that followed since that time, and would imply an increase in the socioeconomic and social inequities.

It was since the debt crisis of the early 1980s that this policy could achieve total legitimacy at national and international levels. However, it was since Carlos Menem´s first presidency -and more precisely, with Minister Domingo Cavallo's Convertibility Plan of 1991- that a model with social and economic viability emerged based on the objectives of the Washington Consensus, and designed to meet the commitments of the external debt. During the previous period, even when the adjustment was already running, it could neither be fully performed nor applied in the orthodox terms of the Mememist period either. Internal and external factors prevented it from being established during the military dictatorship as well as during the democratic government of Raúl Alfonsín. The causes were the lack of social consensus and the instability of the economic and social situation that did not offer enough guarantees to the external investor. On the other hand, this was both cause and consequence of the successive economic crises, of the hyperinflationary periods and of the unsuccessful negotiations with the International Monetary Fund (IMF) and even with local businessmen.

The convertibility plan included the privatizations and de-regulations that led to the dismantling of public bodies of institutional and political control. In this context, the population with the lowest incomes suffered severe impacts in their socioeconomic situation. Even vast sectors of the middle classes added up to the masses of those excluded from the productive system.

The unemployment rate in May 1989 (when Menem became President) was 8,1 % and in October 1999, when he finished his two governmental periods, it increased to 13,1% (with an underemployment rate of 14,3%). The highest unemployment rate of this governmental period was in May 1995 (18,4%). Then, it decreased, with some ups and downs, although it always kept above the two digits, reaching 21,5% in May 2002.

The notorious increase in unemployment and the violent transformation of a wide social sector into exceeding population opened the door to a succession of poverty, hunger, insecurity and social riots that dominated the scene in the mid-1990s. In some provinces, the unemployment rates were close to, or even higher than 20% -Jujuy, Tucumán, Bahía Blanca, Mar del Plata, Salta, Concordia, Gran La Plata, Gran Santa Fe, Río Cuarto, Gran Rosario, Gran Catamarca-. It was a process of national de-structuring expressed in impoverished provinces with high debts.

Besides, the adjustment and restructuring was escorted by institutions adequate to its own interests. The viability of the model was possible because it acted through degraded institutions; through which Argentina would have no chance to develop its economy or to insert itself in the competitive global context.

This leads us to ask ourselves about the feasibility, in the mid-term, of the self-sustainability of the potential improvements in the income and/or in the occupation of the families of poor farmers that are promoted by different Programs of Rural Development existing in Argentina since the 1980s. Which is the scope and the feasibility of the strategies of rural development in Argentina in the context of the neoliberal socioeconomic adjustment? Do proposals centered in the expansion of production and agricultural productivity of poor families achieve their productive inclusion or do these families remain in their situation of poverty and exclusion? Is it only an economic problem or is it also affected by the present institutional weakness in Argentina?

NEOLIBERALISM, INSTITUTIONS AND DEVELOPMENT POLICIES

The neoliberal period led to a gradual process by which the State abandoned its traditional roles of promoting development and guaranteeing equality of opportunities in education, health and housing.

Widespread privatizations and de-regulations were the main instrument of this policy to ensure a differential profitability and, consequently, intensify the concentration of capital. Concessions, powers and advantages in prices and conditions were granted to private investors, frequently in strategic areas such as natural resources, transport, energy and communications.

At the same time, the National State restricted itself in its competence as a market regulation entity, for example, by disarticulating the regulatory institutions for food and raw materials (grains, meat, cotton, *yerba mate*, tobacco). The State also gave in specific functions of the Central Bank, as happened with the convertibility plan by Minister Cavallo. From then on, the dollar became the actual exchange standard.

Likewise, the participation of international organizations was encouraged for the funding of specific projects and programs. This involvement reached even the design and implementation of such projects. This contributed to the increase of the external debt because *funding came through international loans*. Jointly, the government fostered the implementation of social policies by NGOs (non-governmental organizations) under the argumentation that this would imply operational benefits due to their lower operating costs and NGOs would contribute to increase the participation of civil society in public issues.[1]

The programs aimed at the rural poor were inserted in the context described above, with a growing social polarization and with a State that disregarded and/or lacked instruments for the implementation of a national development policy. Some of them (as the PNEA -Program for Small Producers of the Argentine Northwest-, PRODERNEA -Program of Rural Development of the Argentine Northeast-, PSA -Agricultural Social Program-, PROINDER - Program of Rural Development Initiatives-) were intended to implement and reach an integral proposal of productive transformation and improve the income or standard of living of the rural poor. These strategies are contradictory at a national scale since they are part of

[1] In the rural environment there are few NGOs specialized in rural development with many years of expertise. The NGOs dealing with family farmers tend to have a lower scope regarding the number of beneficiaries and the kind, diversity and extent of the services they offer; occasionally they can exceed 2.000 beneficiaries by NGO. Those with most experience are: INCUPO –Institute of Popular Culture -, INDES -Institute of Social Development and Human Promotion -, FUNDAPAZ –Foundation for the Development of Justice and Peace.

macroeconomic processes characterized by the systematic discrimination and exclusion of the small agricultural producing sector.

These processes were not restricted to Argentina; they appeared in the whole of Latin America with local, national and regional specificities. Latin America was the first goal of the Washington Consensus, of the macroeconomic adjustment. Chiriboga (1997: 14-17) in a specific analysis of the subject says: "...the fiscal austerity that characterized the reforms in the Region has implied an important decline in the supply of public services, such as roads, communications infrastructure, electrification, irrigation, education and rural training... *With only a few exceptions, what characterizes the Region as result of the economic reforms, is the weakening, and even the vanishing, of sector-aimed policies and of organizations in charge of supporting the agricultural producers...* The implemented reforms have not been able to promote an alternative institutional system in support of small agricultural producers either. In fact, the main effect was a big reduction in loans programs, technical assistance or commercialization among this kind of producers" (translation and italics are ours).

RURAL DEVELOPMENT IN ARGENTINA

The State concern for implementing programs to improve the situation of the families of the poor agricultural producers had it first attempt in the democratic period that began in 1973 with a Program of Re-conversion of Small Holding Areas, which, unfortunately, had a short duration due to the sudden political changes typical of that period. The rural development issue would re-appear ten years later, with the following democratic period (by the end of 1983).

Previous programs –from the 1960s and early 1970s- had different characteristics. The concern about poverty was minor, having as a priority the insertion and sectorial, agro-industrial, mercantile and capitalist development of family producers with a certain degree of capitalization. They were plans of colonization of integral rural development, such as that of the Río Dulce in Santiago del Estero or that of the Institute for Development of the Lower Valley of the Río Negro -IDEVI-.

Lombardo and Tort (1998: 6) mention the Agricultural National Program -PRONAGRO- designed by the National Secretary of Agriculture, Livestock and Food -SAGPyA- in 1984, as the first case in the period of democratic restoration under the radical administration of Raúl Alfonsín. However, they say it could not be fulfilled because of the opposition of the middle and large farmers of the Pampas and also for the economic plan known as Austral.

The first actions in rural development of this period could be performed only at the beginning of the 1990s; we are referring to the PNEA, although its design began in the mid-1980s, with the return of democracy.

In 1987, the Coordination Unit for Research Projects and Plans for Small Holding Producers was established within the National Institute for Agricultural Research -INTA- dependent on SAGPyA. This unit was aimed at generating and validating agricultural and forestry technology for these producers. This was a totally new experience for the INTA since, until then it had only assisted medium and large producers.

In all aspects: institutional, professional, programmatic and political, rural development is a recent experience (just a bit longer than a decade). Actually, it was only towards the 1980s that Argentina began to be considered a country with rural poverty.

The reason for this fact may be traced in the historic development of the country that had shown, until then, an economic dynamics very different from the rest of Latin America. Its extraordinary and varied agricultural production and its scarce population marked the initial difference. Since the end of the XIX century and well into the XX, the gross domestic product and the foreign currency came from exports of grains and meat, and these products (in the hands of medium and large farmers) had a differential profitability in the world due to the natural high productivity of the Pampas. The economic dynamism resulting from the period of the substitution of imports is also very important to build the image of a rich country: the development policies and the Welfare State of the 1950s to 1970s allowed for the insertion of many small rural producers in the dominant economic model, either producing food for the growing domestic market or migrating and finding jobs in the new national industry. This caused an early urbanization centered in the main Pampean provinces: Buenos Aires, Santa Fé and Córdoba. It was a period of massive migrations from the country to the city responding to the intense employment demand from the industries located in the most urbanized areas (Manzanal 1993: 28-34).

In the mid-1970s, a process of structural transformation started together with the beginning of the neoliberal model. Since then, a set of measures, historically demanded by the most concentrated exporting sector, began to be systematically implemented: the dissolution of the Grain and Meat Board, the elimination custom duties to exports, the establishing of a unique exchange rate and the reduction of the custom duties to imports. The impacts of these measures varied according to the productive insertion type (agro-exporting or domestic). Those producers related to the domestic market had to face the recessive effects of the crisis on this market.

Therefore, the exporting agriculture began to grow rapidly. The fishing activity had also a very important dynamics in relative terms. Oilseeds and cereals showed the biggest productive increases while the traditional products (meat and regional crops) lagged behind.

At the same time, the socioeconomic situation of the small producers worsened due to the decrease in the process of their products as a result of the adjustment, the de-regulation and the privatizations. The small producers were affected by: a) the elimination of quotas for sowing, harvesting, manufacturing, and marketing of traditional production. b) The suppression of the grant they received through the Commerce Employees' Family Grants Office -CASFEC- as in the case of the cotton producers. c) The decrease in the resources distributed as overprice for tobacco producers. d) The absence of subsidized loans as a result of the privatization of the provincial banks. e) The implementation of a regressive tax system, which implied a heavier load for the small producers (the biggest revenue comes from taxes on consumption such as the Value Added Tax -VAT). f) The trend to the elimination of informal economy, in which the small producers were operating at that time.

THE BENEFICIARIES OF RURAL DEVELOPMENT PROGRAMS

One of the characteristics, or requirements, of the programs to alleviate rural poverty promoted by the international funding organizations is the focus on the potential beneficiaries. Soverna and Craviotti (1998: 18) affirm that in the projects of rural development, "focalizing" is a requirement to guarantee that the benefits of a project be directed to those that meet the poverty criteria defined for each case.

To focus on the programs' beneficiary groups it is necessary to define, beforehand, the potential population universe, its relative importance and its location. Then, the Programs set up their respective eligibility criteria. However, this task has turned out to be very complex for different reasons, ranging from the theoretic-methodological difficulties emerging from the different conceptualizations and interpretations of the beneficiary subject to the inadequate data base available.

There is a great diversity of situations that compose the universe of agricultural family production, as well as an overlap of different interpretations that try to identify and make the concepts of peasantry, small agricultural holding and rural poverty, operational.

Neiman (1997:1 a 4) when he refers to "rural poverty" says that: "it does not refer exclusively to geographical contexts of relative isolation, to institutional deficiencies and/or to social subjects typical of the country, but it refers to a more complex notion given by the present re-structuring of the activity" (translation is our). He emphasizes that the trends towards globalization and re-conversion imply: (i) an expansion of the non-agricultural rural activities; (ii) modifications in the relation capital-labor that accelerate the decrease in the welfare of the rural population and make the labor markets more flexible; and (iii) an increase in the regional differences due to the fragmented and unequal character of the current development.

Carballo (1996:57) states that the agricultural family production is: "a heterogeneous universe that includes families producing for their own consumption as well as units with important levels of capitalization totally connected with markets" (translation is our).

Based on data from the Population Census of 1991, the SAGPyA (1997[a]:4) estimated that in that moment there were 128.000 poor agricultural rural families (that is to say with Unsatisfied Basic Needs -UBN-).[2] This figure refers to family heads in rural zones and includes small producers as well as temporary workers.[3]

In spite of the complexity of the respective informative and methodological context, we know through different indicators (information surveyed locally in different provinces) that the poor farms have decreased considerably lately. This is a consequence of the neoliberal policy that made many small producers leave their farms and led to the bankruptcy of their economic activities. These holdings are located basically in the northern and northeastern provinces.

Finally, ¿what do Argentine small family farmers cultivate? They do not produce the basic food included in the household expenses. Cereals, meat, and oilseeds are grown by the capitalist agricultural sector. The small family producers of the non-pampean economies

---

[2] This national estimation was made within the SAGPyA to calculate the target population for the PROINDER program.

[3] However, to identify and quantify the peasant families, or small holdings or small family producers, it is better to use data from Agricultural Census that include specific data from families working in an agricultural holding (unfortunately, the Agricultural Census was carried out 14 years ago, in 1988).

produce basically traditional agro-industrial crops. According to Carballo (1991: 157) at the end of the 1980s they produced: 10% of sugar cane production, 15% of grapes for wine, 25% - 30% of cotton, and 10% of tobacco. They also raised *yerba mate*, tea, vegetables, sheep and goat stocks.

This production must have decreased considerably in the last decade because of the degradation of the small holding sector and the increase in the participation of the large agricultural holdings in the total volume of these products.[4] Since the liberalization and deregulation of the market, the productive boom of cotton, sugar cane, tobacco and *yerba mate* is well known. This expansion was shown in the notable productivity increases led by big agricultural companies, many of them new in the sector.

THE SPECIFICITIES OF THE RURAL DEVELOPMENT PROGRAMS

The different rural development programs described in this paper can be situated in the general context described above. These programs do not constitute a State policy given that there is no legal and institutional framework that gives consistency to the development model, designs the strategy, coordinates the particular actions of each program and rules its institutional, administrative and territorial organization as well as its respective benefits.

The current rural development programs whose target population are the small poor agricultural producers and which have an "integral" strategy for the transformation and the productive insertion of the sector and whose loans and subsidies have a central role, are: the PRODERNEA (prolongation of the PNEA, ended in 1997), the PSA and the PROINDER (enlargement of the PSA). Additionally, we can mention the PRODERNOA (Program for Rural Development of the Argentine Northwest) with similar characteristics to the PRODERNEA but centered in three provinces of the Northwest (Jujuy, Salta and Catamarca) and that has not started yet (although the loan contract was signed in the year 2000).

We must mention that within the SAGPyA there are other programs such as Peasant Woman from the Argentine Northwest, Rural Change, Small Holding Unit, Pro-Huerta, Project for the Restructuring of Tobacco Areas (PRAT), Forestry Project of Development (CAPPCA), and Regime for the Promotion of Forest Plantations (RPPF). But, generally, these programs are not basically aimed at small producers, or they lack an integral strategy for their transformation, or their main component is the technical assistance instead of loans and subsidies.[5] Anyway, they should be taken into account in other analyses related to the small holdings population because some of them support or complement their own actions with the ones of the programs analyzed in this paper. For example, in certain activities or locations the PSA, the PNEA, the Small Holding Unit, the Pro-Huerta and the Peasant Woman have shared the implementation of their projects.

In other areas of the national and provincial public sector, there are also programs that benefit small producers. This is the case of the Secretary of Social Development of the Presidency, with the Participative Fund of Social Investment -FOPAR- and the Participative

[4] The lack of a new Agricultural Census prevents us from giving accurate information on this issue.

[5] Besides, they usually have a wider definition of target population (Rural Change, Pro-Huerta, PRAT) or have only one specific component for small producers (CAPPCA, RPPF) within other broader actions (Pfr. SAGPyA, 2000).

Fund of Capitalization -FONCAP-; and the Ministry of Labor with the Youngsters' Project and the Work Plan. They matter precisely because, together, they contribute to the different services and actions directed to the small agricultural producers. However, these benefits cannot be adequately profited from due to the absence of a policy and a coordinated strategy.

We will now introduce some characteristics of the main current programs which are the subject of this paper. The following data were obtained from SAPyA (1996: 69 - 82):

1. Prodernea

This Program is an extension of the PNEA and, therefore, has many things in common with it. The PNEA was one of the first experiences in rural development and although its design began in 1984, it was implemented only at the beginning of 1991 and it concluded in 1997.

The institutional organization of both programs was based on a National Coordination Unit, with headquarters in the SAGPyA, and the implementation bodies were the Agriculture Ministries of Chaco, Corrientes, Formosa and Misiones (in the PNEA Chaco was not included). Both were funded through a loan from FIDA – BID (International Fund for Agricultural Development –Inter-American Development Bank) subscribed by the Nation and transferred to the provincial governments by the SAGPyA. The provinces were responsible by law of the external debt, guaranteed by the Federal Co-participation, and they implemented the Project through their agriculture Ministries and contributed with counterpart resources (SAGPyA; 1999).

The PRODERNEA (and the PRODERNOA as well) are aimed at a group of small agricultural producers whose economic level is higher than that of the beneficiaries of the PNEA. Its objective is to increase the family income and the self-management capabilities of small producers and indian population of the region. This goal is achieved through the diversification and re-conversion of the production, an improvement in the access to the markets, the establishment of a special fund for small producers and the empowerment of small producers' organizations.

The provincial governments are responsible for its implementation; having started by the end of 1998 and lasting for 5 years (Pfr. SAGPyA; 1997: 62 and ss). In fact, in January 1999 it began in Misiones only. Apparently it should be deferred beyond the year 2003 due to the delays in its implementation. The provinces joined gradually, one per year (in May 2002 Corrientes had not started the Program yet and Formosa had not disbursed the money). Only Chaco and Misiones were able to start with the Program.

In this project, the national Director was replaced twice (February 2000 and April 2001) according to the political modifications at the national level (and therefore in the SAGPyA). This has implied a delay in the implementation.

The disbursements for Misiones amounted to u$s 650.000 until November 2001 (from a loan of u$s 16 million). Chaco went through political problems and difficulties in the technical implementation. As this province was not included in the previous stage of the PNEA, it had less availability of people with expertise specific in strategies and actions for small producers.

The program demanded a strong effort from technicians with producers, because it was based on a loan that required repayment. And this meant a lot of technical support and training from the National Unit which was somewhat dismembered because of the political changes derived from the removal of most of the technicians that had worked in the PNEA for many years. Similarly, in some of the participating provinces, there may have been interference from the provincial government with the decisions related to the projects.

During 1999, another project -the PRODERNOA- was designed. It was approved by FIDA in September 1999, with similar characteristics to the PNEA and the PRODERNEA but intended for 3 provinces of the Northwest: Jujuy, Salta and Catamarca. The loan contract was signed in November 2000 but the project has not started its activities yet. Salta, Jujuy and Catamarca have not approved the law allowing them to receive the loan, and therefore the respective contract with the SAGPyA was not signed either (this loan has no commitment commission). The debt is of about u$s 5 million for Jujuy (being its counterpart 2 million), u$s 4,5 million for Catamarca (u$s 1,5 million counterpart) and u$s 8 million for Salta (u$s 3 million counterpart)

One important difference between the PRODERNEA and the PNEA is that the former is aimed at producers with entrepreneurial skills, that is to say, producers with a higher economic profile.

2. PSA

By the end of the 1990s another line of action was born within the SAGPyA for the rural poor: the PSA, which started in April 1993 without due date and with national scope. The whole country is included with the exception of Santa Cruz and Tierra del Fuego.

When the PSA started working, the PNEA was already running in the northeastern provinces with similar strategies and target population. During the first half of the 1990s, the PSA and the PNEA were the most important programs focused on the poor small agricultural producers, and so it was necessary for both programs to agree on coordinated guidelines to avoid overlapping and friction among provinces. Key informants state that these guidelines could not always be fulfilled. This demonstrates the need to develop a unique policy for the target group with a central coordination.

The main support for the PSA comes from funds from the national budget. In the beginning $10 million were assigned for the launching of the sub-programs. Later it received annual funds of about $ 4 and $9,5 million, depending on the year. The amount transferred to the beneficiaries (accumulated up to the end of 2001) was approximately $28 million (SAGPyA, 2000: 40).[6]

Its goals are: (i) contribute together with the small agricultural producers to the search of alternatives to face the economic crisis; and (ii) increase the income of small agricultural producers and promote its organized participation in political decisions about programs and projects.

The PSA works through a decentralized structure composed by a National Technical Coordination Unit -UTCN-, the National Coordination Committee and the Advisory Council on the national level; and a Provincial Technical Coordination Unit -UTCP- for each of the 21 participating provinces. In each UTCP there are representatives from the provincial

[6] Due to the convertibility plan, between 1991 and the end of 2001 all figures in pesos are equivalent to US dollars.

governments, the INTA, the NGOs and the producers. The provincial coordinator of each UTCP depends on the UTCN.

In the National Coordination Committee there are representatives from other programs of the SAGPyA, the INTA, the Inter-American Institute for Agricultural Cooperation -IICA-, the Inter-Cooperative Agricultural Confederation Ltd -CONINAGRO-, and the main NGOs related to rural development.

3. Proinder, Project of Rural Initiatives

In the mid-1990s a new stage started which focused on groups of extreme poverty through donations or subsidies. The most representative example is the PROINDER, with headquarters within the SAGPyA but funded by the World Bank -WB-. This program is an extension of the PSA. Its principal component, a granted fund, depends on the PSA.

In early December 1998 the PROINDER was formally launched, being its total funding budget u$s 100 million, being 70 % provided by the WB and the rest by the Nation. Its ending is expected by the year 2003.

This program was being designed for many years, as happened with the PNEA. In 1994 the diagnostic stage started (Soverna and Craviotti, 1998:3). In the preliminary versions of this program the "improvement of income" was not included among its objectives. However, in the last revision, it appeared as a goal but without any quantification. Its explicit objective is: "to improve the standard of living of the rural poor population in a framework in which such population may participate in an organized way in the decision-making which affects them and in conditions of sustainability of natural resources and the environment". Some of its intermediate objectives are: increase quantity and/or quality of the production, inclusion of new productive activities, improvement of the production for self-consumption, better positioning in the market, better equipments.

Its main component is a fund (FAIR –Fund of Support to Rural Initiatives) that subsidizes investments of beneficiaries. This is its main difference with the PSA that gives loans that require repayment. This Fund has an application methodology similar to the one applied in the PSA: the beneficiaries, gathered in groups, participate in the diagnosis, design, implementation, follow-up and evaluation of sub-projects or initiatives (Pfr. Soverna and Craviotti, 1998: 2).

As the main component of this program is based on subsidies for rural workers and vulnerable population (indians, women and young people) it may be considered as a new trend in the design of rural development programs. The emphasis is on rural poverty in general, and not on agricultural producers only, and the actions are oriented towards assistance rather than towards self-sustainability. The heterogeneousness and seriousness of poverty in rural environments reduce the concern about production and agricultural holdings as an exclusive issue. Therefore, we can conclude that the concern is focused on "assisting and alleviating the situation of extreme poverty" of the poor living in rural environments (working in the agricultural sector or not) rather than on making structural transformations.

This approach is also evident in the transfer of PROINDER funds to the Program for the Recovery of the Productive Capacity of the Small Producers affected by floods (PROEMER) during 1999, although its aim was to alleviate the social emergency situation brought about by the natural disaster related to El Niño phenomenon. The PROEMER, which started functioning as a PROINDER component since August 1998, received U$S 31 million that were distributed as individual subsidies to 39.000 producers in emergency situation in the following provinces: Corrientes, Santa Fe, Misiones and Santiago del Estero.

The lack or scarcity of additional national resources to face this social problem led to the use of PROINDER funds, which were originally intended for other objectives. This transfer of funds had direct effects in the delay in the implementation of the original components of the PROINDER until the end of 1999. Additionally, this fact is somewhat connected with the low priority assigned to this project by some groups related to the political power.

The following tables show a summary of some variables that characterize the three current programs (the PNEA, ended in 1977, is not included).

Table 1. National Programs of Rural Development in Argentina, Institutions in charge and Target Population

Acronym	Institution in Charge// Executing Institution	Target Population
PSA	SAGPyA//SAGPyA	159.712 small producers
PROINDER	SAGPyA//SGPyA	127.565 families with UBN related to agricultural production.
PRODERNEA	SAGPyA// SAGPyA y Provincial Agricultural Ministries	41.700 families with agricultural holdings of less than 25 hectares[7] has in the provinces of Misiones, Formosa, Corrientes and Chaco and 10.550 indian families from Misiones, Chaco and Formosa.

Source: SAGPyA (2000: 37) "Los programas nacionales de desarrollo rural ejecutados en el ámbito de la SAGPyA", *Serie Estudios e Investigaciones 1*, PROINDER, Buenos Aires.

Table 2. National Programs of Rural Development in Argentina, Target population, Eligibility criteria, geographic location and assistance types

ACRONYM	TARGET	ELEGIBILITY CRITERIA	LOCATION	SERVICES OR ASSISTANCE TYPE
PSA	none	Groups of at least 4 families in Patagonia, 6 in the rest of the country, the producer works in the agricultural holding, permanent household in the holding, lack of permanent salary job and contract of transitory labor only in moments of high demand, extra-holding income coming from transitory labor or handcraft not surpassing the salary of rural worker, income level coming from holding not higher than two monthly rural worker salaries, and capital level not higher than $20.000, excluding family household and land.	National scope, except Santa Cruz and Tierra del Fuego.	Technical assistance. Training. Marketing Support. Assistance with solidary payback of $200 per family, $2.000 per self-consumption projects group. Loan up to $1.200 per family, $50.000 per group in associative productive initiatives.

[7] 1 hectare ("ha") is equivalent to 2.5 acres

Table 2. (Continued)

ACRONYM	TARGET	ELEGIBILITY CRITERIA	LOCATION	SERVICES OR ASSISTANCE TYPE
PROINDER	40.000 small producers and transitory poor workers	Rural household, the producer works in the agricultural holding, not hiring more than 60 annual wages, family work outside the holding, not higher than 270 annual wages, fixed capital not higher than $15.000, livestock existences not higher than 500 sheep or goat heads or 50 cattle heads, not having a shed of brick or metal sheets of more than 50 m2, have any of the needs listed in the UBN indicator.	National, except Santa Cruz and Tierra del Fuego. Focus per department	Funding not reimbursable for investment initiatives. Limits of $200 per family and $4.000 per group for self-consumption projects; $1.500 per family and $22.500 per group for projects of community use and/or holding infrastructure, and $1.500 per family and $50.000 per group for projects of community use infrastructure. Technical assistance. Training. Marketing support. Institutional empowerment.
PRODERNEA	10.570 small producers' families and 3.450 indian families.	Small producers with some productive resources and entrepreneurial management skills but who face multiple limitations. Requirements: living in the rural area corresponding to the Project and working in their own holding with predominant use of family labor, working in an agricultural holding of up to 25 ha or bigger but with only 25 ha of apt land; not to be in debt with the PNEA or other credit programs; most of the family income should come from the agricultural holding, with possible outside income complement from a family member; keeping a productive structure with a clearly commercial orientation, that can exist together with self-consumption production (the latter represents a minor part in the family income). Indian communities are also eligible, whether they practise agriculture, handcraft, fishing, hunting or recollection.	Chaco, Corrientes, Formosa and Misiones. Focus per department except in Chaco.	Credit up to $5.000 per producer and $50.000 per group; lower limits in innovative activities or rural non-agricultural. Promotion of organization and technical assistance. Training and communication. Commercial and agro-industrial development. Support Fund to indian communities. Gender consideration and activities with rural youngsters.

Source: SAGPyA (2000: 38-9) "Los programas nacionales de desarrollo rural ejecutados en el ámbito de la SAGPyA", *Serie Estudios e Investigaciones 1*, PROINDER, Buenos Aires.

Table 3. National Programs of Rural Development in Argentina, operating period, total amount and funding agencies

N°	Acronym	Starting Date	Ending Date	Total Ammount	Funding Agency And % Of Funding
1	PSA	April 1993	Still operating	Subject to budget items. $ 9 million per year (average).	National Government (SAGPyA)
2	PROINDER	May 1998	May 2003	$100 million	75% BIRF 25% National Government
3	PRODERNEA	January 1999	January 2004	$36 million	45,7% FIDA 52,6% Provinces 1,6% SAGPyA

Source: SAGPyA (2000: 41) "Los programas nacionales de desarrollo rural ejecutados en el ámbito de la SAGPyA", *Serie Estudios e Investigaciones 1*, PROINDER, Buenos Aires

Some Limitations of the Rural Development Programs

When analyzing the operation of all these programs, it is clear that there is overlapping of objectives, territory coverage, subjects and actions and, therefore, we can conclude that the coordination and complementation among them has not been enough so far. Without any doubt, there is no institutionalized rural development policy, producing as a result a sum of different programs and actions rather than a coordinated strategy aimed at common objectives.

If we compare the strategy of rural development programs with the social and regional impacts of adjustment policies in Argentina, some contradictory aspects arise. For example:

1) There is no national, regional or local instrumentation to face the restrictions posed by a recessive, concentrated and highly competitive market, especially for small family producers, who have no control over it.
2) There is a lack of regional diagnosis indicating the specific and essential actions to be developed in each zone to be promoted, as well as the particular projects of rural development for target groups. The programs work without any coordination with regional or provincial development policies that could act as framework and boost it. At the provincial level, we notice a lack of connection between public organizations and institutions in charge of rural development and small producers' organizations and support NGOs.
3) The information about small producers at national and provincial levels is not updated; this brings about ignorance about the productive and socioeconomic characteristics of small producers and agricultural transitory workers. This is consistent with the lack of a national strategy of rural development defined in a coordinated and centralized fashion and, at the same time, of provincial strategies.
4) The loan or subsidy amounts given to the beneficiary families do not match up with the necessary resources to start with the modifications the sector needs to overcame its situation of poverty and structural deficiency. The two most important national

programs have distributed $1.200 (the PSA) and $1.700 (the PNEA[8]), in average per family. These amounts can be very important for each family. Due to the low annual income of most of these small producer families, these subsidies may represent more than 30 % of their total annual income, plus the additional value that it is cash. Nonetheless, they do not mean or allow structural changes in the productive development of small producers.

5) The total amount destined for loans and subsidies is small if compared with the funds assigned to training for organization, for the productive, technical, administrative and financial activity in the agricultural holding, and for the development of self-consumption orchards –Rural Change, Small Holding Unit, Pro-Huerta, Peasant Woman (some of them may have been lacking funds for a long time and particularly at present -2002). Although the poor agricultural producer families have received some assistance, this does not mean that they have been able to find "solutions" or autonomy to become independent because each small producer needs *loans, specific technical assistance and multiple actions performed in a coordinated fashion.* Furthermore, there are about 100.000 poor agricultural producer families that require an improvement in their productive conditions and standard of living to achieve a self-sustainable insertion in the market and not just a simple relief. During the year 2001 the PSA distributed $917.927 in direct financial assistance (loan or subsidy), the PROINDER $2.823.273, and the PRODERNEA $807.937.[9]
6) They reach a limited number of beneficiaries. The available data regarding the number of beneficiaries of the running programs is imprecise and overstated: between 1991 and 1997 the beneficiaries from the PNEA were 8.000 and those from the PSA were 39.000 families between 1993 and the end of 1998. However, we cannot assure that this information is accurate or free from overlaps because beneficiaries are not identified year by year. They usually sum up the beneficiaries of the whole period under analysis, or all the "operations" (loans, technical assistance, and training) and consider this as the "total amount of assisted families". This procedure gives as a result a total amount quite higher than that resulting from individual follow-up, name by name, independently from the benefits each person/family has received. According to data from the year 2001, there were 11.046 beneficiaries in the PSA, 11.721 in the PROINDER and 1.447 in the PRODERNEA (figures with similar problems, including loans, technical assistance, training, adaptive experimentation)[10].
7) There is an overlapping and multiplication of actions that do not compose a consistent policy. As we have already mentioned, there is a sum of different programs which only in particular cases reach some coordination. As a consequence, the beneficiaries find it difficult to understand the different operating modes of each program.

---

[8] These figures were equivalent to US dollars until the devaluation of January 2002.

[9] Source: PROINDER, SAGPyA Institutional Strengthening Area, data base. It should be taken into account that during 2001 the budget for all programs was low due in part to the restrictions in the availability of resources imposed by the national government.

[10] Source: PROINDER, Fortalecimiento Institucional, SAGPyA, Base de datos.

8) Most programs are funded through an increase in the external debt. The social and economic consequences implied by this fact demand that these programs be directed to a real productive transformation of the poor small producer sector. That is to say, debt would only be acceptable when changed for growth and a better participation of the small producers in the gross national product; because debt means an economic embargo on the development of the country and endangers the potential of future generations. This is not to question the generation of the debt itself. On the contrary, we accept it replaces the lack of resources in the national budget for social policies. Additionally, the responsibility of these programs in the debt increase is actually lower due to their tiny amounts. It is clear that the groups of higher economic power are the true beneficiaries from the increase in the external debt.
9) If rural projects do not lead to structural transformations and remain as relief programs, they can turn into facilitators of political patronage. The "relief" to extreme poverty situations favors the discretionary acting of local administrations. The patronage spoils the projects really intended for reinforcing values and labor culture in the country. One example is what is going on in some areas with the "Work Program" of the National Ministry of Labor which gives transitory subsidies to the unemployed. It is common that poor agricultural producers participate in these programs given that, due to the seasonal characteristic of their jobs they appear as "unemployed" in different moments of the year (although, in fact, they are not unemployed). When these producers get used to obtaining a fixed monthly subsidy, they refuse to do their normal activities because of the effort and uncertainty they represent. This situation is very common in provinces with a high component of public jobs. We have seen this in La Rioja, Catamarca and Formosa, where the rural population that used to work in the country and now receives a public salary or an unemployment subsidy, is moving away from the possibility of re-inserting themselves as producers because they are getting accustomed to another kind of life and job dynamics having the security of getting a salary every month without the sacrifice and uncertainty associated with agricultural work.

Most of the restrictions mentioned above are the result of and can be explained within the framework of the present neoliberal policy. Thus, dividing little money among many people and reaching more beneficiaries has to do with the political interests of governments, their lack of resources due to the adjustment and their lack of interest in the problem of poverty. For governments, reaching more people is a goal that favors political consensus. Additionally, the increase in the number of beneficiaries could also benefit the officials from international funding agencies as an indicator of their efficiency and professional productivity.

Furthermore, the rural development programs are not the only ones that reach the beneficiary population, because it is trapped in a productive and economic framework where most impacts are negative and come from the macroeconomic adjustment. Frequently, the beneficiary population feels that the adjustment-associated loss in acquired and universal rights (in subsidies to their products, in health care, in education services and welfare system) surpasses the benefits they receive through focused social programs. This situation worsens when the benefits only apply to some sectors, to those that fit with the "eligibility criteria" for being the poorest.

The adjustment and the de-regulation had other consequences for small producers: many of the social benefits they received for free during the Welfare State, have at present to be bought from the private sector. That is why families claim for the lost social benefits, such as the social security that cotton, tobacco and *yerba* producers obtained from their regulating institutions. They also feel unsafe and chased by the State because they are neither registered under any Welfare System nor pay taxes, when, in fact their condition of economic marginality means they do not have the capability to make regular monthly payments because their income is seasonal and rarely higher than $ 6.000 or $ 7.000 per year[11]. We knew that the General Tax Office has pressed the producers with rural inspections when they deliver their products to the stockpilers.

FINAL REMARKS: THE POSSIBLE DIRECTION OF FUTURE ACTIONS

The characterization made above suggests that it is not very probable that the mentioned rural development actions turn into self-sustainable benefits for the poor agricultural sector. As they are designed so far, it is not very likely that these actions enable poor families to:

(a) Improve their income in the mid-term in a self-sustainable way.
(b) Achieve their "actual" productive integration.
(c) Overcome their historical instability, precariousness and flexibility as regards labor.
(d) Have their social security guaranteed.

The rural development strategy described in this paper is not designed to be imposed on or overcome the obstacles and conditions of the macroeconomic context, which systematically tend to the exclusion, marginality and invalidation of the agricultural small producer sector.

Of course, there are mechanisms to face these processes: institutions, groups and NGOs that are trying to do it, but in order to succeed they have to fight an "unfair battle" with sectors of higher economic and political power with other objectives.

It is also true that the beneficiaries themselves, through their stronger participation in the decision in different programs, are a very important factor in order to achieve these transformations. Furthermore, if we consider that most programs have components to promote the organization, training and participation of beneficiaries with the aim of de-structuring the historic limitations they have been facing. The way to achieve this goal is by giving them skills, power and knowledge so that they can assume responsibilities, make decisions, have authority and, in the long run, build processes of change.

All this is feasible only if beneficiaries can organize themselves and make demands free from the assistance of their respective programs. This entails a participative capability totally different from the one they presently have. They have to overcome many restrictions (economic, social, political, ideological, educative and participative) imposed by the current economic development model, which is exactly the opposite of the empowerment and consolidation of the small producer sectors.

---

[11] Amounts equivalent to US dollars until January 2002. From then on, incomes kept their values in pesos but remained highly devaluated compared to the dollar (to July 2002 the relation peso-dollar was $3,6/ dollar)

In other words, it seems that the rural development strategy and the economic policy are contradictory and they do not go after complementary objectives. Therefore, the explicit objectives of the rural development strategy are only apparent or their actual aim is to complement the adjustment with "relief".

This contradiction is more evident if we take into account that the present context is characterized by a weakening of social popular movements, a new organization or "social stabilization" where the "social change" issue is not relevant.

Then, the viability of a change in favor of the excluded -or precariously included,- majorities is higher if it emerges from the political action of these majorities rather than from their economic action. That is why their organizational empowerment against the negative consequences of the model (such as reduction in income, unemployment, insecurity, the deterioration of education, health and environment) is so important. In order to re-insert the groups "invalidated" by the present situation in the social game (Pfr.Castel; 1997: 23), they also have to play a relevant role through their opposition to the model that excludes them and stops them from being part of society as a whole. It is only through this action that the State will be able to play a suitable role.

Consequently, we should ask ourselves if there is another way of action in the present restriction context. We think there is.

First, if we consider that the production is *really* important for the training and labor re-insertion of these families but resources are scarce: Why not focus only on projects which actually promote integral cooperative or group work in the use of land, raw materials, and labor, in the agroindustrial transformation and in marketing? That is to say, carry out an exhaustive survey of the projects to be approved in order to choose the best.

This might imply accepting a lower number of beneficiaries and focusing only on those with potential to generate a real socio-productive transformation, knowing they can turn into a multiplying model for future projects and beneficiaries; exactly the opposite of the disappointment resulting from a succession of unfulfilled goals. Precisely, in a previous paper (Manzanal; 1998:73) we concluded regarding a frustrated experience of joint marketing of vegetables among peasants from Cachi, Salta: "The frustrated experiences add restrictions to the already existing ones."

Furthermore, the opposition between universal and focused policies has no support. On the contrary, they could complement each other, as Rubén de Dios (1998:130) affirms. Focusing *should mean solutions, actual transformations,* if not; the focused programs act as a double exclusion instrument. On the one hand, because of the magnitude of the potential beneficiaries they leave out, as this author says. On the other hand, because they do not provide any solution for the target population, producing a drawback in trust, in organizations, and in the will of participation.

Within the same line of action, programs should promote participation and commitment from the beneficiaries. This can only be achieved by applying "transparent" methods in all decisions and actions. For example, the generation of debt associated with programs and projects -which although minor is not innocuous- should be known about by the beneficiary population. Precisely, because these programs foster their participation and they should participate with full knowledge of the present and future possibilities and limitations. From our contacts with producer families we found out that most of them had no idea of the origin of the funds they were receiving. We think that if they learnt about it, their attitudes and demands regarding objectives and results would surely change and, probably, the need to promote actions tending to modify their marginal, socioeconomic and productive insertion would be more relevant.

The suggested way of acting requires a social agreement that guarantees a high degree of consensus, awareness and commitment from the involved population about the priorities and distribution of resources for social purposes. This leads, again, to the need of coordination and complementation among State programs. It is a priority that should not be ignored in order to favor short-term group and personal interests or in order to show differential results by government areas. Even when there have been many compilations about programs with external funding depending on different State Secretaries, there have been no results regarding complementation and coordination among them. We believe this is so because high governmental areas put specific and personal interests before the interests of society as a whole.

Therefore, it is urgent to train and inform about issues such as types and origin of funding, type of fostered activities and coordination and complementation among programs. In short, make the beneficiary population participate through ways of democratic representation.

It is from this knowledge that the beneficiaries can participate in the decision-making, which leads to transparent procedures and the decline of patronage and of individual or corporative advantages. In addition, the awareness of the beneficiaries about the processes they are involved in, is the first step in the understanding of their socioeconomic framework and, therefore, in the search for alternatives and solutions to their own problems.

Obviously, the feasibility of these training processes requires a long maturing time, which we think should be measured in decades rather than in five-year-periods, as it is the case with the programs analyzed in this paper (generally 4 to 5 years terms).

Besides, these programs work under strict schedules that are compatible neither with participation and training processes nor with the intrinsic characteristics of the target population. In particular, in Manzanal (ibid: 74) we affirmed that these families need a continued assistance instead of training from teams that may change or disappear within a short term: "The processes aimed at training, awareness, participation and organization of the sectors require time; a slow, consistent, sustained and long practice... a decade in the history of marginality suffered by these families and in their family life cycle is a very short time. However, it is too long in terms of the actual projects currently being performed".

So that rural development actions may build effective and sustainable improvements in the standard of living of the rural poor, it is necessary for these actions to have connection and coordination with one another.

This means that we need *a rural development "policy" that is part of a local and regional development strategy and fosters the commitment and the effective participation of beneficiaries in its different stages.*

Organizing and implementing several public programs from a central strategy would avoid many problems related to the scarcity of funds and, basically, it would reach beneficiaries with proposals *according to* their capacity to assimilate different projects; *integral*, due to the coordination among different areas; *sustainable* in the long term because of the addition of resources; and *decisive* in order to achieve the initial objectives. This would also avoid the excess of bureaucracy.

No doubt this is a difficult task because it implies an effort at organizing technical and human resources available individually and unequally in each State area and/or in each program.

However, the most important fact is that we need will and decision from high political levels. This implies not only the intention of "coordination", but, basically, *determination* to face the socioeconomic transformation of the rural poor as one of the priorities in the State policy.

The advance towards the opposite interests, typical of every process of change, demands: (i) *a deep knowledge about the specific problem*, (ii) *to allow the participation* of the different involved sectors (producers, officials, technicians), (iii) to have the *capability to manage* conflicts of interests, and (iv) *to show determination and strength* to initiate a real transformation to improve the previous situation.

REFERENCES

Aspiazu, Daniel (1994) "La industria argentina ante la privatización, la desregulación y la apertura asimétrica de la economía", en D. Aspiazu y H. Nochteff, *El desarrollo ausente*, Tesis, Buenos Aires, 1994.

Basco, Mercedes (1997) *Modalidades de asistencia técnica a los productores agropecuarios en la Argentina*, IICA, Buenos Aires.

Carballo, Carlos (1991) "Los pequeños productores y el desarrollo rural en la Argentina", en *Realidad Económica 110*, IADE, Buenos Aires.

-------------------------(1995) "Programa Social Agropecuario y Cambio Rural. Dos intentos para atenuar la crisis entre los agricultores familiares", en *Realidad Económica 136*, IADE, Buenos Aires.

Castel, Robert (1997) *La metamorfosis de la cuestión social. Una crónica del salariado*, Paidós, Buenos Aires.

Chiriboga, Manuel (1997) "Desafíos de la pequeña agricultura familiar frente a la globalización", *Perspectivas Rurales 1*, Univerisidad Nacional, Heredia, Costa Rica.

Chudnovsky Daniel, López, Andrés y Porta, Fernando (1995) "Más allá del flujo de caja. El boom de la inversión extranjera directa en la Argentina", en *Desarrollo Económico Revista de Ciencias Sociales*, N° 137, abril-junio, IDES, Buenos Aires.

De Dios, Rubén (1998) "Políticas para la pequeña producción agropecuaria o el derecho a permanecer", *Realidad Económica 158,* IADE, Buenos Aires.

Forni, Floreal y Neiman, Guillermo (1994) "La pobreza rural en la Argentina", Documento de trabajo N° 5, mimeo inédito, CEPA (Comité Ejecutivo para el Estudio de la Pobreza en la Argentina), Ministerio de Economía y Obras y Servicios Públicos, Secretaría de Programación Económica, Buenos Aires.

González, María, Pagliettini, Liliana et al (1996) *Habitat rural y pequeña producción en la Argentina. Situaciones de pobreza rural y pequeña producción agraria,* Subscretaría de Vivienda, Secretaría de Desarrollo Social, Buenos Aires.

Kosacoff, Bernardo (1995) "La industria argentina, un proceso de reestructuración desarticulada", en Pablo Bustos (comp.), *Más allá de la estabilidad*, Fundación Friedrich Ebert, Buenos Aires.

Lombardo, Patricia y Tort, María Isabel (1998) "Estrategias de intervención para pequeños y medianos prodcutores agropecuarios en la década del ´90", mimeo *Jornadas Extraordinarias de Estudios Agrarios 'Horacio Giberti',* Facultad de Filosofía y Letras, Universidad de Buenos Aires.

Manzanal, Mabel (1993) *Estrategias de sobrevivencia de los pobres rurales*, Biblioteca Política Argentina, Centro Editor de América Latina, Buenos Aires.

------------------------ (1995) "Desarrollo y condiciones de vida en asentamientos campesinos. El caso de Cachi en los valles calchaquíes salteños", Buenos Aires: Tesis de Doctorado, Facultad de Filosofía y Letras, Universidad de Buenos Aires.

-------------------------(1998) "Vicisitudes de la comercialización de hortalizas entre los pequeños productores agropecuarios. El caso de la producción de tomate fresco en Cachi, Salta", *Realidad Económica 153,* enero/febrero, Buenos Aires.

Murmis, Miguel (1995) "Pobreza rural: datos recientes y diversidad de situaciones ocupacionales", mimeo PROINDER, Dirección de Planeamiento y Desarrollo Agropecuario, SAGyP, Buenos Aires.

Neiman, Guillermo (1997) "Empobrecimiento y exclusión. Nuevas y viejas formas de pobreza rural en la Argentina", mimeo, I Congreso Internacional de Pobres y Pobreza en la Sociedad Argentina, CEIL - UNQ, 4 al 7 de noviembre.

Petras, James y Vieux, Steve (1995) *¡Hagan juego!,* Icaria - Más Madera, Barcelona.

Redar Argentina (1993) "Boletín Redar Argentina, Red de Agroindustria Rural", Año 2, N° 3, INTA, Buenos Aires.

---------------------- (1994) "Boletín Redar Argentina, Red de Agroindustria Rural", Año 3, N° 5, INTA, Buenos Aires.

-----------------------(1994ª) "Boletín Redar Argentina, Red de Agroindustria Rural", Año 3, N° 6, INTA, Buenos Aires.

SAPyA (1992) "El minifundio en la Argentina", Dirección de Planificación y Desarrollo Agropecuario (inédito), Buenos Aires.

------------(1996) "Programas y proyectos agropecuarios y pesqueros", Dirección de Planeamiento y Desarrollo Agropecuario, Buenos Aires.

SAGPyA (1997) "Programa de Crédito y Apoyo Técnico para Pequeños Productores Agropecuarios de Noreste Argentino, Informe Final", Unidad Nacional de Coordinación PNEA, Buenos Aires.

------------- (1997ª) "Proyecto de Iniciativas Rurales, PROINDER, Resumen del proyecto", Dirección de Desarrollo Agropecuario, Buenos Aires.

....................(1999) "Políticas para pequeños productores con potencial empresarial en el norte argentino", Gobiernos Provinciales, FIDA, SAGPyA, mimeo, setiembre 1999, Buenos Aires.

.....................(2000) "Los programas nacionales de desarrollo rural ejecutados en el ámbito de la SAGPyA", *Serie Estudios e Investigaciones 1*, PROINDER, Buenos Aires.

Soverna, Susana y Craviotti, Clara (1998) "Los estudios de caso: su utilidad para el análisis sociológico y la formulación de programas de desarrollo rural", mimeo *Jornadas Extraordinarias de Estudios Agrarios 'Horacio Giberti',* Facultad de Filosofía y Letras, Universidad de Buenos Aires, agosto de 1998.

In: Economics, Politics and Social Issues in Latin America ISBN 1-60021-182-8
Editor: Mary P. Lassiter, pp. 195-221

Chapter 10

Active Labor Market Policies: Evaluative Evidence

Amit Dar
World Bank

I. Introduction

Over the past several decades, "active" labor market policies (ALMPs) have emerged as an important employment policy tool, particularly in developed countries. ALMPs include a wide range of activities, intended to increase the quality of labor supply (e.g., through retraining); to increase labor demand (e.g., through direct job creation); or to improve the matching of workers and jobs (e.g., through job search assistance). The objective of these measures is primarily economic -- to increase the probability that the unemployed will find jobs or that the underemployed will increase their productivity and earnings.[1] However, more recently the case for active labor market policies has also emphasized the potential social benefits in the form of the inclusion and participation that comes from productive employment.

ALMPs are usually regarded as a useful alternative to "passive" (e.g. unemployment insurance, safety net) type of programs, especially in cases of high unemployment. Aside from the political attractiveness of these programs for the government as "seen to be doing something" to mitigate unemployment, it also makes sense at a conceptual level for these programs (specifically retraining) to have heightened importance as technological change increases both skill requirements and the pace of obsolescence. However, as the experience of the past few decades has repeatedly demonstrated, actually implementing an active labor market policy poses many different types of challenges.

The immediate question is whether these programs have any impact. Evaluations of their impacts are mixed, with many programs assessed to have little or no impact on the

[1] Objectives can focus on the needs of employers as well, for example, to ensure a supply of appropriate workers. This may assume priority in times of rapid expansion when vacant jobs rather than unemployed workers are the predominant form of labor market imbalance. In fact, this was at least partly the case in the 1960s when active labor market programs were first introduced on a significant scale.

employability or earnings of participants. Even where policy-makers judge the evidence more favorably, or where they feel compelled to introduce ALMPs for political reasons, they must confront a host of complex design and implementation issues in order to maximize the probability for success. Not surprisingly, most experience with ALMPs have been in developed countries although that is changing to some degree now. It is clear though, that the role and nature of active programming will vary at different stages of development. And, as the experience in OECD countries has shown, culture and institutions matter a great deal as well.

The purpose of this chapter is to review the international experience with active labor market policies and to discuss their applicability in developing countries. The empirical literature on evaluations of ALMPs is vast and often provides contradictory conclusions depending on country, time period and specific program characteristics under consideration. The aim of this review is to provide a summary of these evaluations and attempt to draw some lessons.

This chapter is structured as follows. In the next section, we provide a brief overview of active labor market programs and the level of expenditures on these programs. Section 3 briefly discusses the techniques used when evaluating ALMPs. The evaluation evidence on the impacts of ALMPs is reviewed in section 4 and the key variables associated with successful outcomes are identified. Finally, in section 6, we discuss the applicability of ALMPs to these countries and we assess the key considerations involved in balancing active and passive policies.

II. Active Labor Market Programs: An Overview

Active Labor Market Programs include three main elements (OECD, 1993):

- Mobilizing labor supply with job creation schemes, job subsidies and so on;
- Developing employment-related skills with measures such as retraining;
- Promoting efficient labor markets with employment services, job-matching and counseling.

Within this framework, the more common ALMPs are:[2]

- Direct job creation (public works schemes/public service employment)[3];
- public employment services/job search assistance agencies;
- training/retraining for unemployed adults and those at risk of unemployment;
- support to unemployed persons in starting up small businesses (micro-enterprise development);
- wage/employment subsidies to firms to hire unemployed individuals.

---

[2] A short description of each of these programs is provided in Annex I.

[3] While we use the terms public works and public service employment interchangeably, public works usually refer to physical/civil works to develop infrastructure usually carried out in developing countries. In OECD countries, similar programs are denoted as public service employment and may be used to employ individuals as, for examples, nurse aids and teachers.

In theory, ALMP policies can lower structural unemployment in two ways: by promoting more efficient matching between job-seekers and vacancies, and bringing discouraged and socially excluded workers (such as the long-term unemployed or women workers who dropped out of the labor force) back into the labor market. Targeted retraining and employment services would enhance their ability to re-enter the labor force and compete effectively for jobs. However, while ALMPs can positively affect employment and incomes their potential benefits may be diminished because of substitution, deadweight or displacement effects. These issues will be addressed in more detail in the next section.

Expenditures on Active Programs in OECD Countries

The OECD has collected expenditure data by member countries on active labor market programs since the mid-1980s. Figure 10.1 illustrates trends on government spending over time on ALMPs by showing average national expenditures throughout the OECD region as a percentage of national GDP between 1985 and 1998. The overall picture shows that the relative spending level increased early in the 1990s and has continued at that new and higher level through the decade. This increase likely reflects both an increasing preference on the part of governments for active programming and the higher unemployment in most countries in the 1990s compared to the 1980s.

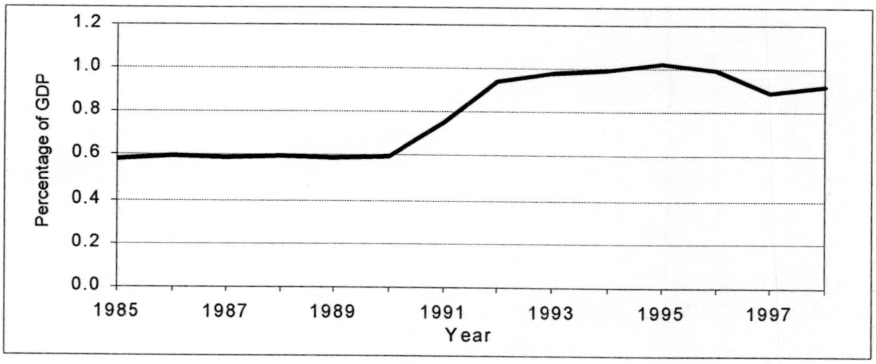

Figure 10.1. OECD Average ALMP Expenditures

A second point emerging from the OECD expenditure data is that countries generally see active and passive programming as complements rather than substitutes. In 1990, the correlation coefficient between national spending on active and passive programs was .60 (OECD, 1993). After diverging in the early nineties when income support jumped to accommodate workers laid off in the recession, the strong correlation resumed in 1993, with spending on active programs slightly increasing relative to passive (Figure 10.2).

Thirdly, it should be pointed out that while they still remain relatively high, expenditures on labor market programs have declined since the early 1990s. The general trend among most OECD countries has been either consistent with a decline in total labor market spending or considerable variances from year to year with no apparent long run trajectory.

Finally, there are major differences across OECD countries in terms of the level and composition of spending on ALMPs (as well as passive programs). Table 10.1 highlights these differences for a subset of countries using the latest expenditure data available.

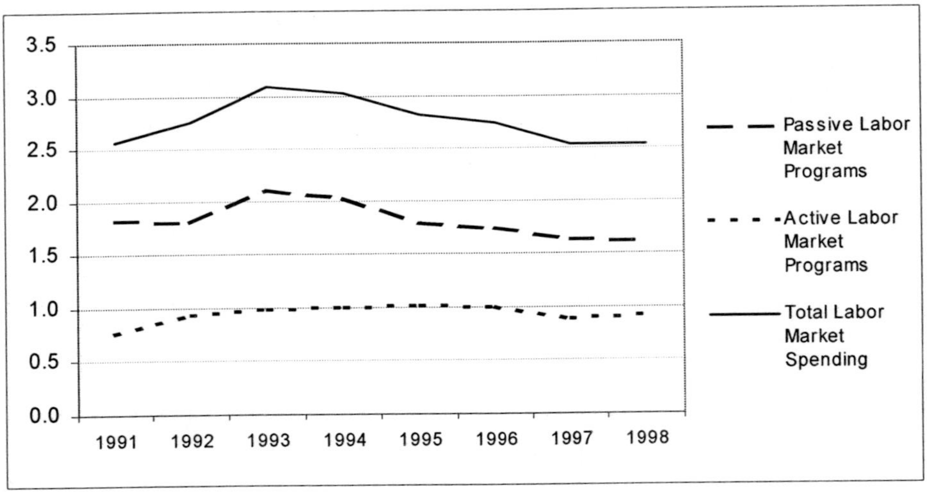

Figure 10.2. Labor Market Expenditures (measured in percentage of GDP)

III. The Importance of Good Evaluations

In spite of the large public expenditures on active labor market programs, rigorous evaluations of ALMPs have been relatively uncommon. In the continuing effort to improve the targeting and efficiency of social programs, policymakers are now increasingly realizing the importance of rigorous evaluations. They want to know what programs accomplish, what they cost, and how they should be designed to achieve maximum efficiency and cost-effectiveness. As we shall see in the next section, the evaluations we have reviewed in this paper are almost exclusively "impact" evaluations. Here we discuss some of the techniques used in performing an impact evaluation.

Impact Evaluation Techniques[4]

Techniques for evaluating the effectiveness of labor programs can be either scientific and non-scientific. The scientific evaluations are of two types: experimental and quasi-experimental. Experimental or classically designed evaluations require selection of both the "control" and "treatment" groups - those who receive the assistance and those who do not - prior to the intervention. Quasi-experimental studies, select treatment and control groups after the intervention.

[4] This section draws from Dar and Gill (1998) and Dar and Tzannatos (1999).

Table 10.1. Expenditures on Labor Market Programs (Selected OECD Countries)

Labor Market Program	Australia {1997/8}	Denmark {1998}	France {1997}	Germany {1998}	Japan {1997/8}	Italy {1996}	Spain {1998}	Sweden {1998}	U. S. {1997/8}
Public Employment Services and Administration	0.21	0.14	0.16	0.23	0.03	0.04	0.07	0.30	0.06
Labor Market Training	0.07	1.07	0.35	0.34	0.03	0.01	0.21	0.48	0.04
a. Training unemployed adults and those at risk	0.06	0.73	0.31	0.35	0.03	-	0.10	0.47	0.04
b. Training employed adults	-	0.34	0.04	-	-	0.01	0.11	0.01	-
Youth Measures	0.06	0.08	0.26	0.07	-	0.42	0.07	0.03	0.03
a. Measures for unemployed and disadvantaged youth	-	0.08	0.07	0.06	-	0.04	0.07	0.03	0.03
b. Apprenticeship and related forms of general youth training	0.05	-	0.19	0.01	-	0.38	-	-	-
Subsidized Employment	0.13	0.30	0.52	0.39	0.02	0.61	0.35	0.58	0.01
a. Subsidies to employment in the private sector	0.04	0.03	0.32	0.03	0.02	0.56	0.24	0.15	-
b. Support of unemployed persons starting enterprises	0.02	0.04	-	0.03	-	-	0.03	0.09	-
c. Direct job creation (public or non-profit)	0.07	0.23	0.20	0.32	-	0.04	0.07	0.35	0.01
Measures for the Disabled	0.06	0.30	0.08	0.25	-	-	0.02	0.62	0.04
a. Vocational rehabilitation	0.02	0.30	0.02	0.10	-	-	-	0.04	0.04
b. Work for the disabled	0.04	-	0.06	0.15	-	-	0.02	0.58	-
Unemployment Compensation	1.17	1.86	4.50	2.29	0.43	0.68	1.64	1.91	0.25
Early retirement for labor market reasons	-	1.88	0.35	-	-	0.20	-	-	-
TOTAL	1.69	5.63	3.22	3.56	0.52	1.96	2.36	3.93	0.43
Active Measures	0.52	1.89	1.37	1.27	0.09	1.08	0.72	2.01	0.18
Passive Measures	1.17	3.74	1.85	2.29	0.43	0.88	1.64	1.91	0.25

Non-scientific techniques do not use control groups in evaluating the impact of interventions, relying instead on statistics compiled by program administrators. These evaluations are of little use in determining whether program participants are doing better: without a control group, it is difficult to attribute success or failure of participants to the intervention, since these effects are contaminated by other factors, such as worker-specific attributes. However, in some cases, these evaluations (e.g. interviews with employers and employees) can provide some information on deadweight loss, as well as substitution and displacement effects (Box 1 lists some of the commonly used terms in the impact evaluation literature).

Classically Designed (Randomized) Experiments

This technique was originally developed to test drug-effectiveness, with program participants and those excluded from treatment randomly selected prior to the intervention. If large samples are randomly assigned to treatment and control groups, observable and unobservable characteristics of the two groups should not differ on average, and so any difference in outcomes can be attributed to program participation. The main appeal here lies in the simplicity of interpreting results - the program impact is the simple difference between the means of the samples of program participants and control group members on the outcome of interest.

However, there are some problems with randomization (Benus and Orr, 2000; Baker, 1999). Some of the main ones are: (i) failure to assign randomly. This could be simply because of nepotism or could involve excluding high risk groups in order for the program administrators to show better results; (ii) ethical questions about excluding some people from the intervention. This is somewhat related to the issue above. Program administrators may often resist implementing the programs on the ground that services are denied to the control group; (iii) changed behavior upon learning of assignment to either group. For example, individuals who are denied entry into the program may end up enrolling in a similar private program or may intensify their job search – this will lead to biases in the data; and (iv) these techniques require extensive data collection before the project begins. Other than being very costly, this can often be impractical as in many countries – particularly developing countries - rigorous evaluations are only emphasized and designed after the program is in place.[1]

While randomization is thought to ensure the absence of selection bias among participants, proponents of randomized experimentation make a controversial assumption: that randomization does not alter the program behavior being studied. This may not be the case, and in fact the bias induced by randomization may be quite strong (Heckman, 1992). For example, individuals who might have enrolled in a nonrandomized regime may make plans anticipating enrollment in training. With randomization they may alter their decision to apply or undertake activities complementary to training (the Hawthorne effect). Thus risk-averse persons will tend to be eliminated from the program.

[1] Heckman (1992) documents other limitations of this technique when applied to social experiments that arise due to selectivity biases, as randomization may differentially affect the decision of people to participate in such programs. For example, relatively risk-averse persons may decide not to enroll for randomized experiments, preferring instead to enroll in private training.

Box 10.1. Some Commonly Used Terms in the Impact Evaluation Literature

- **Deadweight Loss:** Program outcomes are not different from what would have happened in the absence of the program. For example, wage subsidies place a worker in a firm which would have hired the worker in the absence of the subsidy.
- **Substitution Effect:** A worker hired in a subsidized job is substituted for an unsubsidized worker who would otherwise have been hired. The net employment effect is thus zero.
- **Displacement Effect:** This usually refers to displacement in the product market. A firm with subsidized workers increases output, but displaces/reduces output among firms who do not have subsidized workers. This can also occur in helping individuals start up enterprises.
- **Treatment and Control Group:** Program beneficiaries are the "treatment" group. In a scientific evaluation, their outcomes are compared with a "control" group of individuals who did not participate in this program. The treatment and control groups could be assigned at random ex-ante (before the program) or chosen ex-post. This will be discussed in detail in Section III.
- **Selection Bias:** Program outcomes are influenced by unobservable factors not controlled for in an evaluation (e.g. individual ability, willingness to work). Such factors can also arise as a by-product of the selection process into programs where individuals "most likely to succeed" are selected into programs ("creaming").
- **Randomization Bias:** This refers to bias in random-assignment experiments. In essence, this says that the behavior of individuals in an experiment will be different because of the experiment itself and not because of the goal of the experiment. Individuals in an experiment know that they are part of a treatment group and may act differently, and the same could hold true of individuals in the control group. The potential change in behavior is referred to as the Hawthorne effect.

Quasi-Experimental Techniques

In these techniques, the treatment and control groups are selected *after* the intervention. In order to get unbiased estimates of program impact, the comparison group must be similar to the treatment group in characteristics that affect the outcome of interest. While some of these characteristics, such as age, gender and level of education are observable, others, such as innate ability and motivation are not. To get the effect of the program, econometric techniques have to be used that will correct for the differences in characteristics between the two groups.

The main appeal of these techniques lie in the fact that they can use existing data sources and are hence relatively low cost, and that these evaluations can be done at any point in time after the program has commenced. However, there are several disadvantages of these programs. The main disadvantage is these techniques - if done properly - are often statistically complex. The attributes of individuals in treatment and control groups are different; techniques for adjusting for differences in observable attributes (e.g., sex, education, age, region) are relatively straightforward but subject to specification errors; correcting for unobservable characteristics (e.g., motivation, family connections) requires a convoluted procedure that can yield significantly different results depending upon specification. Quasi-experimental evaluations are of different types - regression-adjusted for observables, selectivity-corrected (regression-adjusted for both observables and unobservables), and matched pairs:

Regression-adjusted for observables. This technique assesses the impact of participation in a program when the observable characteristics (e.g. sex, age, education) of the participant and comparison groups differ. This method is appropriate for computing program impact estimates when the difference between the participant and comparison samples can be explained by observable characteristics.

Regression-adjusted for observed and unobservable variables (selectivity-corrected). When selection into programs is not random, and participation in a program is due to both observable and unobservable characteristics, program impacts computed using the technique in (i) above are likely to be biased. The concern is that even if participants and non-participants have similar observable characteristics, there are some unobservable characteristics (e.g. innate ability) which would cause non-participants to have different responses to the program if they had participated. This technique uses the Heckman selectivity method to try to control for these unobservables.

Instrumental variables. This approach can be applied if selection into the program can be expressed as a function of variables that do not affect the outcome in the absence of the program. Hence, this technique can be used if there is a variable that affect an individual's participation in the program but do not affect program outcomes. For example, the distance between a training center and an individual's home may impact on his/her ability to participate in the program, but should have no impact on earnings, given the individual participates in the program.

Matched pairs. As observable characteristics of the individuals chosen in the control and treatment groups are bound to be different, these groups are likely to have different success rates in finding employment, even in the absence of active labor market programs. To control for these spurious differences, synthetic control groups are constructed using a matched pairs approach. The synthetic control group, a subset of the entire control group, is composed of individuals whose observable characteristics most closely match those of the treatment group. An alternative approach is to use the "propensity score" approach which computes the predicted probability of participation in a program given observed characteristics – the closer the propensity score, the better the match (Baker, 1999) (see Annex 2).

Relative Strengths of Techniques

It is clear from the above that non-scientific techniques present the least reliable picture of program impacts. As they give no explicit estimate of what would have happened in the absence of the program, they provide little indication of the effects of the program. While these techniques may be useful to get some indication of the gross outcomes of programs, policymakers should not rely on them to make comparisons across programs or decisions relating to the allocation of resources.

Hence randomized and quasi-experimental techniques are preferable.[2] As specified above, there are pros and cons to both experimental and quasi-experimental techniques. While

[2] A weakness shared by both the experimental as well as non-experimental evaluations is that they do not take into account displacement effects of the retraining program. Thus, for example, in countries where demand for labor

randomized experimentation is theoretically the best technique to estimate the effects of interventions,[3] using the dual criteria of rigor and feasibility, randomized experiments are not necessarily superior to quasi-experimental techniques. Factoring in the high costs of setting up such experiments, and the fact that the labor market programs which need to be evaluated are often already in place, randomized evaluations should not necessarily be the chosen alternative, especially in developing countries.

Within quasi-experimental techniques, selectivity-correction may not add much, especially when information is available for a considerable number of observable individual and labor market characteristics (education, age, sex, household wealth, and region of residence). Besides being cumbersome and somewhat unintuitive, this method often gives arbitrary results depending on the selectivity-correction specification used. Similarly, while the instrumental variable approach is appealing in theory, it is often difficult to identify variables that meet the requirement for being a good instrument. Even when such variables exist, the precision of the resulting estimates tends to be somewhat low (Benus and Orr, 2000).

This leaves the matched pairs and the regression-adjusted techniques. Between the two, the matched pairs technique is preferred for the following reasons: First, the procedure is less arbitrary because, since the observable differences between the treatment and comparison group are minimized, functional form assumptions become less important. Second, because program impact measures are a simple difference of means of the variables of interest (re-employment probabilities and wages) between the control and treatment groups, they are easier to interpret by non-statisticians. However, the technique is dependent on having adequate data on both the control and treatment group.

The Importance of Costs

For the purposes of informing policy decisions, an evaluation is not complete until one considers the costs of both the ALMP and its alternatives. Cost-benefit analysis is the standard method of aggregating benefits and costs across outcome categories and across time. A program may be effective, in the sense of creating benefits for participants (e.g. higher earnings, lower recividism) but these effects may not be worthwhile if they are less than the costs involved. Hence a program may be effective in the sense of creating net benefits for participants but not efficient if costs outweigh benefits (Ryan and Grubb, 1999). Similarly, when comparing active labor market programs, if, for example, training is shown to be twice as costly as job search assistance to the unemployed, but only as effective as job search assistance in facilitating access to jobs and wage gains, then job search assistance is twice as cost-effective as retraining even though the two are equally effective. At least at the margin, this would constitute a case for reallocating resources from training to job search assistance.

is constrained, retrainees may simply "bump" or displace previously employed workers so that aggregate unemployment may not change despite the size of the program. In general, displacement implies that the social benefits - from higher re-employment probabilities due to the retraining program - are lower than indicated by the evaluation, however well done.

[3] Estimating the effect of trainee earnings on an employment program using randomized and quasi-experimental techniques, Lalonde (1986) has shown that randomized experimentation yields significantly different results from quasi-experimental techniques. Policymakers should be aware that some non-experimental evaluations, especially those that rely on functional specifications, of training programs may contain large biases.

Unfortunately, costs appear to be the least analyzed aspect of active labor market programs and hence policymakers cannot make informed decisions about the cost-effectiveness of one program with respect to another. Hence it is important to get a good idea about the costs of a program. The main steps involved in estimating costs can be thought of as follows (Valadez and Bamberger, 1994):

- Identify all costs, whether or not they will be charged to the project (e.g. even if premises for a training project are provided free of charge by the government, a cost should be imputed for these premises).
- Estimate the accounting costs. This is the actual amount paid for the goods and services (e.g. salaries and benefits for staff, cost of equipment, rent of buildings etc.).
- When costs are being paid over a number of years, prepare a separate cost stream for each year.

Even the most careful impact evaluations of ALMP's cannot be used for *social* cost-benefit analysis. The main reason is that retraining programs may simply result in displacement of previously employed workers by the retrainees, so that aggregate unemployment rates remain unaffected by the intervention. But when done correctly, evaluations are good guides for *private* cost-benefit analysis, which policymakers can use to institute cost-recovery in public programs and to promote private provision. Evaluations may also help in deciding whether ALMPs programs contribute to reduced budgetary expenditures by moving people off unemployment benefits into productive employment, or whether? are a net drain inspite of being effective in doing so.

IV. An Interpretation of Evaluation Results[4]

This section presents *our reading* of the evaluative evidence - mainly from OECD countries but also some from developing and transition countries - of active labor market programs.[5] These programs have been evaluated using a variety of techniques that have been described in Section 3 above.

Public Works Programs/Public Service Employment

Public works programs are one of the most heavily funded ALMPs in OECD countries. We summarize the results of 18 evaluations of public works programs, 14 of which are quasi-experimental and four of which are non-scientific. The evaluations point to some general conclusions.

While non-experimental evaluations show some desirable short-run effects in the form of employment increase/unemployment decline, some scientific evaluations suggest

[4] This section is based substantially on Dar and Tzannatos (1999).

[5] Appendices which summarize the studies upon which our synthesis is based are available separately. The reader is encouraged to refer to them for a more objective presentation of individual studies.

displacement effects which can reach 100 percent (as they did in Sweden; Skedinger, 1995). Participants have a smaller probability of being employed in a non-assisted job after participation in the program, and are likely to earn less than their counterparts in the control group. Finally, these programs do not seem to have a significant impact on reducing long-term unemployment in the economy – and whatever small short-run impacts that exist tend to dissipate over time (Webster, 1998).

These conclusions are to a large extent predictable: unlike other ALMPs, such as training, retraining and support program for self-employment, public works provide mainly current benefits (temporary safety net) and are only temporary escape routes from unemployment. Irrespective of the merits of public works, an economist's first impression is that public works can be generally expensive and are not an effective instrument if the objective is to get people into long-term gainful employment.

However, public works can be a short-run anti-poverty intervention. That's why some developing countries have used them extensively in periods of hardship, such as in Botswana, where 21 percent of the labor force was employed in public works in 1985-6, in Chile (13 percent in 1983) and Honduras (5 percent between 1990-3). In Argentina's Trabajar program, the average gain in earnings was about half the gross wage. Even allowing for forgone income, the distribution of gains was decidedly pro-poor as more than half the beneficiaries were in the poorest decile nationally and 80- percent were in the poorest quintile (Jalan and Ravallion, 1999). In other cases, such as the Maharashtra Employment Guarantee Scheme in India, year-round employment is guaranteed. However, the wage rates have been set very low, so that only the poorest are targeted.[6] In East Asia, public works were extensively used during the crisis as anti-poverty measures. While rigorous evaluations of the program are not currently available, initial evidence suggests that these programs were not highly successful in reaching their target population as wage rates were set too high which may, in fact, have led to some distortions in the labor market (Betcherman and Islam, 2001).

Job Search Assistance/Employment Services

Expenditures on these programs range anywhere from five percent of active labor market program budgets (in Denmark) to over 70 percent (in the Czech Republic). On average, OECD countries spend about a quarter of their active labor market program budgets on these programs. It should be noted here that this expenditure is often not used solely to finance job search assistance programs, but also to finance the administration of the unemployment benefit system, as well as the administration and costs of the other active labor market programs.

A total of 20 evaluations were examined, all except two are scientific. Six of the scientific evaluations are experimental and 12 are quasi-experimental. The evaluations suggest that job-search assistance is in some sense one of the most successful active labor market programs: in the general case, it costs little to provide and the program is not any less effective than alternative ALMPs. It is, therefore, the low cost that drives this conclusion.

[6] Recent evaluations of this scheme have showed that, due to a significant increase in the wages, the self-targeting nature of the program has been somewhat compromised.

However, as argued below, much depends on whether the economy is growing or in a recession (as far as effectiveness is concerned).

More specifically, while some evaluations yield "negative" results, most studies indicate positive results, and in a few cases large ones.[7] Less successful programs are generally associated with periods of recessions and rising unemployment rates. For example, job search assistance to those laid off *en masse* in Canada in the late 1980s did not raise their probability of employment or earnings (as compared to a control group) at a time when unemployment was rising. In fact, participants who had been laid off *en masse* spent a significantly greater amount of time searching for jobs than their counterparts who did not use this service (Fay, 1996). Similarly, these services were not very successful in Korea during the East Asian crisis –less than eight percent of job seekers found jobs through these services in 1998[8] (Betcherman, Dar, Luinstra and Ogawa, 2001). On the other hand, the effectiveness of job search assistance seems to increase when economic conditions improve; that is, when new jobs are generated. During the decline in unemployment rates in the Netherlands in the mid-to-late 1980s, program participants were more likely to be employed than those in the control group (OECD, 1993). Evaluations in Hungary and Poland also show that while the overall effectiveness of this intervention is not significant in terms of increasing probability of employment, if the economy is improving, some subgroups of program participants - particularly women - fare significantly better than non-participants (O' Leary, 1998(a), 1998(b)).

Studies which examine both cost and effectiveness data conclude that job search assistance is also supposed to be one of the most-cost effective of the active interventions. Leigh (1995) summarizes his findings of selected programs: job search assistance measures cost less than training and retraining (two to four times less), but appear at least as effective. This of course does not mean that job-search assistance is a substitute for training - it is possible, for example, that those who use job search assistance are more "employment-ready" than individuals who get training. However it does mean that if job search assistance and training programs cater to roughly the same clientele, policymakers can substitute one program for the other. Similar results were also found in experimental demonstrations carried out in the U.S. during the 1970s and the 1980s (Meyer, 1995).[9]

Overall, the evidence suggests that job search assistance can have some positive effects and is usually cost-effective (relative to other ALMPs). There does seem to be a positive correlation between the likelihood of success of a program and local labor market conditions. Programs that have not yielded positive results are generally associated with rising unemployment rates, while economic conditions have been generally favorable in the case where programs have succeeded.

---

[7] Deadweight loss is rarely measured in these evaluations. It may happen that those who benefit from these services are those who would have got jobs anyway because they were the most motivated in looking for jobs.

[8] This low rate of effectiveness is also partly attributed to low personnel and technological capacity in employment offices. Other countries in East Asia which expanded their job search assistance programs during the crisis faced similar problems.

[9] In a study by White and Lakey (1992) the duration of search of non-participants was on average 8 weeks longer than those of program beneficiaries.

Training and Retraining Programs

Training (and re-training) generally accounts for a significant share of expenditures on ALMPs ranging between 40-60 percent in many countries and reaching 77 percent in Denmark in the early 1990s. Spending on training can reach many different groups, and in our review, we concentrate on retraining programs geared towards those laid off *en masse*; training and re-training programs for the long-term unemployed; and training programs geared towards youth.

We have reviewed close to 50 studies - 11 experimental, 30 quasi-experimental and nine non-scientific. A few of these studies are longitudinal, so it is also possible to study the long term impact of the programs.

Compared to scientific evaluations, nonscientific evaluations usually provide an inflated picture of the effects of training and retraining programs on the long-term unemployed. Scientific evaluations suggest that the programs for the long-term unemployed can have a positive impact but this is not always the case, and the impact is usually small.

The success of programs tends to be heavily dependent on the business cycle: programs have performed better when they were instituted at times when the economy was expanding. A good example of this is Hungary, where training outcomes seem to have improved over time as the economy started to grow (O' Leary (1995, 1998(a)). In general, programs seem to be more effective for women (Puhani, 1998; Friedlander et. al., 1997; Goss, Gilroy et. al., 1989, Keum, 2001). For example, in Korea the probability of employment for women after training was significantly higher than that for women who did not undertake training, while the impact for males was insignificant. However in some cases, training has little overall impact – for example Mexico's Probecat program was ineffective in reducing the duration of unemployment or increasing wages post training (De Ferranti, Perry, Gill and Serven *et. al.*, 2000).

Longitudinal studies indicate mixed results - while in some cases the positive effects dissipated within a year or two after program completion, in a couple of cases the impacts persisted. For example, in Sweden, labor market training provided to the unemployed raised their earnings in the short-term but the long-term impact (over two years) was somewhat negative (Meager and Evans, 1998). Conversely, unemployed provided training as part of the New Jersey Reemployment Demonstration project in the mid 1980's were earning more than the control group more than two and a half years after program completion (Anderson, Corson and Decker, 1991). In most cases, training programs are generally no more effective than job search assistance in increasing either re-employment probabilities or post-intervention earnings. For example, evaluations of the Texas Worker Adjustment Demonstration (WAD) program indicate that participants were likely to be employed more quickly than non-participants. However, by the end of the first year after program completion, employment opportunities for male participants were no better than those for non-participants, or for those who only got job search assistance (Bloom, 1990).

Evaluations results for youth training are the most discouraging of all (that is, compared to training programs for the long-term unemployed and those laid-off *en masse*), even though the programs examined here were often introduced in periods of relatively stable or declining youth unemployment They show that training rarely has an effect on earnings or employment probabilities of program beneficiaries compared to their counterparts in some control groups. In almost all cases, participants did no better than the control group either in enhancing their post-training employment probability or their earnings (Fay, 1996; DOL, 1995). A more mixed, and more promising, picture arises from the evaluation of the Canadian Job Entry Program. Though a quasi-experimental evaluation of the program showed that youth who only undertook classroom training did no better than their comparators, those who undertook enterprise training did significantly better than the control group (OECD, 1993). This positive effect was attributed to youngsters staying-on with the training firms.

Costs, when known, vary significantly between $900 and $25,000 per person. This makes training programs between two and four times more expensive than, say, job search assistance (JSA). Combined with the finding that retraining and JSA have roughly similar impact, this implies that JSA can be more cost-effective in assisting displaced workers than retraining. However, it again needs to be stressed here that these programs may be serving different groups of the unemployed and hence may not be direct substitutes for one another.

In *most* cases the costs are found to be so high compared to the benefits of the program that, even if the effects persisted for 10 years, the social return of the program could remain negative (especially for males) (Friedlander et. al., 1997).[10] The U.S. JTPA program appears to be a rare exception - both male and female participants were doing significantly better than the control group and the training program was relatively inexpensive However, in spite of the positive results, evaluators caution that the aggregate effects of JTPA are likely to be modest, both on the target population and on the labor force as a whole.

One of the major implications emerging from the analysis is that training should not be seen as a panacea for reducing unemployment - it usually does not work, especially if the economy is not growing. The evidence shows that programs aimed at the long-term unemployed, usually established in periods when the economy is doing better, are somewhat more effective (at least in the short-run). Evaluations also show that tightly targeted on-the-job training programs, usually aimed at women and other disadvantaged groups among the long-term unemployed, often offer the best returns. For youth, the evidence suggests that it is very difficult to correct what appears to be a failure of the education system during the previous 5-10 years of the youth's life with some kind of training which is usually short in duration and takes place relatively late in life. While rigorous cost-benefit analyses of these programs are seldom carried out, where done, the evidence shows that these programs are not usually cost-effective.

Wage/Employment Subsidies (WES)

We examined 22 evaluations - six of which were experimental, eight quasi-experimental, and eight non-scientific. WES programs are among the least funded active labor market programs in OECD countries. In most OECD countries, they attract less than 10 percent of expenditure on active labor market programs - in fact, in both the U.S. and the U.K, funding for this program is negligible.

[10] The social return is based on a comparison of measurable economic costs and benefits and does not take into account possible externalities associated with the reintegration of the long-term unemployed into the labor force or of reducing high levels of unemployment in specific regions.

Both non-scientific and scientific evaluations tend to agree that WES have high deadweight loss and substitution effects. In the extreme case of Ireland's wage subsidy program, the deadweight and substitution losses combined totaled over 95 percent – alternatively, the net incrementality of the program was a meager four percent (OECD, 1993). Evaluations of programs in Australia, Holland and the U.K also indicate high deadweight and/or substitution effects. Similarly, initial indications on programs instituted in Korea during the East Asian crisis in the late 1990s point to deadweight losses of around 70 percent (Table 10.2).

Equally disappointing are evaluations which compared wages and employment outcomes of participants with those of a control group. For example, the U.S. Targeted Job Tax Credit program, which is a longitudinal study, saw earnings of participants significantly higher than those of individuals in the control group in the first year. This effect declined in the second year and disappeared after that (OECD, 1993). Similarly, evaluation results for Hungary show that participants were significantly less likely to be employed and did not earn any more than those in the control group (O' Leary, 1998(a)). There is also some anecdotal evidence that employers use these programs as a permanent subsidy program - hiring workers as cheap labor and laying them off once the subsidy period ends and then hiring another subsidized workers in their place.

However, a few exceptions exist. One seems to be the U.S. Job Training Partnership act program, where employers were provided subsidies to hire workers in conjunction with on-the-job training. Evaluations of this program show that single mothers who are AFDC recipients benefit significantly from these subsidies, and males also benefited to some extent (Bloom, 1994). In Australia, even though the deadweight loss associated with these programs is around 30%, they have a significant positive impact on post-program employment – participants are 15% more likely to be employed than the control group (Webster, 1998).

While very few studies carried out a direct cost-benefit analysis, the high deadweight losses and substitution effects associated with this program strongly suggest that WES are unlikely to have positive social returns in the way measured by economists, though they may contribute to some reduction in social exclusion among older workers and single mothers.

In summary, evidence indicates that these programs are not likely to be effective; substantial deadweight and substitution effects are associated with them. Wage and employment outcomes of participants are also generally no better than that for a control group. Careful targeting can reduce, but not eliminate, substitution and deadweight effects, and further controls may be necessary to ensure that firms do not misuse this program as a permanent subsidy program.

Micro-Enterprise Development (Self-employment Schemes)

We have summarized the results of 15 evaluations of programs aimed at helping unemployed individuals start up their own businesses: two of the evaluations are experimental, seven are quasi-experimental, five are non-scientific and one evaluation is of various types. These programs come under a variety of names such as micro-enterprise schemes or self-employment schemes but below we generically refer to them as "micro-enterprise development assistance" (MEDA).

Table 10.2. Effectiveness of Wage Subsidy Programs

Country	Deadweight and Substitution Effects (%)	Additionality (%)
Australia in mid 1980s (Jobstart Program)	Deadweight=65%	35%
Belgium in the early 1990s (Recruitment Subsidy	Deadweight=53% Substitution36%	11%
England 1986-1990 (Training and Employment Grant	Deadweight=69%	31%
England late 1980s (Workstart I)	Deadweight=45% Substitution30%	25%
England mid 1970s (Small Firms Employment Subsidy	Deadweight=70%	30%
England early 1980s	Deadweight=63% Substitution10%	27%
Germany in mid 1970s (Wage Subsidy Scheme)	Deadweight=75%	25%
Ireland in the 1980's (Employment Incentive Scheme)	Deadweight= 70% Substitution21% Displacement=4%	4%
Korea in the late 1990s (Subsidy Schemes)	Deadweight=70%	30%
Netherlands during early 1980s (Vermeend-Moor Act)	Deadweight=25% Substitution50%	25%
Netherlands during the late 1980s (JOB scheme)	Substitution =80%.	20%
U.S. in mid 1980s (Targeted Job Tax Credit)	Deadweight=70% Substitution10%	20%

Note: Additionality is the employment effect after accounting for deadweight, displacement and substitution effects

As usual, non-scientific evaluations provide more encouraging results than scientific evaluations. Still, there is general agreement that takeup rates of MEDA programs is low – below 5 percent[11] - and that they have high deadweight loss. Estimates of deadweight losses vary from about 30 percent in the self-employment experiments in Massachusetts and Washington State in the late 1980's and early 1990's (Fay, 1996) to over 50 percent in Canada's self-employment assistance program in 1992-93 (Graves and Gauthier, 1995) and Denmark's enterprise startup grant in the late 1980's (Balakrishnan, 1998).

Evaluations show that businesses are short-lived – typically one-third to half of MEDA created businesses close down in the first year of their operation. For example, the failure rate of businesses is over 50 percent in various schemes in the U.K (Taylor, 1999), 60 percent in the first year in Denmark, and in Australia it is more than 70 percent in the first two years. In France the failure rate is 50 percent but over a period of five years (Table 10.3). Evidence seems to show that businesses assisted through mentoring and business counseling are more likely to succeed, and even though a majority of businesses may close – individuals are likely to move to employment in another industry rather than into unemployment.

[11] In Korea, a somewhat different type of scheme is used – existing small businesses are given subsidies to assist in their development. However less than two percent of firms with less than 100 workers availed of these subsidies in 1998 during the crisis (OECD, 2000).

While there are high deadweight losses and high rates of business failures, MEDA participants seem to fare reasonably well in terms of employment outcomes as compared to a control group. Scientific evaluations show that participants are more likely to be employed than individuals in the control group. However, this does not necessarily translate into higher earnings. For example, in the Washington self-employment experiment, while participants are more likely to be employed than the control group, they earn significantly less (Fay, 1996). In Hungary and the Czech Republic, participants were more to be employed compared to individuals in the control group, but earned $30/month less (Fretwell, Benus and O'Leary, 1999). In the case of Poland, on the other hand, participants were 25 percent more likely to be employed than the control group and earned significantly more. In the Hungarian and Polish programs, women and older workers generally had better outcomes than individuals in other sub-groups.

Table 10.3. Failure Rates of MEDA Business

Program	Failure Rate of Businesses
Australia (New Enterprise Initiative, late 1980s)	58% failed in first year and 71% in two years.
Canada (Self-Employment Assistance Program, early 1990s)	20% failed within first year
Denmark (Enterprise Allowance Schemes, late 1980s)	60% failed within first 12 months
France (Micro-Enterprise Development early 1980s)	50% failed within 4.5 years.
Hungary (MEDA, mid-1990s)	20% failed within first 15 months.
Netherlands in the early 1990's	50% failed within four years.
Poland (MEDA, mid 1990s)	15% failed within first two years.
U.S. in Washington (Self-Employment Experiment 1990)	37% failed within the first 15 months

Even in cases of businesses that survive, there is only a small multiplier effect. Most surviving businesses create, on average, half an additional job. In Hungary, each surviving enterprise created 0.3 additional jobs, in France, 0.5, and in Australia, during a period of declining unemployment, 0.7 (OECD, 1993; Wilson and Adams, 1994).

While there is some scattered data on costs, the cost-benefit issue has rarely been addressed. Where available, data indicate that the cost of starting up a small business vary from $4500 (in France) to $13,000-$14,000 (in Canada and Denmark). The Canadian evaluation states that the long-term cost-effectiveness of these programs is uncertain, while preliminary analysis from Poland and Hungary indicate a loss to the unemployment insurance system with both the average duration and level of unemployment benefits paid to participants being greater than those paid to individuals in the control group. However, it would be premature to draw any conclusions on the cost-effectiveness of these programs on the basis of so little evidence.

In all, evaluations suggest that these programs work for only a small subset of the unemployed population (generally below five percent) and are associated with high deadweight and displacement effects rendering the "net" effects of these programs to be quite low. The failure rate of these businesses are quite high in most cases (though businesses assisted through mentoring and business counseling are more likely to succeed). As in the case of training, assistance targeted at particular groups - in this case women and older individuals - seems to have a greater likelihood of success.

Summary of Evaluative Evidence

In this section we have examined over 120 impact evaluations (some of which are summaries of a group of evaluations) - both non-scientific as well as scientific - of active labor market programs in an attempt to draw some lessons about the efficiency and cost-effectiveness of these schemes. While the evidence covered is probably not exhaustive, this study has managed to look at most of the evidence available on different issues for these programs.

While the paucity of rigorous evidence on the costs and effectiveness of active labor market programs does not allow a definitive conclusion as to whether such interventions can be justified economically, the general conclusion is that large scale application of these programs should be avoided without knowledge of their effects. Table 10.4 summarizes the lessons for each program.

Table 10.4. Overview of Active Labor Programs

Program	Appear to Help	Comments
1. Public Works Programs (17 evaluations)	Severely disadvantaged groups in providing temporary and a safety net.	Long-term employment prospects not helped: program participants are less likely to be employed in a normal job and earn less than do individuals in the control group. Not cost-effective if objective is to get people into gainful employment
2. Job-search assistance/ Emp. Services (19 evaluations)	Adult unemployed generally when economic conditions are improving; women may benefit more.	Relatively more cost-effective than other labor market interventions (e.g. training – mainly due to the lower cost, youth do not benefit usually. Difficulty lies in deciding who needs help in order to minimize deadweight loss.
3. Training of long-term unemployed, those laid-off *en masse*, and youth (47 evaluations)	Women and other disadvantaged groups generally when economy is improving. However, little positive impact on youth.	No more effective than job-search assistance in increasing re-employment probabilities and post-intervention earnings and are 2-4 times more costly. For youth, employment/earnings prospects not improved as a result of going through the training Taking costs into account - the real rate of return of these programs is negative for youth.
4. Employment/ Wage subsidies (22 evaluations)	Long-term unemployed in providing an entry into the labor force.	High deadweight and substitution effects. Impact analysis shows treatment group does not do well as compared to control. Sometimes used by firms as a permanent subsidy program.

5. Micro-enterprise Development Programs (15 evaluations)	Relatively older groups the more educated.	Very low take-up rate among unemployed. Significant failure rate of small businesses. High deadweight and displacement effects. High costs – cost-benefit analysis rarely conducted but sometime show costs to UI budget higher than for control group.

V. Conclusion

What can policy-makers conclude from our review of active labor market programs? While there are various types of interventions addressing different policy objectives, our review of the evaluation evidence in section 4 certainly sends out cautionary signals. Ultimately ALMPs are judged by their performance in improving the employability and earnings of workers and the evaluations indicate that the investments made often not had an appreciable impact on these outcomes.

There are polar positions on the effectiveness of active labor market programs. On one hand, proponents of these programs argue that active labor market programs are both necessary and useful, short only of a panacea for reducing unemployment and protecting workers. Opponents of the programs tend to summarily dismiss these programs as a waste of public money with high opportunity costs to other social programs and labor market efficiency as a whole. Based on a thorough evaluation of evidence, this paper shows that some programs can be useful to some workers in some cases. There are also good design features for each program, but external (to the programs) conditions need to be taken into account (a good program in one country can prove to be a bad one for another; a program found to be useful in the past may no longer be the case). This calls for realism in setting the objectives of ALMP and also setting standards against which active labor market programs should be evaluated. However, due to lack of evaluative evidence, the conditions under which programs will succeed have not been fully identified. A very *broad generalization* on the effectiveness of these programs leads to the conclusions that:

- Some of these programs - such as wage subsidies or training for youth - are unlikely to be cost-effective instruments in reducing unemployment.
- Some programs - such as job search assistance - are likely to have positive impacts on the probability of finding employment if they are well-designed and implemented.
- However, the impact and cost-effectiveness of most of the active labor market programs depends on their design, and also on the overall macro and labor market framework in which they are designed.

However, in putting forward this evaluation evidence, we are not arguing that policy-makers in countries without major ALMP investments should avoid this area in the future. First, active labor market programs can serve social objectives, as well as economic. Researchers have not addressed the question of these social impacts, which may be more positive. Second, workforce development, the social and economic integration of marginalized and at-risk groups, and the situation of unemployed workers are central concerns for policy-makers and ALMPs are obvious instruments to address these. Third, the disappointing performance of these programs in the aggregate masks the fact that some program designs do seem to lead to positive outcomes for some types of workers. The challenge is to learn from existing experiences and to direct future programming along lines that appear to work..

But the evaluation evidence does suggest that policy-makers should be realistic about what ALMPs can do and that investments in this area should be made carefully and modestly. As policy-makers in Brazil look down the road, we recommend that they carefully consider the following issues relating to the formulation of an active labor market policy:

Priority setting. As we have noted, active labor market programs can have various policy objectives including reducing unemployment in cyclical downturns, correcting structural imbalances, improving labor market functioning, and assisting disadvantaged groups of workers. In designing an overall strategy, it is important to identify which of these are the priority objectives since it is the objectives that should determine program choices and program design.

The roles of the public and private sectors. This is a key consideration both in developing an overall strategy and in designing and implementing programs. At one time, governments in the OECD region developed and delivered virtually all ALMPs but, increasingly, governments have reconsidered the respective roles of the public and private (and non-profit) sectors. In many countries, possibilities have opened up for the other sectors to play important roles, at least in the delivery of services. This can lead to more diverse, innovative, and cost-efficient services and to programs that are more closely oriented to labor demand. However, even where the scope for private sector involvement is considerable, governments retain the central role. They must be responsible for the overall system, ensuring that it remains focused on public priorities. They must also address distributional issues (e.g., adequate service for all types of workers) and provide critical public goods.

Promoting partnerships and dialogue. The identification of priorities for active labor market policy and program choices can benefit from ongoing dialogue between government, business, labor, and other relevant organizations (e.g., service providers). Where this dialogue is conducted effectively, policy-makers can maintain a close connection with the needs of the labor market and can maximize support for ALMPs. The dialogue needs to be carried out both at the level where priorities are set (e.g., nationally) and where programs are delivered (e.g., locally). Governments typically must be the leaders and catalysts for ensuring this process.

"Infrastructure" for the labor market. Infrastructure services are critical if ALMPs are to be a useful policy instrument. By "infrastructure," we mean labor market information, a viable and complete network of employment service offices, and certification and accreditation systems. These services are the cornerstones of an effective system: They inform the program choices that should be made. They provide the bridge between the labor market, service deliverers, workers, and employers. And they are necessary for ensuring quality throughout the system. As largely public goods, these are inevitably the responsibility of governments. In countries where the development of an active labor market policy is at an early stage, these infrastructure services should be the first priority.

Coordination within government. In many countries, ALMPs are complicated by the fact that many government agencies are involved and that coordination among them is insufficient. There are two problems associated with this coordination issue. First, multiple departments often are responsible for various aspects of active labor market programming and mechanisms are not in place to ensure that they are working together in an efficient manner which often leads to a duplication of effort. Second, priority-setting and programming in the ALMP area are often not sufficiently coordinated with overall economic planning. Both of these problems need to be addressed through intra-government coordination to ensure the relevance and efficiency of active labor market programming.

Policy and administrative/operational capacity. Designing and implementing ALMPs requires considerable capacity within government. In many ways, this is a more complicated area than passive income support programming. Capacity needs do differ significantly by program. For example, public works can be relatively straightforward to design and implement; as a consequence, these are often the major active labor market interventions in many developing countries. On the other hand, employment services require a network of facilities with extensive geographic coverage, the resources (technological and know-how) to generate and disseminate accurate and timely labor market information, skilled counselors, and reliable connections with the employer and educational communities. Training programs also require labor market information plus training and occupational standards, monitoring and evaluation capabilities, and capacity (increasingly in the private or non-profit sectors) to deliver good programs. Governments must recognize that capacity building is a slow but essential process.

Monitoring and evaluation. This is a key part of capacity and deserves special mention. In spite of the large public expenditures on ALMPs in OECD countries, rigorous evaluations of these programs have been relatively uncommon. In an effort to improve the targeting and efficiency of social programs, sound impact evaluation techniques should be used to evaluate active labor market programs. A good evaluation compares labor market outcomes for individuals who have gone through a particular program with those of a control group of their peers, and also utilizes data on program costs to attempt to answer questions such as: what are the impact estimates of the program on the individual; are the impacts large enough to yield net social gains; and is this the best outcome that could have been achieved for the money spent.

There are clearly many considerations involved in developing a strong active labor market policy. And the experience of the OECD countries, plus the resources required, suggest that countries should move slowly to build on what already exists. Nevertheless, over the long run, building ALMP capacity will be important as formal labor markets grow and as a skilled workforce becomes more important. Nations now need to think about priorities, the role of government, and a range of issues related to how ALMPs should be carried out. Given its foundation role, "infrastructure" needs to get immediate attention.

References

Anderson, P., W. Corson and P. Decker (1991). *The New Jersey Unemployment Insurance Re-employment Demonstration Project Follow-up Report.* Unemployment Insurance Occasional Paper 91-1, U.S. Department of Labor.

Baker, J. (1999). Evaluating the Impact of Development Projects on Poverty: A Handbook for Practitioners. World Bank, Washington D.C.

Benus, J. and L. Orr (2000). *Study of Alternative Quantitative Methodologies.* Working Paper, Abt Associates.

Betcherman, G. and R. Islam (eds.) (2001). *East Asia Labor Markets and the Economic Crisis: Impacts, Responses and Lessons.* The World Bank, Washington D.C.

Betcherman, G., A. Dar, A. Luinstra and M. Ogawa (2001). *Active Labor Market Programs: Policy Issues for East Asia* in *East Asia Labor Markets and the Economic Crisis: Impacts, Responses and Lessons.* The World Bank, Washington D.C.

Bloom, H. (1994). *The National JTPA Study: Overview of Impacts, Benefits and Costs of Title II-A.* An Abt Associates Study.

Bloom, H. (1990). *Back to Work: Testing Re-employment Services for Displaced Workers.* Working Paper, W.E. Upjohn Institute for Employment Research.

Dar, A. and I. Gill (1998). *Evaluating Retraining Programs in OECD Countries: Lessons Learned.* The World Bank Research Observer, Vol. 13(1).

Dar, A. and Z. Tzannatos (1999). *Active Labor Market Programs: A Review of the Evidence from Evaluations.* SP Discussion Paper 9901.

De Ferranti, D., G. Perry, I. Gill, L. Serven, F. Ferreira, N. Ilahi, W. Maloney and M. Rama (2000). *Securing our Future in a Global Economy.* The World Bank, Washington D.C.

Fay, R. (1996). *Enhancing the Effectiveness of Active Labour Market Policies: Evidence From Program Evaluations in OECD Countries.* OECD Labor Market and Social Policy Occasional Paper No. 18.

Fretwell, D., J. Benus and C. J. O'Leary (1999). *Evaluating the Impact of Active Labor Programs: Results of Cross Country Studies in Europe and Central Asia.* SP Discussion Paper 9910.

Friedlander, D., D. Greenberg and P. Robins (1997). *Evaluating Government Training Programs for the Economically Disadvantaged.* Journal of Economic Literature, Vol. 35(4).

Goss, Gilroy and Associates (1989). *Evaluation of the Job Development Program: Final Report.* Report prepared for the Program Evaluation Branch, Employment and Immigration Office (Canada).

Graves, F. and B. Gauthier (1995). *Evaluation of the Self-Employment Assistance Program.* An HRDC Working Paper.

Heckman, J. (1992). *Randomization and Social Policy Evaluation* in C. Manski and I. Garfinkel, eds., "Evaluating Welfare and Training Programs", Harvard University Press.

Jalan, J. and M. Ravallion (1999). Income Gains to the Poor from Workfare: Estimates for Argentina's Trabajar Program. Working Paper Series No. 2149, The World Bank, Washington D.C.

Keum, J. (2001). *Review of the Effectiveness of Korean Public Employment Services* in *Economic Crises and Labor Market Reform: The Case of Korea.* Korean Labor Institute, Seoul.

LaLonde, R.J., (1986). *Evaluating the Econometric Evaluations of Training Programs with Experimental Data.* American Economic Review Vol. 76(4).

Leigh, D. (1995). *Assisting Workers Displaced by Structural Change : An International Perspective.* W.E. Upjohn Institute for Employment Research.

Meager, N. and C. Evans (1998). *The Evaluation of Active Labor Market Measures for the Long-Term Unemployed.* Employment and Training Papers No. 16, ILO, Geneva.

Meyer, B.D. (1995). *Lessons from U.S. Unemployment Insurance Experiments*. Journal of Economic Literature, Vol. 33.

OECD (1993). *Employment Outlook*.

O'Leary, Christopher (1995). *An Impact Analysis of Employment Programs in Hungary*. W.E. Upjohn Institute for Employment Research Working Paper 95-30.

O'Leary, Christopher (1998(a)). *Evaluating the Effectiveness of Active Labor Programs in Hungary*. W.E. Upjohn Institute for Employment Research Draft Working Paper.

O'Leary, Christopher (1998(b)). *Evaluating the Effectiveness of Active Labor Programs in Poland*. W.E. Upjohn Institute for Employment Research Draft Working Paper.

Puhani, P. (1998). *Advantage Through Training? A Microeconometric Evaluation of the Employment Effects of Active Labor Market Programs in Poland*. ZEW Discussion Paper No. 98-25.

Grubb, W. and P. Ryan (1999). *The Roles of Evaluation for Vocational Education and Training: Plain Talk on the Field of Dreams*. ILO, Geneva.

Skedinger, P. (1995). *Employment Policies and Displacement in the Youth Labor Market*. Swedish Economic Policy Review, Vol. 2(1).

Valadez, J. and M. Bamberger (1994). *Monitoring and Evaluating Social Programs in Developing Countries: A Handbook for Policymakers, Managers, and Researchers*. The World Bank, Washington D.C.

Webster, E. (1998). *Microeconomic Evaluations of Australian Labor Market Programs*. The Australian Economic Review, Vol. 31 (2), pp. 189-201.

Wilson, S. and A.V. Adams (1994). *Self-Employment for the Unemployed: Experience in OECD and Transitional Economies*. World Bank Discussion Paper No. 263.

ANNEX I: DESCRIPTION OF ALMPS

I. Direct Employment/Public Works and Public Employment

Some governments attempt to alleviate cases of severe and continued mass unemployment by creating jobs and hiring the unemployed directly. In other arrangements, the government contracts with non-profit organizations or private businesses to provide jobs. Participants are provided jobs in various sectors of the economy, e.g. construction, health and municipal government. Although most programs target the displaced and the long-term unemployed ("the hardest to place groups"), youth in some countries also participate as a way to introduce them to the world of work. For example, unemployed youth have been provided temporary employment through public works projects in Angola, Ecuador and Zambia, among other countries, while long-term unemployed have been employed in similar programs in many OECD and developing countries during the 1980s and 1990s.

These programs may assist disadvantaged and the long-term unemployed groups to regain contact with the labor market and can lead to the production of public goods and develop basic infrastructure. Another advantage is that these programs can be self-targeting, particularly when the wages are set at an appropriate level. Conversely, if wages are set too high, public works jobs may end up crowding out jobs in the private sector. There is usually a stigma attached to such jobs which decreases individual's employability in a non-subsidized job.

II. Employment Services/Job Search Assistance

The main objective of employment services is brokerage - matching jobs with job seekers. Job-search assistance comprises many different types of services; for example, initial interviews at employment offices, in-depth counseling during the unemployment spell, job clubs etc. They assist a varied group of unemployed and job seekers - including the long-term unemployed in the U.K, women on welfare in the U.S., individuals laid off as a result of industrial restructuring in Canada, and the youth in Holland. As mentioned above, job seekers are usually provided a wide range of services. In Hungary and Poland in the mid 1990s, for example, they were provided with job referrals, job counseling, skills assessment, job search training, resume preparation and job clubs (O' Leary, 1998(a), 1998(b)). In New Zealand they were assisted through a job screening interview, workshops, follow-up interviews and personal case management (NZ DOL, 1995). In Australia they were helped in resume writing and interviewing techniques (Fay, 1996).

These services are relatively inexpensive and by providing job seekers with better information on jobs, they can also help in shortening unemployment spells. On the negative side, opponents of these interventions argue that they usually have deadweight losses - individuals who get jobs through employment services are generally the most qualified and would have also gotten jobs in the absence of these services.

III. Labor Market Training

This includes training where there is some form of public support. That support can come in the form of direct provision of training (e.g, through public training institutes), financial support for trainees (e.g., funding direct costs of training and/or subsidizing trainees), and providing "infrastructure" services (e.g., labor market information, licensing and other quality monitoring, certification and credential services). In this paper, we focus on three types of training programs:

- Programs aimed at the long term-unemployed. Though there is no generally agreed definition of what constitutes long-term unemployment, the term usually refers to those who have been unemployed for more than 12 months (OECD, 1993). Overrepresented in this group are "older" workers who used to be employed in what turned out to be a declining industry or region.
- Retraining programs aimed at those displaced. This group generally tends to be more homogenous than the long-term unemployed. Retraining programs are usually offered when individuals are laid-off *en masse* (e.g. in the automobile, shipbuilding, mining, steel and pulp industries). Generally, these losses occurr during periods of contraction of a particular sector; and

- Training programs aimed at youth. These programs usually aim at assisting school dropouts (often paying special attention to youngsters who drop out prior to completing upper secondary education) or youth who come from severely disadvantaged families. The assisted individuals are typically below the age of 20.

While publicly provided training programs can lead to increases in productivity and enhance the skills of the unemployed, youth and those at risk, they have a number of limitations. Firstly, they are relatively costly. Secondly, then tend to have little impact when the economy is not performing well (i.e. when growth is slow). Unfortunately, this is usually the situation during which they are likely to be instituted. Finally, training programs can also result in deadweight loss – i.e. those who benefit from the programs may have more skills to begin with and who would have gotten jobs anyway.

IV. Micro-Enterprise Development Assistance/Self-Employment Creation Measures (MEDA)

However, technical assistance, credit and other support can contribute to the creation and promotion of small-scale new businesses and self-employment. In countries with embryonic financial infrastructure, private banks are often unable to conduct comprehensive risk assessment and offer credit to unemployed workers who want to create their own business. Small business loans can contribute to the removal of this distortion arising from credit rationing.

In general, MEDA programs are not targeted at any particular group. For example, such assistance has been given to the newly unemployed (such as in Massachusetts, U.S., in the early 1990s), to those who have been unemployed for at least five months (such as in Denmark in the 1980's) and those who were laid-off in Hungary and Poland in the 1990's. Similarly, they are available under varied economic conditions. In Ireland, for example, these programs were instituted in the mid 1980s at a time when unemployment rates were high (around 15 percent) and rising. In Australia, on the other hand, they became more common in the late 1980s when unemployment rates fell from eight to six percent.

Program conditions also vary. For example; participants may receive assistance to set up their businesses as a lump-sum payment or periodic allowances. Often there is "screening", that is, potential beneficiaries undergo a rigorous assessment which evaluates their likelihood of success (for example, in Germany) but in other countries, such as the US, screening is more cursory (Wilson and Adams, 1994). In most cases participants may also receive post-startup business advisory services and business counseling.

Though theoretically the idea that someone who cannot get a job as an employee will be inclined to become self-employed makes sense, very few among the unemployed – usually less than five percent - are tempted to take up opportunities for self-employment (Wilson and Adams, 1994). One explanation for this may be that individuals are generally risk averse, and given a choice between getting unemployment benefits or money to start up a - possibly unsuccessful - venture, prefer to get the unemployment benefits. Furthermore there is some danger of displacement of small businesses who do not get this assistance.

V. Wage/Employment Subsidies (WES)

These programs have been used for the long-term unemployed, those coming from severely disadvantaged areas (e.g. areas with high unemployment), and youth. They aim to reduce social exclusion, that is, to help these individuals regain contact with the world of work. They are instituted under varying economic conditions (though usually during slack periods) - in Australia during periods of falling unemployment in the mid 1980s (Mangan, 1988) as compared to Scotland where unemployment rates rose from six to 10 percent while the program was underway between 1989-1992 (NERA, 1995).

Subsidy programs can assist the unemployed, particularly the long-term unemployed to maintain contact with the labor market and they may lead to permanent employment by helping individuals develop some work-related skills. However, opponents argue that these programs are associated with deadweight losses - those that are provided subsidies would be hired anyway in the absence of these subsidies. They can also have low net employment effect as workers taken by firms in a subsidized job substitute for unsubsidized workers who would have otherwise been hired. Furthermore, employers may end up abusing the system by hiring workers as cheap labor and laying them off once the subsidy period ends.

ANNEX II: ALTERNATIVE MATCHING TECHNIQUES

The aim of the matching technique is to create a "synthetic" control group that closely matches the characteristics of the treatment group. Characteristics should be based on the following criteria: (i) they should be observable (e.g. education, gender, age, education); and (ii) they should be relevant – i.e. these attributes should be correlated with the outcomes of interest (.e.g earnings and employment probability). The control (and treatment) group samples can come from a representative sample survey. The larger the sample of eligible non-participants the better, to facilitate good matching. If the two samples come from different surveys, then they should be highly comparable surveys. The synthetic cohort can be created in one of two ways:

Method I

For each treatment group observation, a distance measure is computed for each control group observation using the Mhalonabis distance measure:

$$Dij = \sum_k (Zik - Zjk)^2$$

where the index i represents observations in the treatment group and the index j represents observations in the comparison group. The index k runs over the exogenous characteristics on which the observations are matched, and Z represents the standardized value of a characteristic where the mean and standard deviation of the characteristic is computed on the pooled sample of treatment and control group observations. Thus for each individual in the treatment group, a Dij is computed for every control group member. The control group observation for which the Dij is the smallest is chosen as the "matched" observation. It is possible that a single control group observation can be a match for more than one treatment group observations.

The impact of the program is measured as the difference in outcome sample means for the treatment and synthetic control groups.

Method II

This method is known as the propensity score method and works as follows:

- Pool the treatment and control group samples and estimate a logit regression of program participation as a function of all the variables in the data that are likely to determine participation in the program.
- Create the predicted values of the probability of participation from the logit regression; these are called the "propensity scores." There will thus be a propensity score for every sampled participant and non-participant. The range of propensity scores estimated for the treatment group should correspond closely to that for the retained subsample of non-participants.
- For each individual in the treatment sample, an observation is found in the non-participant sample that has the closest propensity score, as measured by the absolute difference in scores. This is called the "nearest neighbor."
- Calculate the mean value of the outcome indicator (or each of the indicators if there is more than one) for the five nearest neighbors. The difference between that mean and the actual value for the treated observation is the estimate of the impact due to the program for that observation.
- Calculate the mean of these individual gains to obtain the average overall impact.

This is the simplest form of propensity score matching.

In: Economics, Politics and Social Issues in Latin America ISBN 1-60021-182-8
Editor: Mary P. Lassiter, pp. 223-246

Chapter 11

AUTONOMOUS PARTICIPATION AND POLITICAL INSTITUTIONS IN RECENT BRAZILIAN DEMOCRACY*

Alberto Tosi Rodrigues
Universidade Federal do Espírito Santo, Brazil

INTRODUCTION

In the political sociology, the conservative thought always indicated a direct correlation between social mobilization and the appearance of systemic political troubles, with disorganizing and separative characteristics.

Samuel Huntington, who had a strong influence in the Brazilian debate since the sixties, proposed a model – in line with several other researchers – according to which the processes of socioeconomic modernization would generate a fast dissemination of certain aspirations (consumption, well-being etc) in the lower layers of society. This would cause an overload of unprocessed and not attended demands on the political system in developing countries. Consequently, would cause an anomic political mobilization. "The relationship between social mobilization and political instability seems to be reasonably direct. The urbanization and the increase in the indexes of literacy, education and exposition to the mass media provoke an increase of aspirations and expectations which, if not satisfied, galvanize the individuals and the groups to the politics. In the absence of strong and adaptable institutions, such increases of participation produce instability and violence. (...) The faster the instruction of the population occurs, more frequent is the government brought down" (Huntington, 1975, p. 60).

Under the impact of the crisis of the central capitalism in the seventies, that same conservatism, through the well-known Trilateral Commission, started to associate the disfunctionalities of the political system due to the processes of social mobilization to the governments' incapacity of using appropriate mechanisms of economic administration

* First published in *Revista de Sociologia Política*, v. 12 june 1999, p. 99-119.

(related basically to the fiscal crisis of the State) and implementation of public policies in general. It was introduced the debate on "governability" of democratic regimes: the "excessive" mobilization of society was linked directly to the overload of demands on the political system and the decisory paralysis, and to the governments' incapacity, in central capitalist countries, to apply policies to overcome the crisis (cf. Crozier; Huntington; Watanucki, 1975). The difficulties to combat the economic crisis were attributed to the democratic political process itself and, more specifically, located, by the conservatives, "in the institutional mechanisms of mass democracy of the Welfare State" (Offe, 1984).

According to this point of view, higher the social differentiation, better the conditions of organization and mobilization of society. In other words, higher the participation, higher the risks to the governability. As a consequence, during the sixties and seventies in the "developing" countries (specially Latin America), the eclosion of authoritarian regimes was interpreted and justified as a legitimate restoration of governability conditions, by national States threatened by the ailment of masses. These masses would be mobilized by action of the irresponsible populism.

In Brazil, for three decades, between the thirties and sixties, a clientelistic incorporation of the urban masses to the political process occurred.

Such incorporation was based fundamentally on the State Corporatism and the populism; both aspects have their deepest cultural and organizational roots in the traditional patrimonialism, patriarcalism and coronelism. I won't discuss such political practices here, but it is important to mention, on one hand, that patriarcalism (cf. Duarte, 1939; Holanda, 1992), patrimonialism (cf. Faoro, 1979; Schwartzman, 1988), and coronelism (cf. Leal, 1975) concern the historical processes of privatization of public issues in contexts without competition or controlled political competition; on the other hand, the populism (cf. Weffort, 1980) and the populist corporatism (cf. Diniz and Boschi, 1991) are institutional responses to the advent of political competition imposed by a wide social differentiation (cf. Santos, 1993).

The movement of 1964 finished the populist cycle. After a decade of bureaucratic-military regime, more specifically after the moment of larger social repression and political closing (1968-1974), the traditional knots of the Brazilian politics were untied partly. Since the end of the seventies, a change in the mechanisms used by political leaderships to call the urban and rural masses to participate in the political conflicts has occurred. In this change, the exclusiveness of populist patterns of leadership/mass articulation and political mobilization was broken. Although the old format still persists considerably – in a variety of levels of the electoral processes, and especially as a practice incorporated to the political culture – and leaderships on the right and on the left are still using it to guide their own conduct, its validity started to be contrasted with the emergency of an organized section of the civil society that was able to articulate a new, more autonomous, form of political "combat" and a new type of public ethics.

The social bases of the Brazilian political conflict were separated, at that time, between an organized section, which had its autonomous participation expanded – from localized claims to the participation in the public space at national level –, and a disorganized section, that was maintained as object of the populist manipulation or "new" types of use. During the transition to the democracy, those new outlines of the political practices of the society interacted strongly with the process of reorganization of the institutional order. Once again, there was a counterpoint between the demands expressed by the political mobilizations of the organized society and the "objective needs" defended as a governance issue, by the technocracy. The point, according this technocracy was to combat the economical crisis associated with the growing inflation and the external debt.

The objective of this article is – based on the context described above – to identify analytical elements to understand the social mobilizations in a different perspective, rather than the view of sociological conservatism. A perspective which sees mobilizations and demobilizations of the organized society as the compensation of the enlargement and narrowing processes of the political system or, in other terms, as movements of "socialization" or "privatization" of the sociopolitical conflict. Also, based upon the Brazilian process of democratic "transition" and "consolidation", I intend to identify some elements related to the tension between the processes of social mobilization and the construction of the new political institutions of the democracy.

THE DEMOCRATIC PROCEDURE

Bobbio (1985 and 1988) states that the democracy is, basically, a method. With the advent of modernity, the linkage between old democracy and liberalism was reciprocally useful: the last would provide the former with the civil warranties indispensable to the actors' freedom, as the former would give to the last a method, a procedure for taking collective decisions.

Robert Dahl (1971) has proposed a minimal definition of the democratic procedure. A polyarchy would be the regime capable of had developing the institutionalization of procedures and the growth of participation of the citizenship.

Any decision-making process includes, according to Dahl, two analytically distinguishable states: the composition of the political agenda (the decision on which themes will be object of deliberation) and the decision itself ("decisive stage", the results) (cf. Dahl, 1989, p. 107). To a given political order be considered democratic, the decisions are supposed to be legitimately taken by the members of that association, that is, by whom the decisions are applied to and are, in fact, obliged to follow them. This decision should be made in conditions of equality. Each adult member of the association is supposed to be "the best judge of him or herself", which means that he or she is a citizen.

Under a democratic political order, there will be a fully democratic political process if a group of ideal-typical criteria were observed, as follows:

(1) In the decision making process, the citizens should have appropriate and equal conditions among themselves to introduce questions in the political agenda and to express the reasons for which they prefer a certain result.
(2) In the decisive stage of the decision making process, it should be guaranteed to each citizen equal opportunity for expressing his or her choice; and that choice should be computed with the same weight as those of other citizens. (That criterion does not implicate in prohibition of proportional representation or delegation of powers in certain decisions).

According to Dahl, these first two criteria are sufficient to consider a government according to the democratic process.

(1) The third criterion tries to answer the objection regarding the intellectual capacity of components of the demos to make certain types of decision. Dahl reminds us that the democracy is historically and theoretically associated to the problem of the knowing, as it is the decision-making concerning what people want or what they think to be the best, which requires some degree of information. So, a third criterion is justified, according to which "[e]ach citizen ought to have adequate and equal opportunities for discovering and validating (within the time permitted by the need for a decision) the choice on the matter to be decided that would best serve the citizen's interests" (Dahl, 1989, p. 112).

(2) But there is still the risk that the agenda of themes to decide be excessively limited. The control on the agenda may be expropriated of the citizenship by individuals or oligarchies, as in the case of holders of executive positions that intend to minimize the attributions of the parliament. Thus, it emerges the need for another criterion, according to which "[t]he demos must have the exclusive opportunity to decide how matters are to be placed on the agenda of matters that are to be decided by means of the democratic process" (Dahl, 1989, p. 113), without the demos loosing the possibility of delegating the decision on a theme of the agenda.

(3) Finally, there is the risk that the demos be excessively restricted. In other words: what is the size of the citizenship for a system to be considered democratic? That subject involves both the problem of inclusion (which people should be legitimately included in the demos) and the problem of scope of the authority (how the decisive power of the demos can be legitimately alienated). Then, the fifth general criterion states that "the demos must include all adult members of the association except transients and persons proved to be mentally defective" (Dahl, 1989, p. 129).

In short, based on the democratic theory point of view, the two basic criteria, presented by Dahl, already guarantee the existence of a democracy or a democratic process in its wide sense, or a "procedural" democracy. "I have suggested, might be regarded as procedurally democratic in a narrow sense. In contrast, one that also meets the criterion of enlightened understanding can be regarded as fully democratic with respect to an agenda and in relation to a demos. At a still higher threshold, a process that in addition provides for final control of the agenda by its demos is fully democratic in relation to its demos. But only if the demos were inclusive enough to meet the fifth criterion could we describe the process of decision-making as fully democratic" (Dahl, 1989, p. 130).

Dahl also states that, although these are ideal-typical criteria, they cannot be simply considered as unreal or disconnected to reality. He argues that the assumption of political equality is not invalid even with inequalities of resources among different actors, which obviously occurs in reality. Differently, Dahl explains that the fundamental point is that the inequalities of resources (economical, ideological, of status etc) should not generate formal inequalities of individual citizens in the political process. "For when differences in political resources cause citizens to be politically unequal, then that inequality necessarily reveals itself by a violation of the criteria" (Dahl, 1989, p. 131; see also Beethan, 1994 and Saward, 1994).

Authoritarian Brazil: Demobilization, Contention and Resurgence of Civil Society

The history of change from the autocracy established by militaries in 1964 to a regime that could be submitted to the proof of Dahl's criteria, as we know, was complex, long and truncated. And, nevertheless, the results of the proof are controversial.

Under the bureaucratic-military regime, the State not just deepened the Brazilian capitalism as also, in terms of its relationship with the society, enlarged the political significance of the traditional corporatism, at the same time that banished – at least as effective practice, in that period – the populist pattern of competition, responsible for the mobilization of the urban masses. There was then a new narrowing of the political arena, allowed by the military reaction to the radicalization of the political and economical instability, placed in populist period and guaranteed through the enlargement of corporatism (O'Donnell, 1976).

At the same time, Brazil was urbanized radically (the urban population was higher than the rural one for the first time in the history) and reindustrialized on new bases (based essentially on the external capital). This promoted an occupational restructuring of large proportions (mainly in the secondary sector, to the detriment of the primary sector, and with relative growth of the tertiary sector) and a considerable improvement of some social indicators, like educational level (Santos, 1985). The corporatism was used again by the regime as the more appropriate institutional technology to control the traditional social actors, especially the working classes.

It should be considered that the economic and political goals of the military regime, in response to the "pretorianism" (Huntington, 1975, p. 204-273) present in the crisis of the populism, were to "clean the market of 'inefficient' producers, created during the first stages of industrialization and, not casually, local capitalists in their majority; to minimize the 'excessive' or 'premature' demands of political and economical participation of the popular section; to eliminate elections and political parties, that were channels of transmission of those demands (...); 'to discipline' the workforce in its direct relationships with the businessmen; and to subordinate the class organizations – especially the unions – that could support the reappearance of the leaderships and demands that were planned to be eliminated. Obtaining those goals was seen as the stabilization of the social relationships that would allow the internal and external inversions (...)" (O'Donnell, 1976, p. 16).

The retaking of the State corporatism is the fundamental instrument for achieving those objectives. In contrast with the populist corporatism, this new authoritarian intervention of the State is characterized by the concomitant "nationalization" of the society organizations and "privatization" of certain areas of the State, in a segmented way, that is, differentiated according to the separation of class. In short: there was a deeper retaking of the corporativist protection on the workers' unions, not trying only anticipating their autonomous organization, but deliberately repressing the populist activation; and, simultaneously, franchises were established to certain business sectors access the State, such as financing, exemptions and incentives. "Bureaucratic rings" are consolidated at this time, they are typical in the "Brazilian political model". It was established – there is a certain consensus among the analysts on that – a new dominance pact or a new alliance of classes, sections or social groups, structured on the State, the foreign capital and, in a subordinate manner, the national capital (cf. Cardoso, 1975).

Under such conditions of extreme political closing, it is not possible to think comprehensively about political participation of the society in the initial ten years of military regime. Starting on Geisel's government (1975-1979) and, especially, under the Figueiredo's government (1980-1984), three dynamics (evidently linked) become more visible: the called *political opening*, especially concerning to the restrictive legislation of the minimum liberties, to the parliamentary dynamics and to the revival of the importance of the electoral process (cf. Velasco E Cruz and Martins, 1983; Diniz, 1985); the *development of the associativism and the eruption of the urban social movements* (cf. Boschi, 1987; Sader, 1988; Doimo, 1995); and the *appearance of the new combative syndicalism*, of which the most visible representation appeared in the metropolitan area around São Paulo city, in the last years of the seventies (cf. Keck, 1988).

Regarding the political parties organization, the reform of 1979, first, allowed the continuity of the effective political parties in the bipartisanist period (1965-1979): was created PMDB (Brazilian Democratic Movement' Party) and PDS (Social Democratic Party), substituting, respectively, MDB (Brazilian Democratic Movement, oppositionist) and Arena (National Renovating Aliance, situationist). Second, promote the revival of populist tendencies existents before 1964, like PTB (Brazilian Labor Party, more rightist) and PDT (Labor Democratic Party, more leftist). A surprise, however, was the appearance of PT (Workers' Party), which fundamental social bases are constituted as a consequence of the mentioned economical modernization. In the beginning of the eighties, a centralized organization of trade unions, the Unique Central of the Workers (CUT) and a movement of rural workers (MST) appear as the most important expressions of the autonomous organization of the urban and rural working classes; that means, particularly, a clear cut with regard to the populism and to the coronelism, respectively.

Great mass mobilizations also emerge, such as the Campaign of "Direct Elections Now!" in 1984 (cf. Rodrigues, 1993 and 1995), which is followed by the establishment of a civil government, managed by Democratic Alliance (a linkage between PMDB and moderate sectors of PDS). This government (1985-1989) promote unsuccessful attempts of containing the inflationary process that progressively increased since 1983, the attempt of reformulating the legal mark of the new regime through a process of reviewing the Constitution in 1987-88 and, finally, the first presidential election since 1960, in 1989.

One important aspect is that the wide economical modernization operated by the military regime between 1964 and 1984 was associated to the extreme repression of the praetorian-populist social participation in the initial moment – of which the "new" corporatism highlighted above was an important aspect –, also allowed the social differentiation, based on which the associative boom and the appearance of the urban social movements, the new syndicalism and PT were generate in the last decade of the regime.

CONJUNCTURE, PROCESS, MOBILIZATION

In order to discuss the analytical elements needed to the study of situations related to the enlargement of the participation of the organized society in the political conflict, it is necessary to establish some basic points about conflictive conjunctures and about processes of political mobilization.

Political conflicts are situations in which the opposition among actors with their objectives, resources and different strategies is verified. The conflict result cannot be established *a priori*, just for evaluating intrinsic capabilities or stocks of available resources to the political actors. It should be related to the analysis of the unfold of the conflictive process itself, that includes the constraints of institutional order and the opposition of other actors, as well as the intervention of absolutely random or unexpected events.

> "It is extremely difficult to predict the result of a dispute observing the beginning, because we don't even know who else will enter in it. The logical consequence of insisting too much on the determinism of the private origins of the conflict is to attribute a zero value to the political process" (Schattschneider, 1967, p. 50, no italics in the originals; see also Hindess, 1982, p. 500).

A conflict, however, is established among agents in a specific arena (or in different arenas at the same time) and around a certain agenda. According to the jargon of the area, arena refers to the given conditions of a conflict or group of conflicts, as well as to its specific action modes (vote, strikes, dismissals etc) and to the limitations concerning the possible results. For example: if we are talking about a conflict in the parliamentary arena, the possible results will probably be laws, regulations, supervisions etc. In the same vein, agenda can be defined as the list of themes and questions around which the conflicts are armed, its content is also object of the conflict, as well as the time disposition of those themes. For example: it is possible to occur a conflict around a program of privatization as well as a conflict for the theme of the privatization entering the agenda.

In sum, the conjuncture is a moment of a longer political process, structured on certain political (and economical, social, cultural, ideological) parameters, in which certain actors, owners of resources and strategies, conflict themselves around specific arenas and agendas to obtain certain results. In the progress of the conjunctural conflict, the structures that work as orientation to the actors, the arenas and agendas around which the actors conflict, the resources they have, their initial objectives, and also the actors themselves as unitary entities, are subject to several transformations, wanted or not, expected or not. Political conflict, in this context, is every situation in which the obstacles to the achievement of certain actors' objectives include the opposition of other actors (cf. Hindess, 1982, p. 498). Consequently, the final result of the conflict is a direct function of its amplitude.

I use here three propositions of Schattschneider, that state, on one hand, a direct relationship among the amplitude of the conflict and the actors' profile (if individuals or collectives, if many or few, if rightists or leftists), and, on the other hand, the composition and the resolution of the political agenda.

a) First, the result of any political conflict is a function of its reach, its possibility of involving a larger or smaller number of actors;
b) Consequently, the proposition that the most important political strategy is that according to which the actors are in charge of expanding or controlling the reach of conflicts; and

c) Implicitly in the previous ones, it is the notion that the constraint of the conflict to the limits of its initial contenders tends to perpetuate the correlation of forces given at first, while the expansion of the conflict reach tends to unbalance it in favor of the contenders interested in (and effectively capable of) enlarging it.

According to the actors' tendency and the given situation, the strategies will tend to the "privatization" or the "socialization" of the conflict. As suggested by Schattschneider, "the political conflict is not as a soccer game, that occurs in a measured field, with a pre-determined number of players, and in the presence of a audience strictly excluded of the game field. The politics is much more similar to the original and primitive soccer game, in which everybody was free to participate, a game that the whole population of a town could play against the whole population of another town, running freely to one or another place across the open field. Many conflicts are narrowly confined through a variety of strategies, but the distinctive quality of the political conflicts is that the relationship among the 'players' and the audience was not defined precisely, and in general there is nothing that avoids that spectators participate in the game" (Schattschneider, 1967, p. 24).

But, certainly, the reach of a conflict will also be a function of the scale of organization, motivation and potential of the actors' mobilization and, at the same time, of the degree of competitiveness of the system, that is, the nature of the political institutions. It is necessary to attend especially those conflicts capable of taking place in the great national political arena.

In the new articulation and organization opened in the Brazilian society starting in the seventies, the discussion on participation requires the approach of some analytical perspectives that may help to clarify the phenomenon of political mobilization of society, under the conditions of both the transition from authoritarian rule to democracy and the formal validity of the democracy.

The first question is: how to conceptualize the political mobilization of society in a context of enlargement of the political arena – from the point of view of both the new institutional spaces opened gradually by the transition to democracy, and the entrance in the game of new political actors? How does the relationship among the political conflict, the new rules of the game and the new players (placed side by side with the old ones) start to occur? How to analyze the impact of this enlargement on the unfolding of the game? How to understand the political mobilizations not as mere sporadic irruptions or how anomic mass behaviors, but as a political throw which are part of the democratic conflict itself?

The literature on mobilizations has several answers to these questions. The present study is not supposed to be an exhausting review – that can actually be found in Mann (1991) and Tarrow (1988, p. 421-428) – but I can indicate some pertinent answers here to the general question about the relationship between the political mobilization of mass, often called of "political protest" and the institutionalized political system, especially the democratic regimes.

Mobilizations are not usually treated in the literature as mass participation in important questions of national politics, which it is our more direct interest here. Initially linked to the social psychology of the turning of the century (cf. Le Bon, 1954; Canetti, 1983) or the development sociology in the fifties and sixties (cf. Smelser, 1963; Huntington, 1975), the research about mobilizations grew a great extent between the end of the sixties and the eighties, in the United States and Western Europe, motivated by the waves of political protest that broke out. While the European specialists emphasized the structural causes of the movements, the collective identities that they expressed and their relationships with the advanced capitalism (cf. Tilly, 1978; Touraine, 1981), the Americans preferred an "attitudinal" focus, stressing the participation (or embarrassments to the participation) of the organized groups in the mass protest and their forms of collective action (cf. Gamson, 1968; Lipsky, 1970; Oberschall, 1973; Olson, 1978; among other). In previous works during the eighties, with exceptions, the emphasis in the innovation of the movements (called "new social movements") made the political institutions be treated as residual category in the analysis, simply as source of demands satisfaction or protest repression. However, since the last decade more specific studies in Europe and United States started to focus on the political process as the center of the social mobilizations approach (cf. Tilly, 1978 and 1985; Offe, 1985; Dobry, 1986; Tarrow, 1989; Gamson, 1990).

The recent literature shows analytical approaches on the interfaces between mobilizations and the institutional political system: one based on the conjuncture and the other one based on the process. The first one is the model developed by Dobry (1983 and 1986) on *fluid conjunctures*, that is, conjunctures of political crisis associated, in the short term, with ample processes of mass mobilization. The second one is the approach developed by Sidney Tarrow (1981 and 1989) on *cycles of protest and reform*, that is, an aggregation of mobilizations episodes and the measurement of responses given by the political system, in the long term.

In the Dobry's perspective, the specificity of conjunctures of political crisis is the complex relations between the mobilizations and the changes in the states of the political systems. "In opposition to all forms of reification of the institutions [he says] it refers to analyzing the 'structures', 'organizations', or 'apparatuses', considering their sensitivity to mobilizations, plays, and tactical activities of the crisis protagonists. But it also refers to deciphering simultaneously the situation logic which, in such contexts, tend to impose itself to actors and structure their perceptions, calculations and behaviors" (Dobry, 1986, p. 39-40, no italics in the original).

Such perspective evaluates critical conjunctures as moments in which important national political questions mobilize a group of "new" actors, increasing, in a significant manner to those conjunctures, the group of actors normally present in the everyday political situations. The assumption is that the society is sufficiently dynamical and pluralist to stop the sectors socially organized and conjuncturally mobilizable. Such amplification forces all protagonists to change references for their usual political calculations, that is, in the logic of specific social field to which its political activity is delimited. In such conjunctures, they start to base their tactical activity in a situation logic, which they helped to elaborate and are influenced by. This logic breaks the insulation of different social spaces and different everyday political arenas that live within a complex society and create a common thematic basis on which the conjunctural conflict starts to occur.

For example, in 1984 (in the popular campaign to restore direct elections for president) or in 1992 (in the campaign for the impeachment of President Collor), Brazilian syndicalists and workers, capitalists and business entities leaders stopped acting politically on the basis of the logic normally applied to the relation between businessmen and workers; students stopped acting on the basis of university issues; and even the congressmen stopped acting exclusively on the basis of the logic and routine proper to the parliamentary force disputes; and so all cited actors started acting on the basis of the major national political issue in the agenda (direct elections or impeachment). They temporarily abandoned their sectorial political arenas, that is, the spaces socially circumscribed where they normally act, to play the major game (amplified) of the national politics, during that critical conjuncture. In other words, these restricted arenas were momentarily unified in a major national political arena.

As an immediate consequence, the political resources used by the actors in everyday situations change their value (they may increase or decrease), altering the relative weight of the contenders. Given the velocity in which that occurs in conjunctures of crisis, the all strategic routine usually used is unstructured. It incurs a situation of generalized uncertainty among different actors, increasing the difficulty of each one to calculate their own and opponents' actions, and also to anticipate their possible results. As the situations are new and the interactions unusual, the level of impredictability of the game increases so much, as well as specific objectives, certain preferences of actors, and even rules of the political game become unstable. The result is that actors become even more dependent on the plays of other players to decide which will be their own following plays. In short, the perturbation of the actor's calculation ability, given the velocity, uncertainty and unpredictability of the conjunctural game, causes an increase in the tactical interdependency among actors.

Dobry named these moments of instability, unpredictability, break of usual political procedures, and change in the arenas of the game as *fluid political conjunctures*. In the center of the crisis, it is the enlargement of the game, that is, a political (conjunctural) mobilization of the society. In these conjunctures, the social space is simplified; everything moves according to few issues or the only "main" political issue placed at the national arena, and, at the same time, the political game becomes infinitely more complex due to the instability and velocity of the relations. In the end, the solution of the central issue will break the articulation of the situation logic and the political game will be restructured upon new and old sectorial arenas and institutionalized relations (in part, the same relations, in part, the old ones). In sum, the game returns to its "normal" mode, but the cards may be significantly mixed (cf. Rodrigues, 1993).

Based on the previous discussion, it is possible to make two inferences. First, if a larger period of time is considered, more than one (maybe several) conjunctures of mobilizations as described above can be detected, involving simultaneously national issues and more restricted, sectorial issues. Such observation in a longer time scale may allow for detection of connections and interrelations between different episodes apparently isolated, as well as their respective impact on the "usual" institutional political game. Secondly, considering larger time scales could facilitate to state occasional relations between institutional responses given by the political system and the episodes of conjunctural mobilization. Thus, it would be possible to verify whether the political system reorganized itself somehow in response to the advent of mobilizations that generated critical conjunctures. And, in the affirmative case, it would also be possible to verify if the reorganization intended to attend the demands or build instruments capable of dismotivating new social pressures (that is, develop "technologies of contention").

These seem to be the questions made by Sidney Tarrow. As seen above, perhaps the main novelty of the more recent literature on mobilizations is the fact of breaking the analytical barriers between "institutional" and "non-institutional" politics. Consequently, some important formulations on the interactions between mobilization and institutions emerged.

First, consider the concept of *structure of political opportunities* and, connected to it, on one side, the relation among the emergence, the strategy and the dynamics of protest and contest movements, and, on the other side, the cultural frame and the traditions of the national politics. If there is not solution of continuity between politics made in the institutions and politics made on the streets (as Dobry's analytical model shows), both politics should be submitted to constraints or opportunities that complicate or facilitate the action of some political actors to the detriment of others according to the situation (which is usually called "structural selectivity").

More specifically, it should be considered – in the evaluation of the political impact of mobilizations – the degree of opening or closing of the political system, the profile of the regime; the stability or instability of the political alignments done at the level of the institutional politics; the presence or absence of allied and organized supporting groups with solid institutional engagement; presence or absence of divisions within the political elites and their degree of tolerance to protest; the capacity or incapacity of the government to formulate policies as well as its velocity in elaborating responses to demands. Of course, this called "structure of opportunities" must be considered according with its variation in time, which forces us to think the relation between the mobilizations and the political institutions on the basis of an enlarged time scale that extrapolates the analysis of conjuncture (cf. Tarrow, 1988, p. 429; 1989, p. 32-40, p. 82-90).

Secondly, consider the importance of the social space built by the social movements, where they obtain adhesions, conduct battles, compete with other potential movements, and develop political identity. According to the focus of each author, this social space is called "sector of social movements", "subculture of social movements", or "net of social movements". This sector, subculture or net of movements, as understood by Tarrow, involves all individuals and groups engaged in some sort of direct action for collective or public benefits. That includes the formal organizations that give support to social movements (Non-Governmental Organizations, for instance), as well as the group of sporadic participants or those who give informal support to the movements (in Brazil, for example, entities like Brazilian Lawyers Order, Brazilian Press Association, Catholic Church etc). It can also include eventually group of common interests (such as unions and syndical associations). This is similar to the notion of "*ethical-political field*" developed, for example, by Doimo (1995) in the analysis of the Brazilian social movements during the Seventies, which is also related to the "discursive matrices" mentioned by Sader (1988), regarding the same movements. In Tarrow's perspective, "people and groups can move in and out of the social movement sector, and even organizations founded for nonmovement activity may cooperate in it for brief periods .... The size, the shape, and the composition of the social movement sector change over time, as groups mobilize and demobilize, issues move on and off the political agenda, and elites respond with different combinations of facilitation, repression, indifference, and reform." (Tarrow, 1988, p. 432).

In sum, it refers to a space of potential protest, in which circulates themes and mobilizing experiences among movements and, at the same time, individuals and groups compete for space and hegemony, they develop "political relations" as the organized groups do around the institutionality.

Thirdly, consider the themes of cycles of protest and the relations established within these cycles between protest and political reform. Based on the studies of Tilly on the movements in the Nineteenth century and Pizzorno on industrial conflict, Sidney Tarrow observed that the magnitude of the conflict, its diffusion channels, the forms of action used, the actors themselves and the types of organization vary enormously as a function of time. Considering the cycle, he abandons the idea of "structural stability" of the political systems in order to work with the idea of "dynamical stability", which implies understanding the mobilizations as successive realizations, but in different formats, of the same principle of interaction between the social actors and the political institutionality. Such approach allows identifying, throughout the period, different phases of consensus and mobilization, ideological or organizational change, and institutional transformations, all factors that impact the emergence of a given issue in the political agenda. Thus, new lights are thrown on conjunctures of strong mass mobilization. Because, if on one part, they explain themselves by the capacity of organization of the movements or by the structure of opportunities found at the moment in political system, "another part may be explained by the externalities in protest cycles, in which groups that emerge on the crest of a wave of protest may profit from the general atmosphere of discontent created by the efforts of others during earlier phases of the cycle" (Tarrow, 1988, p, 434-435).

In sum, cycles of protest can be defined as aggregations of partially autonomous and independent mobilization episodes. In its trajectory, new forms of action emerge and evolve, the sector (net or subculture) of movements grows and changes its composition, and the political opportunities appear and stop, in part due to the points set in the agenda, the mobilizing practices and conquests obtained by the movements that appear during the cycle.

Tarrow thinks the cycles of protest as something similar to the economical cycle, that is, as a series of individual and collective decisions made in a context marked by the action of systemic factors that are not uniformly experienced, but rather diffusely perceived. The factors, that generate the cycle are certainly "structural", but once the cycle has started, there is a feedback in which results of past protests increase the expectations with regard to new confronts. Such perspective, therefore, emphasizes the perception of the ongoing process, without forgetting the specificity of the conjunctural plays. "*A cycle of protest is a fundamentally political process*" (Tarrow, 1988, p, 435, no italics in the original).

Accordingly, the cycle can be analyzed in three phases. An ascendant phase, that originates the cycle based on a structural situation of accumulation of "injustices" or repression on certain social sectors (as in the first decade of the Brazilian military regime, 1964-1974), and/or the appearance of new opportunities of political actors (as in its second decade, 1974-1984). Given this situation, the appearance of disruptive movements grows "by imitation". In this phase, the protest is spread out from a group to another and tends to pressure the structure of political opportunities in order to open new opportunities (as the Brazilian process of political "decompression" and "opening" in second decade of military regime). These mobilizations grow until the peak of the cycle. This moment, described in the literature as the "moment of madness", can be satisfactorily analyzed as a "fluid conjuncture" (as in the campaign for direct elections, named "*Diretas Já*" in Brazil, in 1983-84). Next, a descendent phase occurs, characterized by demobilization, resulted from the depreciation of the central theme that monopolizes the agenda, and marked recycling of movements and organizations as well as their themes (cf. Tarrow, 1989, p. 50-56). Note that the descendent moment could be seen as the front door to a new ascendant phase.

Based on this conception of cycle, Tarrow considers the "reform" in the institutional political level as indicative of "success" of a protest cycle (the approval of a new democratic Constitution in Brazil, 1988, can be seen in this perspective). *According to the situation, a cycle of reforms could begin as a response to a cycle of protests.* It does not refer to a linear temporal sequence: interpenetration of processes may occur. Thus the effectiveness of social agents mobilization is associated with the processes of institutional change.

Now we will look closer, and from a distinct point of view, the called "structure of political opportunities". What seems to be a change in the opportunities of action, from the movements' perspective, may be perceived as changes in the political regime, from the institutional perspective.

Mobilization, Transition and "Consolidation" of Democracy

We have already asked ourselves about the effect of engagement of a large number of new actors in a given political conflict. But the same question could be done from another perspective: Which institutional conditions would allow and/or facilitate or, on the other hand, constraint and/or make difficult the entrance of an ample spectrum of new individual or collective actors in a given conflict? Or, another question: What is the impact over an institutionality which is "modestly tolerant to participation" of the entrance of a large number of new actors in the dispute on the main political conflicts of the agenda?

It is clear that these questions intend to relate the understanding of conjunctural mobilizations and the cycles of protest to the configuration of the political regime. More specifically, the interest here is to relate these elements to the process of democratization, or what is conventionally called *transition from authoritarian rule* and *democratic consolidation.*

As a comprehensive review of the enormous literature available would be impossible here, I will use a representative example, the called "first generation" of studies on transition, which includes the work of O'Donnell and Schmitter on South Europe and Latin America, especially its conceptual generalizations. After fifteen years of publication, this analysis seems a kind of academic common sense. However, I believe that the role attributed to the political mobilization of the organized society in it does not correspond to what has been empirically verified throughout the enlarged Brazilian transition.

These authors emphasize the indetermination and uncertainty characteristic of the regime transition. They refer to it as a situation in which several alternatives are possible (entry to democracy, return to authoritarianism, emptiness of power), but none is defined; situation in which the *worth* of the agents would prevail on the *fortune* of structural determinations; interval of a regime placed between the breakdown of the authoritarianism and the establishment of some form of democracy; when the rules of the game are primarily the object of conflict; rules that "will define, in a large scale, the resources to be used and the actors allowed to go into political arena" (O'Donnell and Schmitter, 1988, p. 23).

Besides so much indetermination, there seem to be a "normal" way utilized by the process. The central principle is the "liberalization", moment of gaining the elementary formal rights by citizens, acquisition of freedom and the consequence of dropping the costs of the expression of individual and collective interests. Once lowered this cost, the trend is the eclosion of focuses of disagreement and contest against the regime, which will have a "multiplying effect". The next step is the "democratization", understood as the set of "processes according to which the rules and procedures of citizenship are applied to political institutions previously driven by other principles (...), or they are expanded to include individuals who did not have these rights before nor were submitted to these obligations (...)

or, yet, extended to cover themes and institutions in which the citizen participation was not possible previously (...)"(O'Donnell and Schmitter, 1988, p. 25-26).

Thus, although distinct, liberalization and democratization are associated, as more advances the former, harder becomes keeping the constraints to the effective advent of the latter.

The liberalization begins, in this perspective, with the appearance of tensions between "hard" and "soft" groups within the authoritarian forces, because "there is no transition which is not a – direct or indirect – consequence of important divisions in the authoritarian regime itself" (O'Donnell and Schmitter, 1988, p. 41-42). The next play is the formation of democratizing alliances between the "soft" groups of the regime and the moderate ones from the allowed opposition. The important threat, omnipresent in the calculations of this very small group of actors, is a *coup d'état* that reverts the opening and worsen the authoritarianism. But the effectiveness of alliances and oppositions only becomes evident when, based on the called "resurrection of the civil society", the political mobilization of an ample profile of social forces.

Very similarly to the phases of protest cycle proposed by Tarrow, O'Donnell and Schmitter define three phases in the process of social mobilization during the transition of the regime. In the *first phase* – when new actors start to perceive their potential space, but before an oppositionist mobilizing "explosion" – the soft/moderated groups seem to represent the best alternative; in the *second phase*, when the protests reach a peak, the situation of "disorder" seems to favor the hard groups, that sign a high possibility of a *coup d'état*, pressuring the soft/moderate ones; in the *third phase*, when a relative demobilization occurs, "the tolerance capacity of several actors will increase. The soft and undecided elements of the ended regime, as well as the classes and social sectors that support them, will learn to handle new conflicts and demands, with modifications in the rules of the game and the institutional configurations, as well as levels and patterns of popular demands and organizations that never would have accepted it in the beginning of the transition" (O'Donnell and Schmitter, 1988, p. 53-54).

Throughout the transition of the authoritarian regime – which is similar to a typical "cycle of protest" in the O'Donnell and Schmitter's description – the liberalization, its first phase, spends accumulated energies and allows the discovery of deactivated public spaces and forgotten or non-configured collective identities: "it can involve the reappearance of previously existent political parties to make pressure in favor of the democratization or even a revolution; the sudden appearance of books and magazines dedicated to topics previously prohibited by the censure; the conversion of old institutions – unions, class associations and universities – of government control agents into instruments of expression of interests, ideas and anger against the regime; the emergence of base organizations that articulate demands previously repressed or ignored by the authoritarian regime; the expression of ethical preoccupations by religious and spiritual groups previously known by their prudent accommodation to the authorities; and so on" (O'Donnell and Schmitter, 1988, p. 85).

Even the privileged groups that initially gave support to the authoritarian regime, and now do not see necessity in staying, become supporters of the transition followed by liberal professionals and waged sectors of the middle class, who brings to the public scene the intervention of their class entities, receiving the status of "representative entities of civil society", and also, the articulation of workers and the syndical movement. In addition, there is "the literal explosion of base movements", especially linked to the churches.

This context represents what Tarrow termed sector (subculture or net) of social movements, based on which conjunctures of disruptive collective action emerge in the scene of regime transitions ("fluid conjunctures" in Dobry's language; "popular revolt" according to O'Donnell and Schmitter). "In some cases and in particular movements of transition [they describe], many of these several layers of society meet to form what we call "popular revolt". Unions, base movements, religious, intellectual, artistic, clergy, defenders of human rights groups and professional associations give mutual support to their efforts towards the democratization and form a larger whole which identifies itself with "the people", *el pueblo, il popolo, le peuple, ho laos*. This emergent front makes strong pressure to expand the limits of the mere liberalization and partial democratization. A fantastic convergence that this revolt involves is threatening to both the soft groups of the regime, who support the transition expecting to control its consequences, and some of their quasi-allied ones; the moderate opponents of the regime, who expected to dominate, without this loud interference, the following competition for the highest positions of the government" (O'Donnell and Schmitter, 1988, p. 91-92).

The final phase of this cycle is the demobilization. "In any case, independently of the intensity and the background that emerges, the popular revolt is always ephemeral. The selective repression, the manipulation and co-optation done by the responsible ones for the transitional regime; the fatigue produced by frequent demonstration on the streets; the internal conflicts regarding to the choices of substantive procedures and polices; a feeling of ethical disillusion with respect to 'realistic' compromises imposed by pacts and/or authoritarian patterns of leadership within some component groups – all these are factors that contribute to the dissolution of the revolt. The ascension and decline of this revolt frustrate many expectations and many actors" (O'Donnell and Schmitter, 1988, p. 94-95).

During these different movements of the transitional cycle, spaces for setting pacts (or for a cycle of reforms, as Tarrow says) between restrict groups of actors, in order to redefine the rules according to which they act, through the statement of mutual guarantees. According to O'Donnell and Schmitter, this is a form of entering the democracy "through non-democratic ways", as the participants of the pact (usually "oligarchies") "tend to reduce the competition and the conflict; intend to limit the responsibility with the ample public; try to control the agenda of political priorities, and deliberately distort the principle of equality among the citizens. However, these pacts can alter the power relations, promote new political processes and conduct non-anticipated results" (O'Donnell and Schmitter, 1988, p. 68).

Although this type of agreed political change is capable of opening new possibilities to the democracy, it implies the constitution of repertoires of institutional containment, as different pacts are celebrated.

According to these authors – although they always emphasize that the phases are not so linearly presented in real cases – we could distinguish three moments corresponding to three types of pacts: the *military moment*, characterized by the pact between the soft and hard groups regarding the political liberalization and the disposition of the soldiers to return to the headquarters; the *political moment*, perturbed by the mobilizations, in which the necessity of reestablishment of basic mechanisms of political competition could be articulated through a pact intended to "limit the agenda of political alternatives, to share proportionally the benefits, [and] to restrict the participation in the decision making of those who were not involved in the pact. To compensate, the participants of the pact agree to give up on the appeal to military intervention and effort for the mass mobilization" (O'Donnell and

Schmitter, 1988, p. 73); and, finally, an *economic moment* of the transition, in which would be fundamental to face up to the effects of the economical crisis and the increase of social inequalities usually left by authoritarianism, that could be minimized, in possible cases, through a pact of nationally centralized corporative organizations of the capital and work.

The "normal" end of the transition, in this model, would be marked by political pacts based on containment technologies, as if social mobilizations were, at the same time, a necessary resource to help to "extend" the authoritarianism and an inconvenience to be dismissed as soon as the accumulate resources by the "democratic" opposition were sufficient to celebrate the intra-elite agreements. In this end, a convocation for elections reasonably competitive to the fundamental positions of the government occurs; when its rules, in agreement between the main actors of the process, are successfully established, they represent the basis of a "contingent consensus" around which the new democracy is established. The impact of these initial election, O'Donnell and Schmitter indicate, will differ according to the results obtained by the forces on the right or on the left. The authors suggest that there are greater chances of stabilization if the results of center-right were satisfactory.

In sum, the "transition ends when an 'abnormality' is not a main characteristic of the political life; it occurs when the actors establish – and respect – a set of more or less explicit norms that define the channels to be utilized for accessing to the government positions, the ways that can be legitimately used in their conflicts, the procedures to be applied in the State decision making, and the criteria used for exclusion of the game. In other words, the normality becomes the main characteristic of the political life when those who are active in the politics expect that all act according to the rules – and to the set of the game rules called regime" (O'Donnell and Schmitter, 1988, p. 107).

As the procedures start to become a routine, those authors tend to consider that we have begun the "consolidation" of the democracy. What is expected in this phase is to structure and legitimate the collectivities, political identities, specific arrangements and resources appeared during the transition. It is the institutionalization of the uncertainty characteristic of the democracy, based on a "stabilized" reference frame. It is not a simple enlargement of the transition. According to the authors' approach, the consolidation has its own dynamics. The tormenting, conflictive, and uncertain days in which the authoritarian regime is brought down are slowly substituted by moments of "normalization", "routinization" – now in democratic patterns – of the political life. "Whereas during the transition a purer form of political causality tends to predominate in a situation of rapid change, high risk and indeterminate strategic choice, during the consolidation, actors have to 'settle into the trenches' (to uses Gramsci's metaphor). They have to organize their internal structures more predictably, consult their constituencies more regularly, mobilize their resource base more reliably, consider the long-term consequences of their actions more seriously, and generally experience the constraints imposed by deeply-rooted material deficiencies and normative resistances much more saliently" (Schmitter, 1985, p. 6).

Based on the regular functioning of a legislative power freely and competitively elected, always considered a central institution of the new democracy, some crucial questions would be defined: the nature and the character of territorial representation; the relation among parties (in the electoral plane and in the parliament); the autonomy of the state and para-state agencies; the strategies of the interests association; the forms of relationships with social pressure etc. Finally, it is the process of stabilization of the representation being structured, via two generic channels of access: the territorial, controlled by the parties; and the functional, manipulated by the interests associations.

So, what is the meaning of the eventual presence of political interest protest or mass mobilizations if the social demands started to be expressed by the routine channels, the vote or the organizational membership?

According to Schmitter and O'Donnell, after starting the processes mentioned above and the routinization of alternation (or larger realignment) of the parties in the power, the internal regulation of the main political structures would be completed: party competition, actuation of the interests associations, parliament functioning, responsible executive power. Contingent patterns would become the started structures, practices and norms would be converted in laws and regulations based on the state authority and the Constitution. Regarding the actors and arenas of conflict characteristic of the change from authoritarianism to democratic regimes, Schmitter observes that "... just as O'Donnell and I argued that movements were the crucial sites for determining the outcome of the demise of authoritarian rule and parties were central to the transition to democracy, now I would argue that parliament and ... interest associations are the sites where consolidation will be decided" (Schmitter, 1985, p. 22).

In sum, what occurs from the "transition" to "consolidation" of democracy is a transformation of the contingencies (typical in the conflictive period of authoritarianism fall), in a structured, routinized and normalized institutional pattern. A process in which the political actors of disruptive vocation, on one side, or repressive, on the other side, would simply leave the scene or transform themselves in institutionalized groups (internally speaking) with structured interests, occupying positions in the political-juridical institutionality. A process in which the constitutive rules of the regime would not be the object of uncertainty anymore and would start to define mutually normalized expectations. A process that would relocate – with or without rearrangements – those asymmetrical social relations that give support to the political domination into a economic domination.

In O'Donnell-Schmitter's model, the mobilizations, that were at the center of the arena during the moment of forcing the doors of the "liberalization", and the parties, that were privileged channels during the process of "democratization", provide space, with the advent of "democratic consolidation", to the prevalence of the parliament in the center of the public scene as an arena of ruled conflict, and of organized corporative interests, which are privileged political actors in a game with rules that tend to be universally known and routinely accepted, because they were previously agreed.

It seems to me that this model is empirically insufficient. For instance, Huntington understands social mobilization as the dysfunctional eruption and produces an analysis that is rather a conservative explanation of the emergency of the authoritarianism as an institutional response to mobilization. Differently, O'Donnell and Schmitter see the social mobilization from the point of view of its functionality, in terms of the erosion process of the authoritarian institutionality. In both analyses there were not analytic instruments to explain the eruption of conjunctures of strong social mobilization in institutionalized democratic contexts. Mobilizations in democratic contexts, taking such model strictly, constituted abnormalities. The functional forces and the insistence on the disjunctive transition/mobilization *versus* consolidation/demobilization, inherent to O'Donnell-Schmitter's model, limit its explanatory power and deny the contribution of the organized society to the positive construction of a democratic institutionality.

As a final comment, I intend to emphasize that, in the Brazilian process of democratic transition and consolidation, the new institutions did not routinize a political competition in a polyarchic mode because the transition pacts, started among actors of oligarchic profile, extended the previous authoritarian pattern of relation between the society and the state; also, as a consequence, the institutional reforms offered by the political system as a response to the transition mobilizations intended to limit the range of political socialization rather than institutionalize the extended competition; and, finally, because the social exclusion, sub-product of conservative modernization, composed a social field divided into organized and mobilized society, on one hand, and a inorganic and demobilized mass, on the other hand, making the engagement of ample sectors of the population in the process of political participation impracticable. I will develop this line of thinking in the next topic.

Now I will just remind that O'Donnell, in a more recent article (1996), suggests that in social formations, such Latin American ones, the comparison between the effective processes of democratic construction and Dahl's polyarchy model shows only the gaps and insufficiencies of the real political systems. Its positive aspects, therefore, should be analyzed in its own political tradition. Differently, I believe that Dahl's construct, due to its ideal-typical character, is the most appropriated instrument to reveal the negative influence of the clientelistic and authoritarian political tradition of countries like Brazil on the present possibilities of the institutionalization of democracy. It is exactly from the advent of "democracy through non-democratic means" that these limits emerge. So, rebuilding the crescent mobilization process of the organized society during the transition, we are able to see that there were always historical alternative for this contradiction.

Democratization Without Democracy

It is clear that, and in line with the prediction of O'Donnell and Schmitter's model, the parliamentary arena increases its importance during and after the writing and promulgation of the Brazilian constitution in 1988. However, parliamentary arena does not construct itself as institutional locus where social demands are processed.

The image associated with the academic common sense of a linear counterpoint between a conflictive transition and a stable democratic political competition centered on the parliamentary arena and the social representation via groups of interest, in the case of Brazil, do not correspond to the facts due, partially, to the following reasons.

First, it is due to the fact that the stated political pacts, although guaranteed the overcoming of the regime, did not intended to change the political system towards the institutionalization of a new order of relations between the state and society. The way the transition pacts occurred contributed to create, during the New Republic (1985-1989), an "atmosphere" of ample dissatisfaction of the society with the results of those pacts, in terms of both the failure of the experiments of monetary stabilization and the dissemination of traditional clientelistic practices incompatible with the moment of institutional construction. The crisis of the State, as the crisis of the domination pact under the authoritarianism (cf. Sallum Jr., 1995), that cannot be discussed in the narrow limits of the present study, was associated with other difficulties of the democratic routinization of political competition, confronting during the transitional conflict, the trend to socialization of the political game characteristic of the logic of the organized and mobilized society to the trend to the privatization of the game, characteristic of the technocratism of economical administrators under a situation of fiscal crisis and external debt (cf. Loureiro, 1997).

The heterogeneity of the coalition that allowed the transition made impossible the effectuation of the expectations created by itself – the idea of institutionalizing new articulations between emergent organized interests and public power. Neither the State nor its form of intervention on the economic and political processes were substantially altered, what represented a long immovability of the corporativist and authoritarian pattern of relationship with the organized society. The effect of eclosion of the organized and autonomous participation of new and old sociopolitical actors was to discard part of this regulamentation, what however does not solve the institutional problem. It is also clear that, on the society's perspective, the sectorialization of traditional actors (the syndical and business organizations) made impossible the formulation of projects globally or partially consistent at the level of interests associations, and changed the management of the institutionalization to the Executive power and the congress – especially at the moment of write the new Constitution in 1988, making the disperse or exclusively corporative demands reach the legislative level (Diniz, 1992).

Secondly, the recent trend of constituting a "modern, dynamical and pluralist" (Dahl, 1989) society, working as the basis of political competition in horizontal modes (similar to the American political system) was not able – especially due to the strong resistance of the old clientelistic structures and the right segments that used them – to endow the new evolving regime with a formal institutionality typically polyarchic, despite acting towards it. The increase in social complexity observed through the sixties had a non-immediate and weak impact on the changes in the formal political institutionality, although it did impact directly the process of emergency of new actors and the political mobilization of the society. The political system, attached to the clientelistic pattern responded with a partial and limited "cycle of reforms" (and, specially, incapable of instituting an effectively polyarchic pattern) to the "cycle of protests" occurred during the transition.

> "There were substantial changes in the associative patterns and mobilization forms", that is, "the process of urbanization was intensified, the social differentiation was deepened, the capacity of organization was increased and strengthened", and, as a consequence, "the pressures and demands on the institutional and political system were substantially amplified". On the other hand, "the political effects of these changes were overestimated" by both the involved political actors themselves and the analysts' theoretical formulations. The political limitations related to these socioeconomic changes can be attributed to the following two causes. On one hand, as mentioned by Camargo and Diniz, "the process of change obeyed to an incrementalistic logic rather than a dynamics of rupture with established patterns in terms of both elite's segments and popular organizations" (1989, p. 11). Put in a different way: the pacts established in transition ending limited the reach for retaking the process of crescent political mobilization of the society, that occurred through the increase of social complexity created by the economic modernization. As shown in other study, in the decisive episode for reestablishment of direct elections to the Republic President, in 1984, a situation of intra-elite disputes – although these are not comparable, in terms of social exclusion, to those that dominated the period previous to 1964 – prevailed on the logic of "socialization" of the conflict (cf. Rodrigues, 1993). On the other hand, the "improvements of the organizing capacity are not translated automatically into satisfactory absorption for the institutional

political system", that is, the conflict from which the post-authoritarian institutionality emerged, resulted in the prevalence of the positions of those actors who are interested in building mechanisms that rather limit the absorption in an autonomous manner and allow the organized social intervention on the political process. "It was crystallized, therefore, the gap between society and State, generating a chronicle and permanent focus of the crisis" (Camargo and Diniz, 1989, p. 11).

Thirdly, given the socially exclusionary profile of the modernization occurred in the country, the organized portion of the society has composed the social ground of enormous economically and politically marginal masses, compromising the volume and efficiency of the substantive demands. If the organized social sector requests compensation from the State in terms of the efficient formal institutionalization of access channels to the political processes, the crescent inorganic masses continue under the control of the clientelistic informal institutionality (specially coronelism and populism, understood here not as a dated historical phenomenon, but as a behavioral matrix). As observed by Francisco Weffort, "the political order inaugurated in 1988/89 in Brazil reflects a transition process in which these two dimensions of democratization (liberalization and participation) had an extremely unequal growth. The increase of liberalization (of the right to information and expression) was much larger than that of participation – that is, the capacity of the people of influencing the government and its politics for elections and other democratic means" (Weffort, 1992, p. 21-22).

This occurred besides the possibilities of participation formally allowed by the 1988 Constitution (cf. Benevides, 1991). According to Weffort's perspective, Brazil lives a dual system at the moment, which opposes the marginal and integrated ones, these latter the only ones to access the mechanisms of participation. Thus, although the formal democratic institutionality allows a possibility of influence, the socioeconomic marginalization, that decreases the organization capacity of social groups – and also the influence of clientelistic institutionality still existents on the behavior of these disorganized sectors – has prevented its true exercise.

Based on these and other questions not discussed here, it would be at least enigmatic speaking of "consolidated democracy" in Brazil. The political crisis lived in the Brazilian transition is characterized as eminently institutional crisis. More specifically, it was a crisis of incompatibility between formal institution candidate to polyarchy (but marked by an authoritarian conception of government-demos relationship) and effective political processes in which the organized society, intervening with mobilizations that tended to amplify the public space, was confronted with institutional technologies of containment. Thus technologies are realized through traditional practices, which are restrictives of the public space, and so anti-democratic practices. "The social displacements of the last decades [as Wanderley Guilherme dos Santos points out] produced the emergency of unseen social realities, and redefine the political meaning of older situations. The most significant aggregated result of these modifications consists in the intensive confrontation between the political processes created by these new realities and the old political process characterized by underdeveloped corporatism associated to the not responsible populism (...). In a few words, the essence of the contemporary institutional crisis is defined by the fact that the real political process left behind, and very distant, the institutions created fifty years ago. The underdeveloped corporatism is in crisis because it cannot keep the normal process of competition between several social segments encapsulated anymore. At the same time, the institutional marks which will orient the future historical evolution were not cleared designed" (Santos, 1993, p. 37-38).

And the problem is not limited to the system of organized interests. The "big politics" (parliament, parties, elections) still maintained as hostage of a informal institutionality heir of the clientelistic and authoritarian tradition that occurs with the polyarchic "institutional package" and make difficult its effective implementation.

It is important to emphasize here that in different opportunities, throughout the democratization process – in the critical moment of the direct election campaign (1984), or in the process of Constitution making (1987-88), or in the presidential election in 1989 – there were historical opportunities for political choices that privileged the institutionalization of the polyarchy rather than the maintenance of autocratic and traditional institutional tracks.

In this vein, I just indicated a question – developed in another work (see Rodrigues, 2000) – that can throw some light in the analysis of the construction of this hybrid institutionality and the relative narrowing of mobilization spaces, under the recent democracy. It is the construction, in the eighties and nineties, of the two distinct political-ideological poles in the Brazilian politics. Each one generating and trying to implement several ways of facing the fundamental questions of the process of democratization, that is: *the problem of the State* – the fiscal/financial crisis and the public power crisis (power of justice and police, maintenance of the order etc) –, *the problem of the structuring of the regime* – regarding the respect to the mentioned conflict between the institutionalization of the polyarchic "full package" among the oligarchic reminiscences –and *the problem of participation* – relative to the institutional technologies to contain the participation of the organized and mobilized society, inserted or maintained even in democratic contexts, and also the participation of ample inorganic sectors of Brazilian society.

On one hand, the ethical-political field based on the urban popular movements and the new syndicalism of the seventies was spread out to the public space of national level, especially with the formation of Worker's Party (PT) in 1980 and its electoral ascension during the eighties and nineties. These actors, polarized around the left parties and combative syndicalism, treated the problem of the State based on the idea of deprivatization, that is, the removal of business enclaves of its privileged position regarding the State apparatus and the increase of transparency in the relation of this State body with the society, and this a formula for overcoming the financial and public authority crisis that the Brazilian State suffers; they also treated the problem of the regime in the sense of ruled equalization of political competition, and, therefore, in route to polyarchy. And, finally, they treated the problem of participation as mobilization of the organized society in an autonomous manner (and not populist anymore), because it allowed the political resources necessary for facing the adversaries controlling the State apparatus.

On the other hand, the reception of the neo-liberal ideology in Brazil, in the eighties, occurred in order to opposing the "tocquevillean" public ethics that appeared in the seventies. To this associativist and solidary ethics was opposed a market-oriented, privativist and pre-liberal-democratic ethics, by the neo-liberal ideology, as one of its contributions to the formation of attitudes and referencing of the actors' behavior. A market-oriented ethics that was intimately associated with the clientelism and autocratism, traditionally cultivated by the right. In Brazil – where there are not relation between the organized interests and Welfare State, that became the more immediate target of neo-liberal critiques in industrialized countries – neo-liberal attack was against the very recent political organization of workers and popular segments. The actors who composed this pole tried to face the financial crisis of the State base on the notions of "minimum State" and market-oriented reforms (that are supported by the idea of deregulamentation of social rights) and, in this process, used the institutional oligarchic reminiscences rather than trying to stabilize a institutional order of polyarchic profile. In the same way, to obtain adequate conditions for the technocratic and centralizing focus of the economical management and the policies implementation of monetary stabilization adopted – in the name of, once again, the governability – they believed in the containment of mobilization of the organized society and the co-optation (via media and political marketing, at this time) of the ample disorganized portions of the population, regarding both the distributive conflict and the electoral process.

The second pole, as known, was hegemonic in Cardoso's government (1995-2002), but the repeated international economic crises and the electoral advances of the domestic left indicate to the possibility of new conflicts between these poles and, so, new peaks of mobilization. In fact, this occurs in 2002 elections, that put in power Luis Ignacio Lula da Silva and the Worker's Party (PT).

REFERENCES

Beethan, D. 1994. "Key Principles and Indices for a Democratic Audit". *In* Beethan, D. (ed.). *Defining and Measuring Democracies*. London, Sage.

Benevides, M. V. M. 1991. *A cidadania ativa*: referendo, plebiscito e iniciativa popular. São Paulo, Ática.

Bobbio, N. 1985. *Estado, governo, sociedade*: para uma teoria geral da política. Rio de Janeiro, Paz e Terra.

Bobbio, N. 1988. *Liberalismo e democracia*. São Paulo, Brasiliense.

Boschi, R. R. 1987. *A arte da associação*: política de base e democracia no Brasil. São Paulo/Rio de Janeiro, Vértice/IUPERJ.

Camargo, A. and Diniz, E. 1989. Dilemas da consolidação democrática no Brasil. *In* _____.(eds.). *Continuidade e mudança no Brasil da Nova República*. São Paulo, Vértice.

Canetti, E. 1983. *Massa e poder*. Brasília, Editora da Universidade de Brasília.

Cardoso, F. H. 1975. *Autoritarismo e democratização*. Rio de Janeiro, Paz e Terra.

Crozier, M.; Huntington, S.; and Watanuki, J. 1975. *The Crisis of Democracy*: Report on the Governability of Democracies to the Trilateral Commission. New York, New York University Press.

Dahl, R. 1971. *Polyarchy*: Participation and Opposition. New Haven, Yale University Press.

Dahl, R. 1989. *Democracy and Its Critics*. New Haven, Yale University Press.

Diniz, E. 1985. "A transição política no Brasil: uma reavaliação da dinâmica da abertura". *Dados*, v. 26 n. 3, p. 329-346.

Diniz, E. 1992. "Neoliberalismo e corporativismo: as duas faces do capitalismo industrial no Brasil". *Revista Brasileira de Ciências Sociais*, v. 20, Oct.

Diniz, E. and Boschi, R. 1991. "O corporatismo na construção do espaço público". *In* Boschi, R. (ed.). *Corporatismo e desigualdade*: a construção do espaço público no Brasil. Rio de Janeiro, lUPERJ/Rio Fundo Editora.

Dobry, M. 1983. "Mobilisations multisectorielles et dynamique des crises politiques: un point de vue heuristique". *Revue Française de Sociologie*, n. XXIV, juillet-septembre.

Dobry, M. 1986. *Sociologie des crises politiques*. Paris: Presses de Ia Fondation Nationale dês Sciences Politiques.

Doimo, A. M. 1995. *A vez e a voz do popular*: movimentos sociais e participação política no Brasil pós-70. Rio de Janeiro, Relume Dumará-ANPOCS.

Duarte, N. 1939. *A ordem privada e a organização política nacional*: contribuição à sociologia política brasileira. São Paulo, Cia. Editora Nacional.

Faoro, R. 1979. *Os donos do poder*: formação do patronato político brasileiro. 5ª ed. Porto Alegre, Globo.

Gamson, W. A. 1968. *Power and Discontent*. Homewood, Dorsey Press.

Gamson, W. A . 1990. *The Strategy of Social Protest*. 2ª ed. Belmont, Wadsworth Publishing Co.

Hindess, B. 1982. "Power, Interests and Outcome of Struggles". *Sociology*, vol. 16 n. 4, p. 498-511.

Holanda, S. B. de. 1992. *Raízes do Brasil*. 24ª ed. Rio de Janeiro, José Olympio.

Huntington, S. 1975. *A ordem política nas sociedades em mudança*. Rio de Janeiro/São Paulo, Forense-Universitária/Edusp.

Keck, M. 1988. "O 'Novo Sindicalismo' na transição brasileira". *In* Stepan, Alfred. (ed.). *Democratizando o Brasil*. Rio de Janeiro, Paz e Terra.

Leal, V. N. 1975. *Coronelismo, enxada e voto*: o município e o regime representativo no Brasil. 2ª ed. São Paulo, Alfa-Ômega.

Le Bon, G. 1954. *Psicologia das multidões*. 5ª ed. Rio de Janeiro, F. Briguiet and Cia. Eds.

Lipsky, M. 1970. *Protest in City Politics*. Chicago, Rand, McNally.

Loureiro, M. R. 1997. *Os economistas no governo*: gestão econômica e democracia. Rio de Janeiro, Fundação Getúlio Vargas Editora.

Mann, P. 1991. *L'action collective*: mobilisation et organisation des minorités actives. Paris, Armand Colin.

Oberschall, A. 1973. *Social Conflict and Social Movements*. Englewood Cliffs, Prentice Hall.

O'Donnell, G. 1976. "Sobre o 'corporatismo' e a questão do Estado". *Cadernos DCP*, n. 3, p. 1-54, mar.

O'Donnell, G. 1996. Illusions About Consolidation. *Journal of Democracy*, v. 7 n. 2, April.

O'Donnell, G. and Schmitter, P. C. 1988. *Transições do regime autoritário*: primeiras conclusões. São Paulo, Vértice.

Offe, C. 1984. "A 'ingovernabilidade': sobre o renascimento das teorias conservadoras da crise". *In* _____ . *Problemas estruturais do Estado capitalista*. Rio de Janeiro, Tempo Brasileiro.

Offe, C 1985. "New Social Movements: Challenging the Boundaries of Institutional Politics". *Social Research*, v. 52 n. 4, p. 817-868.

Olson, M. 1978. *Logique de l'action collective*. Paris, Presses Universitaires de France.

Rodrigues, A. T. 1993. *Mobilização e conflito político*: a campanha das diretas já. Dissertação (Mestrado). Campinas, IFCH/ UNICAMP.

Rodrigues, A. T . 1995. "A massa na praça: mobilização e conflito na campanha das diretas já". *Comunicação and Política*, v. 1 n.3, p. 163-178, abr.-jul.

Rodrigues, A. T. 2000. *O Brasil de Fernando a Fernando*: neoliberalismo, corrupção e protesto na política brasileira de 1989 a 1994. Ijuí, Ed. Unijuí.

Sader, E. 1988. *Quando novos personagens entraram em cena*: experiências, falas e lutas dos trabahadores da grande São Paulo (1970-1980). Rio de Janeiro, Paz e Terra.

Sallum Jr., B. 1995. "Transição política e crise do Estado". *In* SOLA, L. and Paulani, L. (eds.). *Lições da década de 80*. São Paulo, Edusp/Genebra/UNRISD.

Santos, W. G. dos. 1985. "A pós-revolução brasileira". *In* Jaguaribe, H. (ed.). *Brasil*: sociedade democrática. Rio de Janeiro, José Olympio.

Santos, W. G. dos. 1993. "Fronteiras do Estado mínimo: indicações sobre o híbrido institucional brasileiro". *In* _____ . *Razões da desordem*. Rio de Janeiro, Rocco.

Saward, M. 1994. "Democratic Theory and Indices of Democratization". *In* Beethan, D. (ed.). *Defining and Measuring Democracies*. London, Sage.

Schattschneider, E. E. 1967. *El pueblo semisoberano*. México, Unión Tipográfico Editorial Hispano Americana.

Schmitter, P. C. 1985. *The Consolidation of Political Democracy in Southern Europe and Latin America*. Firenze, Instituto Universitário Europeo. Datilo.

Schwartzman, S. 1988. *Bases do autoritarismo brasileiro*. Rio de Janeiro, Campus.

Smelser, N. 1963. *The Theory of Collective Behavior*. New York, The Free Press.

Tarrow, S. 1988. "National Politics and Collective Action: Recent Theory and Research in Western Europe and the United States". *Annual Review of Sociology*, v. 14, p. 421-440.

Tarrow, S . 1989. *Struggle, Politics and Reform*: Collective Action, Social Movements and Cycles of Protest. Ithaca, Cornell University Press.

Tilly, C. 1978. *From Mobilization to Revolution*. London, Addison-Wesley Publishing Co.

Tilly, C. 1985. "Models and Realities of Popular Collective Action". *Social Research*, v. 52 n. 4, p. 717-747.

Touraine, A. 1981. *The Voice and the Eye: An Analysis of Social Movements*. Cambridge, Cambridge University Press.

Velasco e Cruz, S. C. and Martins, C. E. 1983. "De Castello a Figueiredo: uma incursão na pré-história da abertura". *In* Sorj, B. and Almeida, M. H. T. de. (eds.). *Sociedade e política no Brasil pós-64*. São Paulo, Brasiliense.

Weffort, F. C. 1980. *O populismo na política brasileira*. Rio de Janeiro, Paz e Terra.

Weffort, F. C. 1992. *Qual democracia?* São Paulo, Cia. das Letras.

In: Economics, Politics and Social Issues in Latin America ISBN 1-60021-182-8
Editor: Mary P. Lassiter, pp. 247-272

Chapter 12

THE PROCESS OF POLITICAL TRANSITION IN BRAZIL: ISSUES AND CONSTRAINTS IN THE CONSOLIDATION OF THE DEMOCRATIC REGIME [1]

Carlos S. Arturi
Professor in the Department of Political Science at the Federal University of Rio Grande do Sul, Brazil

INTRODUCTION

The process of transition to a democratic regime in Brazil, beginning in 1974, developed simultaneously with a new slant in the analytical perspectives on changes in political regimes. Analyses centered on macro-structural variables, which had prevailed throughout the seventies, were strongly contested by the attention now given to other factors, the eminently political and institutional factors, in the study of the transition from authoritarian regimes.

The long duration and the gradualism of the Brazilian transition has facilitated the use of diverse approaches in the analysis of the process, thus making it a privileged case for the verification of hypotheses regarding recent processes of democratization. This paper aims to contribute to the theoretical debate on the topic, presenting the results of the author's doctoral research, which studied the strategy of political liberalization implemented during the presidential terms of Ernesto Geisel (1974-79) and João Figueiredo (1979-85).[2]

The study of the attempts that those in power made to liberalize the authoritarian regime gradually and under strict control and to institutionalize a "strong" democracy in which the military would maintain the right of veto over the country's political life, revealed that the

[1] This paper was originally published in *Revista de Sociologia Política*, volume 17 nov. 2001, p. 11-31. Translated by Meryl Adelman.

[2] My doctoral dissertation, entitled *Le Brésil: une tentative de démocratisation octroyée (1974-1985),* defended at the *Institut d'Etudes Politique de Paris,* was published in France under that title in 2000. The primary source of data used for this work were two dozen interviews conducted with the main leaders of the authoritarian regime, including ex-presidents Ernesto Geisel and João Figueiredo, and with the most outstanding opposition leaders of the period. See Arturi (2000).

latter were relatively successful in their efforts[3]. In effect, the process of political liberalization in Brazil was, among all recent cases of transition processes, the one that was most kept under control by authoritarian leaders and the one whose civil elite guaranteed not only the political survival but the broad participation of the military in political power after democratization. The Armed Forces obtained extraordinary political prerogatives, which have maintained them as key political actors with a large degree of informal power, particularly in moments of political crisis. The old authoritarian leaders were also able to obtain the guarantee that there would be no "revenge" against the State agents who had committed crimes of repression against members of the opposition, which was another one of the most pressing problems in the consolidation of the new democratic regimes established within the last two decades.

This chapter presents a synthesis of doctoral research on this singular political phenomenon. It poses the question of how the leaders of the authoritarian regime were able to obtain results similar to those that they had in mind when they began the liberalization process in the early seventies, in spite of the large growth and diversification of the opposition during the period, the resistance of "hard-liners" to the political opening, and the difficult economic constraints they had to face.

To answer this question also means making a contribution to theoretical knowledge and scientific debate on political regime transition processes.. Academic production on processes of transition in political regimes come up against a series of obstacles, originating from insufficient empirical research and methodological difficulties linked to the absence of a general theory of political change (Nohlen and Thibaut, 1994). In this regard, the "third wave" of democratization (Huntington, 1991) produced a particular slant in the theories of political transition, as well as a series of generalizations on the topic, that need to be tested and honed by case studies, as we will do in this article through the study of the Brazilian experience.

The main hypothesis of this paper is that the major constraints in consolidating the democratic regime in Brazil are due to the successful strategy of regime liberalization that was implemented under the Geisel and Figueiredo administrations, maintaining a high degree of voluntarism and control over political processes. Such is the case, in spite of the difficulties that General Figueiredo encountered in guiding the political process and its succession in the final years of his government, resulting from the pressures and growing mobilization of the opposition and the broad social sectors that were demanding the effective and immediate democratization of the country. As a complementary hypothesis, we look at the long duration and extremely gradual evolution of the phase of political liberalization, as well as the use of electoral competition as a privileged political transition. Resource. We consider the notion that these factors created in the Brazilian political arena the impression of a "normalization" of the process as it was being conducted under the control of and according to the rules unilaterally imposed by those in power. These rules were in effect "naturalized" in the

[3] The outcome of this long process of political liberalization was certainly more democratic than what authoritarian leaders had intended it to be when they initiated it in the mid-70s. The indirect election of moderate opposition leader Tancredo Neves to the presidency in 1985 ran counter to the initial plans of authoritarian leaders, who had hoped to elect one of their civilian representatives to that office. Complete political democratization of the country during José Sarney's presidency (1985-1990) marked by the implementation of the new Constitution in 1988 and direct presidential elections in 1989, certainly went further than the authors of the "democratic opening" wanted it to.

evaluations, calculations and elaboration of strategies by the main political actors of the period.[4] This "time factor" has shown to be fundamental in the progressive widening of the moderate sector of opposition as well as the reformist wing of the regime. In this regard, the loss of control over the transition process, at the end of the Figueiredo presidency, meant that the logic of the process became more autonomous.[5] It derived from the voluntarism of the regime's leaders and was modeled on the most traditional characteristics of Brazilian political life: an "authoritarian praxis associated with a liberal logic" (Trindade, 1985), the political centrality of the military and the tradition of conciliation "at the high levels" of the political elite.

The Theoretical Debate on Transitions to a Democratic Regime

The definition of a democratic regime, even when restricted to its exclusively political and institutional dimension, demands that the following conditions be fulfilled: 1) that all relevant political actors must submit to free and peaceful competition for power, whether due to the fact that they place value on democracy or to political calculations of the costs and risks of not playing by its rules;[6] 2) that no political actor holds veto power over the participation of others or over the results of political competition; 3) that there are no state institutions that remain independent and autonomous in relation to democratically elected political power. A "minimalist" definition of democratic regimes like this one is far from being unanimously accepted in the literature, but the definition of democracy as a political regime whose main basis is peaceful and free competition for power and the guarantee of basic civil liberties has been shown to have operational value for research purposes. In the case of our work here, this political and institutional definition is pertinent, since it deals in the same dimension as our research topic, that is, change in political regimes.

The main thematic approaches and orientations in the study of regime transitions have been modified in the attempt to capture the rapid changes in ongoing processes (Nohlen and Thibaut, 1995, p.15) Thus under the influence of history itself, that is, the transitions that have recently been negotiated in Southern Europe and Latin America, the analysts – many of whom had been actors in those processes – have gone on to give primary emphasis to typically political variables, such as the quality of leadership, rational choice, and actors resources, as well of the interaction effects of actors' strategies on the way transitions to a democratic regime were configured. As of the 80s, this change in perspectives has taken place

[4] This hypothesis is based on two articles by Bolivar Lamounier on the importance of the elections in the Brazilian transition. See Lamounier (1985; 1988, p. 110, 194)

[5] This argument was originally developed by Renato Lessa through his analysis of what the election results of 1982 meant for the transition process (LESSA, 1989, p. 90-103) In turn, in Lamounier's view (1988, p.111), the transition process acquired autonomy after the triumph of the opposition in the 1974 elections. We take another stance, which is that the process gained autonomy only at the point in which none of the actors involved have the concrete ability to change its rules. In the case in point, as Lessa argues, this occurred after the 1982 elections, at which point opposition politicians were elected as governor to some of the most important states of the nation.

[6] According to several authors, this condition expresses itself in different ways. Thus, for Linz, main political forces should consider democracy as "the only game in town"; for Przeworksi it should be considered "the lesser evil"; for Whitehead, the regime could be chosen among other variables, by default. (cf. Moisés. 1995)

in detriment of "macro-level" explanations, which had given primary importance to the influence of social and economic variables – the level of economic development, class structure, and phases of industrialization – in processes of political change[7]. This radical change in analytical orientation is itself linked, in the first place, to the third wave of democratization beginning in the early 70s. It came as a great surprise to the majority of political scientists and supplied undeniable empirical counter-evidence to the theories that posited macro-level variables, whether economic (degree of economic development), social (modernization) or cultural (civic culture) as necessary pre-conditions for the existence of democracy[8]. In effect, as noted by Banegas, "these macro-historical approaches were criticized for their bias toward determinism and 'ultimate causes', and principally for their tendency to confound statistical correlation with historical causality". (Banegas, 1993). In the preface to the Brazilian edition of Dahl's *Polyarchy,* Fernando Limongi provides a concise and accurate evaluation of the influence of recent processes of democratization on theories of political change: " The constitution of this research object – regime transition – was concomitant with the assertion of the explanatory autonomy of specifically political variables. In other words, this literature is one of the vehicles through which political science has freed itself from modernization theory and its characteristic type of explanation based on the historical process of the transformation of social structures." (Limongi, 1997, p.12). The participation of many intellectuals as political actors in the very processes that they have studied has certainly influenced this analytical perspective, centered on choice and on political action; after all, someone "thus devoted to political practice needs a heroic illusion to inspire action."[9]

The "micro-political" approach starts from the assumption that the transition from an authoritarian to a democratic regime is a process that is dependent primarily on variables that refer to the intervention and voluntarism of the political actors participating in the transition. According to this perspective, it is in the "fluid moments" of transition (Dobry, 1986) when uncertainty in relation to the rules and the continuity of the political game become a defining trait, that the conditions of political processes normally determined by the social and economic structure find themselves "suspended". (Karl and Schmitter, 1991). In systematizing the "micro-political" approach, O'Donnell and Schmitter maintain that analyses of the transition from authoritarian regimes should be guided by a "theory of abnormality in which the unexpected and the possible are as important as the common and the probable ... [since] the 'methodology of normal science' is not appropriate in situations of rapid change, in which parameters for political action are shifting" (1988, p. 18-19). Thus, for these authors, under such circumstances both unexpected events and the action and ability of political elites and leadership take on greater import in determining political processes. From a methodological point of view, political research veers toward methodological individualism, the theory of rational choice and strategic interaction.

Thus, many authors seek to build explanatory models of regime transition based on the identification of key actors, the formalization of their goals and the distribution of their preferences. These approaches tend to run into problems: they often incur in excessive

[7] For a critical review of academic production on transition processes and democratic consolidation, see Santiso (1993), Banegas (1993) and Moisés (1995).
[8] For a critical analysis of these theories, see Hermet (1986) and Heper (1991).
[9] This expression was used by Michel Dobry in a seminar organized by Guy Hermet at the *Institut d'Etudes Politique de Paris* Feb. 16, 1994.

formalization and simplification, confound analytical levels, neglect the political and institutional history of the countries that they study and the contextual data of the transition, and above all, tend to overestimate the rationality of actors, many of whom are just in the process of self-constitution during this particular juncture. (Banegas, 1993). Some authors, such as Di Palma, exacerbate the role of political voluntarism in the construction of democracy and thus neglect other variables that do not directly refer to political actors and the transition context. (Di Palma, 1990). This position leads to the attempt, in many authors, to elaborate prescriptive "formulas" and norms destined to guide the behavior of political actors and the construction of institutions that are supposedly more adequate in leading processes of transition and democratic consolidation toward better outcomes. The series of guidelines for democratic political actors that Huntington put together, as well as the intense academic debate about what form of government (presidential or parliamentary form) would be better suited for consolidating the new Latin American democracies – are examples of this normative tendency, inspired by attempts at "political engineering".[10] With regard to the identification of actors' interests and their choice formation, it should be taken into account that their rationality is limited, especially during processes of transition in which the rules of the political game undergo constant modification. Furthermore, political actors and individuals do not act exclusively in response to rational interests, but are also guided by ideologies, values and "symbolic" motivations. In this regard, gaining legitimacy becomes a significant factor in the stability of democratic regimes and a serious obstacle in the exercise of authoritarian power. Przeworski's observation that a lack of legitimacy is not in itself enough to provoke the crisis of an authoritarian regime, unless associated with the existence of a viable power alternative, is in fact pertinent. Nonetheless, no regime can achieve stability without the legitimacy of its political order. Linz was a pioneer in pointing to the legitimacy deficit of authoritarian regimes. He identified this lack in the Brazil of the early 70s as a serious obstacle to institutionalization, exactly at a time in which other scholars were predicting institutionalization on the basis of macro-level analyses[11]. In turn, the establishment of democratic regimes in the majority of Latin American countries, as of the 80s, coincided with major economic crisis and with the radical reform of the model of State-guided economic development. The survival of democracy in these adverse conditions strongly suggests that the population's normative support for this regime has been stronger than the economic and social crisis in the region (Remmer, 1992-1993, p.5) In turn, wherever the democratic regime was overturned, as in the Peruvian case, this has been due to other factors, as Nohlen and Thibaut (1994) remind us.

The major risk involved in analyses centered on actors' actions and choices consists in retrospective rationalization and the "finalist" tendencies involved in attempts to reconstruct the past (Linz and Stepan, 1995). The action of political actors is in reality almost always submerged in uncertainty as to the context of their actions and the effects and reactions that that they will produce upon other actors. This is particularly pertinent for transition situations,

[10] The Brazilian transition process even before it began was the center of this type of speculation. In mid 1972, Huntington was invited by Leitão de Abreu, the Minister in Chief of the Civilian House of the Médici administration, to formulate a series of political forms for the liberalization of the authoritarian regime's, which at that moment was at its peak moment of political repression. The suggestions that he made, perhaps the first-ever explicit attempt at "political engineering", were only put to use two years later, by General Golbery do Couto e Silva, the Geisel government's chief political strategist.

[11] For a critical review of this debate, see Lamounier (1988).

in which habitual and stable political references cannot be counted on. Analysis therefore should not underestimate actors' feelings of risk and uncertainty when they engage with junctures that are "in flux." The tendency that not only researchers but also individual political actors themselves have is to reconstruct the motivation behind the action and the logic of events that have occurred according to their final outcome. The political analyst must therefore seek to comprehend the evaluations, choices and action of actors as they were experienced while they were happening. In spite of the limitations we have referred to and the precautions that must be taken when a micro-political perspective is adopted, this approach has had quite positive effects on the specialized literature, insofar as it points out the risks of reifying the study of political processes, that is, taking the State, the Armed Forces, social classes and actors as "one and the same man" with regard to interests and political action.

The lacunas in both macro-structural and micro-political approaches led Terry Karl to propose a middle-range approach which seems more promising to us in promoting an understanding of processes of transition to democracy. The author has elaborated a notion of "contingency" in order to escape the dichotomy "structural determination vs. actor's freedom" and for capturing the connections between macro-structural factors, a country's institutional and the options that political actors have. It must be demonstrated "how, in particular moments, the range of available options is contingent upon the structures created in a previous period and how these decisions are conditioned by institutions that were established in the past." (Karl, 1991, p. 423) From this perspective, pre-existing political institutions play a mediating role between socio-economic structure and the actions of political actors, since they supply the parameters of political space as well as the institutional resources that are available to actors (Badie and Hermet, 1990). For example, in the Brazilian case, the project of political liberalization that was carried out through the electoral process was not exactly the "choice" of the Geisel administration, as if it had been implemented for this purpose and with a clarity as to the goals that were being pursued. In truth, this project was implemented basically due to the fact that there was an available and functioning political party system and electoral calendar. The existence of elections and the survival of liberal political institutions, even throughout the most dictatorial phase of the authoritarian regime, can be explained by a traditional characteristic of the Brazilian political system dating back to the time that the country obtained its independence: inter-elite competition for political power. Nonetheless, actors' options and actions "should not only be interpreted in relation to pre-existing opportunities and constraints but also with regard to those that emerge through the process of transition itself." (Banegas, 1993.)

In short, the interaction of pre-existing social, economic and political structures and the strategies of political actors allows for institutional and behavioral arrangements which condition the possibilities for democratic consolidation. In this regard, choices and decisions carried out previously gain importance in the outcome of the transition process, however minor they may have been at the moment they were made and taken; they can have a decisive impact on later stages of democratization, facilitating or encumbering their success. For example, the agreements made between the military and the opposition during the stage of political liberalization remained in effect for quite a long time, bringing about a democracy marked by "birth defects'. (Karl and Schmitter, 1991, p. 286) In this manner, characteristics of the country's political culture, historically rooted patterns of behavior and structural constraints may or may not be reinforced by the choices and actions of political actors within a particular conjuncture. The persistence of economic crisis and the adoption of plans for economic stabilization, often without any prior discussion with the rest of society or within Congress, aggravated central aspects of the "delegative democracy" of the region (O'Donnell, 1994) This concept refers to the regimes of the "third wave" of democratization that according to O'Donnell are "intrinsically hostile to the normal patterns of representation of established democracies, the creation and consolidation of political institutions and especially, horizontal accountability". (O'Donnell, 1993, p. 165) These non-institutionalized democratic regimes are characterized by the way they delegate to elected officials the ability to carry out whatever measures they deem most adequate to alleviate acute economic crisis[12]. Plebiscite and personalist elements of this type of democracy have their roots in the populist style and the low level of institutionalization that mark the region's political past.

With further regard to the relative weight of diverse variables in explaining phenomena of transition from authoritarian regimes, the preponderance of political and institutional factors should not lead us to underestimate the impact of macro-structural variables in these processes. In fact, as Linz and Stepan (1996) have verified, those authoritarian regimes that allow for some limited political pluralism, as well as the existence of social and economic arenas that are extensive and relatively free from State control, have been more favorable to democratic transition and have generated positive elements for the eventual consolidation of the latter. Insofar as the political micro-variables that are related to the previous regime are concerned, these authors give salience to two in particular, both linked to actors: the leadership of the earlier regime and the question of "who initiates and who controls the process of transition." The question here refers to whether the transition was initiated by the regime itself or from the opposition, and whether the process was controlled by authoritarian leaders or by an interim government after the collapse of the previous regime. Linz and Stepan focus on the analysis of actors and political leadership, but bring structural and historical variables into their analysis. The authors attempt to identify which traits linked to the formation of the nation State – practices and institutions – and which paths taken by transition processes (for example, through the establishment of pacts of via collapse) facilitate or encumber the consolidation of democracy.

THE AUTHORITARIAN REGIME AND THE INITIATION OF TRANSITION

A completed process of democratization generically involves three stages: the beginning of the dissolution of the authoritarian regime, the creation of democracy and the consolidation of the new regime (Bermeo, 1992, p. 273), Brazil's long and gradual transition makes these three phases clearly distinguishable. The first begins in March of 1974 and goes through March of 1985, covering the two latter military regimes, that is, the presidential administrations of General Geisel (1974- 1979) and Figueiredo (1979-1985). The second stage – the construction of democracy – covers Jose Sarney's civil administration (1985-1990). The new democratic regime's process of consolidation, which can be considered a second transition, begins with Fernando Collor de Mello's presidency, starting in March 1990

[12] In Brazil, the Cruzado Plan, in 1986, and the Collor Plan, in 1990, were examples of this type of plebiscite delegated to the population, which in fact thus lent its support *a posteriori* to a series of harsh economic measures that had been imposed in an authoritarian manner.

(elected through universal suffrage and removed from power through an impeachment process in December of 1992). It continues at present.

For our purposes here, a more accurate analysis of the first period – the period covered in this paper – becomes a must. Some scholars of recent democratization processes in Latin America believe that there is strong affinity between the preceding types of authoritarian regimes, the modes of transition to democracy and the dilemmas that the particularities of these processes placed on the consolidation of new democratic regimes (Nohlen and Thibaut, 1994). This relationship is however not as direct as it seems at a first glance; in this regard, a brief analysis of the significant political change that occurred in Brazil in recent decades will make an empirical evaluation of the most common theses on democratization processes possible and will allow us to hone our initial hypotheses.

One important specificity that should be emphasized that distinguishes the Brazilian autocracy from similar regimes of the region is that it lasted longer, was more economically successful, and involved less repression than the others. Furthermore, in Brazil, "the military as a corporate group, rather than one military man, took responsibility for power and adapted political institutions to the new authoritarian order." (Soares, 1994, p. 13) In fact, Brazilian military regime leaders always considered authoritarianism to be a transitory political form, maintaining the functioning of political parties, an electoral calendar, and the Congress throughout almost the entire period, albeit under that restrictions that we will soon discuss. This institutional ambiguity of the Brazilian dictatorship is of extreme importance for our analysis, since the characteristics of the authoritarian regime that preceded the democratic transition should be considered a fundamental political micro-variable influencing the mode of transition and resulting type of democracy. Another fundamental trait of the Brazilian process of democratization is the fact that it was carried out through negotiations that were under the tight control of authoritarian leaders. In this regard, it is similar to the Spanish case, as authors Share and Mainwaring emphasize (1988). Nonetheless, a notable difference between the two countries was the military predominance, in the Brazilian case, in both the authoritarian regime and the initiative taken to liberalize it. In Spain, Franco's regime was less militarized and civil forces led the transition. This distinction between the two cases helps us to understand the centrality of the problem of democratic political control over the armed forces as fundamental for the consolidation of democracy in Brazil (Aguero, 1992). Another key difference between the two countries is the velocity of the Spanish process and the renovation of its political elite, in contrast to the long lasting and extremely gradual nature of the Brazilian process, also characterized by the high level of continuity between the leadership of the old regime and the new democratic one. All these factors contributed heavily to the difficulties of consolidation (Lessa, 1989). This in and of itself demonstrates the limited value of the generalizations made by transition theories.[13]

[13] For a critique of the explanatory power of theories of regime transition based on comparative perspectives, see Hermet (2001).

LIBERATION FROM THE AUTHORITARIAN REGIME. VOLUNTARISM AND CONTROL UNDER PRESIDENT GEISEL (1974-1979)

One of the most widely disseminated theses in the specialized literature, advocated by O'Donnell, maintains that in the authoritarian regimes in which repression was less brutal and periods of economic growth were significant, leaders held political resources that enabled them to take the initiative to "open up" the regime and negotiate the transferal of power with the opposition, protecting certain prerogatives of their own as well as their very political survival. Thus, the greater the political support that the authoritarian regime had at the beginning of the transition, the more gradual and controlled was the process and therefore, the greater the difficulties of democratic consolidation, given the presence of "authoritarian vestiges" within the new regime (O'Donnell, 1988). In effect, when the Geisel government began political liberalization in 1974, the military had already consolidated the model of conservative modernization whose motto, "security and development" summed up its characteristics. The high growth rates of the "economic miracle" (1968-1974) and the decimation of armed revolt supplied considerable social support and political and economic resources to the new government, allowing it to implement a bold strategy of political transition that had not yet found majority support within the ruling elite.

The beginning of the political liberalization can be situated at the moment when an authoritarian regime's leaders announce their intentions to promote such a process and are seen by the country's main political actors as having credibility. In the Brazilian case, this moment came at the end of 1974, when the Geisel government accepted the wide and unexpected victory of the opposition party, Movimento Democrático Brasileiro (MDB), in the elections that took place in November of that year. Those elections involved seats in the State legislatures, as well as for Congressional representatives and Senators. In effect, Geisel's promise to initiate a "slow, gradual and secure political détente" which was formulated only a few days after he took office in the month of March, was met with considerable skepticism on the part of the opposition and civil society, since all earlier military presidents had also promised to restore democracy once they took office. Furthermore, in the 1976 municipal level elections, the regime imposed strict restrictions on electoral propaganda, through the modification of specific legislation. In April of 1977, the government closed the Congress down for several days in order to promulgate a series of constitutional amendments that made some drastic changes in electoral legislation and placed constraints on democratic opposition. Their objective was to guarantee the government party Aliança Renovadora Nacional (ARENA) a congressional majority in 1978, as well as in the Electoral College that was in charge of choosing the next president in early 1979. They also postponed direct elections for State governors until 1982, among other arbitrary measures. Thus Geisel was able to obtain a firm control over the process of liberalization, alternately targeting the opposition – with pragmatic measures aimed at securing a congressional majority for the government party – and the military "hard-liners" – especially when at the end of 1977 he fired the Minister of the Armed Forces who wanted to succeed him. Through this episode, all political actors involved in the transition realized that they could be largely sure of the continuity of the process.

Another factor of capital importance was the hegemony of liberal and conservative sectors within opposition forces. Most significant here in the left's general alignment with the rules of transition that the military regime had imposed was the support they gave to General

Euler Bentes Monteiro, for the MDB, against the regime's candidate General Figueiredo, in the Electoral College at the end of 1978. At that same time, General Geisel extinguished the main legal instrument and major symbol of the military dictatorship, Institutional Act n. 5 (*Ato Institucional n. 5)* that had given it unilateral powers in altering the rules of institutional politics. Thus, the transition came to acquire a dynamic of its own, in the sense that the first liberalizing measures that were implemented constituted new rules for the political game, making an institutional retreat almost impossible. The costs of the latter would mean demoralizing supporters of the liberalization project and undermining the regime's own "authoritarian legality". (Santos, 1988).

In short, during General Geisel's administration, the political process was dominated by the government and restricted in fact to conservative forces and parliamentary opposition – grouped around the two parties, ARENA and MDB – in accordance with what the "détente project" had established. During Geisel's presidency, the existence of considerable political support for the regime, the opposition's fragility with regard to the coercive resources the government held and the *virtù* (in the Maquiavellian sense) of the authoritarian leaders allowed the latter success in the implantation and control of their project of democratization "granted from above". Geisel left his hand-chosen successor, General João Figueiredo, with the task of deepening the regime's liberalization. His strategy included the stipulation that, upon finishing his term in office in 1985, power be passed on to a civil politician member of the regime's party. However, as fate had it, events followed another path. With Tancredo Neves' unexpected death; José Sarney, who had been one of the most prominent civil members of the authoritarian regime, took over. Thus, although the Figueiredo government had in the latter years of its administration begun to lose control of the political process, the final outcome of political liberalization was much closer to what had been envisioned by the mentors of the project for a "slow, gradual and secure" transition process.

THE TRANSITION GAINS AUTONOMY DURING THE FIGUEIREDO ADMINISTRATION (1979-1985)

General Figueiredo assumed office as President of the Republic in March, 1979, proclaiming democracy as the final goal of the "political opening" that he was to promote while in office. However, the disappearance of authoritarianism's main legal instrument, the AI-5 – abolished only a few months before he took office – together with economic recession, the emergence of social movements such as the "new unionism", enabled the political process to gain momentum, loosening the government's hold over it. In spite of these constraints, the Figueiredo administration went ahead with its strategy of gradual political reform. In August of 1979, the regime proposed and had Congress approve a broad and intelligent bill of political amnesty, which was made extensive to imprisoned and exiled leftists as well as to all those who while belonging to the regime's organs of security had committed crimes linked to repression. Furthermore, the emergence of an active trade union movement – which began with the big strikes carried out by metalworkers of the state of São Paulo at the end of the seventies – played a major role in the "political opening" of the Figueiredo government and was a novelty for the Brazilian electoral system. In fact, the "new unionism" introduced an "alien" political actor into the scenario in which conservative and liberal forces had previously been engaged as the only protagonists of the ongoing transition.

Insofar as the use of the electoral process as the path of transition is concerned, this resource had been practically exhausted with the last institutional reform of the authoritarian regime: the 1979 extinction of the two existing political parties (ARENA and MDB) and the implementation of a multi-party system. Political amnesty and political party reform made up part of the regime's strategy to divide the opposition, in order to put an end to the growing plebiscite-based organization that, under the two-party election system, was unfavorable to those in power. This maneuver was partially victorious, causing the fragmentation of the opposition into various parties while the regime's cadre remained to a large extent composed of members of the new government party, the PDS (*Partido Democrático Social,* or Social Democratic Party). The opposition, in turn, realized that possibilities for deeper change in the institutional order had diminished. It thus chose to adapt itself to the rules that were in effect and focus its attention on the elections for state governors scheduled for 1982, which were to be carried out for the first time since 1966. The strategy of different segments of the opposition from that moment on was oriented to the consolidation of new parties and electoral campaigns, giving lesser priority to other political issues that did not refer specifically to party and electoral themes, such as the call for a Constituent Assembly. The opposition's division into several parties which took place before the authoritarian regime came to its end facilitated the re-positioning of the political elite, allowing for a "pact-based" transition that was to occur in exclusively institutional terms, without the explicit and substantive pacts that were made among political actors as in the Spanish case. It was this trait that led to the overburdened political agenda of the following period, particularly during the period in which the National Constituent Assembly (*Assembléia Nacional Constituinte)* was at work (Lessa, 1989).

The year of 1981 was fundamental for the Brazilian transition process. The fact that a bomb exploded inside a car occupied by members of the military, in the Riocenter parking lot on April 31st, had various significant consequences for the country's political future. In the first place, the episode meant the end of the acts of violence that since the end of 1979 were perpetrated by an extreme right dissatisfied with the transition process. This provided a guarantee to all the political actors involved that the transition process no longer ran the risk of being interrupted by a coup from the "hard-line" segments of the regime. The second important effect of the Riocenter case was General Golbery do Couto e Silva's dismissal from his post as Head Minister of the *Casa Civil,* which he had been occupying since the beginning of Geisel's administration. This was because he was demanding a thorough investigation of what had gone on and punishment for those responsible for the attacks. The substitution of the regime's most important strategist of the "political opening" with the ex-minister of the Medici government, Leitão de Abreu – a public person respected within the regime's inner circles but not habituated to political and parliamentary maneuvers – meant a break with General Golbery's strategic project. After taking office, Leitão de Abreu pushed an electoral bill through Congress, at the end of 1981, that among other things prohibited the linking of parties and imposed the vote for one party alone for all elected offices. Non-compliance could lead to ballot annulment. Known as the *Pacote de Novembro,* this bill undermined the survival of Tancredo Neves' *Partido Popular* (PP, People's Party) as well as other conservative leadership of the democratic opposition. Maintaining the PP as a potential source of support for the regime's party, the PDS, in order to elect civilian members of the regime to the Electoral College elections that were to be held in January of 1985 made up part of Golbery's plans. The measures adopted by Leitão de Abreu forced the PP to rejoin the PMDB in early 1982 and contributed to a more rigid party scheme. This brought back the plebiscite nature – for or against the military regime – that the elections had had since 1974. Once again, the importance of the abilities that political leadership displayed in guiding the transition process came to the forefront (see Arturi, 2000, chapter 5).

The results of the 1982 elections for state governors and for federal and state congressional representatives gave expressive political victories to the opposition and were directly responsible for the regime's loss of control over the transition process. The senators who had been chosen indirectly in 1978 allowed the government party to maintain a majority in Congress and in the Electoral College that in January of 1985 met to elect the following President of the Republic. However, beginning with the 1982 elections, when opposition parties won 10 of the most important state governments in the country and a majority of chairs in the House of Representatives, the transition process gained autonomy in relation to its actors. Neither members of the regime or the opposition would now be able to change the rules of the political game. In effect, given the extinction of the AI-5, authoritarian leaders no longer had the option of arbitrarily changing their "authoritarian loyalties". Neither did they continue to enjoy the parliamentary majority they needed to approve constitutional amendments, though opposition forces within Congress also lacked such a possibility. The government, confronted with growing political exhaustion, was thus obliged to manage the country negotiating directly with powerful governors belonging to the opposition. This situation marked the return of one of the most enduring characteristics of the national political system: the power of state governors and the centrality of regional politics in the forging of alliances within Congress (Abrucio and Samuels, 1997) The opposition forces of political parties and organized civil society gradually increased the constraints on the military regime's ability to maneuver and were thus able to reverse the prevailing situation of political predominance of the transition process, although always under strict observance of the political and electoral legislation imposed by the military government. This complex political scenario, in addition to the opposition's insecurity regarding the irreversibility of the transition process – especially after the neutralization of the military's extreme right, due to the Riocentro incident in 1981 – led to the multiplication of strategies for the upcoming presidential succession. Both the opposition and those in power held the same political goal: the election of the next President in the Electoral College in January of 1985.

This was the context in which the surprising mobilization for direct election of the President of the Republic – the movement *"Diretas-Já"* – emerged, in 1984. The strongest and most concrete post –1964 demand for the country's democratization, it was also a momentary curb on the regime's political strategy and on the plans of the most conservative opposition leadership that had already been trying to negotiate possible alliances with sectors of the ruling party. The movement for the direct elections for president mobilized millions of people all over the country but was not able to stop the April1984 rejection of the constitutional amendment that would establish them. Nonetheless, the movement was fundamental in stimulating and justifying the support of the regime's dissidence, the *Frente Liberal* (Liberal Front) for the PMDB's presidential candidate, Tancredo Neves.

The immense campaign for direct elections and its ultimate impotence in changing rules imposed by the authoritarian regime was characteristic of the process of "top-down" liberalization through agreements and fractures within the political elite in Congress. If on the one hand it facilitated dissidence within the government and made a hypothetical political and institutional retreat less feasible, it was on the other hand incapable of producing a truly democratic outcome to the transition process, given the simple fact that the majority of the leaders both within the government and the opposition were at that juncture satisfied with "authoritarian legality" and the political gains it promised. The events that followed are well known: the election of the Tancredo Neves/José Sarney slate in January of 1985, Neves' hospitalization due to serious illness in the wake of taking office on March 15, and his death on April 21st. Thus, due both to fate and elite choices, José Sarney, ex-president of the PDS and leader of government forces in the defeat of the amendment proposing direct elections only a few months early, became the first Brazilian civilian president since 1964.

The political pact between the military and the opposition candidate that had certainly been made to protect against any political turbulence in the final stretch of the route to liberalization, in order to guarantee these political prerogatives and safeguards, was facilitated by the gradualism and the lengthy duration of the process which permitted the political transformation of many of its actors. Thus, during the final years of the Figueiredo government, there were practically no more "radicals of the opposition" nor regime "hard-liners" around that theoretically the moderates would have to isolate in order to carry out a successful transition. The privileging of "guarantees" and of the continuity of the process became the trademark of the Brazilian route to democracy – *democracy granted from above* – whose success was due to the combination of the authoritarian regime's strategy of voluntarism and the self-positioning of the majority of the opposition within the logic and rules imposed by the former. The gradualism, slowness and strict control implemented during this period by those who held power transmitted "authoritarian residues" and reinforced the country's traditional political practices, thus leading to the problems that were to characterize the following stage of democratization under Sarney and to constrict the process of consolidation of the new democratic regime as of 1990.

The Democratic Regime and Factors Backing Its Consolidation

When the establishment of the democratic regime proved itself more auspicious than the specialists on the matter had originally imagined it would be, research on the initial phases of the transition turned rapidly toward the issue of the consolidation of democracy. At that point, a critique of the limits of political democracy and its possibilities for consolidation in the absence of profound political and economic reforms was developed. This critique centered around the specifically political limitations of the democratic regime – the tendency to delegate responsibility and the "low intensity" of citizenship (O Donnell, 1993), "low democracy" (Gill and Rocamora, 1992), "democratic liberalism" (Nun, 1994) and on the definition of democracy through socially substantive variables, that is, as a specific kind of society ("social democracy", "popular democracy", etc.) Of course, it is pertinent to take social, cultural and economic variables (high level of social inequality, economic crisis, authoritarian political culture, transformation of the role of the State, neo-liberal ideological assault etc) into account, particularly in order to identify the dilemmas and constraints in the consolidation of a new political order. In effect, the consolidation of democracy can be seen as a kind of second transition; evaluating the stability of the regime and the extent to which it becomes rooted in a particular country demands that a certain amount of time has already passed. As Morlino asserts, the consolidation of democracy "is not a process of innovation. On the contrary, it can be characterized by the solid established of structures and procedures intended to last ... Transition and consolidation phases are considerably distinct. It is basically a matter of the difference between fluidity and what is solidly established." (Morlino, 1992, p. 152-153)

Fundamentally, democratic consolidation requires a tolerance for uncertainty in relation to the outcome of power disputes. It must become acceptable to the main political actors that are involved. In other words, they must agree that those who win the elections, whomever they may be, can effectively take office, and that those who have experienced defeat do not make a political and institutional retreat in an attempt to alter the rules of political dispute *a posteriori*. Przeworski's key contribution in identifying this central element of the rules of democratic political disputes must nonetheless be taken in a relative sense. In fact, uncertainty regarding the outcome of political competition is only accepted by the old leadership of the authoritarian regime and for the ruling classes if other "certainties" come along with it, having to do with restricting possible social, economic and political reforms that any of the forces that could come to prevail as a result of peaceful power struggles could implement (Przeworski, 1984) Thus it is necessary to distinguish between the typical uncertainty of transition processes, regarding the possibility of retreat from the process and the fact that rules are in constant flux, from the limited uncertainty regarding the outcome of electoral disputes that is characteristic of all consolidated democracy. Thus, as Mainwaring (1992) asserts, uncertainty becomes a central element of transitions, but not of democratic regimes. From this point of view, all successful transitions to democracy are basically conservative, involving pacts and agreements –whether these are implicit or made public – that protect private property, guarantee authoritarian leaders and the military that they will not be persecuted by the new democratic regime and that, in the Brazilian case, their political survival is guaranteed. (Przeworski, 1992). Furthermore, those elements that are favorable to transition – moderation and minimalist goals on the part of the opposition, opportunism and control on the part of regime reformers – and that facilitate the acceptability of the process itself later become obstacles and constraints in the consolidation of democracy. As Przeworski maintains, the best strategy for "pact-based" transitions is inherently contradictory: "the forces that promote democracy must exhibit prudence *ex ante* and determination *ex post*. But the decisions that are previously made create conditions that are later difficult to reverse, since they preserve the power of forces associated with the authoritarian regime." (Przeworski, 1994, p. 111) In short, the demand to abandon the forces and arrangements that facilitated the transition but are considered anti-democratic and could bring about the "slow death" of democracy is not very feasible.

There have also been significant changes in the hierarchy of the explanatory value of variables according to the stage of the democratic process. The thematic focus of research has moved from the conditions in which the transition emerged –crisis of authoritarian regimes, causes of political liberalization, alliances and conflicts among actors – to dilemmas relating to the consolidation of democracy – military prerogatives, the building of democratic institutions, reform of the State under conditions of serious economic crisis etc. During the transition process from the authoritarian regime to democracy, the most influential variables are those that concern the quality of the action of political actors and the interaction of their strategies. Conversely, after the democratic regime has been established, macro-social variables (level of social inequality, type of economic policy, influence of international factors, degree of State reform, etc.) and institutional variables (system of government, electoral and party system, etc.) become the most important factors for the success or failure of the new regime's consolidation.

These abrupt changes of approach reflect the absence of explanatory models for the relationship authoritarian regime/ mode of transition/type of democracy. In this regard, Nohlen and Thibaut assert that the primary problems for the consolidation of a democratic regime do not originate in economic crisis nor in the contradictions between the elite pacts and social demand for reforms but in institutional mechanisms such as the relationship between the Executive and the Legislature or political systems' loss of ability to aggregate and represent. (Nohlen and Thibaut, 1994, p. 26) Przeworski (1992) in turn emphasizes that the repertoire of institutional arrangements for the building of a new political order is highly limited and that actors frequently seek refuge in traditional practices and institutions in putting the new regime together. In fact, in Share and Mainwaring's opinion, the way in which democracy is installed does not totally determine its later development, but does establish the rules of the game, the modes of interaction and the limitations imposed on political actors behavior and on political change; in short, the initial conditions of the democratic regime are the most important (Share and Mainwaring, 1988). Having said this, then, it is our point of view that the dilemmas that a democratic regime must confront are political obstacles that either originated in the mode of transition from the authoritarian regime (path dependency) or are traditional characteristics of the Brazilian political system that were reinforced by the controlled and gradual nature of the transition process.

The New Republic (1985-1990) and Dilemmas for the Consolidation of a Democratic Regime

The democratization phase in Brazil unfolded during civilian José Sarney's presidency (1985-1990). Referred to as the "New Republic", during this period the ban on communist parties was lifted and voting rights were significantly expanded, with the latter granted to illiterate persons in 1985. In 1988, the new democratic Constitution was written and approved. Direct democratic elections for President of the Republic were held in 1989, for the first time since 1961. The actual beginning of the democratic regime can be situated at the moment in which the winner of these elections, which occurred in two rounds, Fernando Collor de Mello, took office in March 1990. During the Sarney administration, constraints on the building and consolidation of the new regime were multiple and interdependent: persistent economic crisis marked by growing inflation, the political fragility of the "Democratic Alliance", President Sarney's lack of legitimacy in the eyes of the majority of the population and the presence of important vestiges of authoritarianism linked to the "top-down" form that the transition had taken This set of obstacles were intimately connected with the election-based transition that had been carried out through the last two military administrations and the dynamics of the party and electoral system of the New Republic. In effect, the absence of public pacts during the stage of political liberalization led to a situation, with Tancredo

Neves' death, of transition *à refaire*[14], which served to aggravate President Sarney's political difficulties. The military had accepted Neves' election almost exclusively on the basis of the political security that he personally offered them, in terms of guaranteeing both the political prerogatives of the Armed Forces and that ruling classes' basic economic interests would remain unharmed by possible reforms. Furthermore, Sarney had inherited a ministry that was the product of Neves' isolated political agreements with various sectors of society, the nature of which the current president was largely unaware. Weakened by this situation and by the PMDB's and its new president, Ulysses Guimarães, attempt to direct the administration of the country and guide political reform, Sarney reacted by seeking support in the military and using *clientelista* practices to individually attract parliament members from various parties. He also set up alliances with state governors in order to influence their federal-level representatives. Both types of strategy worked to weaken political parties and the Congress. In fact, they were only possible because those institutions were already in such a fragile state, due to the way in which transition had been carried out and its effects upon electoral legislation and political parties and practices.

The conservative orientation that the President imposed was able to find its instruments of support in traditional characteristics and practices of the Brazilian political party system. In this regard, Sarney used governors' support to cut off the most progressive wing of the PMDB, re-structuring his own administration and getting the parliamentary support that he needed in order to govern. He managed the country through the effective presence of the most conservative members of the Democratic Alliance and other parties, the majority of whom came from the Liberal Front, a group of last-minute dissidents from the authoritarian regime. The liberal and conservative majority in Congress in 1985, which included the "bionic" senators that had been appointed by the regime in 1978, in addition to the President's desires and the pressures of the military led to the imposition of a Constituent Assembly made up of senators and congressional representatives elected in 1986. This meant the defeat of the left's proposal for an Assembly made up of representatives elected for the specific purpose of writing up a new Constitution. Those same forces put successful pressure on the Constituent Assembly to limit the scope of social and economic reforms, particularly with regard to agrarian reform, as well as limiting Sarney's presidency to one five year term and imposing the adoption of the presidential system of government. With specific regard to the party and electoral system, the Constituent Congress was responsible for maintaining the over-representation of the northern and northeastern states and the under-representation of southern and southeastern states in the House of Representatives. In the second place, the Congress' draft of a new constitution was carried out under the strong influence that governors held over their states' federal representatives, a fact which reinforced the traditional articulation of national politics through regional agreements, in detriment of inter-party relationships and the internal strengthening of political parties. Lastly, the Constituent Congress was partly responsible for the internal division of political parties that led to the formation of new ones, such the PSDB, made up of a group of PMDB dissidents. In short, a characteristic trait of the Brazilian party system that had long contributed to its fragility was reproduced: the fact that political parties almost always emerged from intra-elite fragmentation during periods of regime change. (Lima Jr., 1993).

---

[14] Phillippe Schmitter used this expression at a conference he gave at the *Institut des Hautes Etudes de l' Amerique Latine (IHEAL)* in Paris, on March 8, 1993.

The overloading of the economic and social agenda of the Constituent Congress – due to the absence of substantive pacts among social actors in the period preceding political liberalization – together with the corporatist pressures coming from almost all the organized sectors of society in turn produced the lack of definition of many of the political and economic principles of the new Constitution, which were thus left for later regulation, through regular legislation. The PMDB and its president, Ulysses Guimarães – also the President of both the House of Representatives and the Constituent Assembly – torn apart by the conflicts posed as party in power and heir of the opposition, maintained an ambiguous stance that served to discredit the democratic forces that provided leadership during the transition process. In this regard, the 1989 direct presidential elections took on multiple meanings. As they relate to the theme of our research, the election campaign and its results in two rounds marked the actual beginning of the country's democratic regime and the end of a lengthy transition process began 15 years earlier. This election also reveals some important constraints that acted on the party system, caused by the way the transition had been carried out; in particular, some worrisome indications of political parties' loss of legitimacy and the low level of identification with parties on the part of the electorate. In effect, Ulysses Guimarães and Aureliano Chaves, the 1989 candidates from the two main parties, PMDB and PFL, that together retained over half of all congressional seats did not surpass a respective 4% and 2% of all votes in the election's first round. Nonetheless, these candidates had been the leaders of the Democratic Alliance, which had allowed Neves' election through the Electoral College in 1985, and the implementation of the first civilian government since 1964. IN turn, the two candidates who received the greatest amount of votes and whom disputed the second round of elections were Fernando Collor de Mello, with 25% of the votes, from the inexpressive PRN, holding only 21 House seats in 1989, and Luiz Inácio Lula da Silva, from the PT. Both candidates represented the opposition as well as the vast majority of the population's rejection of the government and traditional politicians[15]. When President Collor was impeached and Itamar Franco took office in December of 1992[16], under strict observance of constitutional procedures, the democratic regime clearly demonstrated its vitality. Nonetheless, such events did not mean that the political order had overcome its precarious character, in which the party system itself was one of the most fragile elements.

If we give due value to institutional factors in the processes of democratic transition and consolidation, in the Brazilian case two important characteristics of the country's political traditions that were central in the configuration of the transition process and the constraints on the existing regime come to the fore: military watchfulness and influence over the political regime, particularly consolidated after 1964, and the use of electoral competition, however limited, in order to maintain control over intra-elite conflict. In effect, countries like Brazil that have spent a considerable amount of time under authoritarian military rule must develop two political conditions that are indispensable for democratic consolidation: 1) effective civilian control over the military and 2) true opportunities for the interchange of political forces within positions of institutional power (Rouquié, 1986). Now, in the Brazilian case we see that one of these pre-conditions did not come into being, and the second has only begun to be implemented and tested, since the PT (Worker's Party) candidate took office as President

[15] Leonel Brizola, who came in third in the first round with 13.6% of the votes, also represented the forces of opposition to the New Republic, as a candidate of a relatively small political party, the PDT.

[16] For a more detailed analysis of the multiple political implications of impeachment, see Monclaire (1994).

of the Republic in January, 2003. Both the constitutionally-provided prerogatives and the informal powers of the Brazilian military continue to be quite broad, giving them a high degree of autonomy with regard to the State apparatus (Moraes, 1987; Stepan, 1991; Oliveira, 1994; Zaverucha, 1994; Soares, D'araujo and Castro, 1995). Such a situation can be seen as practically incompatible with a democratic regime (Zaverucha, 2000). Agreements made between the opposition and the military that allowed for a peaceful change of administration were in fact based on a series of guarantees providing for the non-punishment of crimes committed by the military regime's security forces and the maintenance of Armed Forces' privileges which allow them considerable autonomy with regard to political institutions and influence over the process of constitution of the new democratic order. Military tutelage over the political system was in place during the Sarney administration[17], during which time State ministers linked to the military, and the Ministry of the Armed Forces in particular, put heavy pressure on the president and the Constituent Congress towards the restriction of the social and political reforms that were being demanded by certain sectors of the PMDB, which held over half of the ministries, and by left-wing opposition.

The heavy influence of the Armed Forces during this period was due to Sarney's lack of legitimacy in the public view and particularly, on the part of the PMDB, unhappy about having to submit itself politically to a president with such recent connections to the authoritarian regime. In addition to his past as an important member of the previous regime, the President's political fragility was further aggravated by the population's frustration with the failure of the campaign for direct elections and with Tancredo Neves' unexpected death. Thus, in the public eye, Sarney came to be seen as a "usurper". According to Eliezer de Oliveira, Sarney moved closer to the "military apparatus that, in supporting the president, also provided him with a series of limitations to be placed on government policies". (Oliveira, 1994, p. 111) The most visible aspect of the military's political action was the strong pressure they put on the Constituent Assembly, in the sense of imposing the presidential system of government, a five-year presidential term for President Sarney, limited amnesty for the left-wing members of the military who had been punished throughout the military regime, and the veto of the social reforms, especially in the agrarian sector, that might produce serious conflict. Some authors believe that the Brazilian military lost a considerable amount of the political power that it had at the time that President Sarney took office in 1985. In recent research, Wendy Hunter (1997) argues that the reason for this erosion of the power and political prerogatives held by the military during the Sarney, Collor and Itamar Franco administrations is the development during this period of a dynamic of electoral politics like that which is typical of democratic regimes. This process, associated with the end of the Cold War and the decline of the radical Left, led to an effort on the part of politicians to reduce both the budget and spheres of influence of the military, transferring economic and power resources to the political party and electoral arena[18]. There are two grounds on which her

[17] Zaverucha (1994) referred to the military influence over President Sarney as "friendly" tutelage. In his most recent work, *Fragile Democracy* (*Frágil Democracia*) (2000), he analyzes the military's political action under Fernando Collor, Itamar Franco and Fernando Henrique Cardoso's democratic administrations, asserting "there is still a long and difficult road toward the democratization of civilian-military relations in Brazil. Brazil's fragile democracy has not yet reached its point of no return to authoritarianism." (p. 313)

[18] Hunter advocates the thesis that in Brazil, "the competitive dynamics of democratization has produced irresistible incentives for civilian politicians to contest military influence", thus identifying it as responsible for the diminished power and political prerogatives of the Armed Forces after 1985 (1997, p.6) The author nonetheless recognizes that the military remained a factor of power that actors took into consideration,

work can be questioned, however; in the first place, in the face of empirical evidence regarding the "tutelage" that the Brazilian military did in fact exercise throughout the Sarney administration. In the second place, Zaverucha demonstrates that democratic civilian control over the military does not to this date exist in Brazil. He alerts us to the fact that the Brazilian Armed Forces continue to hold considerable prerogatives and political autonomy at today, and that the military dimensions of democratic transition and consolidation have been underestimated by many political analysts (Zaverucha, 2000).[19]

With regard to the constraints imposed on democratic consolidation that were generated from within the recent process of transition itself, a key factor is the high level of continuity between the elite of the authoritarian and of the new regime. These defining characteristics of Brazilian democratization stem from the agreements and coalitions that were established between moderate members of the opposition and old regime reformists. Such agreements were made for the most part within Congress, through the distribution of political resources and positions among these actors in the new civilian government that was established in 1985. These conditions, along with others that we will soon examine, were responsible for the fragility of the new democratic political institutions, and the political party system in particular. In effect, as Hagopian (1992) emphasizes, there was a large migration of political leadership of the authoritarian regime into the opposition during the regime's latter years (1983-1985). According to this author, this type of transformation was induced by opposition leaders and in fact facilitated transition by fomenting the emergence of an organized dissidence (*Frente Liberal)* within the government party that was then able to forge a political alliance with the major opposition party of the moment, the PMDB. The so-called Democratic Alliance (*Aliança Democrática*) promoted the candidacies of Tancredo Neves (PMDB) for President and José Sarney (PFL) for Vice-President within the Electoral College that was responsible for choosing a new president for January of 1985. Tancredo Neves' death led to the most unexpected turn taken by a process of transition in Latin America: the rise to presidency of someone who only a few months earlier had been president of the authoritarian regime's political party.

Thus, both the military and the conservative civilian elite that had undergone severe political and electoral loss starting the mid-seventies were able to keep a large share of their positions within the State after the militaries were removed from power in March of 1985. Since the election of Tancredo Neves and José Sarney occurred in an Electoral College that was still largely populated by members of the government party, the opposition and its "dissident allies" had to negotiate votes. This was done to a large extent through *clientelista* type arrangements, which produced a high degree of political continuity. Later conservative forces were able to further increase their presence in Congress by changing parties, something which was made feasible by the liberal nature of electoral and political party legislation on

---

especially in crises, and on those occasions in which there was only weak popular support for the President of the Republic. We believe that Hunter goes too far in her assessment of the Armed Forces' retreat from the center of political decision making, which she sees as the significant and lasting decline of military political influence. (ibid, p. 144)

[19] Other authors have a more nuanced opinion than Zaverucha does on military power after the transition. They recognize that the Armed Forces maintain prerogatives from the days of the authoritarian regime as well as considerable informal power, but also show that there have been democratic advances in civilian-military relations over the last few years, such as the creation of the Ministry of Defense. They also point to the lack of preparation and attention on the part of civilian elites with regard to military and defense issues. See Oliveira (2000) and D'Araújo & Castro (2001).

the constitution of new parties and the easy switching of party on the part of parliament members. The high level of continuity of the authoritarian elite within the New Republic can be illustrated by the fact that when general elections were held in 1986 and the Constituent Assembly was put formed, 217 elected representatives were from the party that had been the bulwark of the authoritarian regime (ARENA) whereas 212 were from the MDB, the party of the opposition during the period in which a compulsory bi-partite system was in effect (1966-1979). This outcome was also due to the significant prestige and support that the authoritarian regime and its leaders continued to enjoy, in virtue of the economic development that had been achieved and the positions of power that had been retained. Furthermore, the positions of power held by members of civilian political elite of the military regime after democracy was established were actually more numerous than they had been during the Sarney government. In fact, the PFL, as of 1990, became the main base of support for the Collor and Itamar Franco administrations; in 1994, it allied with the PSDB (*Partido da Social Democracia Brasileira)* to elect President Fernando Henrique Cardoso, with Marco Maciel (PFL) ex-senator and ex-leader of the Geisel government in the House of Representatives as Vice. In turn, the presence of parties and politicians linked to the old regime as a influential forces within the parliament as well as within President Lula's government reinforces the notion that is has been the reformists of the old regime who have become the privileged heirs of the transition process. The significant persistence of conservative and right wing forces within all of the new democratic regime's governments can, as Timothy Power warns us, hold back processes of consolidation. (Power, 2000, p. 240)

The institutionalization of the political party system is a fundamental element for the consolidation of a democratic regime[20]. The incipient institutionalization of the Brazilian political system contrasts with the importance that political parties and elections have had in the democratization of the authoritarian regime. The political party system is the institution that has undergone the most influence of the pacts carried out among the political elite, as Hagopian asserts. This is because while social and popular movements may place constraints on the authoritarian regime and can be decisive in the establishment of democracy, they do not determine the institutional design of the new regimes. With regard to factors concerning the fragility of the political party system that are rooted in the country's political history, parties' heavy dependence on the State as well as the centrality of regional politics in the formation of electoral and party alliances are characteristics that, according to Campello de Souza (1988) should be given more explanatory power than the much-referred -to maintenance of continuity by conservative forces. From this point of view, one of the most persistence constraints on democracy linked to the 1964 military coup was precisely the interruption – from 1945 to 1966 – of the political party system which had demonstrated a strong electoral identification. Thus the influence of the authoritarian regime reinforced a secular trait of the Brazilian political system, characterized by a combination of a "liberal logic" and an "authoritarian praxis" (Trindade, 1985), which has in part been responsible for a political culture that has resisted the democratization of the public sphere and the expansion of citizenship. The authoritarian regime, in maintaining persistent control over the political process, produced three different party systems during its 21 years of existence. Heavy State

[20] "A system of institutionalized political parties signifies stability in competition between parties, existence of organizations that have deep roots in society, the recognition of these party organizations and of elections as legitimate institutions for the choice of representatives and the validity of parties that have stable structures and rules". (Mainwaring and Scully, 1994, p.44).

interventionism alongside weak institutionalization of the political system led to a complete eradication of the political party identification that existed prior to the 1964 coup, a one of a kind situation among all Latin American transition processes.

Another series of factors also are critical for the current political order and constitute significant constraints in democratic consolidation. Regarding the obstacles created by economic and social factors, enormous income inequality and the absence of the social reforms that had been promised by the opposition to the authoritarian regime has led the majority of the population to associate the inefficacy of successive government policies to the actions of the democratic regime. These macro-structural variables have had an incisive impact on the political process, constraining democratic consolidation in several ways. High income concentration in Brazil has had serious albeit indirect political effects, such as the shrinking of political community, difficulties in maintaining the public order, and lack of trust in politicians – all factors that in the long range undermine the legitimacy of the democratic regime (Reis and Cheibub, 1993). In effect, the State is not able to neither exercise a "monopoly over violence" nor impose political order over the entire national territory in which things such as slave labor and the private exercise of law and order still occur, particularly in rural areas. In turn, State agencies resist equal treatment and recognition of the rights of the poorest sectors of the population and of minority groups. This is especially true for the organs of public safety, which continue to act in violent and arbitrary ways in relation to those sectors. In the Brazilian case, this pattern of action, highly disrespectful of basic human rights, has its origins in the country's slave regime past, further reinforced by a long period of authoritarianism. O'Donnell has used the concept of "low intensity citizenship" to describe the strange situation in which " the participatory and democratic rights of the polyarchy are respected, but the liberal component of democracy is violated ... this parting of paths is the reverse side of the complex mixture of democratic and authoritarian elements of these States". (O'Donnell, 1993; p. 173)

CONCLUSIONS

Literature of the field emphasized the heavy affinities between the previous regime, the mode in which the transition occurred, and constraints on the consolidation of democracy, as discussed in the introductory section of this chapter. The characteristics of the authoritarian regime, existing political traditions and the institutional patterns that were adopted together make up and establish the limits of the transition process. In turn, the political behavior and institutional patterns established or reaffirmed during these processes have been responsible for a persistent legacy that has affected the new democratic regime and its possibilities of consolidation (Munck and Leff, 1997). These effects of the mode of transition on the new regime act primarily over the patterns of competition and interaction among elite groups, and over the institutional rules and the limitations that are placed on political change, that is, that affect the initial conditions of the new democratic regime. Regarding stages of the transition process, in the cases in which they are distinguishable, something similar can be observed. The stage of liberalization of the Brazilian authoritarian regime, which unfolded gradually through elections and non-public agreements that were made among its main actors created a series of political constraints, that then made the democratic transition difficult.

This chapter has sought to demonstrate that the adoption of a particular institutional route for political liberalization – electoral competition limited by authoritarian legislation – which remained within the confines of the country's political traditions, led to gradual autonomy of the process and the "naturalization" of its rules on the part of its main political actors. From this point of view, the Brazilian case confirms the hypothesis of path dependency: once a given institutional pattern is adopted, it tends to stabilize and to bring all political activity within its boundaries. The possibility for significant modifications of the political tradition and of a country's institutional patterns can occur in certain "critical moments" which is the case in processes of regime transition (Hunter, 1997). However, empirical research on the liberalization of the Brazilian authoritarian regime enables us to qualify this proposition, since it demonstrates that with regard to transition processes that take place in a gradual and controlled manner, changes in political regime can occur without important changes in institutional patterns and traditional political practices. In the case we are analyzing here, the only chance that over the course of more than a decade of political liberalization there could have been a break with the old political regime – in early 1984 when the big campaign for direct presidential elections emerged – was aborted when the main political actors contented themselves with "authoritarian legality". Thus, the choices made by the period's most significant political actors reinforced the Brazilian tradition of "top-down" conciliation with elite groups, the use of electoral competition to measure the power of leaders in relation to their adversaries (counter-elite) and the presence of the military as one of the key actors of the political system.

Political actors' – including the vast majority of opposition forces – strategic acceptance and incorporation of the rules imposed by the regime was also facilitated because the political opening put into motion by authoritarian leaders gradually took on a dynamic of its own which gave the process a relative autonomy in regard to those who got it started. This occurred during the middle of the Figueiredo presidency. In fact, the extinction of the most arbitrary legislation (AI-5) in 1978, amnesty and the return to a multi-party system the following year, the neutralization of the extreme military right due to the Riocentro case, and the direct elections for state governors that were held in 1982, all brought about increasingly democratic and less reversible effects. That is, anything else could seriously jeopardize the transition process itself. Moderate opposition, under Tancredo Neves' leadership, developed a strategy for winning the presidency that adapted itself to authoritarian rules, working within the confines of the perverse effects that the liberalization strategies imposed from above had established. The attempt to "grant democracy from above" did ultimately escape the control of authoritarian leaders and the democratization process then took on autonomy (Lessa, 1989), giving shape to a political game which neither regime leaders nor the opposition could alter at will, unless a highly improbable institutional break were to occur. Thus, when the possibility of a truly democratic path emerged, which would mean a real break with the authoritarian regime (through the campaign in 1984 for direct presidential elections), moderate opposition leaders did not see it as worthwhile. They feared the risk of military veto, but also saw it as contrary to their strategic objectives, which meant getting the Presidency through the Electoral College and in accordance with current legislation.

In conclusion, we believe that we have provided ample proof for the argument that the mode of transition adopted heavily influences the result of transition processes and the constraints that emerge in the consolidation of the new democratic regime. In the case that we have studied here, authoritarian leaders' loss of control over their attempt to grant democracy from above produced an outcome that was quite different from what they had desired. In fact, the autonomy that the transition process took on, instead of bringing about an institutional break from the old regime, reinforced the characteristics that make the Brazilian political system resistant to both classical forms of dictatorship as well as stable democratization (Lamounier, 1989). The political dilemmas behind democratic consolidation originating in the transition process should be seen together with those that emerge from economic crisis, social inequality and the deep changes in the role of the State that is going on in Brazil today[21]. In short, the consolidation of Brazilian democracy today is still just one possibility among others.

REFERENCES

Abrucio, F. and Samuels, D. 1997. "A nova Política dos Governadores". *Lua Nova* n. 40-41, p. 137-166.

Aguero, F. 1992. "The Military and the Limits to Democratization". *In* Mainwaring, S., O'Donnell, G. and Valenzuela, A. *Issues in Democratic Consolidation*: The New South American Democracies in Comparative Perspective. Notre Dame, University of Notre Dame Press.

Arturi, C. S. 2000. *Le Brésil*: une tentative de démocratisation octroyée (1974-1985). Villeneuve d'Ascq, Presses Universitaires du Septentrion.

Badie, B. and Hermet, G. 1990. *Politique Comparée*. Paris, Presses Universitaires de France.

Banegas, R. 1993. "Les transitions démocratiques: mobilisations collectives et fluidité politique". *Cultures et Conflits* n. 12, p. 105-140, hiver.

Bermeo, N. 1992. "Democracy and the Lessons of Dictatorship". *Comparative Politics*, v. 24 n. 3, p. 273-292, April.

Camargo, A. and Diniz, E. 1989. "Dilemas da consolidação democrática no Brasil". In _____. *Continuidade e mudança no Brasil da Nova República*. São Paulo, Vértice.

D'araújo, M. C. and Castro, C. 2001. *Militares e política na Nova República*. Rio de Janeiro, Fundação Getúlio Vargas.

Di Palma, G. 1990. *To Craft Democracy:* An Essay on Democratic Transition. Berkeley, University of California Press.

Dobry, M. 1986. *Sociologie des crises politiques*. Paris, Presses de la Fondation Nationale des Sciences Politiques.

Gills, B. and Rocamora, J. 1993. "Low Intensity Democracy". *World Quarterly*, v. 13 n. 3, p. 521-524.

Hagopian, F. 1992. "The Compromised Consolidation: The Political Class in Brazilian Transition". *In* Mainwaring, S., O'Donnell, G. and Valenzuela, A. *Issues in Democratic Consolidation*: The New South American Democracies in Comparative Perspective. Notre Dame, University of Notre Dame Press.

Heper, M. 1991. "Transitions to Democracy Reconsidered". *In* Rustow, D. and Erickson, K. *Comparative Political Dynamics*: Global Research Perspectives. New York, Harper Collins.

[21] See Sallum Jr. (1996) For an analysis of the Brazilian transition covering a wider period of time, involving cycles of political mobilization and institutional reform, see Rodrigues (2001).

Hermet, G. 1986. *Sociologie de la construction démocratique*. Paris, Economica.

Hermet, G. 2001. "As transições democráticas no século XX: comparação entre América Latina e Leste europeu". *In* Abreu, A. A. *Transição em fragmentos*: desafios da democracia no final do século XX. Rio de Janeiro, Fundação Getúlio Vargas.

Hunter, W. 1997. *Eroding Military Influence in Brazil*: Politicians against Soldiers. Chapel Hill and London, University of North Carolina Press.

Huntington, S. 1991. *The Third Wave*: Democratization in the Late Twentieth Century. Norman, University of Oklahoma Press.

Karl, T. 1991. "Dilemas de la democratización en América Latina". *In* Solano, J. L. and Horcasitas, J. H. *Transiciones a la democracia en Europa y América Latina*. México, Miguel Ángel Porrua.

Karl, T. L. and Schmitter, P. 1991. "Les modes de transition en Amérique Latine, en Europe du Sud et de l'Est". *Revue Internationale des Sciences Sociales*, n. 128, p. 285-302, mai.

Lamounier, B. 1985. "Apontamentos sobre a questão democrática brasileira". *In* Rouquié, A., Lamounier, B. and Schwarcz, J. (eds.). *Como renascem as democracias*. São Paulo, Brasiliense.

Lamounier, B. 1988. "O Brasil autoritário revisitado: o impacto das eleições sobre a abertura". *In* Stepan, A. (ed.). *Democratizando o Brasil*. São Paulo, Paz e Terra.

Lessa, R. 1989. "Reflexões sobre a gênese de uma democracia banal". *In* Diniz, E., Boschi, R. R. and Lessa, R. *Modernização e consolidação democrática no Brasil*: dilemas da Nova República. São Paulo, Vértice.

Lima Jr., O. B. 1993. *Democracia e instituições no Brasil dos anos 80*. São Paulo, Loyola.

Limongi, F. 1997. "Prefácio". *In* Dahl, R. *Poliarquia*: participação e oposição. São Paulo, Edusp.

Linz, J. and Stepan, A. 1995. *Problems of Democratic Transitions and Consolidation*: Southern Europe, South America and Post-Communism. Baltimore, Johns Hopkins University Press.

Mainwaring, S. 1992. "Transition to Democracy and Democratic Consolidation: Theoretical and Comparative Issues". *In* Mainwaring, S., O'Donnell, G. and Valenzuela, A. *Issues in Democratic Consolidation*: The New South American Democracies in Comparative Perspective. Notre Dame, University of Notre Dame Press.

Mainwaring, S. and Scully, T. R. 1994. "A institucionalização dos sistemas partidários na América Latina". *Dados*, v. 37 n. 1, p. 43-79.

Moisés, J. A. 1995. *Os brasileiros e a democracia*. São Paulo, Ática.

Monclaire, S. 1994. "Le quasi-*impeachment* du Président Collor". *Revue Française de Science Politique*, v. 44 n. 1, p. 23-47, fév.

Moraes, J. Q. 1987. "O argumento da força". *In* Oliveira, E. R. (ed.). *As Forças Armadas no Brasil*. Rio de Janeiro, Espaço e Tempo.

Morlino, L. 1992. "Consolidações democráticas na Europa Meridional. Indicações teóricas para análise empírica". *Dados*, v. 35 n. 2, p. 145-172.

Nohlen, D. and Thibaut, B. 1994. "Investigación sobre la transición en América Latina: enfoques, conceptos, tesis". *Arbeitspapier* n. 11.

Nun, J. 1994. "La democracia y la modernización: treinta años después". *In* Sierra, G. *Democracia emergente en América del Sur*. Ciudad del México, UNAM.

O'Donnell, G. 1988. "Transições, continuidades e alguns paradoxos". *In* Reis, F. W. and O'Donnell, G. *A democracia no Brasil*: dilemas e perspectivas. São Paulo, Vértice.

O'Donnell, G. 1993. "Acerca del Estado, la democratización y algunos problemas conceptuales. Una perspectiva latinoamericana con referencias a países poscomunistas". *Desarollo Económico*, v. 33 n. 130, p. 163-184, jul.-sept.

O'Donnell, G. 1994. "Delegative Democracy". *Journal of Democracy*, v. 5 n. 1, p. 55-69, Jan.

O'Donnell, G. and Schmitter, P. 1988. *Transições do regime autoritário:*, primeiras conclusões. São Paulo, Vértice.

Oliveira, E. R. 1994. *De Geisel a Collor:*, Forças Armadas, transição e democracia. Campinas, Papirus.

Oliveira, E. R. and Correa, S. 2000. "Forças Armadas, direção política e formato institucional". *In* D'araujo, M. C. and Castro, C. *Democracia e Forças Armadas no Cone Sul.* Rio de Janeiro, Fundação Getúlio Vargas.

Przeworski, A. 1984. "Ama a incerteza e serás democrático". *Novos Estudos*, n. 9, p. 36-46.

Przeworski, A. 1992. "The Games of Transition". *In* Mainwaring, S., O'Donnell, G. and Valenzuela, A. *Issues in Democratic Consolidation*: The New South American Democracies in Comparative Perspective. Notre Dame, University of Notre Dame Press.

Valenzuela, A. 1994. *Democracia e mercado*: reformas políticas e econômicas no Leste Europeu e na América Latina. Rio de Janeiro, Relume-Dumará.

Reis, E. P. and Cheibub, J. B. 1993. "Pobreza, desigualdade e consolidação democrática". *Dados,* v. 36 n. 2, p. 233-260.

Remmer, K. 1992-1993. "The Process of Democratization in Latin America". *Studies in Comparative International Development*, Washington, v. 27 n. 4, p. 3-24, Winter.

Rodrigues, A. T. 2001. *O Brasil de Fernando a Fernando*: neoliberalismo, corrupção e protesto na política brasileira. Ijuí, Unijuí.

Rouquié, A. 1986. "Demilitarization and Military-Dominated Polities in Latin America". *In* O'Donnell, G., Schmitter, P. and Whitehead, L. *Transitions from Authoritarian Rule.* Comparative Perspectives. Baltimore, The Johns Hopkins University Press.

Sallum Jr., B. 1996. *Labirintos.* Dos generais à Nova República. São Paulo, Hucitec.

Santiso, J. 1993. "La démocratie incertaine. La théorie des choix rationnels et la démocratisation en Amérique Latine". *Revue Française de Science Politique*, v. 43 n. 6, p. 970-993, déc.

Santos, W. G. 1988. "El siglo de Michels: competencia oligopólica, lógica autoritaria y transición en America Latina". *In* Cavarozzi, M. and Garreton, M. A. *Muerte y resurreción.* Los partidos políticos en el autoritarismo y las transiciones en el Cono Sur. Chile, FLACSO.

Share, D. and Mainwaring, S. 1988. "Transições através da negociação: a democratização no Brasil e na Espanha". *In* Selcher, W. A. (ed.). *A abertura política no Brasil.* São Paulo, Convívio.

Soares, G. A. D. 1994. "O golpe de 64". *In* Soares, G. A. D. and D'araújo, M. C. (eds.). *21 anos de regime militar*: balanços e perspectivas. Rio de Janeiro, Fundação Getúlio Vargas.

Soares, G. A. D., D'araújo, M. C. and Castro, C. 1995. *A volta aos quartéis*: a memória militar sobre a abertura. Rio de Janeiro, Relume-Dumará.

Souza, M. C. C. 1998. "A Nova República brasileira: sob a espada de Dâmocles". *In* Stepan, A. (ed.). *Democratizando o Brasil.* Rio de Janeiro, Paz e Terra.

Stepan, A. 1988. "As prerrogativas militares nos regimes pós-autoritários: Brasil, Argentina, Uruguai e Espanha". *In* Stepan, A. (ed.). *Democratizando o Brasil*. Rio de Janeiro, Paz e Terra.

Stepan, A. 1991. *Os militares*: da Abertura à Nova República. Rio de Janeiro, Paz e Terra.

Trindade, H. 1985. "Bases da democracia brasileira: lógica liberal e *práxis* autoritária". *In* Rouquié, A., Lamounier, B. and Schwarcz, J. (eds.). *Como renascem as democracias*. São Paulo, Brasiliense.

Zaverucha, J. 1994. *Rumor de sabres*. São Paulo, Ática.

Zaverucha, J. 2000. *Frágil democracia*. Collor, Itamar, FHC e os militares (1990-1998). Rio de Janeiro, Civilização Brasileira.

INDEX

D

E

F

G

H

I

J

N

O

P

Q

R

S

Y